STREET ART

Project Editor
VALERIA MANFERTO DE FABIANIS
LAURA ACCOMAZZO

Graphic Layout
MARIA CUCCHI

STREET ART

LEGENDARY ARTISTS AND THEIR VISIONS

Text by
ALESSANDRA MATTANZA

Introduction by
CHRIS VERSTEEG

SHELTER HARBOR PRESS
NEW YORK

CONTENTS

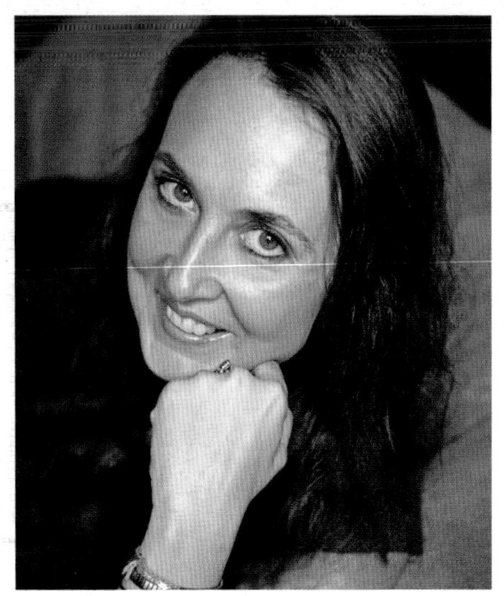

Traveling the World in Pursuit of Graffiti and Street Art

BY ALESSANDRA MATTANZA

A love of street art and graffiti is instinctive: one's opinion is not influenced by the charisma of the – often unknown – author, or the estimation of a respected art critic, or even the price of a ticket. It is simply instinct, like an exchange of glances. Pure chemistry, love at first sight, *coup de foudre*, a joining of souls coming together by chance in the infinite possibilities of the human universe.

Glance by glance, street art has conquered the world, free from the barriers of language, culture or religion, and above all free from economic limits: street art reaches every corner, even in the most neglected and isolated areas of the planet, because it speaks right to people's hearts. And therein lies the real power of street art: it reaches everyone, without discrimination, because it is an extremely democratic form of art. It is free and wild and sensual.

For just as wild animals hunt their prey, so the street artists choose the perfect place and wait for the right moment to abandon themselves to the primitive instinct of creation. Some are swift, striking in a few minutes; others need more time to complete their works. Yet they are all driven by the same obsession that only an artist can understand: they cannot live without their art. Street artists know this feeling well, it is why they often work in harsh conditions, such as in the rain or under a burning sun, in inhospitable settings, such as in the heart of the metropolitan jungle, in shantytowns or under a

bridge where not a living soul ever goes, forgotten corners of the city, often unsafe and dangerous, and often with the fear of being discovered and arrested for an illegal activity. Just what drives a street artist to work in such uncomfortable and perilous conditions? "The unbearable lightness of being that you can't live without . . .," said a graffiti artist I met in Los Angeles, and who prefers to remain anonymous.

What is striking about many muralists and graffiti artists is their courage and temerity, typical of great spirits. Theirs is a genuine artistic revolution, one which continues without an end in sight, increasingly impassioned and which has finally conquered even those who initially didn't want to hear anything about it, such as the great institutions, the museums and the galleries that snubbed the movement until it became impossible to ignore. However, even now that they have won the applause of society, many street artists continue to work in secret, on the margins of the community. Why? To make a difference, to inspire and to be — with their brushes, spray paints, and stencils — the great innovators of an era that is still to come and in which everyone will be truly free.

Freedom and unconventionality saturates the work of one of the artists I most admire: Jean-Michel Basquiat. In 1996, the director and painter Julian Schnabel dedicated a well-known biopic to him, with the actor Jeffrey Wright playing the artist

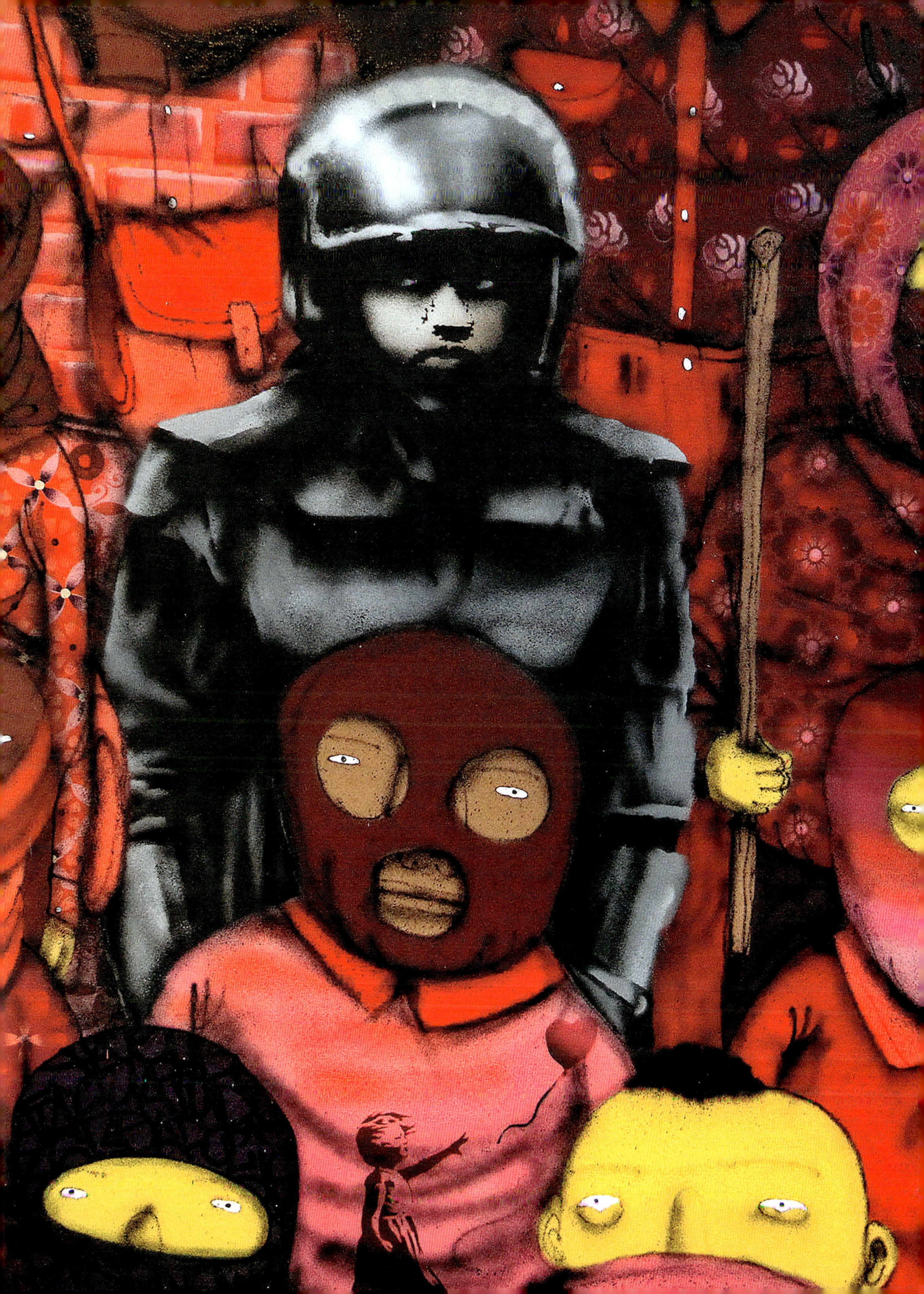

and David Bowie in the role of Andy Warhol. Schnabel, who personally experienced that splendid season of New York art and met Basquiat face-to-face, portrayed the great artist as an unquiet spirit and a soul adrift in the forest of skyscrapers of New York in the late 1970s, full of danger and temptation, a man clinging to his art in order to survive. Born in Brooklyn in 1960, to a Haitian father and a Puerto Rican mother, he died at only twenty-seven from a heroin overdose, in his apartment at 57 Great Jones Street in NoHo; destined to become a legend with his graffiti all over the Lower East Side, capturing hip-hop, post-punk and other street art movements. "There are days when I have no ideas and I think 'heck, I'm out of it', but it's only a passing mood," he used to say. Or, "I don't think about art when I am working, I think about life." And then, "I do paintings that look as though a kid did them."

Basquiat was a great friend of Keith Haring, another artist that I love and another fundamental chapter in street art. Though he died of AIDS in New York at only thirty-one, Haring wrote a distinctive chapter of street art, with his cartoon-like figures, such as the barking dog that was his signature and which has become an icon. Intolerant of the canonical expressive forms and the traditional systems of distributing art, he abandoned the New York School of Visual Art to immerse himself in the metropolitan fabric of the city, making use of empty advertising spaces on the underground as a workshop in which to experiment. Using simple and attractive symbols he denounced important social problems such as racism, social injustice, capitalism, drugs, love, happiness and sex. "We should not [. . .] make bourgeois art for a few and ignore the masses. [. . .] Art is all this and that is why I work in the street."

An expression of pure joy and sunniness, the Brazilian twins Otávio and Gustavo Pandolfo, better known as Os Gemeos, are another of the artists that I love; I discovered them in a New York gallery a number of years ago. In 2016, they organized a thrilling exhibition-event, *Silence of the Music*, at the Lehmann Maupin Gallery, at 536 West 22nd Street in Manhattan. For a number of years they have been exhibiting in institutional settings such as museums and galleries, but they also began on the streets. I adore their Brazilian imagery full of yellow and bright colors and their mythological figures, a dreamlike universe that even includes music boxes and sculptures in which to lose oneself like in a kaleidoscope, discovering new elements that take us to another planet. "Whatever we do in life, we should have fun. If we don't have toys or money, we have to invent and improvise. We derive our work from this background: we grew up in the district of Cambuci in São Paulo, playing in the street. Then came hip-hop, breakdance and graffiti. We fell in love with all this. We grew up in the 1980s, when hip-hop came to Brazil; we would have liked to know more, but it was difficult at that time to find information and we didn't have the money to travel to the United States where hip-hop was born. So, we created our own world. We started creating graffiti with latex, water-based paints and other materials. We used anything we could find, the only *fil rouge*, yesterday as today, is music," they explained during their New York adventure. Then they added with conviction, "We are complementary: every time one of us completes the thought of the other. Our creative process is so natural that it is even difficult for us to explain it. It is as if a thread keeps us united even when we are distant. It is a never-ending bond."

Another great artist is the Frenchman JR, a specialist in the "photographic collage" technique. Everything began by chance when, in 2001, he found a camera on the Paris underground. Wandering around Europe with this fateful gift, he photographed and assembled portraits of everyday people and street artists for the project *Portrait of a Generation*, with which he papered streets, underground railway stations and the roofs of Paris. This was followed by *Face 2 Face*, another major illegal exhibition featuring the faces of Israelis and Palestinians, and *Women Are Heroes*, in which he emphasized the dignity of female victims of conflicts and attacks and the role they play in society. In 2015, he also directed *Ellis*, a short film written by Eric Roth, narrated by Robert De Niro and dedicated to the immigrants who passed through Ellis Island in New York. According to JR, art is meant to change the perception of the world. "Art is not born to change the world, but it can change the way in which we look at it, it can create analogies. When I see people interact with a work, when I notice the impact of art on individual lives, then I imagine that in a certain way, it is also possible to change reality a little bit. That is what I believe. For this reason I want to create as many interactions and as many communications as I can. But this is something that I have understood over time, I began painting on the streets when I was fifteen and at that time I didn't think much, I just did graffiti and I wrote my name everywhere, using the city as a canvas. I went into the tunnels of Paris or onto the roofs with my friends. Every outing was an adventure." According to JR, the city is still the best art gallery possible, "I don't have to worry about finding a gallery in which to present my work and wait for others to decide whether what I do is worth showing to people. I can see for myself on the streets."

Blu, an Italian who lives at various squats and anarchic groups in Bologna and around the world, is an even more controversial figure: in 2016, he destroyed most of his work in Bologna as a protest against the commercialization of art and creativity and against the decision of the municipal authorities to exploit the popularity of his work. This gesture caused quite a stir around the world, but Blu was no stranger to scandal: in 2010 MOCA Museum in Los Angeles deleted one of his murals, considering it politically offensive because it portrayed a number of coffins wrapped in dollar bills rather than in the American flag.

I am also a painter, as well as a writer and a photographer. I have been painting on canvas since I was a child, mainly abstract figures, and I know well the passion for art and the incessant need to create. I am quite shy and reserved, so for me it is very difficult to exhibit in galleries. My art belonged to a space that was only mine. It was my friends who pushed me to hold some exhibitions, but if I were to turn back time, I would choose anonymity, just like so many street artists. Perhaps this is why it is so interesting for me to discover new works of street art, and not knowing who created a mural or a graffito always gives me the shivers. At times, I take a photo of the work with my camera or my iPhone, just to be able to remember it. The first time I saw a graffito I was in an alley near the station of Venice, where I was studying. It was a yellow script, but it looked like a serpent. It struck me immediately; it was so gaudy on that grey wall in a dark, narrow *calle*. It was a surprise that gave me an almost childish thrill, as if I had discovered a secret. What makes street art so fascinating is the aura of mystery that surrounds it, the casual discovery along a street or on a mailbox, on the corner of a house or a tunnel in the subway. This is why I love losing myself in the streets of Venice Beach or downtown Los Angeles, where new works appear overnight, but also in improbable places like West Hollywood, where the cinema stars meet up: it was here, some time ago that a gigantic tiger ambushed me from a wall on the Sunset Strip. In New York, I always find something new on the streets and shutters of SoHo, the Bowery, the Lower East Side, the Meatpacking District or Chinatown, or while I walk the High Line, where the flamboyant mural by Eduardo Kobra, another artist I love, reproduces the famous photograph of a sailor and a girl kissing passionately. Other "hot" areas are Williamsburg, at the moment considered the "kingdom of graffiti," Bushwick, and indeed Brooklyn in general, Hunts Point in the Bronx; and of course there is the Graffiti Hall of Fame in Harlem, where I go from time to time to have a look. Miami is also a very interesting place to discover new and magnificent street art, in particular in Wynwood. In San Francisco, like a sky that can change from one moment to another, there is a "rainbow" of graffiti along Haight Street and its side roads; the area has managed to hold on to some of its hippieness, despite the globalization of Haight-Ashbury. In the Mission District, almost everywhere, along Balmy Alley, Clarion Alley and Lilac Alley, on the façade of The Women's Building, home to the *MaestraPeace Mural*, and in other places, from a supermarket on Nob Hill, to North Beach, the district of the beat poets and writers, or the more touristy Fisherman's Wharf, street art is everywhere.

In London, the best areas are Leake Street, the West Bank and the areas around Brick Lane and Shoreditch. In Paris, street art appears everywhere, but above all on the walls of Seine-Saint-Denis, an incredible cultural workshop, and in the multicultural district of Belleville. Paris loves street art: here and there it hides mosaics by the well-known street artist Invader, who creates pixelated figures similar to the characters in vintage videogames.

Berlin is another hotbed of ideas, especially the Mitte district and the East Side Gallery in Kreuzberg. In the German capital works by El Bocho, amongst others, are truly amusing. Other European cities where it is possible to admire excellent street art are Lisbon, in Calçada da Glória, Rua das Gaivotas, Rua Rodrigues Faria and Avenida Conselheiro Fernando de Sousa, or Prague, where we find the Lennon Wall in the central district of Malá Strana.

Down under, Melbourne is the Australian capital of culture in the fields of music, fashion, design, art and street art, even deserving the nickname of "stencil graffiti capital" thanks to a festival held in 2004 that left a number of colorful memories in the city. Anyone traveling there should wander down Hosier Lane, a central pedestrian street and home to the best of Australian street art.

However, the most amazing places are probably the most unexpected. The side streets of central Reykjavik in Iceland are rich with colorful graffiti. As is Philadelphia in Pennsylvania, where, thanks to the Mural Arts Program (MAP) the Mural Mile is covered in evocative works. In Toronto, the famous Graffiti Alley includes a long lane covered in graffiti that stretches out a few blocks in the fashion district around Queen Street West. Also in Toronto, the Ritz-Carlton Hotel at 181 Wellington Street West organizes a number of programs in support of local artists and tours of the Alley. However, for me, the most surprising experiences were in Tahiti, in

Pages 12–13 **Eduardo Kobra, *We Are All One*, 2016** - For the Olympics in Rio de Janeiro the Brazilian artist Eduardo Kobra painted an immense, colorful mural depicting five faces, dedicated to the indigenous peoples of five continents.

Pages 14–15 **JR, *Ellis Island*, 2016** - The French artist JR, already the author of a series of works in the former Ellis Island Immigrant Hospital, dedicated this work to immigrant children; it is to be found at 100 Franklin Street, New York.

French Polynesia, which has recently been covered in graffiti that recalls the wonderful colors of the Pacific Ocean and the island's luxuriant vegetation. The murals not only animate Papeete, the largest town on the island, where there is now a popular skatepark, another destination for the graffiti artists, but also the walls, houses and mailboxes of the smaller villages. Amongst the most popular figures are indigenous and Polynesian motifs and local myths and legends. It is Tahiti that shows how street art has now reached even the most remote corners of the planet, bringing along its values of peace, love, equality, respect, and the desire for a better world.

Then there are the artists I met during this fantastic journey around the world to discover street art. Vibrant souls charged with positive energy, who talked frankly and courageously about their art and what it means to them to be independent and creative. I chased Banksy for months around the London underground and throughout England, asking his friends and acquaintances for news; then I was able to approach him for the first time through the wonderful documentary he directed *Exit Through the Gift Shop: A Banksy Film* (2010), presented at the Sundance Film Festival and nominated for the Academy Award for Best Documentary Feature. I met Shepard Fairey, who also won over Barack Obama, for the first time at the Tribeca Film Festival where he presented his documentary *Let Fury Have the Hour* (2012). David Choe revealed all his wild artistic sensuality in a surreal and beautiful concert. Ben Eine was as enigmatic as his colored letters. Then there was Specter, with whom I spent an entire winter's day among the urban landscapes and at the Brooklyn loft where he lives and works. ROA, who explained to me how much a society reveals of itself in the relationship it has with animals. Evol and his passion for the "urban people." Aryz who wants to create art that encourages people to create their own art. Vhils, with his splendid project to "humanize" the city. Fauxreel, who makes fun of advertising. C215, the specialist in stenciling, but also a lover of stray cats and wild creatures. Alex Vau, skilled in seducing with music, poetry and words and with his passionate and sunny vein. AEC from Interesni Kazki, who takes inspiration from mythology. Philippe Baudelocque, who compares his technique to a sweet *mille-feuille*. M-City, who as a child was enchanted by naval shipyards. El Mac, virtuoso of faces and bodies. NUNCA, who despite his extreme shyness revealed himself in all his authenticity. Slinkachu, whose very personal and original technique has also conquered the Internet.

Then there were two very special women, because, apart from being extremely talented, they are among the very few important female figures in the still mostly male world of street art. Swoon, who explained to me the "oneiric" origin of her name and told me how she became enthralled by portraits, and Becca, who lives with her animals, dogs, cats and even fawns, at her creative sanctuary in Austin, Texas.

All these great artists are part of a thrilling collage of souls and minds, ideas and dreams, a wonderful mirror of humanity and its infinite facets. During this journey around the world, I gathered visions and testimonies of the most important masters in the sector and I learned that we must never take anything for granted: abandoned railway cars, ruined houses, underpasses lined with dry leaves all hide infinite possibilities for art and creativity, and when a peeling wall is transformed into a colorful mural, something in the world changes.

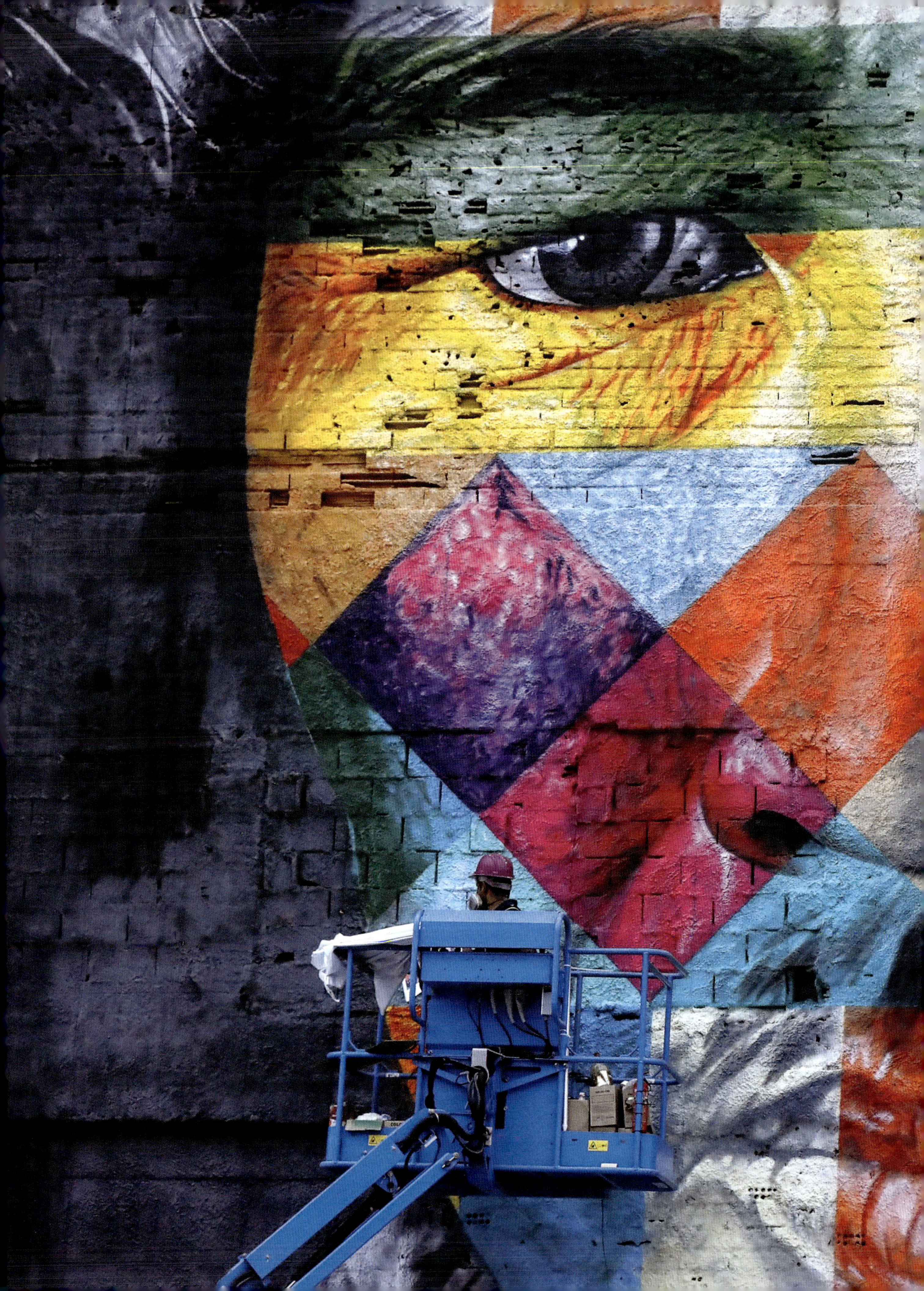

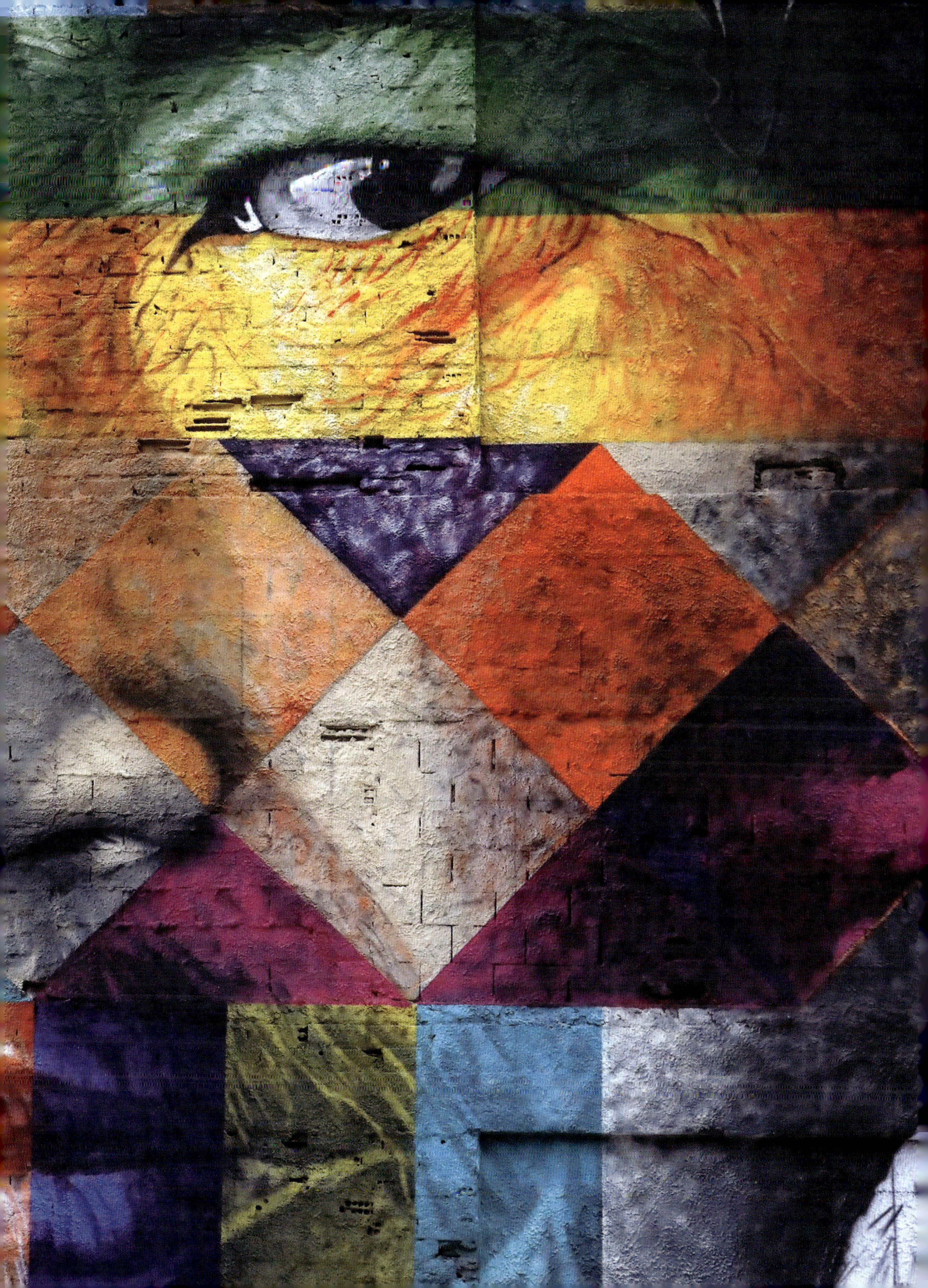

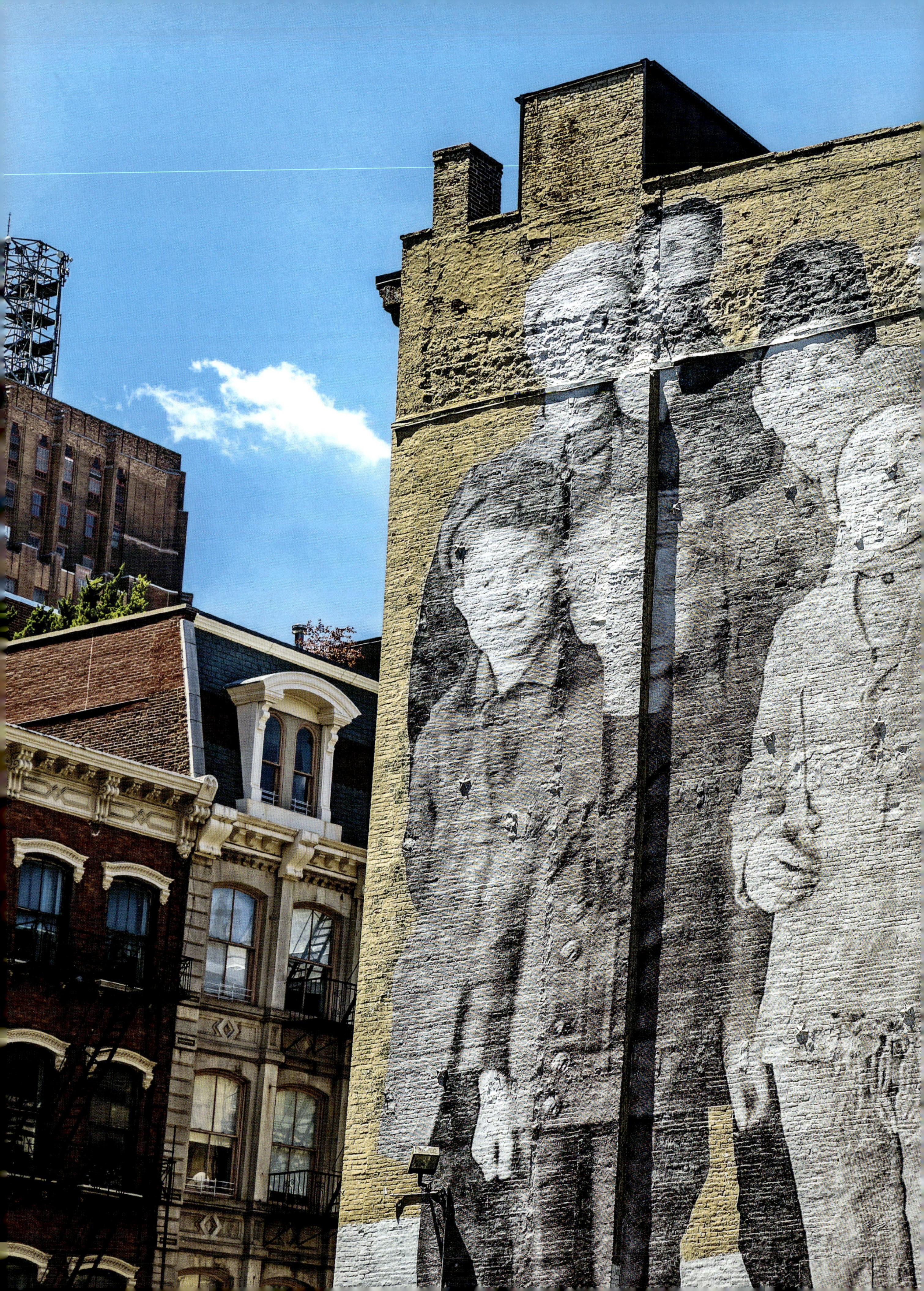

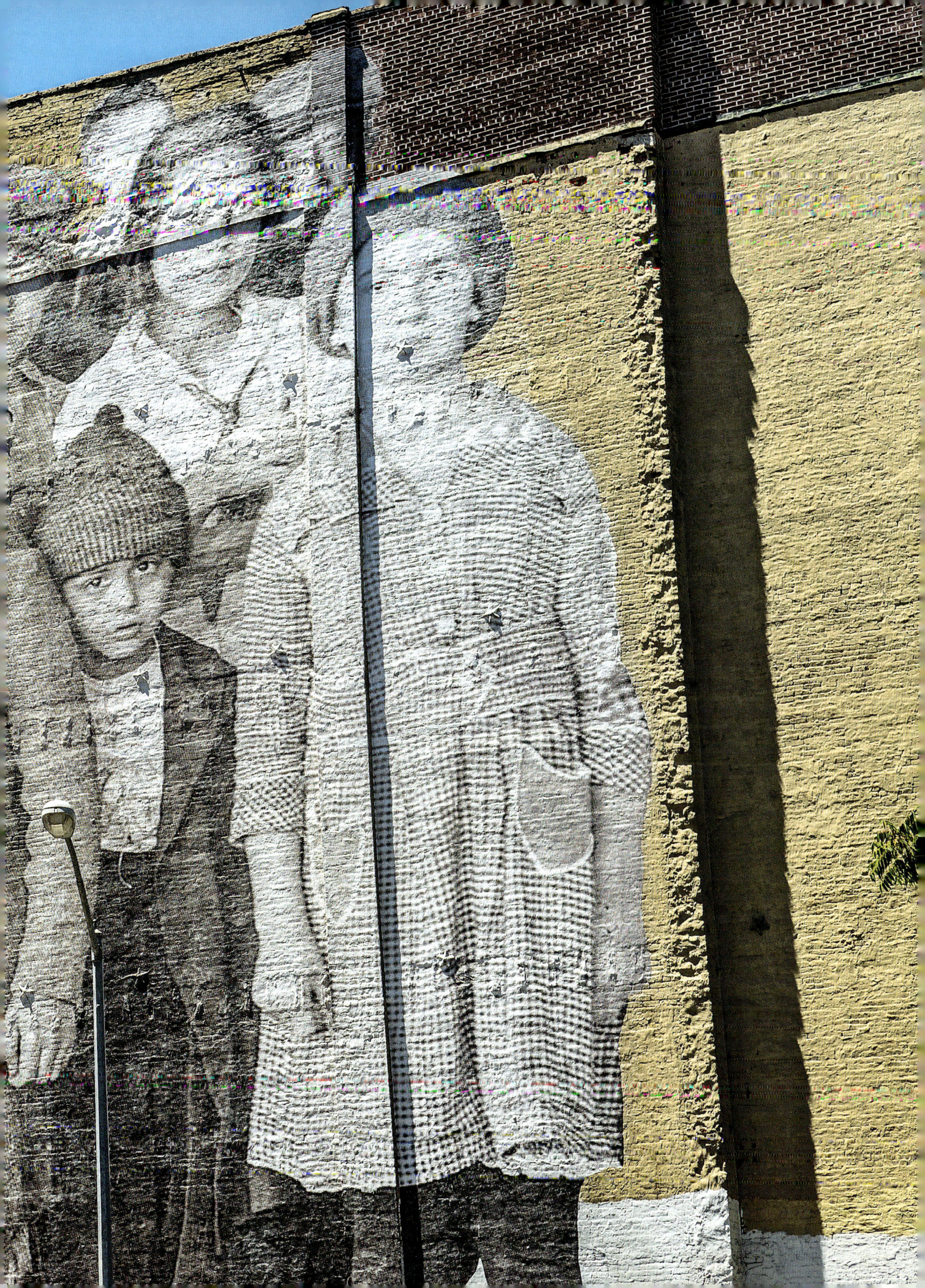

Introduction

by Chris Versteeg

Drawing on walls is an art form that is as old as mankind. From the famous cave paintings in Lascaux, in France, to images, names and messages scratched in stone by the ancient Romans, to early travelers who left their names in old cities. Some people just have to leave a mark, saying 'I was here'. You could fill ten books on the subject, but for now our focus is on street art, so we'll skip the pre-historic works and go straight to modern times. Wikipedia says street art is "visual art created in public locations, usually unsanctioned artwork executed outside of the context of traditional art venues. The term gained popularity during the graffiti art boom of the early 1980s and continues to be applied to subsequent incarnations. Stencil graffiti, wheatpasted poster art or sticker art, and street installation or sculpture, are common forms of modern street art. The terms 'urban art', 'guerrilla art', 'post-graffiti' and 'neo-graffiti' are also sometimes used when referring to artwork created in these contexts. Traditional spray-painted graffiti artwork itself is often included in this category, excluding territorial graffiti or pure vandalism." This description pretty much poses the questions of whether graffiti can be considered street art and vice versa. These two art forms somehow do not always seem to mix so well.

The common opinion is that graffiti as we know it today originated in the early 1970s in New York City and, most of the time, was about 'getting up'; getting people to see your name all over the city. For some it was a game, others loved the adrenaline and yet others had more artistic motives. Some moved on while others built a career around it. Pieces got cleaned, painted over or just faded away. But the key factor was that graffiti was mainly done illegally, painted on walls, trains and venues with stolen paint and had had very little connection to the 'art scene.'

Graffiti painters - or 'writers' as they are called - would form 'crews' and fight other crews when one of their works got painted over by other writers. As a trophy, writers would take photographs of their work. But it was not only writers who documented their art: two New York based photographers, Martha Cooper and Henry Chalfant, eagerly photographed a huge amount of painted trains in the 1970s and 1980s. They won the trust of writers and got tipped when trains were being, or about to be, painted. In some cases, they went along with the writers, shooting the now classic images of graffiti painters.

Their book *Subway Art*, published in 1984, was the first proper publication on graffiti on trains and created a gateway to a bit more social acceptance. However, that wasn't the first book on the subject; in 1982, Craig Castleman wrote *Getting Up, Subway Graffiti in New York*, a series of interviews and stories about young graffiti artists. It was one of the first serious insightful descriptions of what was still a shady world. These books - and the documentary *Style Wars* (1983), also directed by Henry Chalfant - would later inspire a whole generation of new graffiti writers, and lay the foundation for a life style.

Graffiti was considered to be vandalism, and writers could be prosecuted if caught by the police. The public felt somewhat threatened because of graffiti, forcing local governments to step up and take action. This resulted in an even more underground movement with strict codes and rules. Eventually, many big cities created sites where writers could paint graffiti legally, practice and perfect their styles, meet each other and hang out. On the other hand, the punishment for painting illegal graffiti became more severe. In some cases, this made some writers decide to only paint in legal places, or choose the opposite course, a carefully hidden undercover life as illegal artists.

Street art – as we know it today – on the other hand, originated much later and often with the purpose of putting art on the streets, using public space as an open-air gallery where an artist could achieve fame rapidly. In this context, artists would more often cooperate than fight each other and basically their attitude was more peaceful and open. Public opinion also became more favorable; street artists used images that were more like cartoons and more attractive than letters alone, and their works came across as less aggressive. Street art

also re-introduced the use of media-like posters, stickers, stencils and in some cases even mosaics. This in itself lent a more artistic tone to their work and revealed that many street artists have a background in graphic design, illustration or arts. Like graffiti artists, they too wanted to have their name or image known throughout the city, and stickers were the perfect medium. You can post stickers in the daytime, on your way to work or school. Consequently, entire streets were soon covered with stickers by artists from all over the world.

In the early days, famous places to see street art were London, Paris, Berlin and, naturally, New York. And while graffiti was mostly about promoting oneself, street artists also addressed social and political issues or used humor to attract their audience. Even though most of the work was still done illegally, this more open approach caused some galleries and art collectors to embrace street art and soon the first exhibits were organized, quickly followed by advertising agencies, which realized that this was a perfect way to add a bit of 'street cool' to a brand.

But let's go back a bit in time. In the late 1970s, a young man in New York named Keith Haring was inspired by the graffiti he saw all over the city and he too started to make drawings on the streets. But instead of using letters, he developed his own style of line drawings with human and animal shapes, heavily influenced by popular culture.

His work soon drew a lot of attention and he became one of the most iconic artists of the 20th century. Arguably, Haring could be considered one of the first street artists as we know them today, and he is still a major inspiration for many artists. The same is true of Jean-Michel Basquiat, who in the late 1970s started his career as a graffiti writer, but soon turned to painting canvasses and selling them in art galleries. Some people don't consider him a real street artist, because he worked only briefly in the streets, but the influence of his work is undoubted. Of course, there were many others, such as Dondi, Lee, Futura, Rammellzee and Quick, who worked both on the streets and on canvas, but none of them rose as quickly to stardom as Haring and Basquiat. At this point in time, graffiti and street art as an artistic medium were mainly an American affair, but the more European artists visited New York, the more inspiration they brought back to the Continent. One of those artists was the Frenchman Blek le Rat, who visited New York in the summer of 1971. He too was blown away by the abundance of graffiti and, after finishing his studies, he started to try different forms of graffiti himself. At first, he tried just making letters, but he soon found out that he preferred working with stencils. They can be very detailed, yet quick to apply and can be used repeatedly. His work is often a subtle way of creating more public and social awareness, and his art is still widely appreciated. One of the most famous street artists of our time - Banksy - was inspired by Blek le Rat and once said: "Every time I think I've painted something slightly original, I find out that Blek le Rat has done it as well, only twenty years earlier." Here he addresses one of the problems of modern-day art: so much has already been done that it is a great challenge to be original.

These artists travels from the Continent to New York and vice versa resulted in the birth of a network, an exchange of ideas concerning art, and soon the graffiti and street art virus spread through Europe. One member of this new network was JonOne (JonOne156). Born in the United States, he traveled to Paris a few times and finally settled down there to paint in the streets and pursue an artistic career. He's known for his persistent 'street bombing' and for painting pieces in broad daylight, as well for his very colorful canvasses, and he is still a very active artist today. Graffiti and street art flourished those days, with names such as SKKI and Lokiss producing unique works that were a bold mixture of graffiti and abstract art. Another city that really bloomed in the early 1980s was Berlin. The Berlin Wall divided the city. The Wall was almost 12 feet high and more than 90 miles long. Needless to say, this 'canvas' attracted a lot of artists, who were somehow allowed to paint the western side of the Wall, while the eastern side was of course off limits, with a strip of no-man's-land and watchtowers – known as 'the death strip' – guarding it. Most artists painted politically motivated work on the Wall, since it was a political icon, separating two ideologies. Eventually, in 1989 West and East Germany were re-united and demolition of the Wall began.

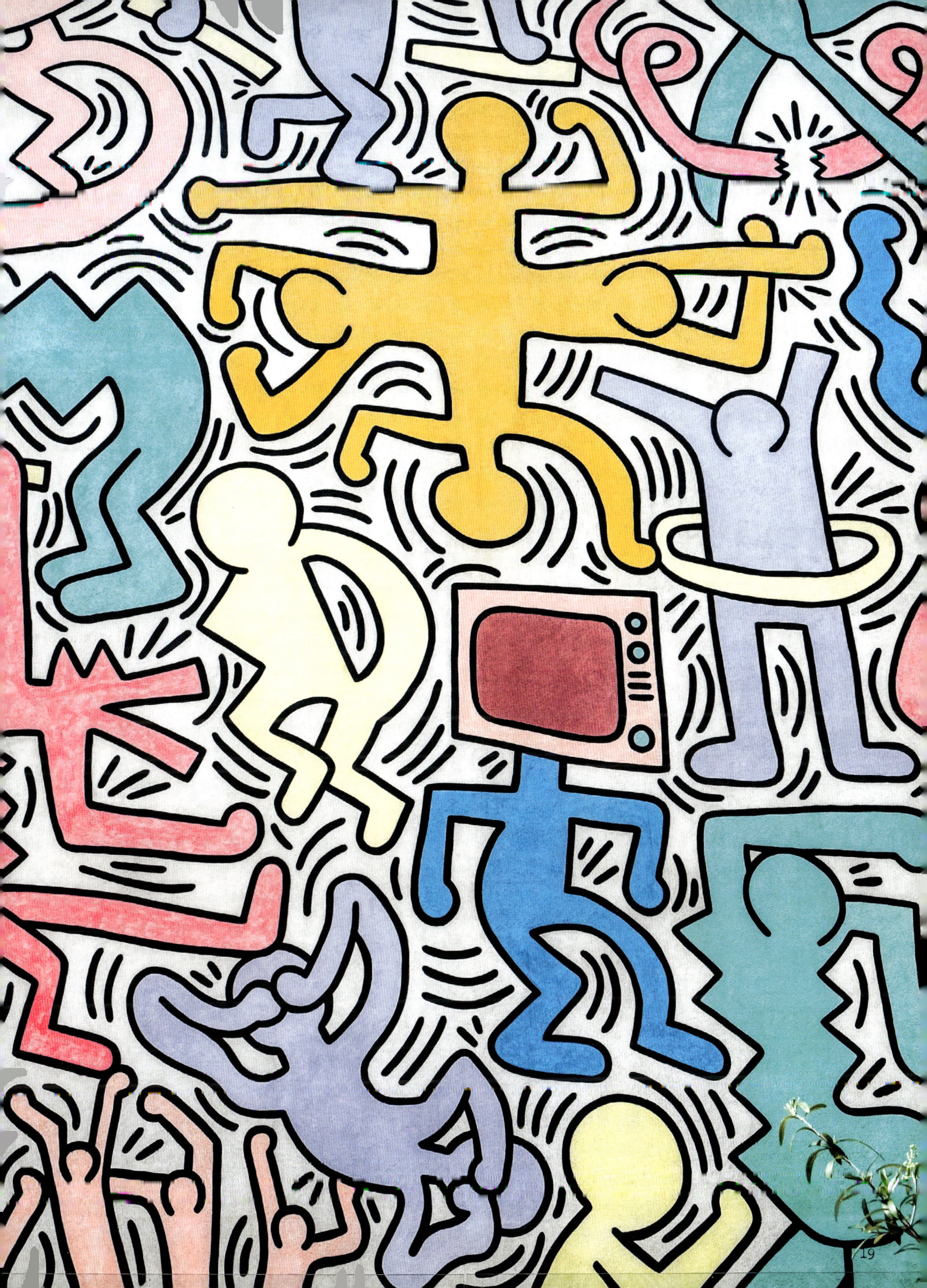

Only a small section still stands, maintained by The East Side Gallery; it is a mile long and is located near the center of Berlin, in the Friedrichshain-Kreuzberg neighborhood. The most famous painting on the remaining section is *My God, Help Me to Survive This Deadly Love*, which shows Soviet leader Leonid Brezhnev and East German leader Erich Honecker, kissing each other. This image was based on a photograph taken in 1979 during the 30th anniversary of the German Democratic Republic and was painted in 1990 by Dmitri Vrubel, a Russian artist.

By that time, most major cities in Europe had established a graffiti and street art scene with artists traveling all over Europe to make their art. Small magazines were published, documenting and spreading work, influencing a new generation. The scene developed further, growing more and more mature, becoming a major presence on the streets. With the advent of the Internet, the scene just exploded! All of a sudden you could see art from every corner of the world. Previously such hard-to-reach places as Japan or Brazil turned out to have a lively scene, and artists could easily contact each other via email and plan visits. International collaborations became more and more normal and artists could exchange tips and tricks and show their works online. Their popularity grew and more of them started to do work in the streets. Some had a graffiti background, while others were working as illustrators, and they all always tried to find a good location for their art. Worldwide, people influenced and motivated one another, which led to an increase in quality and output. Fotolog, Flickr and the New York-based Wooster Collective were important online platforms to see the latest work, and magazines like *Underground Productions* (Sweden), *Stylefile* (Germany), *Backjumps* (Germany), *Bomber Megazine* (the Netherlands), and *Non Stop Magazine* (Switzerland) covered graffiti and street art from all over the world.

Even though it was still an illegal art form, the police continued to focus mainly on 'traditional' graffiti like train writing and street bombing and would sometimes simply not know how to deal with this new thing called street art. Sometimes artists working illegally would be sent off with just a warning, or got their paint or posters confiscated. As was mentioned above, in general street art has been received more favorably than graffiti. A good example of this is building or shop owners commissioning artists to paint their walls or rolling shutters, sometimes over illegally painted work. This is mutually advantageous: the artist gets a good spot to paint works that would last for a long time and also gets paid for his or her work, while the owner has eliminated unwanted graffiti and has an artwork that was appreciated. In some cases, street art was a reaction to the highbrow art galleries that were interested only in the commercial aspects of art. Street artists wanted their work to be public, to bring art to the street for everyone to enjoy.

Every city had its own approach to illegal art. In Finland for example, the city of Helsinki issued a zero tolerance policy in 1998, that made all forms of street art illegal and punishable with high fines, and it was enforced by private security contractors. This policy ended in 2008, after which legal walls and art collectives have been established. Another extreme example is Singapore, a city known for its high fines. There, vandalism is punished with a fine or jail term, plus mandatory corporal punishment of three to eight strokes of the cane. While some cities were able to sustain a strict cleaning and prosecution policy, others sometimes simply didn't have the funds to do so and eventually turned into huge open-air street art museums. One of these latter is Berlin. After the reunification of the city, the eastern part became a run-down, low rent neighborhood with many abandoned or poorly maintained buildings. This attracted a lot of artists, turning this section of town into a cultural hot spot. Another example is Barcelona, a relatively cheap city with good climate that became very popular among street artists. And more importantly, almost all the art painted in the streets stayed there, sometimes for years. Early in 2004, a group of artists from several different countries got together in Barcelona to spend a week just painting every day. Among them were the London Police, Galo, Dave the Chimp, D-Face, Flying Förtress, miss Van, Bo & Microbo, Lastplak, Pez, Mysterious Al, C100 and Captain Rouget. They met with local artists and painted walls, pasted up posters and put up huge numbers of stickers. At that time, Barcelona was considered the world's best city for street art, but that all changed quickly. By the end of 2005, the city removed almost all street art and graffiti and instituted high fines for those caught painting. Eventually, artists got organized and managed to gradually get some art back on the streets, but in the process a lot of good works got lost.

Among the most visible things in the streets are the omnipresent stickers. Traffic light poles are often covered with them, as are lamp posts, mailboxes, phone booths, the back of traffic signs, drainage pipes, bus stops, subway entrances and basically every possible visible surface where a sticker can be fastened and seen by a lot of people. Stickers are a bit like what a tag is for a graffiti writer; you can put up hundreds of them in a day without attracting too much attention to yourself. They became like a business card, easy to carry and to collect, sometimes carefully kept or even peeled off. Some would be simple, homemade, photocopied paper stickers, others would consist of multi-colored printed vinyl stickers, both big and small, but whatever they were they could be seen everywhere. It is pretty safe to say that stickers became very popular then. In 2005, the Italian duo Bo & Microbo published a book called *Izastickup* which is more than 200 pages long and filled back-to-back only with stickers. In the Netherlands, there was a website called *Stick It*, totally dedicated to stickers, and in 2005 a cover of *Art Review* magazine featured a portrait of a man whose face was completely covered with stickers. For the majority of artists stickers were the most effective way of promoting their work.

One of the best known is Shepard Fairey's *André the Giant has a Posse* sticker, created in 1989.

Page 23 **Invader, *Star Wars*, 2013** - Outside the Great Eastern Street car park in London, tiles colored in order to look similar to the pixels of early videogames depict a lightsaber duel: it is the unmistakable style of the French artist Invader.

Pages 24-25 **Blu, Rome, 2014** - In Rome, in via del Porto Fluviale, Italian artist Blu repainted an old barracks that is now occupied with more than 400 people living there: the windows have become the eyes of dozens of colorful faces that are looking out onto the street.

"The sticker has no meaning but exists only to cause people to react, to contemplate and search for meaning in the sticker" he said. He took the image of a French professional wrestler and actor called André the Giant, elaborated on it, and in a few years time tens of thousands of stickers were put up all over the world. This basically sparked the career of Fairey, who is now known as Obey (Obey the Giant) and is famous for his iconic posters, as well as for painting huge walls on commission and running a clothing line. His work often uses iconic historical figures, sometimes addressing social issues, and is strongly influenced by traditional propaganda posters.

Generally, most artists work either by painting murals, putting up posters and stickers or drawing on walls with markers. Naturally, there are a few interesting exceptions to this rule. First, there is Invader, a French artist who uses mosaic tiles to create his images, which look like they just walked out of an old 8-bit computer game. He carefully prepares his work before cementing it on a wall, and the images are all different. He has visited major cities around the world leaving his 'invaders' wherever he goes. Moreover, that's not all; he documents them and marks them on a map, inviting people to go find them all, awarding points to each artwork found and in so doing turns his art into an interesting game.

Special mention is also due to the Portuguese artist Vhils, who makes relief portraits by chiseling into plaster and brick walls, dissects poster ads, and excavates walls.

Today, street art is an established art form, with artists earning a living from their work and gaining the appreciation they deserve. Most of them have worked hard to get where they are, dedicating their life to art and believing in what they do. Art galleries and collectors show their interest in, and realize the artistic potential of the movement, often connecting it to pop art. I won't go so far as to say street art has become mainstream, but part of it is moving in that direction. Most artists started out doing illegal work, while some are now only doing studio or commissioned painting work, and there are even some who call themselves street artists, but have never painted in the streets . . . In conclusion, the label 'street art' is the name of a style of art that doesn't necessarily have to be executed in the streets. Of course, this is crazy: street art - as the name clearly says - is made in the streets, on walls or any other public surface. As soon as it goes indoors, it becomes 'art inspired by street art', stencil art or illustration design. This is merely my personal opinion; street art is still a relatively young art form and is changing shape all the time. Let's see what art history books will have to say about it in 2117.

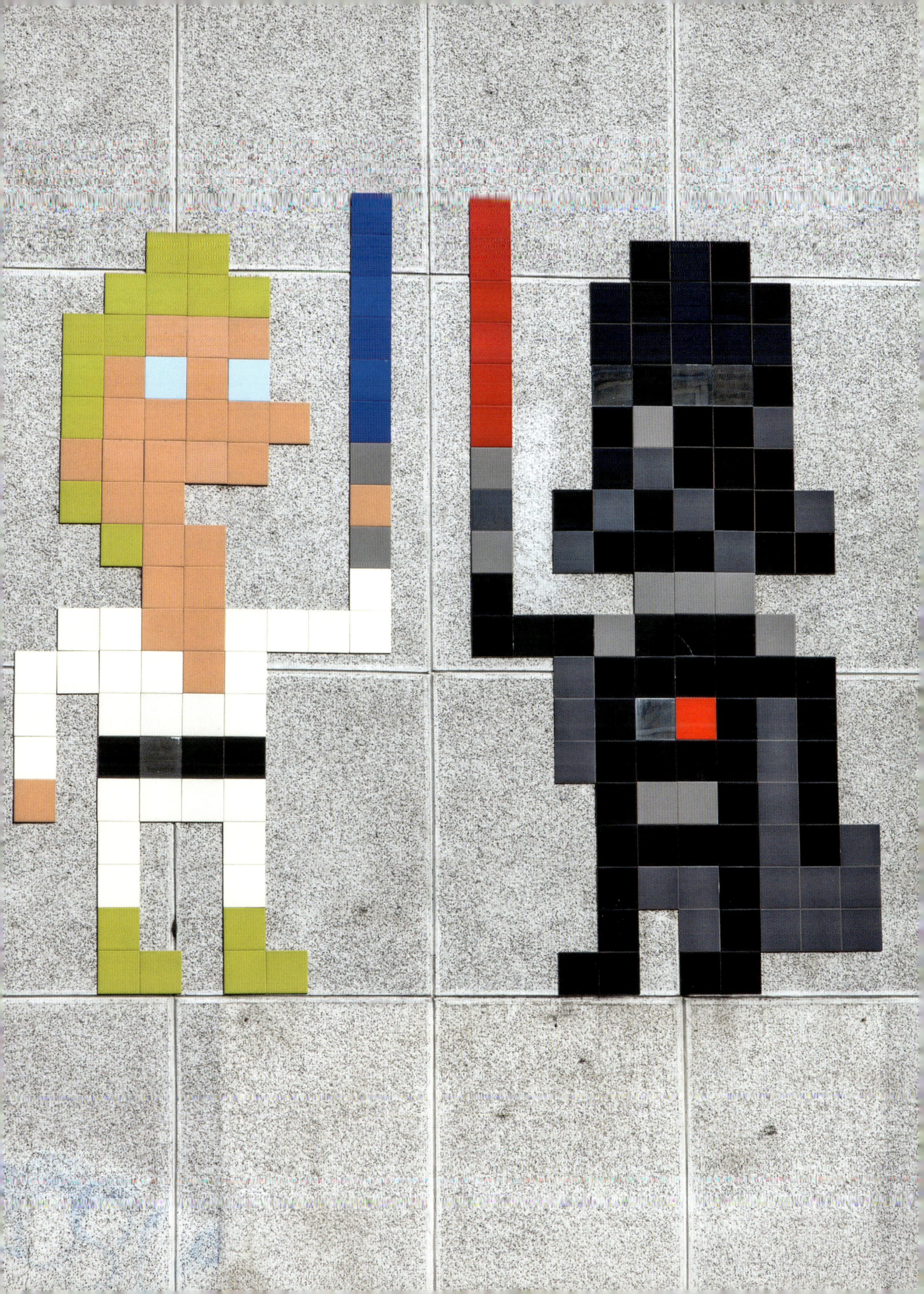

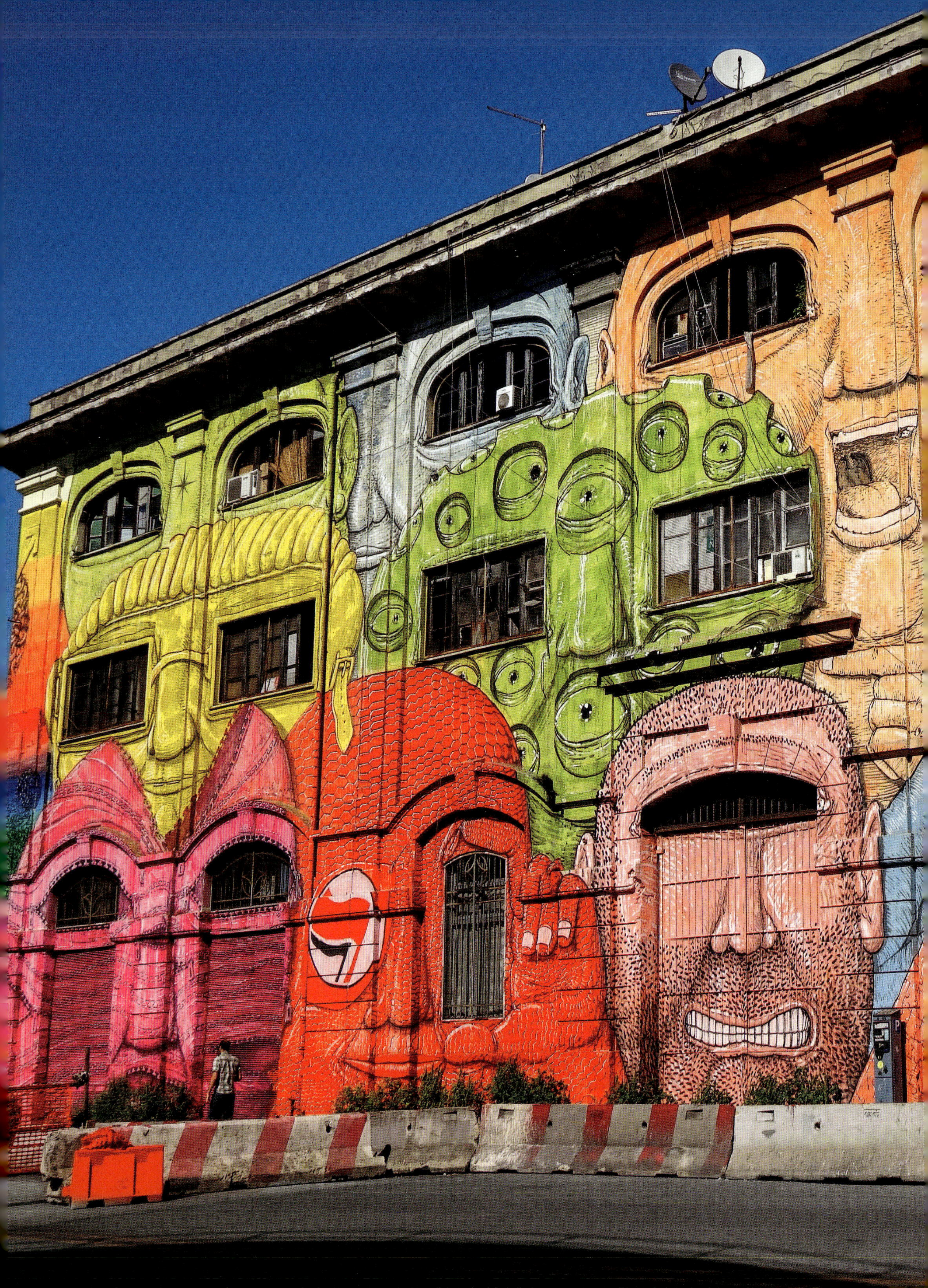

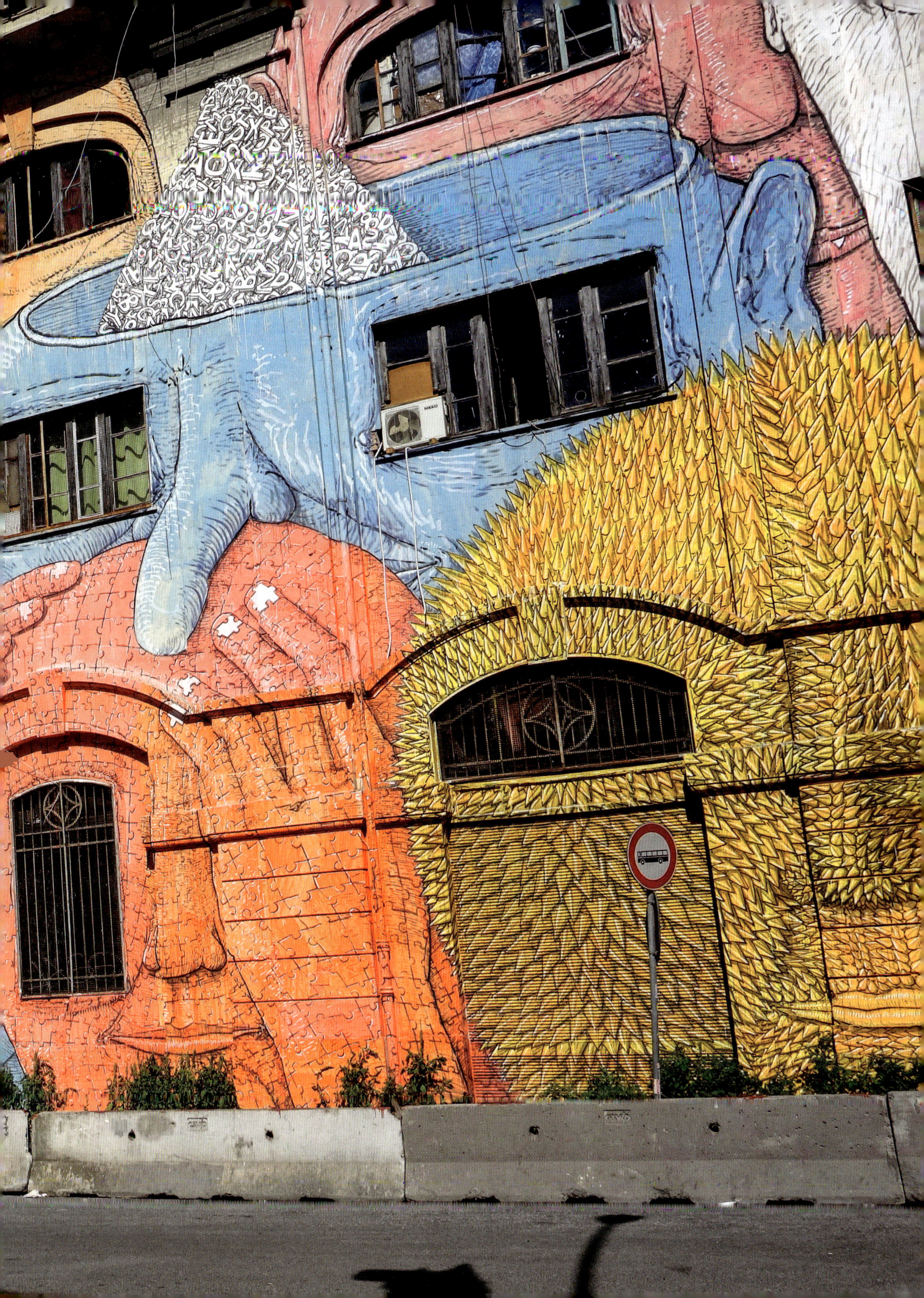

ARYZ

Painter of Emotions

Amongst Aryz's most frequent subjects are skeletons, animals, extravagant and unusual people, but they all have something in common: "I tend to adapt my work to the shape of the buildings and the setting I am working in.

I choose the colors to try to work in accordance to the context that surrounds the wall," Aryz explains. "I live in Cardedeu, about twenty-five miles from Barcelona. It's nice there because nobody cares much about graffiti or street art. When I come back from a project or an event, it's very relaxing there, mainly because not much happens in my town," and he adds that this helps him to remain true to himself.

> I would be satisfied just to know that my creativity has been an inspiration for others.

"When I began, I never would have imagined that I would gain such recognition, I am truly grateful to all those who have supported me."

Aryz was actually born in Palo Alto, California, in 1988, but his parents moved first to Barcelona and then to this small town. Although he is recognized as one of the greatest mural artists in the world, he still considers himself a painter first and foremost. "I don't think of myself as a street artist, what I do is not spontaneous or done illegally, I consider myself just a painter who loves to paint," he tries to clarify.

Still, he admits that everything began with his passion for graffiti. "I grew up at a time when the graffiti artists of Barcelona were enjoying a golden moment, and I was fascinated by the writings and productions that I saw in the streets or magazines, I soon realized that I wanted to take part in it," he recalls, thinking of his training, which began in the streets but soon moved inside.

"First thing I did on the street was some letters, since I was strongly influenced by hip hop. Later, I started to get a bit more interested in Art and that changed a bit the direction of my path . . . at the same time I started attracting wider attention, and slowly I was getting involved in more ambitious projects. I switched from painting big walls in abandoned factories to paint big walls in the middle of cities." Some associate Aryz with large-scale murals, but he does not think in such terms. "It is not a question of size, but of what a surface or a wall inspires me to do.

Grateful Death, 2013 - A mural created during the Cologne Urban Art Festival CityLeaks, in Severinswall, Cologne. The union of the skeleton and the flower reflects the *memento mori* of 17th century iconography.

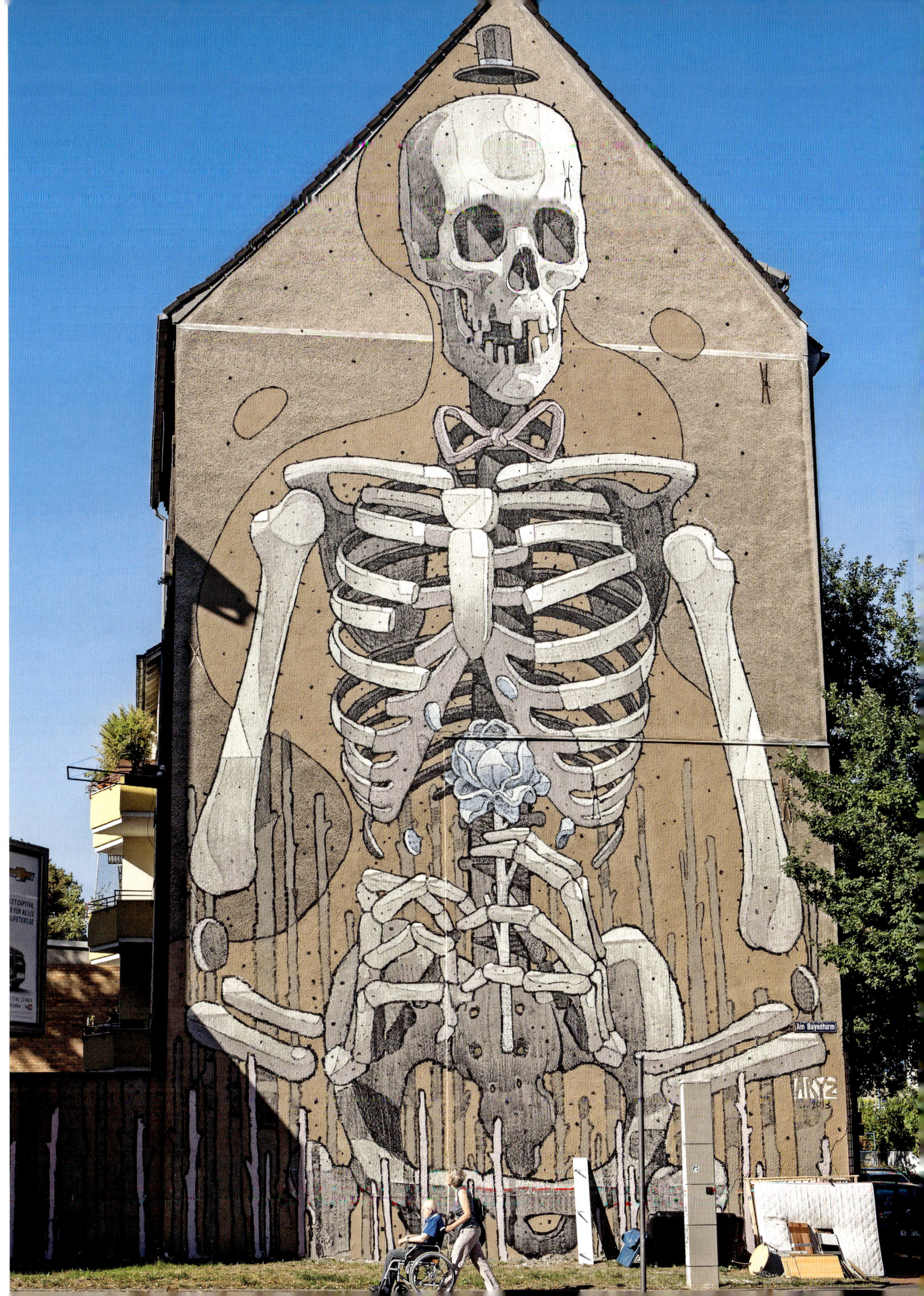

Aim Bayenturm
ARYZ
2012

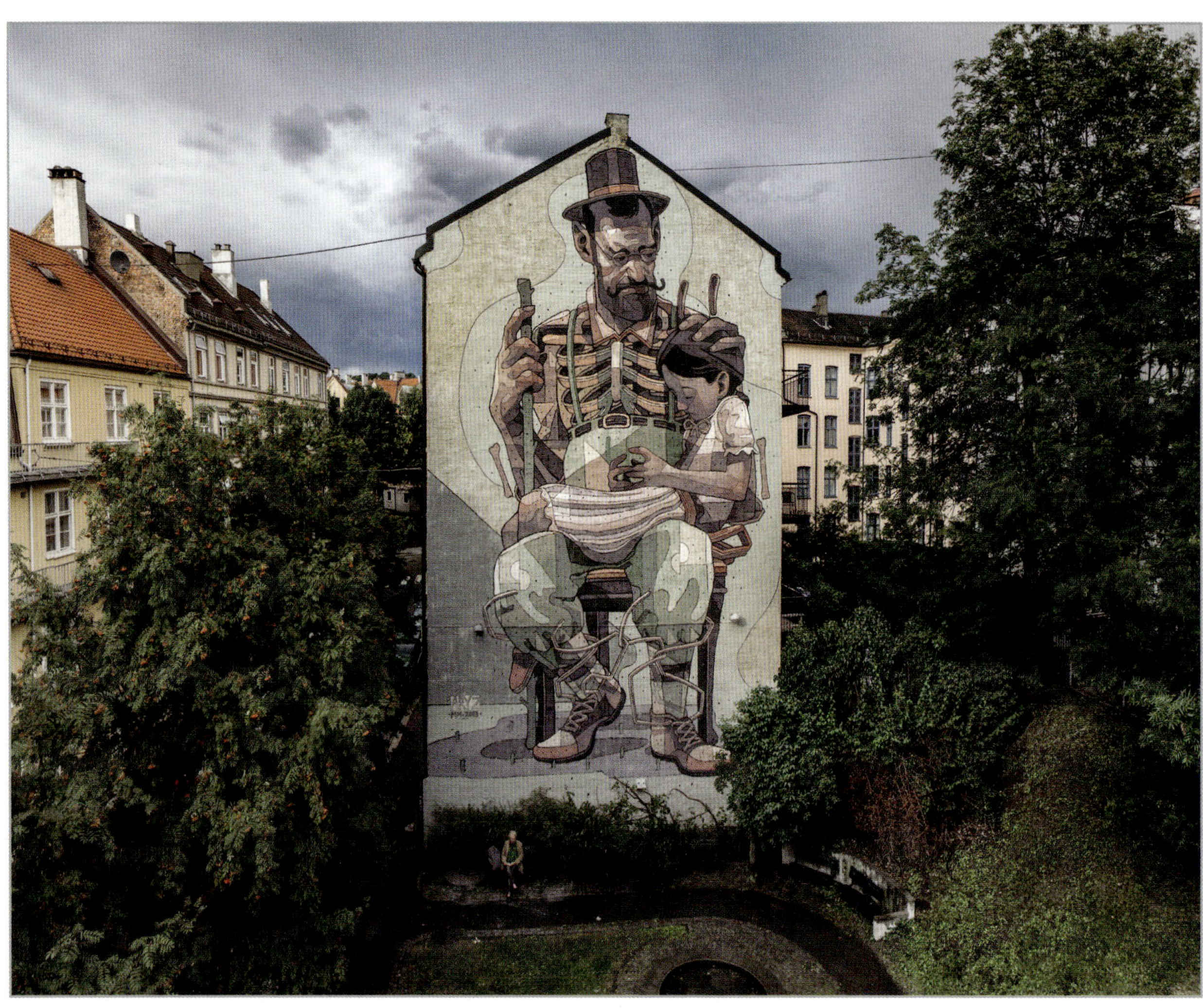

Oslo, 2013 - On the occasion of the *Oslo Triennial of Mural Art*, Aryz painted this mural representing
a father holding his daughter on his knees.

It can be big or small, it doesn't matter. When I know what wall I'll paint, I draw a picture of it, so that way I can see if the idea fits or not to the space I have. Once that's done I can start painting, I never have a rendered or defined idea of what I'll do. It's an evolving process . . . Sometimes it goes well, and many others it doesn't."

Aryz explains his method for choosing and creating the subjects, "To paint façades I mainly use rollers, and some brushes for last touches. I don't like spray paint so much, I like to have a direct contact with the wall, and with the sprays, you rarely touch the surface with the tool. I think that with brushes and rollers you can see more of a human touch, there are more imperfections. In this society where everything needs to be perfectly done by a machine, It's good to see something done by someone who also does mistakes . . ."

"I was certainly influenced by the masters of classic Spanish painters, such as Ramon Casas, Diego Velázquez, or Joaquín Sorolla, but I also enjoy watching the work of contemporary painters such as Neo Rauch, Adrian Ghenie, or Michael Borremans. Everything that surrounds me interests me and drives me to create."

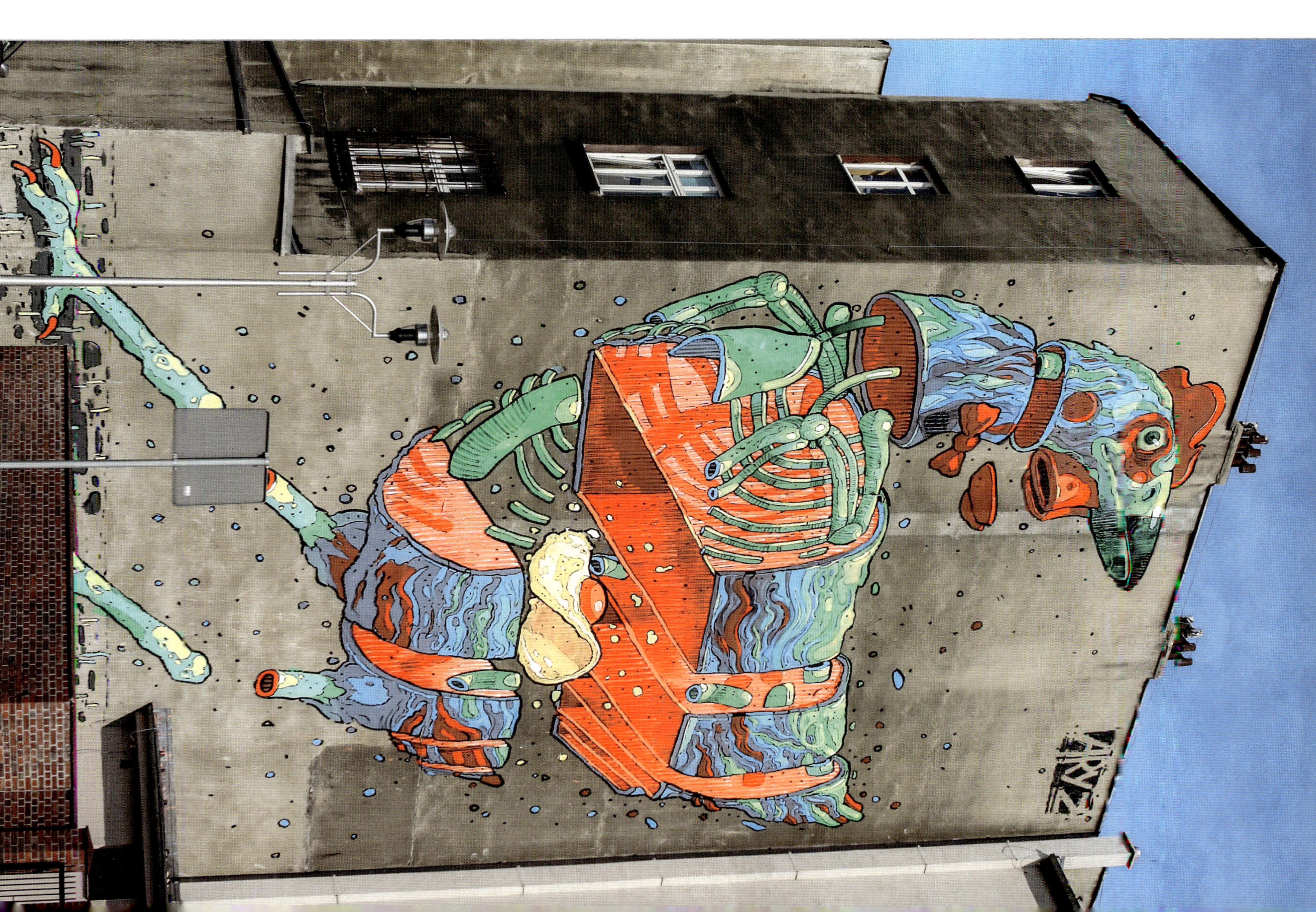

Fried Egg, **2011** – Both animal and psychedelic machine, this chicken that Aryz painted during the Street Art Festival 2011 in Katowice, Poland, reveals itself to be the ironic container of a fried egg.

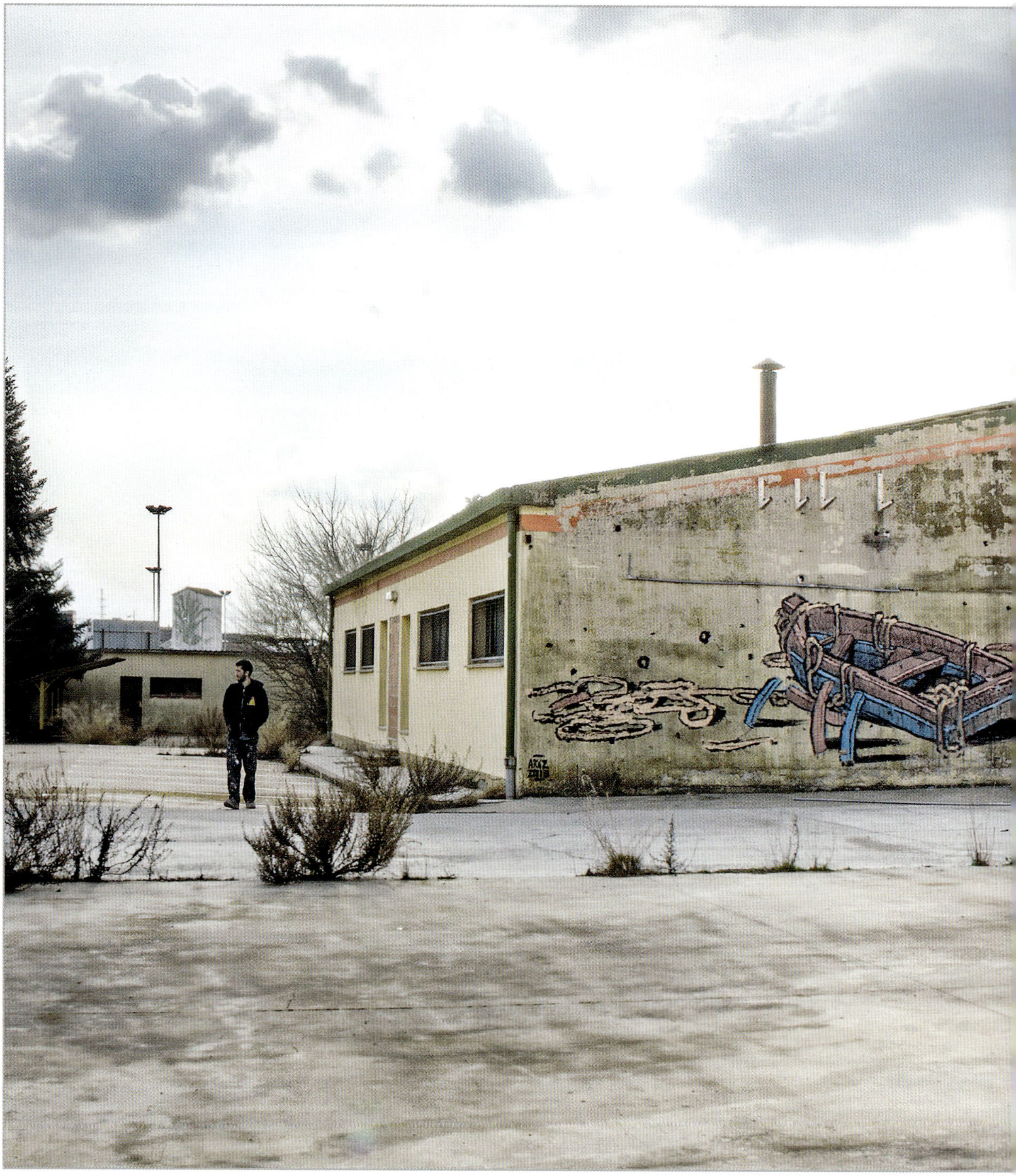

Marina, 2013 – Aryz depicted a derelict vessel on the wall of an abandoned factory in Sant Celoni, a town near Barcelona.

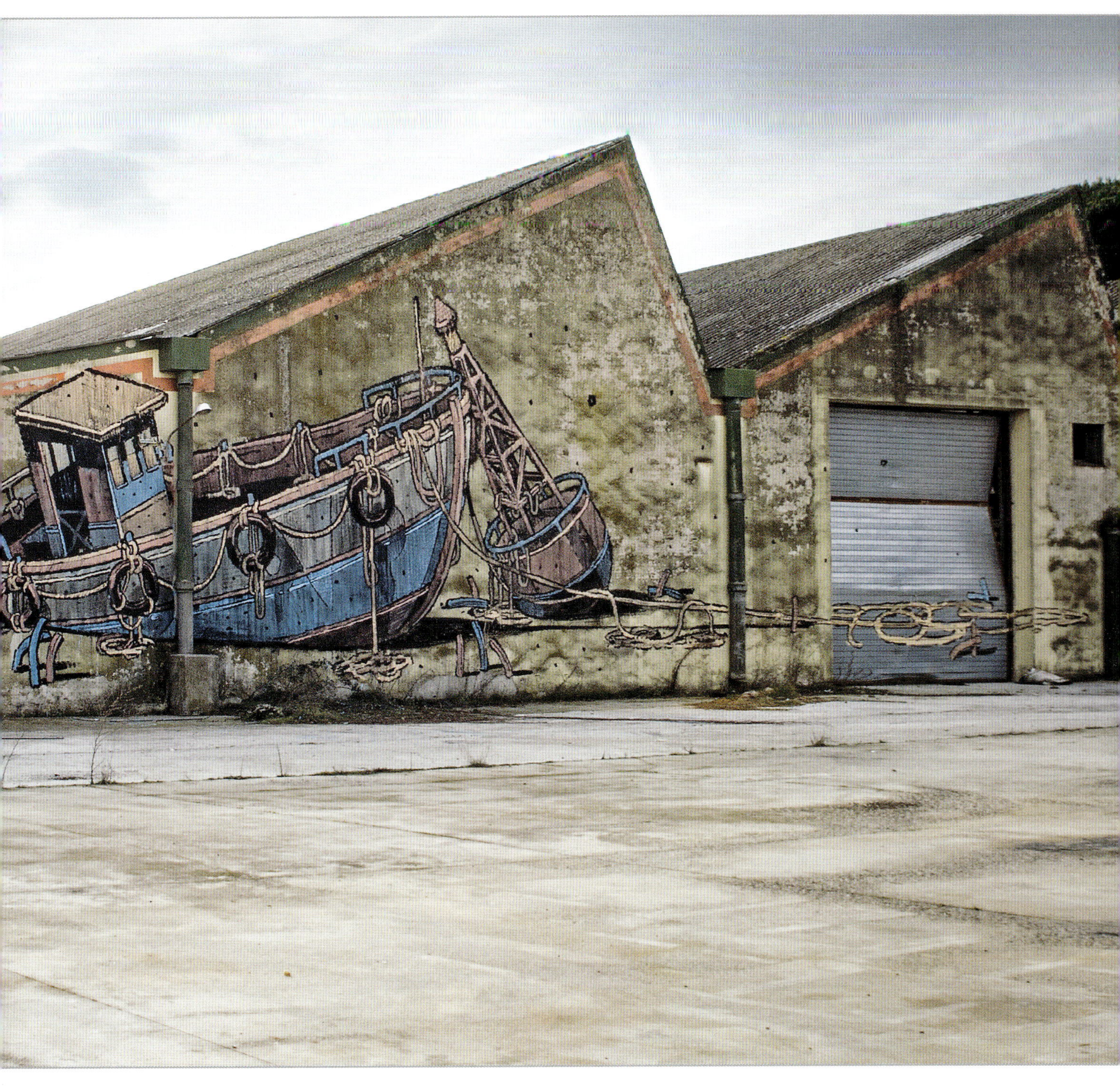

"I'm interested in working in images
that can be seen from a distance,
nowadays people have no time for looking
at something closely and carefully."

"I'm interested in working in images that can be seen from a distance, nowadays people have no time for looking at something closely and carefully. When I paint outdoors I mainly work on images that can be easily seen from far away . . . always playing around with my own visual language. I like what's now happening in contemporary painting, I think that what I do fits into what we are living nowadays. I am not interested in seeking a really defined concept or idea . . . but If I can awake an emotion or inspire someone with what I do . . . I'm more than happy". He also reveals that he is not always certain of the result he attains. "It is as though I were looking at my work from outside and sometimes I don't like it.

But, I am happy that it can evoke something in other people and I hope that it drives people to create," he says. "I would be satisfied just knowing that my creativity has been an inspiration for others. For me, this is what is important. Recently, I have felt more comfortable in my studio, I feel that I need to focus more on my indoor work than on my outdoor stuff . . . plus I like to isolate myself from the outside world . . . and being in the studio is perfect." Aryz's attitude reflects the spontaneity that emerges from his works and the ineffable sensation of surprise and novelty that makes them so magical.

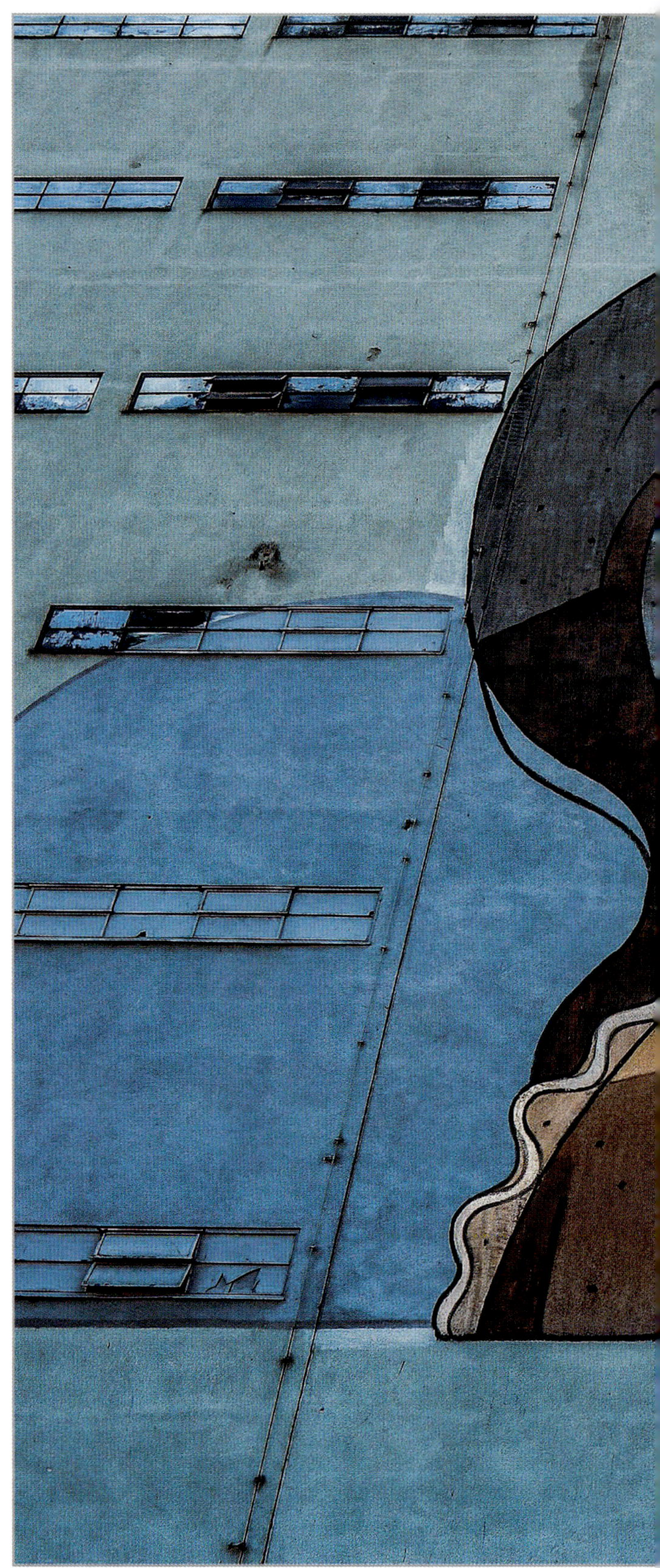

Overprotection, 2014
In the river port of Linz, Aryz portrays a disquieting embrace. "By chance, or not, close to Linz was born one of the most-known villains in the history of the last century," the artist recalls, alluding to Hitler.

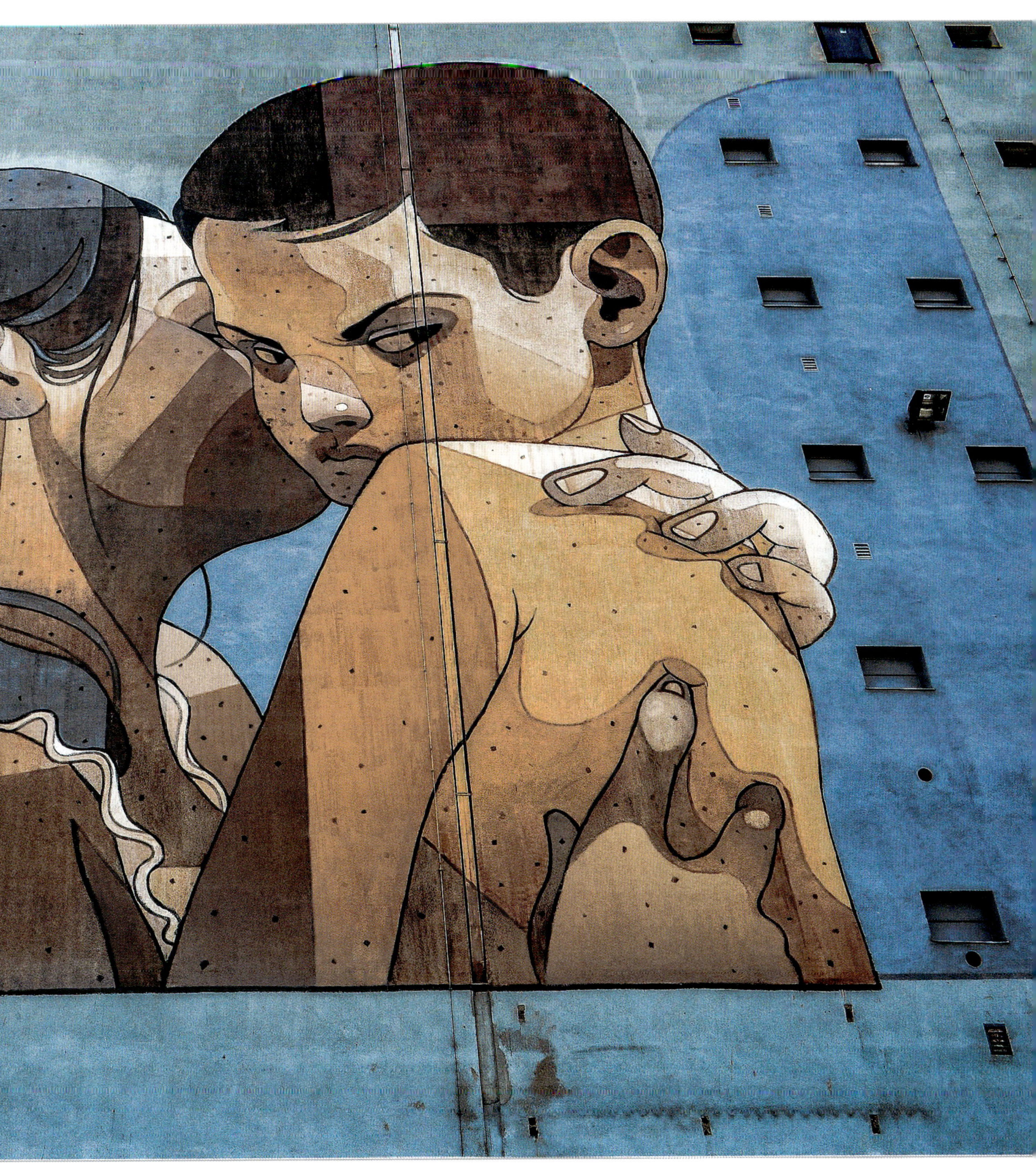

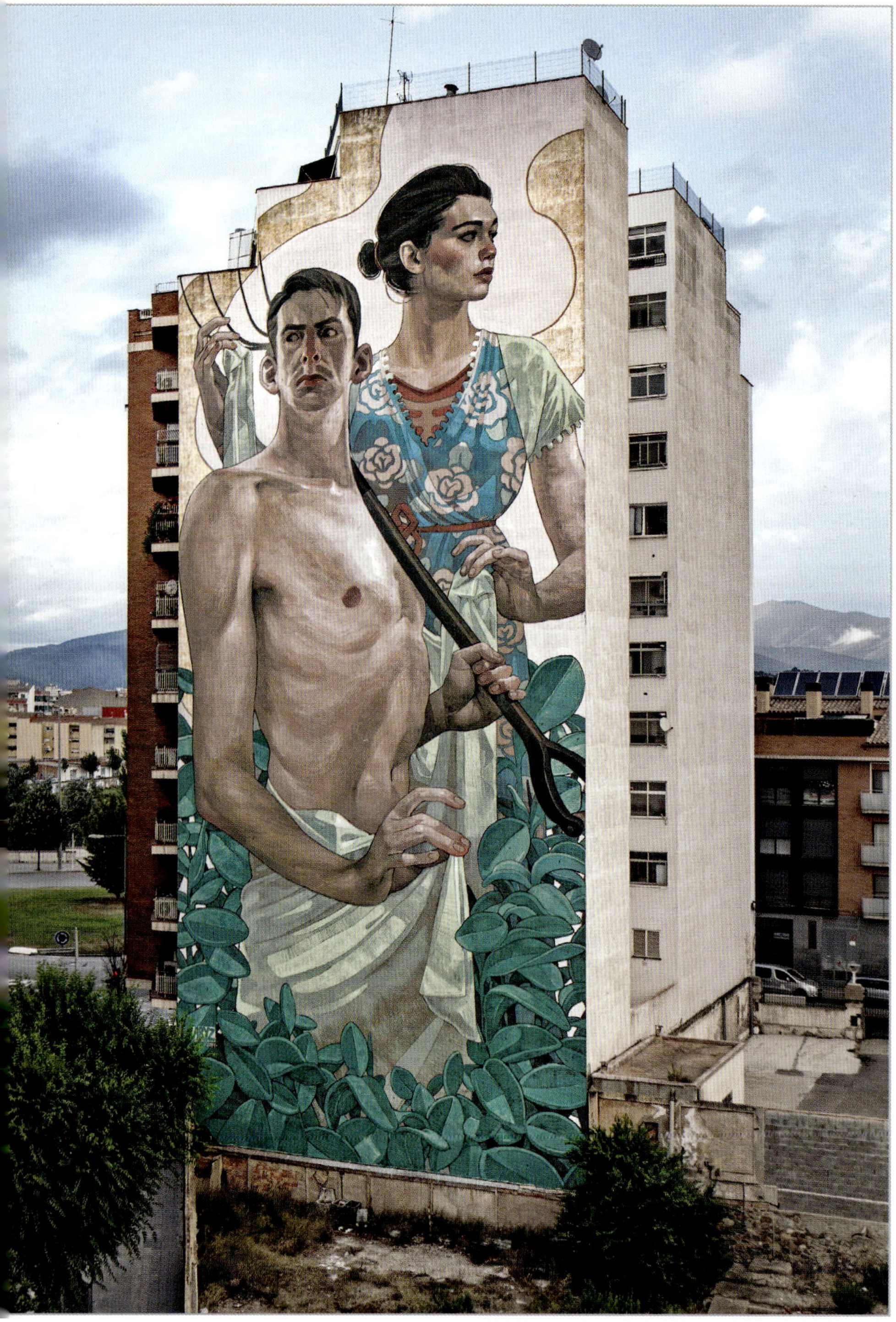

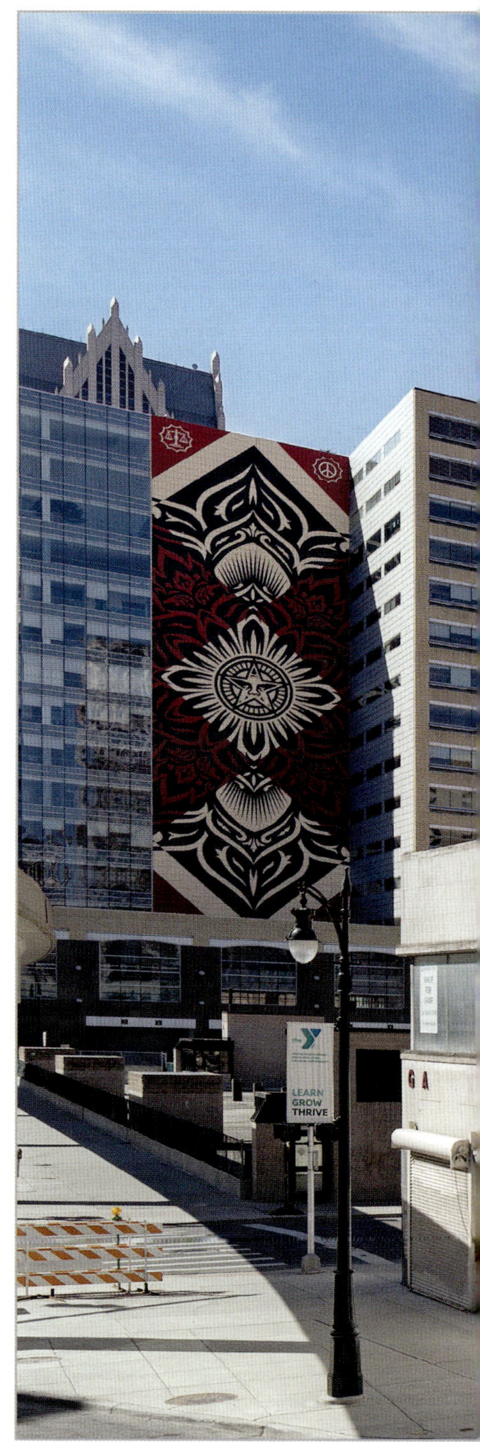

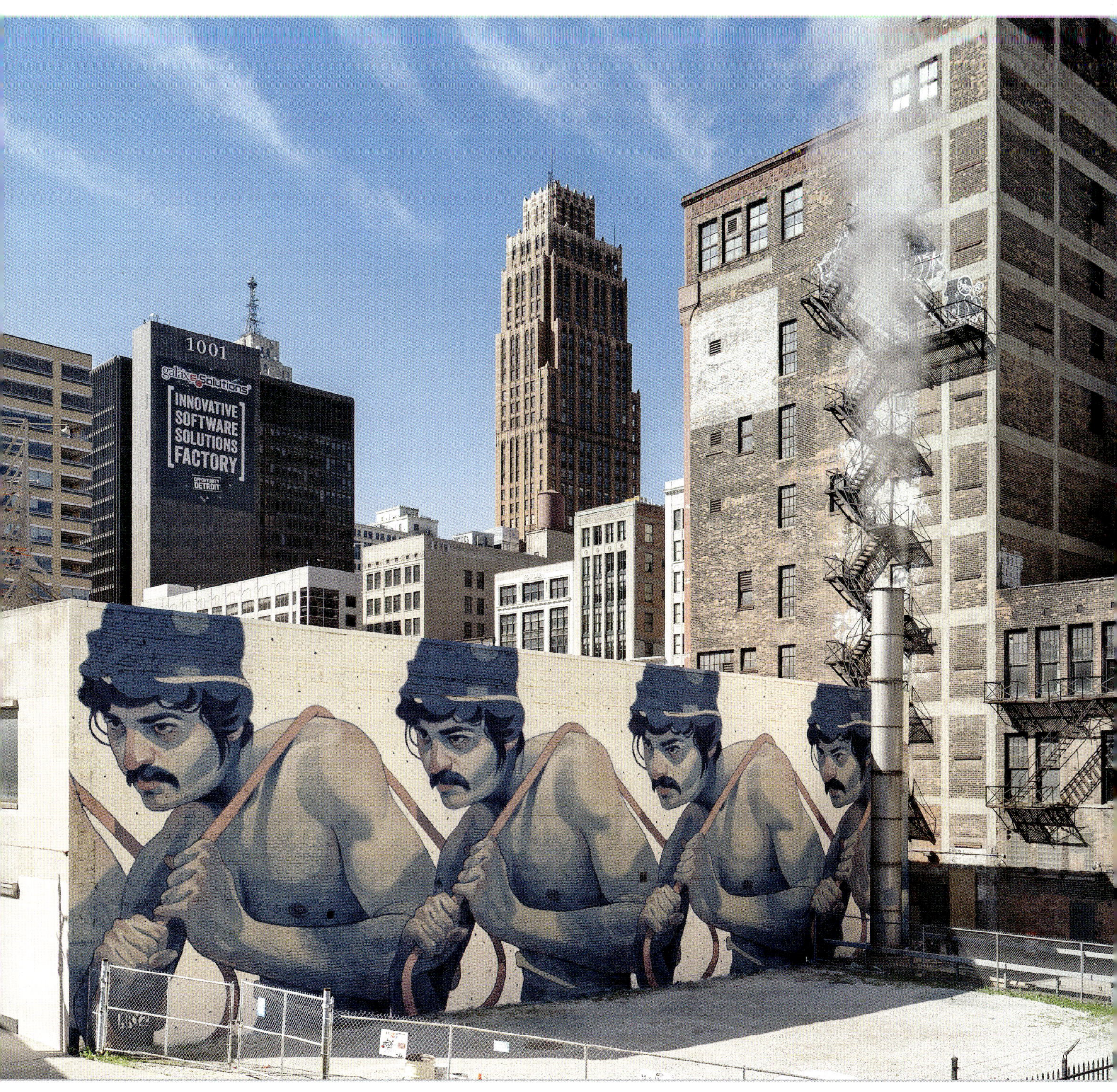

Príap i Demèter, 2014 - In Granollers, center of the great agricultural traditions close to his hometown, Aryz gives a realistic interpretation of the figures of the Greek gods of fertility and agriculture.

One Man Army, 2015 - The epic deeds of industry are founded on the sweat of the workers: the effort of the exploited is the protagonist of this mural created in a Detroit suffering the crisis of the decline of its factories.

BANKSY
Graffiti Genius

The name of Banksy echoes through smudged streaks of color on walls, as if it were a trace of words cast to the wind able to fly and become first a strong message and then an infinite legend. It is, however, his figures that have become still more iconic, and now are engraved in our collective memory. Among the most significant images are that of the man with the Balaklava who is about to throw a bunch of flowers instead of a bomb, the one of a rat announcing the birth of a new race, the one of a girl dreamingly releasing a red balloon, and the one of two policemen who unexpectedly kiss.

There are some recurring characters revisited in his works: the Mona Lisa holding a rocket launcher or showing her behind, a panda carrying two pistols, the British queen with a thunder on her face, Steve Jobs wandering around with a bag. Banksy does not spare anyone.

Everything about him is a kind of mystery. Is it him, or is it not? His identity has never been revealed, even if there have been several theories, and even the police have tried to find clues in his artworks impressed on walls. Banksy does not want to reveal who he is. He prefers to continue using walls as a weapon to express his ideas, to provoke, trying to make a difference and spread the love that is evident in his artistic creation. One cannot label his art: it is better to let it express itself directly through the special language by which it has conquered the world.

It is better to read Banksy through his production and that wild inclination that seemingly lives by pure instinct.

We are now almost certain that Banksy lives in Bristol, in the U.K. He has achieved fame in the world of street art thanks to illegal graffiti, sculptures, and installations. Besides being an artist, he is also a painter, political activist, and film director. He has become a star in spite of himself, he who never did like museums, preferring the street, with all its risks: at the mercy of wind and bad weather, and with the danger of being discovered and arrested. The underground and anonymity are things he would never give up.

> Part of my art is keeping my identity hidden, confusing people to lead them to wonder whether it is really me in front of them.

Rat, 2013 - Banksy leaves again a trace along London's city walls: his famous and irreverent rats are scattered throughout the world, as if to say "Banksy was here."

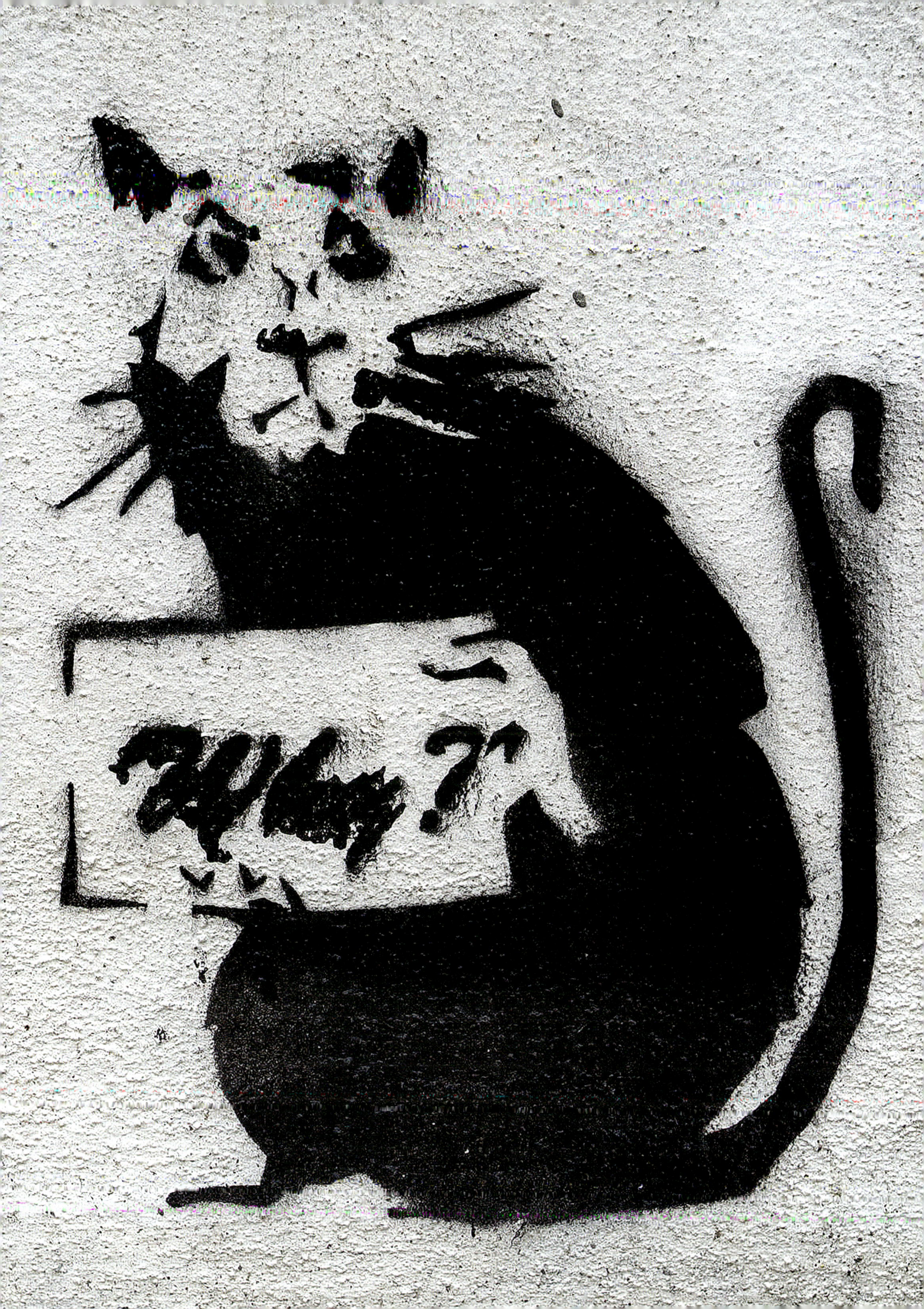

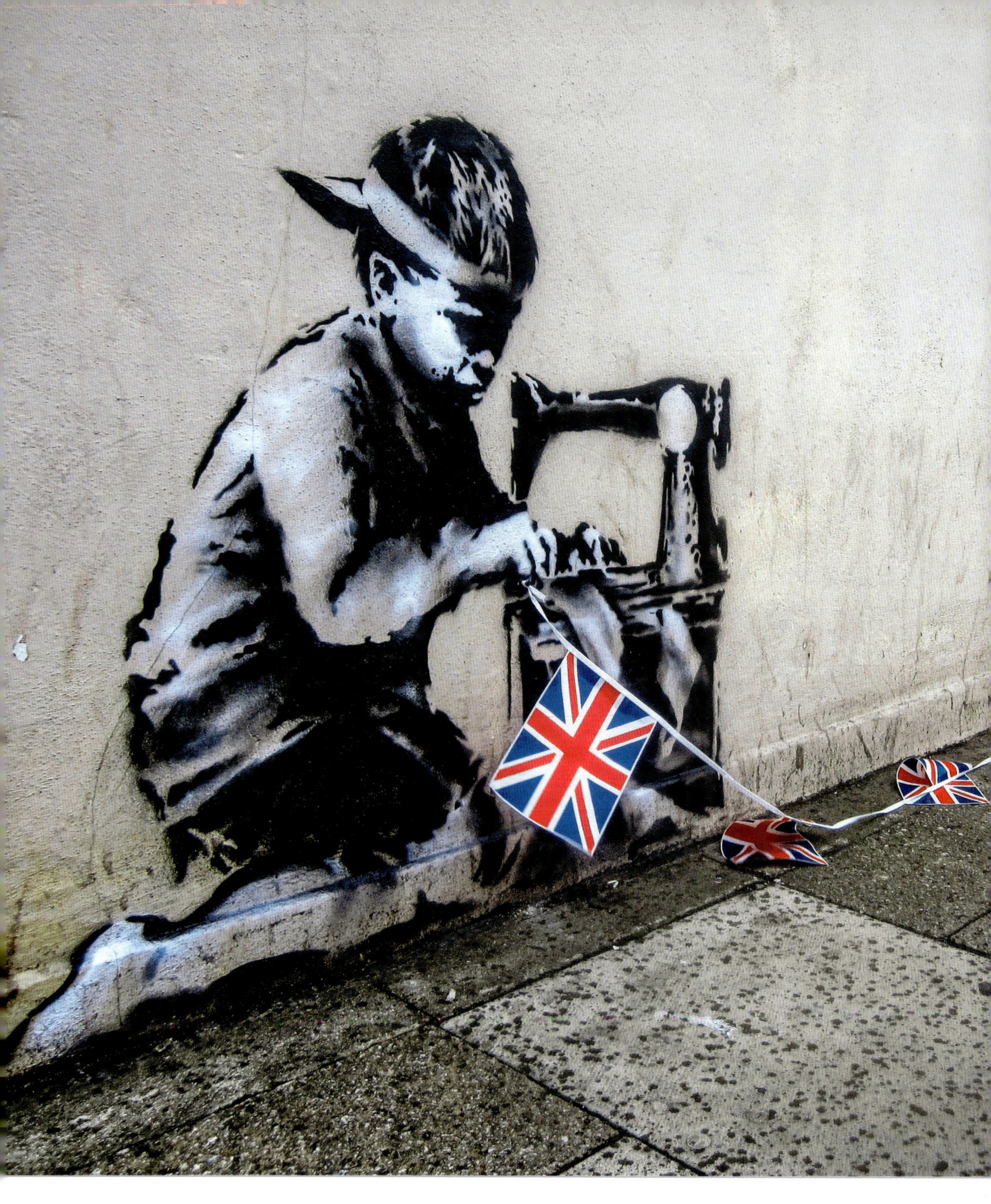

Slave Labour, **2012** – Removed from the wall of a Poundland store in London and put to auction, the work shows a child sewing United Flags: a protest against child labor.

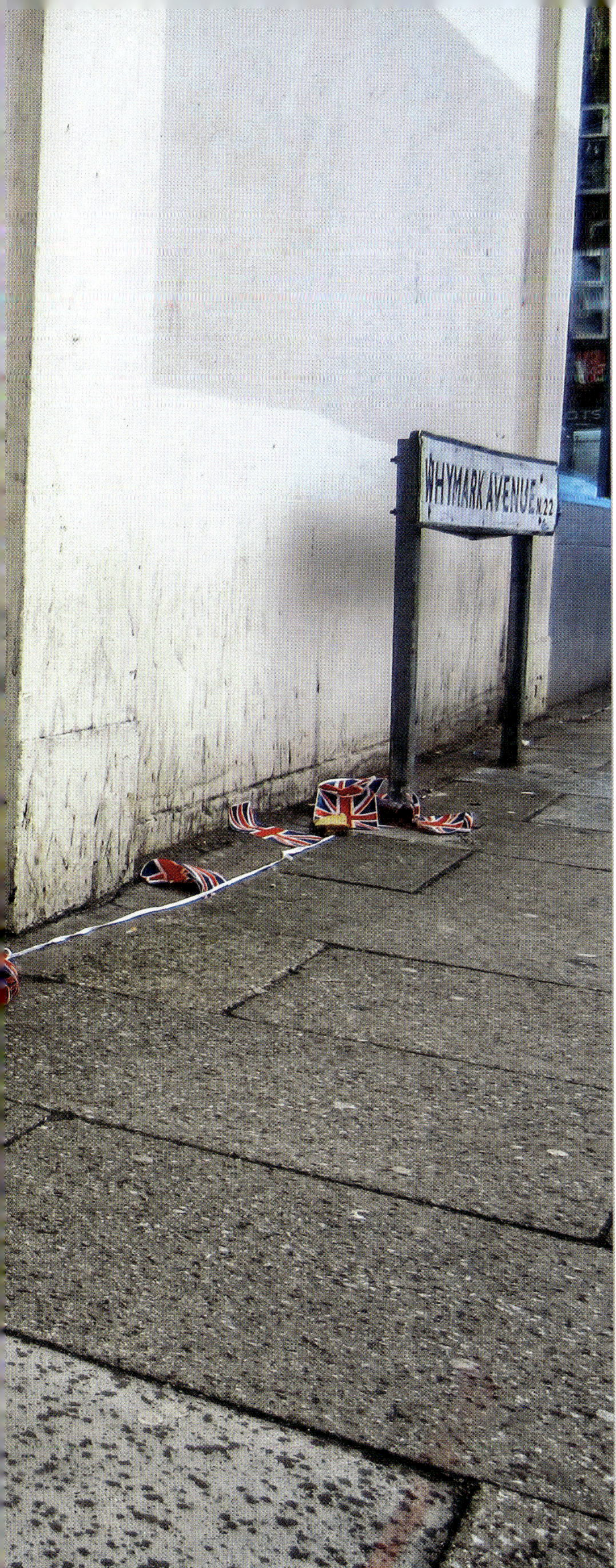

***Young Girl Being Frisked by Policeman*, 2007**
A detail of a larger piece in Glastonbury, showing an English policeman searching a teenager against the wall as if she were a dangerous criminal.

Today his works are often recovered and taken, even cut, from walls and sold to gallery owners or at auctions for stratospheric prices. His admirers keep vigilant watch not only over walls but streets, zoos (he has already "struck" in the London Zoo in an area for penguins and elephants, with graffiti in support of them), and playgrounds, all places where he has left a trace. Like a wild animal, whose keen intelligence and cunning make it impossible to catch, Banksy is unpredictable.

Among his fans are celebrities such as Kate Moss – whom Banksy portrayed in the way Andy Warhol portrayed Marilyn Monroe and who some say commissioned from him a mural for a bathroom in her home; Jude Law; Christina Aguilera; Justin Bieber, who had himself tattooed with the famous little girl and the balloon; Brad Pitt and Angelina Jolie – it seems that the ex-couple spent millions to secure one of his works and that they managed to persuade him to create a work about the dramatic Hurricane Katrina for their French estate; Drake; Chris Martin of Coldplay; Jake Gyllenhaal, who apparently received as a present from his mother, the screenwriter Naomi Foner, a Banksy's print for his thirtieth birthday; the late George Michael; Bono of U2; and many others.

When he is asked whether he is happy to be popular with celebrities and to have achieved fame, Banksy emphasizes: "Becoming famous is like starting a journey. You don't know until you've done it and you can't turn back and start again."

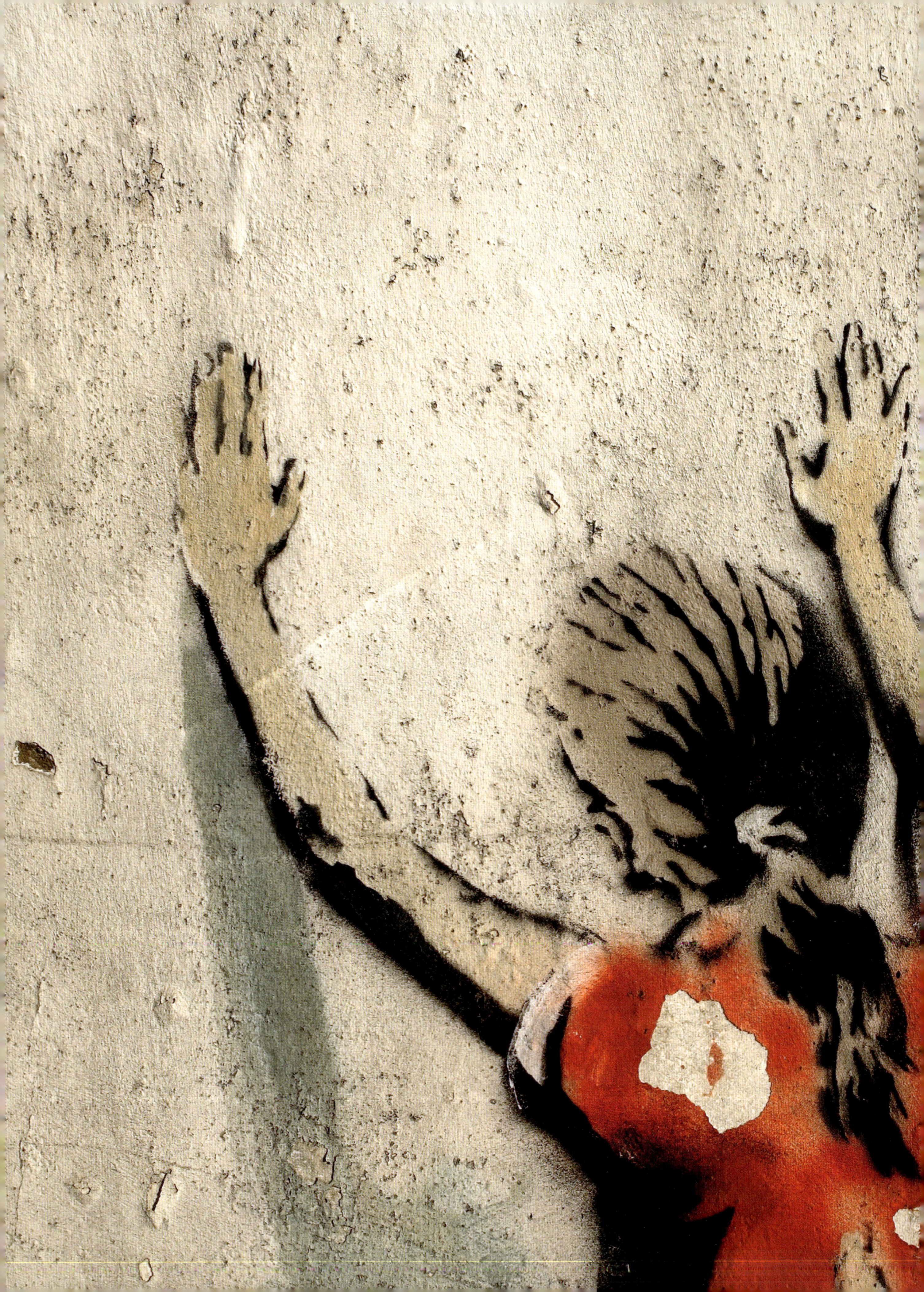

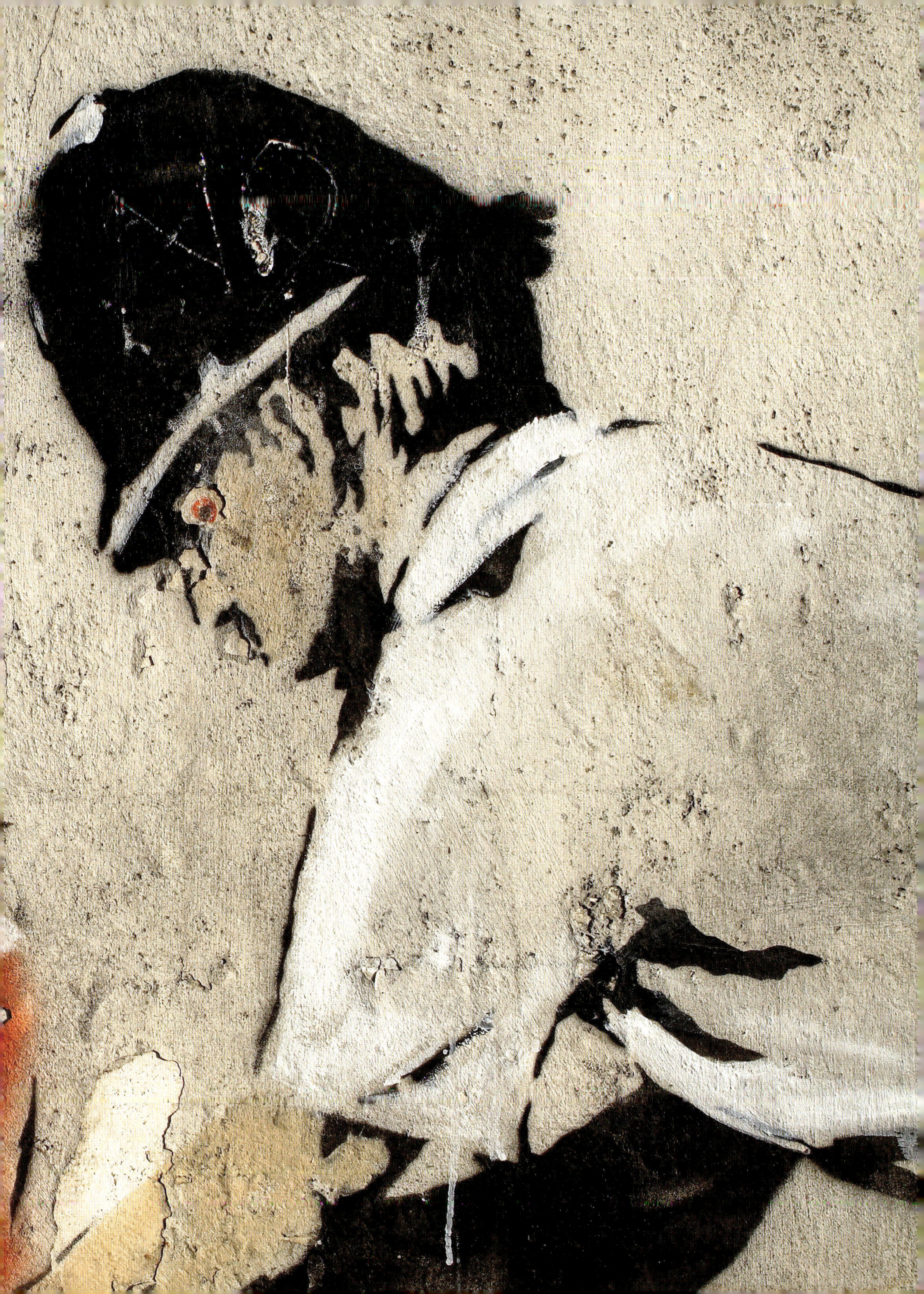

Trying to get in contact with Banksy leads one to meet some of his friends, underground artists who are in their turn equally interesting people, in an intriguing exchange of e-mails and messages that continually makes one fear for the outcome. But at the same time, it gives a positive energy and enthusiasm that stills any doubts, thanks to that common love for art and feeling united in this adventure, like Peter Pan seeking Neverland. In the same way, by lowering one's defenses and allowing oneself to behave spontaneously, without posturing or too many expectations, one enters Banksy's universe.

"Part of my art is keeping my identity hidden, confusing people to lead them to wonder whether it is really me in front of them," he emphasizes, as he does in his documentary film *Exit Through the Gift Shop*, nominated for an Oscar after its debut at the Sundance Film Festival in 2010. On Main Street, in Park City, Utah, where the famous festival founded by Robert Redford is held, we can still admire a Banksy work behind glass: a cameraman picking a red flower. The documentary, directed by Banksy himself, tells the story of Thierry Guetta, a French immigrant in Los Angeles, of his obsession with street art and video cameras and of how he became a famous artist. Banksy appears in front of the camera with his face covered or pixelated and his voice masked in order not to be recognized. It is impossible to resist his glamour, that aura of global hero that surrounds him. It is made still more palpable by those who are close to him, who protect him (Banksy has never asked anyone not to reveal his identity, but spontaneously those close to him do not betray him); they try to learn more about anyone who is trying to approach him. If one wants to contact him, the secret is "to be patient and wait," as a trusted friend confesses. One must be prepared to wait endlessly, for months, while in one's mind pass dreams and traces of memories of his satirical street art, his subversive epigrams, which mix the dark mood of his graffiti with his unmistakable stencil technique.

Then there are his subjects: large rats, children, policemen, soldiers, old people, monkeys and gorillas, cats . . . and his vision of the world: anarchic, existentialist, pacifist, anti-imperialist, anti-capitalist, anti-authoritarian, anti-fascist. And everything is dominated by that free-spiritedness which distinguishes his soul as an artist. He is able to create something universal through a magic that reaches to the ends of the earth and is transformed into poetry, even when it sends political messages, "for good." Everything in spite of the laws or criticisms that consider street art to be a form of vandalism.

"I got a can of spray paint and pointed it at a wall. I put my finger on the nozzle and paint came out and I became an artist," he says in all honesty, about how he began his artistic journey. Regarding certain definitions, like the one by the refined art critic who describes him as "a British Andy Warhol," Banksy responds: "I'm like 'a British Andy Warhol?' I call that *lazy reporting*. You can see they had nothing better to do."

Hanging Man (Adultery Street Art), 2006 - Irony on the theme of adultery in Park Street, Bristol: a jealous husband looks out of a window while his wife's naked lover hangs to the window-ledge.

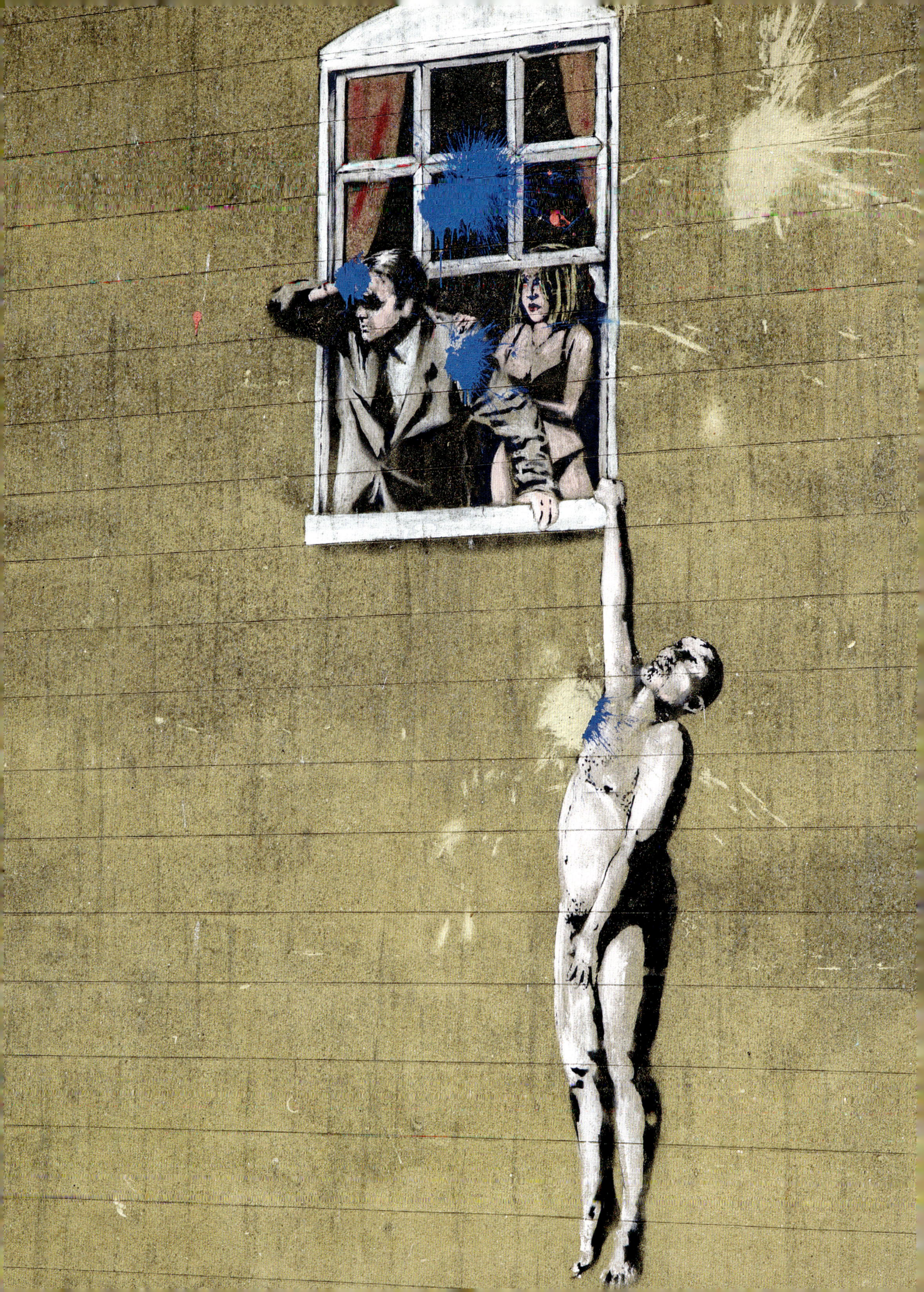

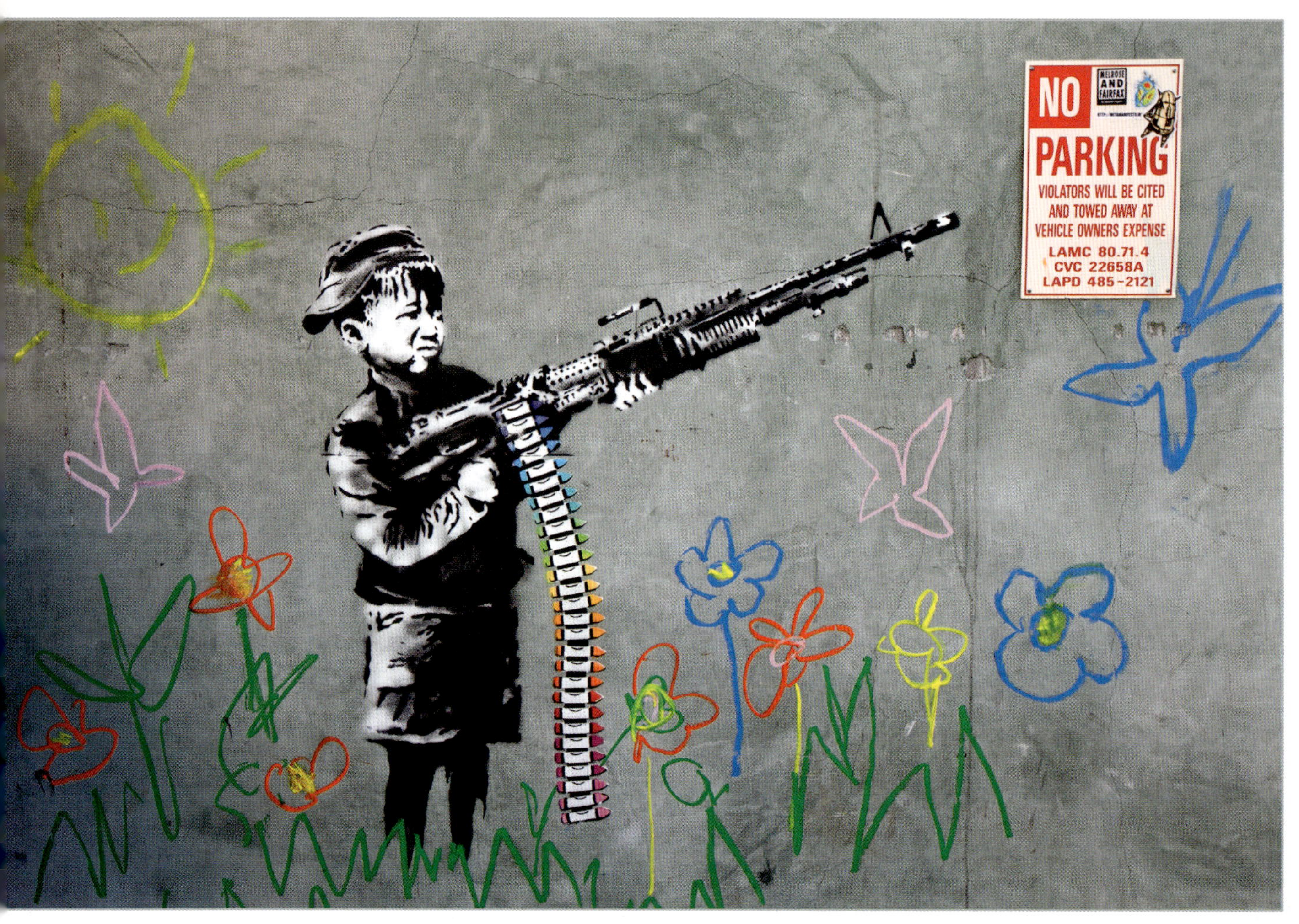

Crayola Shooter, 2010 - On a wall in Los Angeles an Asian boy, in black and white, embraces a machine gun loaded with crayons: a touching way of demonstrating the tragedy of child soldiers.

Apart from the descriptions attributed to him that he himself openly dislikes, the "Banksy phenomenon" has become contagious and has gone forward like a true revolution, appearing in streets, and on walls, bridges, and buildings in the entire world. It unexpectedly appeared on the Israeli separation barrier, during his trip to the West Bank, of course always incognito, until his art appeared and opened the way to him.

Banksy has a sense of his growth on the British underground scene in Bristol, where various artists and musicians collaborated. Some say he was born in 1973, but he does not confirm this. He began with graffiti around 1992, but his real beginning was probably in 2002 in Los Angeles at the 33 1/3 Gallery. There is no direct confirmation, apart from what people write about him . . .

His consecration coincided with the great exhibition in 2003, entitled *Turf War*, where he even painted real animals, provoking protests from animal welfare groups, although he had followed all the relevant regulations. Later he

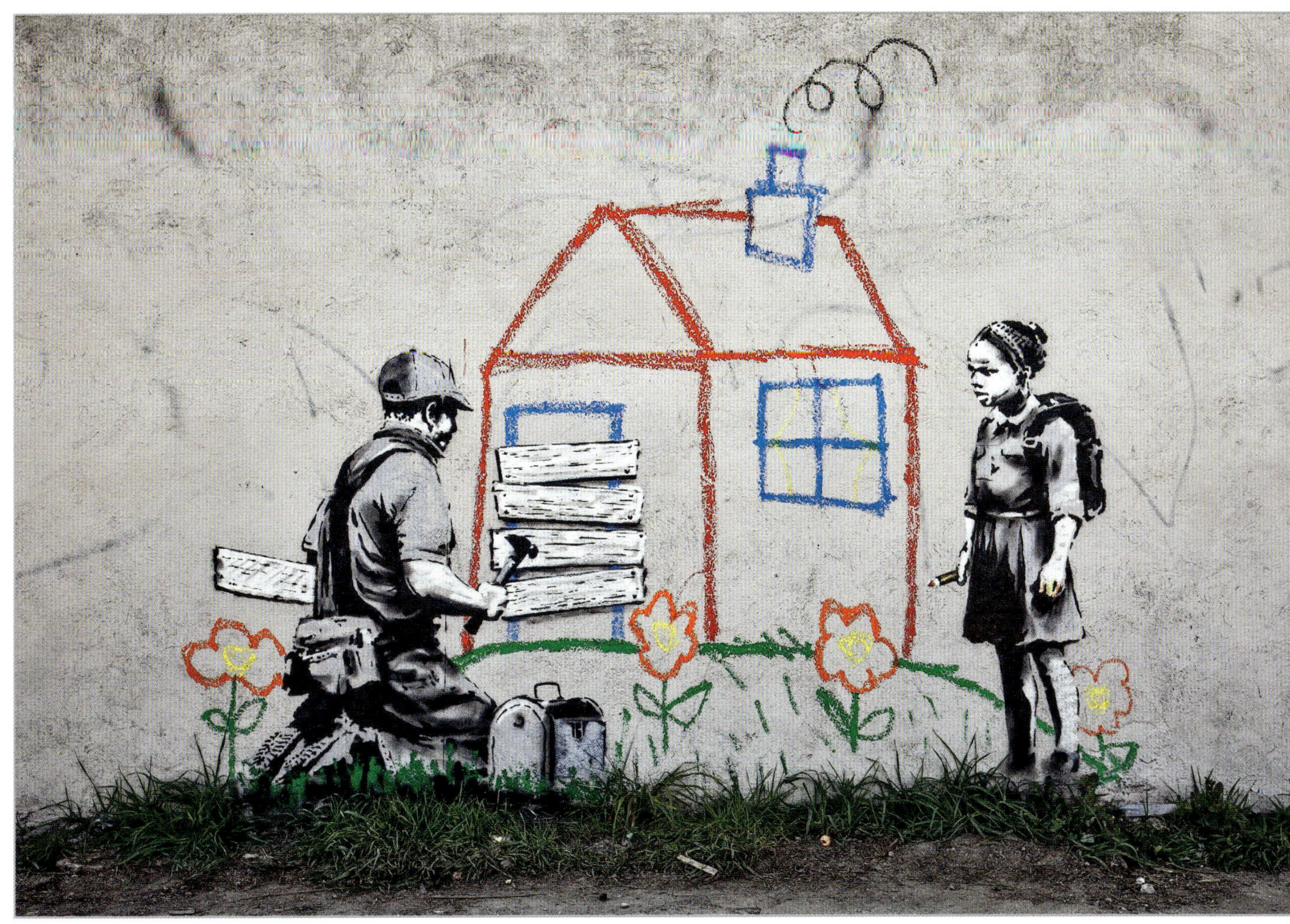

Crayon House Foreclosure, 2010 - The cynicism of adults against the imagination of children: in Los Angeles, coming home from school a young girl can no longer return to her colorful home.

produced the so-called "subverted paintings," inspired by classic works of the past such as those of Monet, Edward Hopper and others, revisiting them in his way.

The 2006 Los Angeles *Barely Legal* exhibit even included a live elephant, which was also completely painted. The title, a play on words, was: *Elephant in the room.*

Banksy admits that he likes puns, as he has shown several times in his art. His vision emerges in the book *Wall and Piece*, 2005, one of several he has written on his art and thought, in which he states: "The people in charge of cities don't understand graffiti, because they think that nothing has the right to exist if it doesn't produce profit, which makes their opinion meaningless. They say that graffiti frightens people and is a symbol of the decline of society, but graffiti is dangerous only in the mind of three types of people: politicians, the managers of advertising agencies and graffiti artists. What really destroys the character of our districts are the large companies that stick enormous advertising slogans

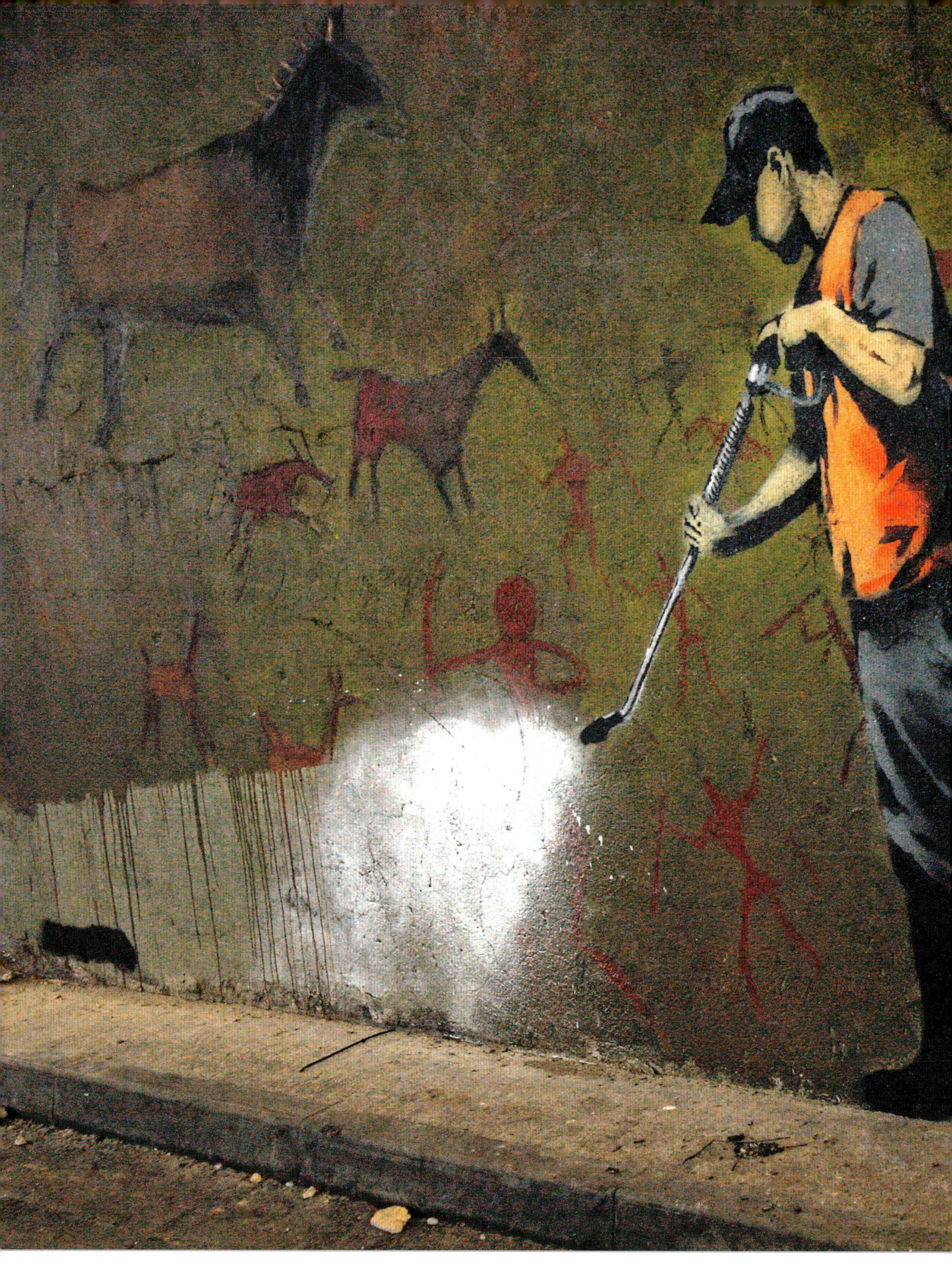

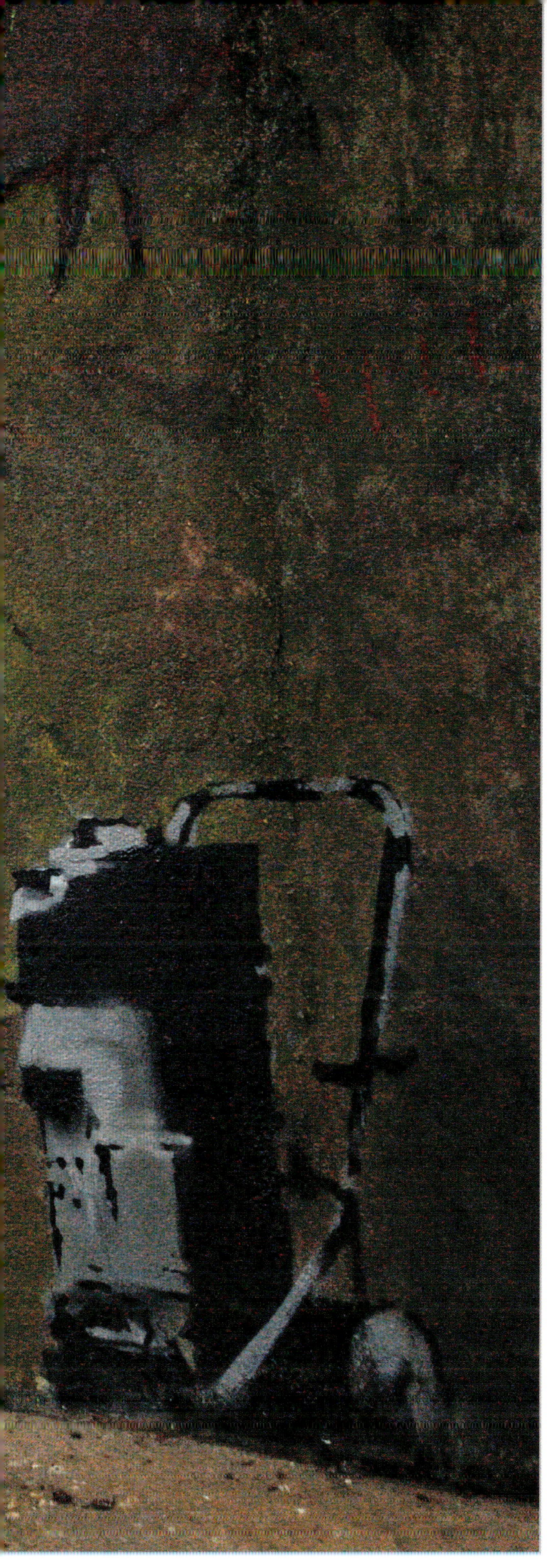

on buildings and buses, trying to make us feel inadequate unless we buy their products and services.

They want to 'fire' a message in people's face from every possible surface, but people aren't allowed to reply. Well, they have begun the struggle and the weapon chosen to react, to give our answer, is the wall. Some people become policemen, because they want the world to be a better place. Other people become vandals, because they want to make the world a better place to look at." He has also maintained that "graffiti doesn't always ruin buildings. It is actually the only way to improve many of them."

If he is asked why some critics and authorities continue to consider street art a form of vandalism, he replies: "There is graffiti and vandalism. They are two different things. The problem is that they are confused."

Regarding the stencil technique developed by him, and which has made him so famous and consists in reproducing images by means of a paper stencil in order to obtain the desired shapes to color inside, Banksy gives a direct explanation: "It's difficult to paint good images freehand. So I decided to take a 'short cut' and to work in this way, even if I have maintained the discipline, the 'hard line', in painting and practicing and developing my art, in continuous experimentation and learning."

Leake Street, 2008
Near Waterloo Station, a garbage man is intent on cleaning a wall in London from rocky landscapes in Lascaux's grotto style. The work was undertaken for the Cans Festival.

He creates most of the work in the studio, since he has little time available to finish the work outside (an urban legend relates that he never takes more than fifteen minutes), where he acts in secret.

When he was younger, and perhaps still not too good at moving fast, he was apparently arrested several times. If one asks him the reason that prompts him, even today when he has become a star of street art, to work undercover, he has no doubts: "*Never Worry, Never Hurry*, this is my motto. This is how I like to work. If something prevents me working one day, I return the next day. I have no deadlines. *Time moves. A building stays still.*"

He has produced innumerable works and it is impossible to condense years of intensive production into a few pages.

In *No Ball Games* two children throw each other a sign that forbids them to play with a ball, but in that case itself represents the means to play. On the 450-miles long wall that separates the West Bank and the State of Israel, he has completed several works portraying children intent on getting around the barrier in the strangest ways, for example holding on to balloons, and others that shows gaps transformed into earthly paradises with the *trompe-l'oeil* technique. During the period he spent in New York, he made a mark with the exhibit *Better Out Than In,* a series of murals which features the works *The Street is in Play* (one boy climbs on another's back to touch a sign which says that graffiti is a crime), *You Complete Me* (a dog urinating on a hydrant), *Mobile Waterfall* (a paradisiacal waterfall built inside a traveling truck). Other noteworthy graffiti: *Gorilla in a Pink Mask* in Bristol, *Madonna with gun* in Italy, the series *Parachuting Rat* in Melbourne, Australia, *Pulp Fiction* in London, *Sniper* in Bristol and *Spy Booth* in Cheltenham, just to mention a few, besides the recent work in Gaza.

Banksy does not like art galleries and museums, which he considers places reserved for an elite, in contrast to the street, to which everyone has access. He has even created works that he has secretly placed, in protest, in these "temples of culture" for the institutional society. Among these, *Show me the Monet* (a typical landscape by the French master, in which shopping carts and a traffic cone triumph), or *You Have Beautiful Eyes*, removed from the Metropolitan Museum of Art in New York a couple of hours after the installation.

When he thinks of a work to which he feels particularly attached, since probably he cannot choose between the various graffiti, he says: "At the moment I'm quite proud of my first feature length film *Exit Through the Gift Shop.* It got nominated for an Oscar and has traveled around the world and been viewed by millions of people, thus all I could wish for my art."

Hammer Boy, 2013 - In the famous Upper West Side stands the silhouette of a child ready to fiercely attack a hydrant with a hammer.

Shower Lady, 2015 - Curious boys watch a woman in the shower: the art offers new – and indiscreet – worldviews, as shown by Banksy in the "temporary theme park not suitable for children," in Dismaland, England.

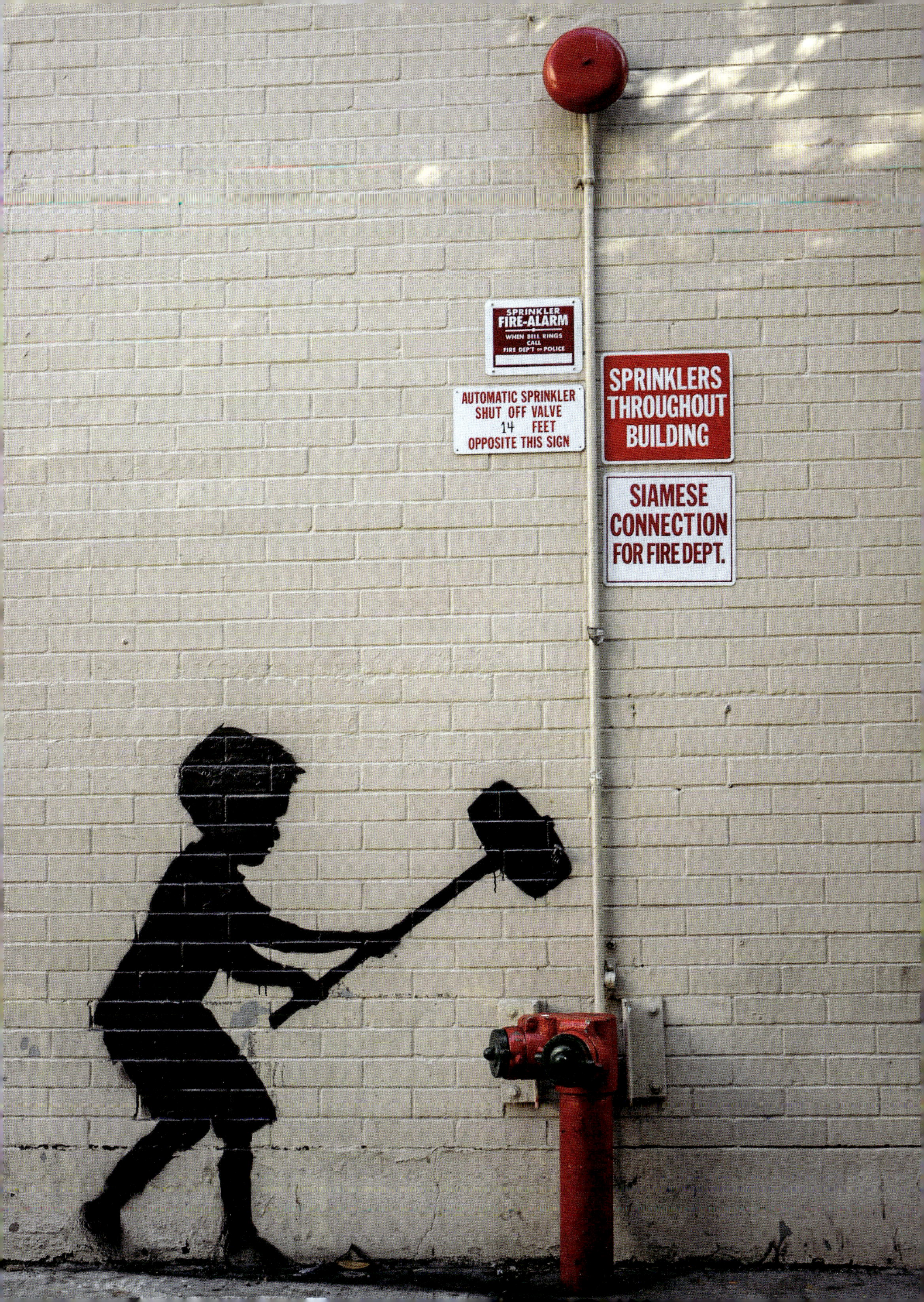

SPRINKLER
FIRE-ALARM
WHEN BELL RINGS
CALL
FIRE DEPT or POLICE
AUTOMATIC SPRINKLER
SHUT OFF VALVE
14 FEET
OPPOSITE THIS SIGN
SPRINKLERS
THROUGHOUT
BUILDING
SIAMESE
CONNECTION
FOR FIRE DEPT.

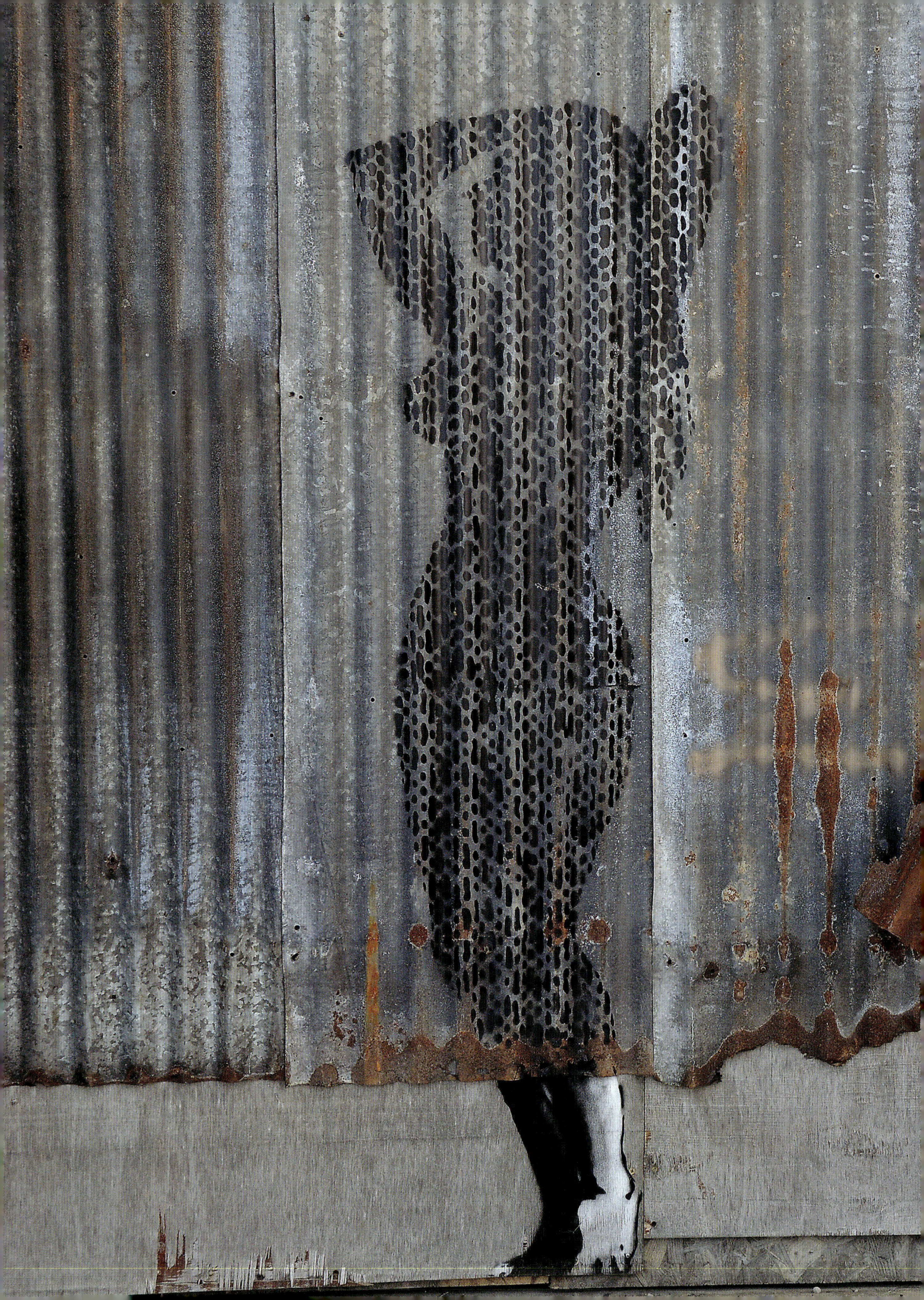

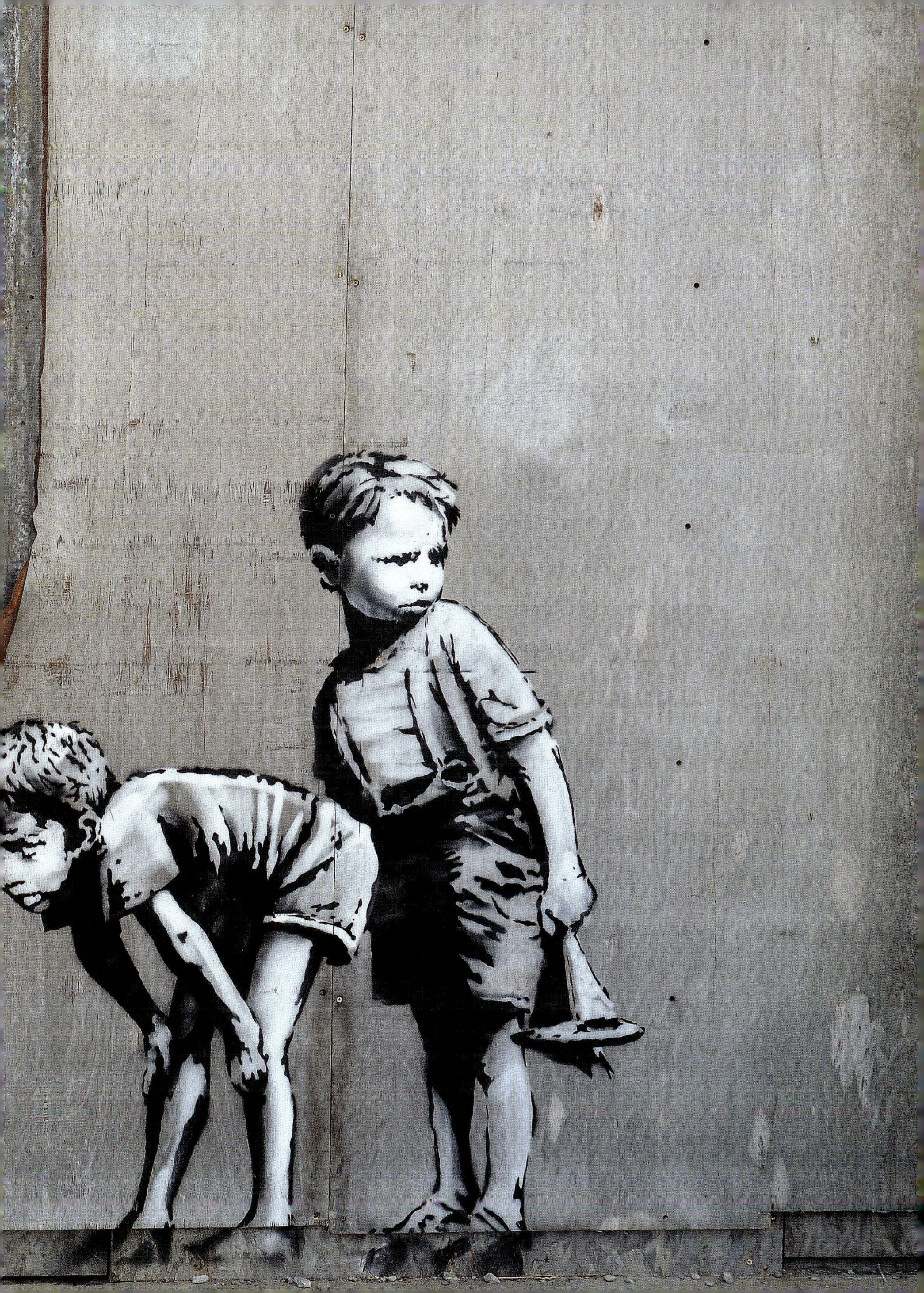

Regarding his source of inspiration, he states: "One percent inspiration, 99 percent perspiration."

Concerning music, on the other hand, Banksy says: "I often listen to the radio when I work, exactly as a decorator would do in his daily profession." He confesses that he feels free to express himself through different art forms, even sculpture. "I'm open. I'm not tied to any medium. First the idea comes and then I use any artistic medium necessary to get across the message I want to communicate." In politics, he is close to whom he admires and is brief, while touching the heart, like his art: "I quote a saying from the great Gandhi: 'Be the change that you want to see in the world.'"

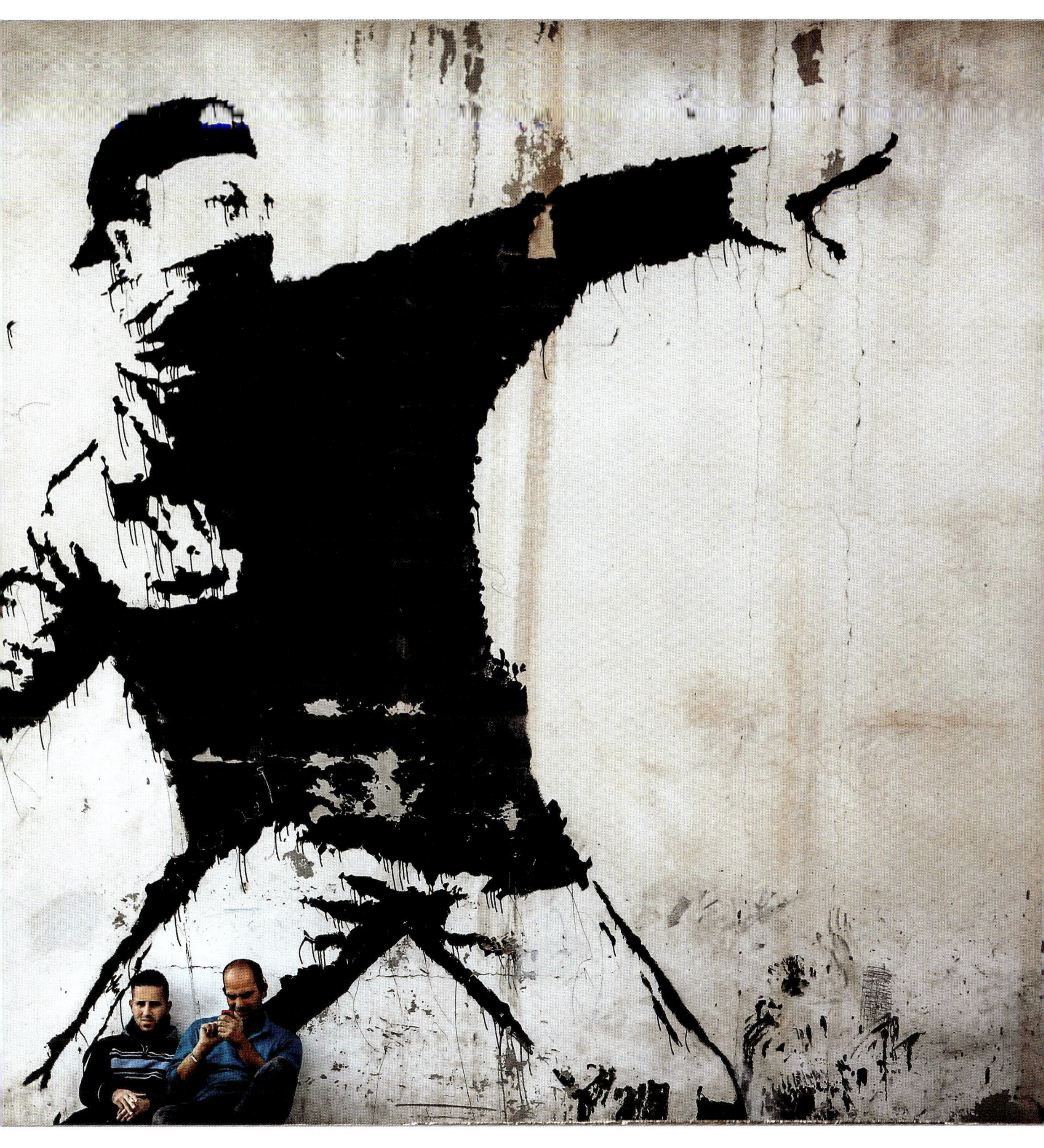

Rage ('The Flower Thrower), **2005** - In a service station in Bethlehem, two men sit against one of the mysterious artist's most famous pieces: *The Flower Thrower*, a symbol of protest against the occupation of Palestine.

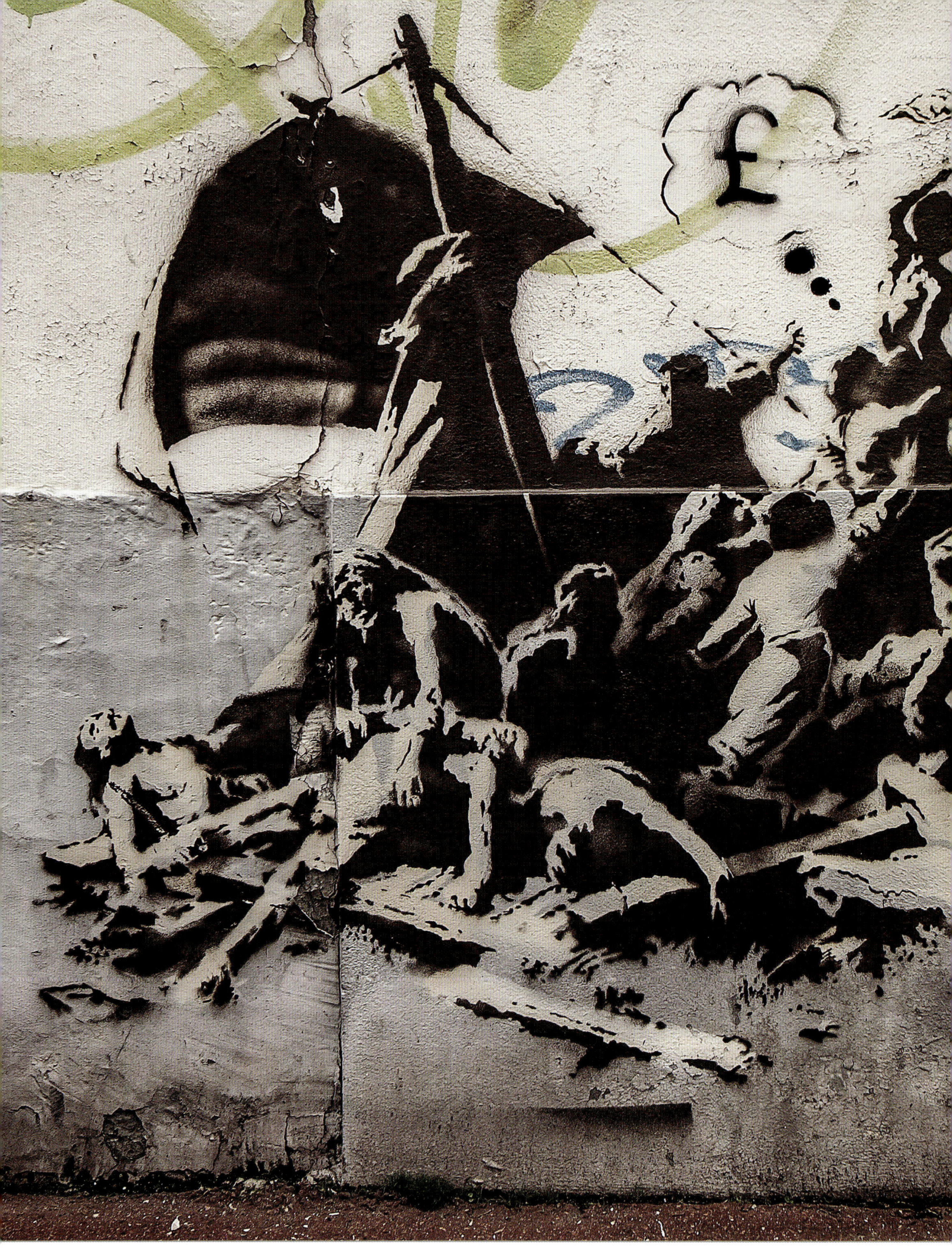

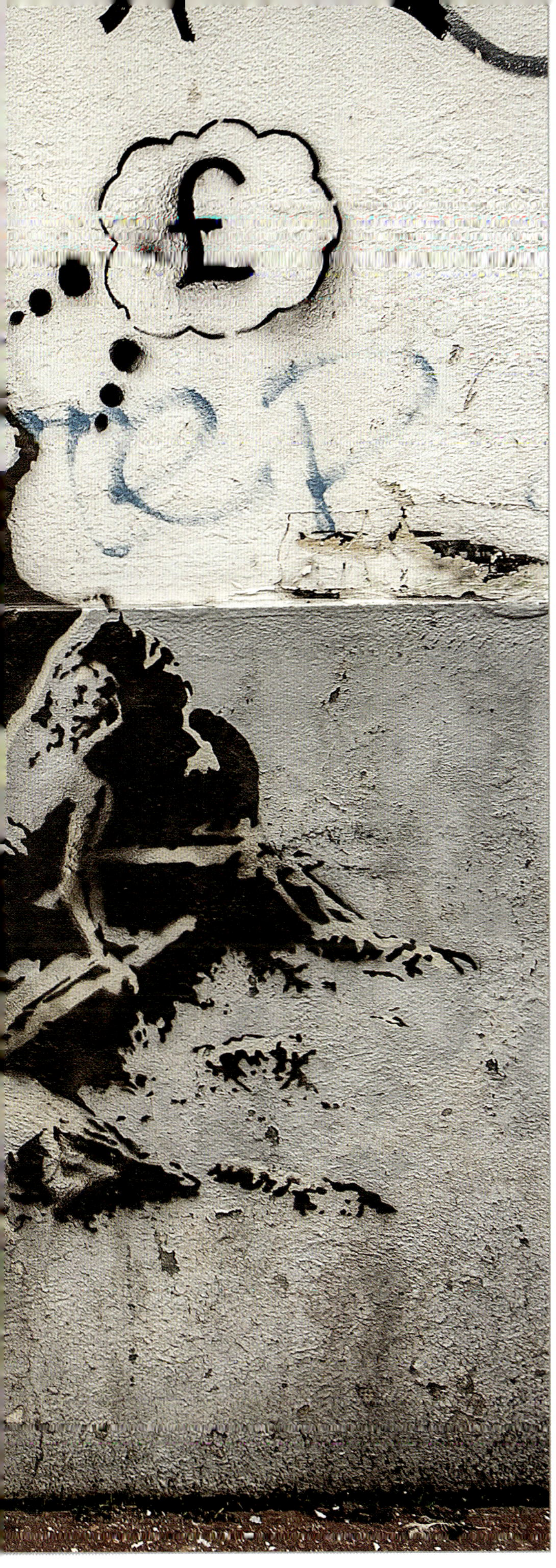

Banksy still has a dream to fulfill, or even many, but he lives in the moment and in fact reveals: "I had a dream last night that I did a piece on the moon. Might not be such a bad idea . . ."

When he is reminded that people still tend to question his identity, he replies satirically: "The question is 'who is the real me?' I often ask myself that question! I'm going to leave it open and let your readers decide! But those who know me know that I'm really me from my answers!" he concludes. And we must remember a message he wrote on a wall, beside the image of an ordinary man holding a bucket and a brush: *WINNERS . . . ARE NOT THOSE WHO NEVER FAIL BUT THOSE WHO NEVER QUIT.*

The Raft of the Medusa, 2015
Banksy uses Géricault's 1819 masterpiece on the shipwrecking of the frigate Méduse on the walls of Calais, where the infamous refugee camp known as the Jungle was located.

PHILIPPE BAUDELOCQUE

The "Constellator" of Animals

"I, Philippe Baudelocque, wish to express who I am and my multifaceted character by any means necessary. My cosmic drawings express this concept. They are comprised of cells, and each cell reflects a facet of myself." In his Paris studio, this famous French artist talks about his work, which has recently attracted a lot of attention in the French capital, in Marseille, and in many cities abroad. "Firstly, I don't see myself as a street artist, because I ask for permission, and the street is just one of many playing fields. I don't have a hierarchy between spaces. A t-shirt is a space, a glass, a stairwell, forest, a gallery, etc . . . I am more interested in their specific qualities and the range of audiences . . . It's not difficult to become a street artist. It's very simple: do something in the street and people, whether journalists or just passers-by will call you a street artist . . . So yes," he says, "I touch upon street art, but not exclusively." He adds: "I would like to remind you that in 2000, when I first became involved in street art other than tagging, this term did not exist."

He was born in Villecresnes, France. He studied at the École Nationale Supérieure des Arts Décoratifs in Paris, and developed his unique style with the series *Cosmic Animals* in 2009. Composed of large drawings of wild animals, the work is almost a mosaic of specificity. "All the elements came together over time. I wanted to connect with myself as much as possible," he recounts, describing how he decided to embark on an artistic career. "I remember the exhibitions that I went to on Sunday mornings with my parents, and this was my preparation."

"I was one of three children. The fact that my father was a Sunday painter, as well as my mother being a musician, must have had a bearing on my life . . . With hindsight, I can see that what was most important was the appreciation, the urge to learn. Books were the most frequently received present by my brother, sister and me when we were little: how to recognize plants, animals, stones, stars, but also history, geography books etc. Not knowing something was nothing to be proud of. When we did not know something, we had to figure it out, to look it up in the dictionary or ask someone when necessary. The need to become an artist slowly came after studying art in Paris.

> It is instinctive for me to return to and reflect on the causes. For me this is the work that artists should accomplish, to find their uniqueness deep within.

Baudelocque walks the catwalk for the fashion designer Agnès B. during the Paris Fashion Week in January 2017.

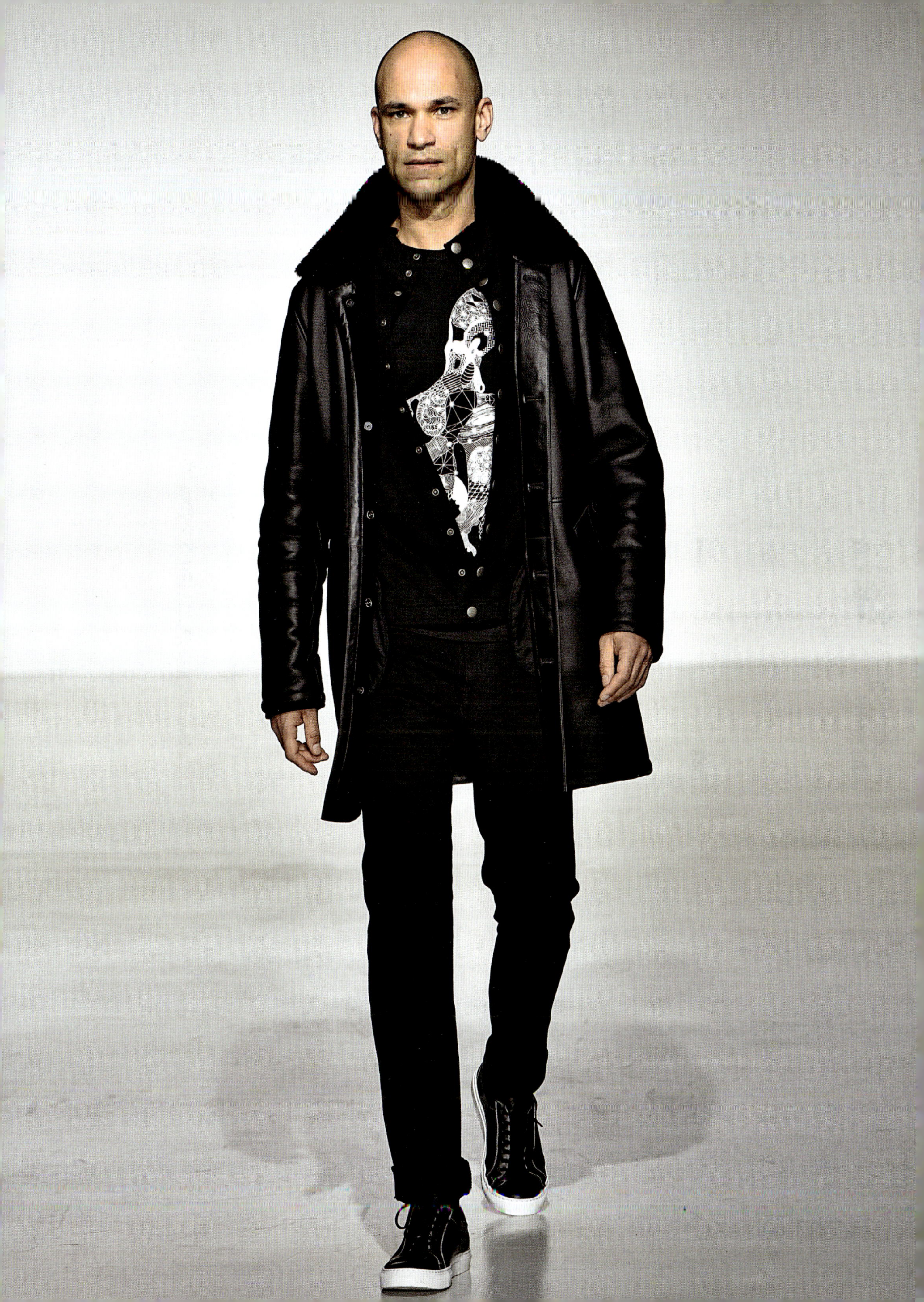

It is instinctive for me to return to and reflect on the causes. For me this is the work that artists should accomplish, to find their uniqueness deep within," he says, revealing his vision. "Graffiti is one of the greatest artistic emotions. When I saw some for the first time I was speechless. I remember when I took it up – it was 1988 – and my feelings at the time: excitement at being part of this movement, fear of not being good enough, fear of not working well, pushing my limits as I entered unknown territory." He speaks passionately about these foundational years. "When the book *Spraycan Art* arrived in France, I did everything I could to get a copy. It was my bible. And it still is today, among the others," he confesses.

"About my technique – people usually focus on the most fundamental aspect of my work, that is, the white on a black background with pastels and oil or chalk. It is clean and economical, and therefore a very practical technique. It enables me to evoke the fragility of existence, beautiful fragility in the highest sense of the term. Calm and powerful, sure of itself and fearless," he says about the style that has made him famous. "These drawings are like a *mille-feuille*," a French pastry formed with layers of flaky pastry and cream. "The first layer is visually accessible to everyone irrespective of sex, age or nationality. Then, if you so desire, you can gradually distinguish other elements, symbols. You can also link them, macrocosm and microcosm for example," he continues. At the same time, he says, he does not have a specific message. "Meanings form without there being a need to write them. These drawings are mirrors in which people are reflected and revealed. They tell me what they see, but it is always what they see of themselves," he emphasizes.

It is not by chance that animals have long been his favorite subject. "I began with animals because I value their lack of political and social concepts. Everyone understands them, everywhere in the world. With animals, there's no dispute. They are the first level, as I mentioned before, and everyone can grasp this. They are only in black and white. But I also love color despite using it exclusively for a series whose name is also a pseudonym. It's called *Phil MASALA*.

The color is the subject of this work through all the media, figurative and abstract, at our disposal: the web, painting, drawing, photography, the installation . . . "

Humanity Constellation, **2015** - A great hand comprising numerous patterns: this is the work created by Baudelocque on public housing in Tor Marancia, Rome, in the context of the project *Big City Life*.

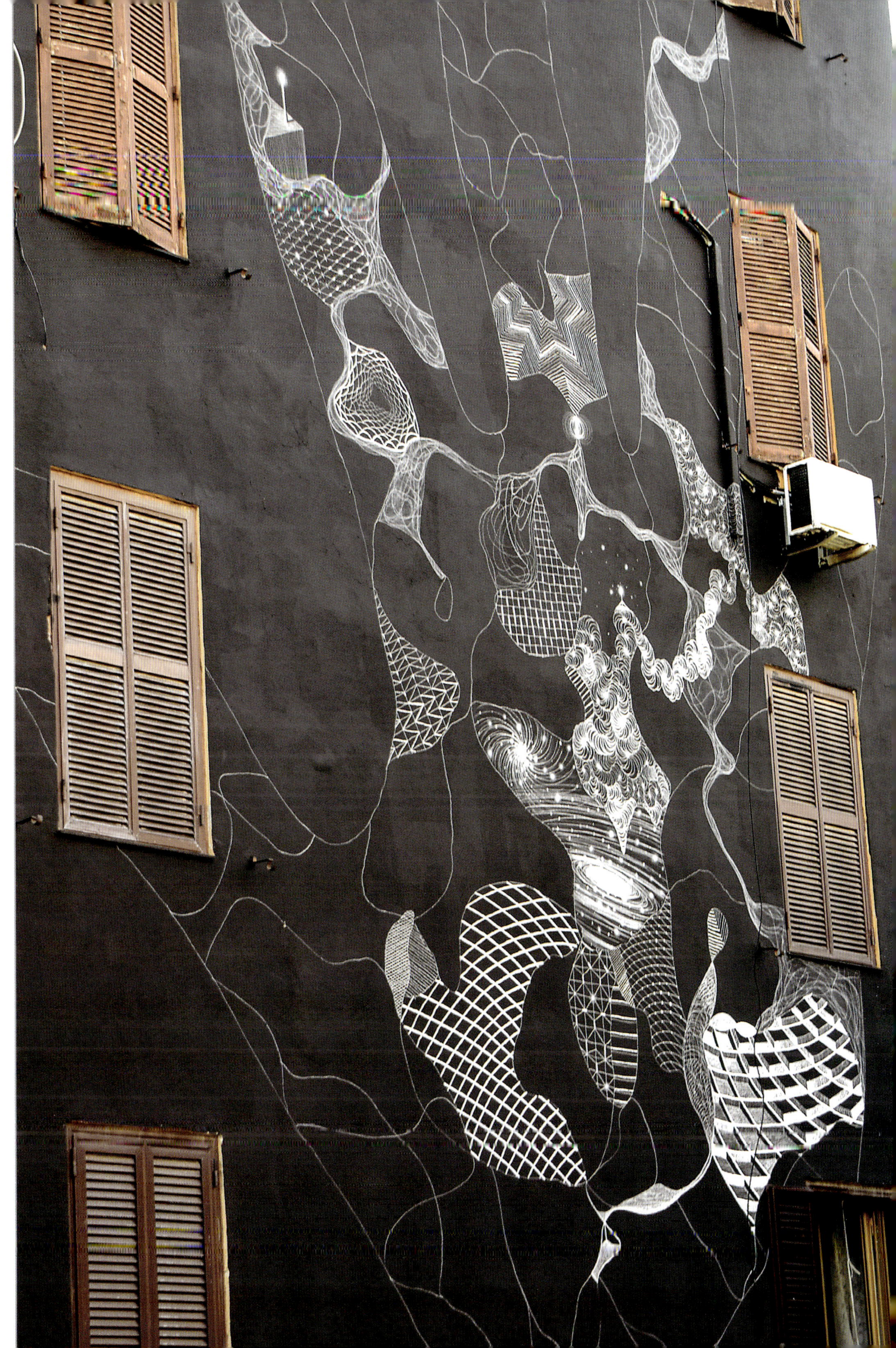

"It's not difficult to become
a street artist. Do something
in the street and people, whether
journalists or just passers-by will
call you a street artist . . .
So yes, I touch upon street art,
but not exclusively."

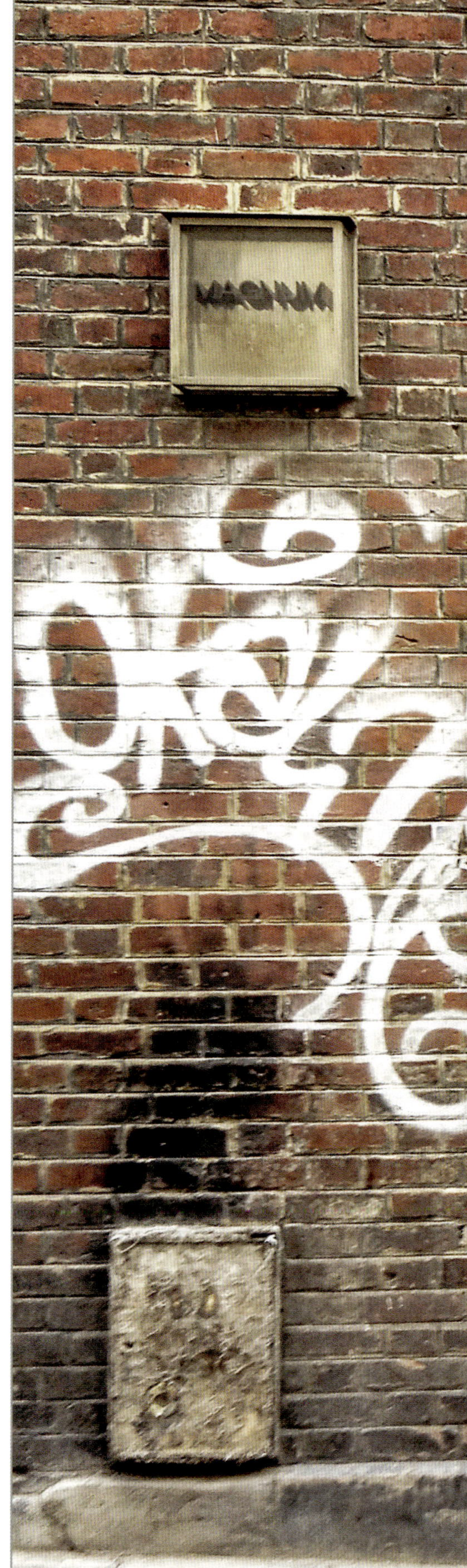

***Gorilla*, 2012**
In 2012, a gorilla that seems to contain all the wisdom of the universe makes its appearance in Rue Hégésippe Moreau, in Paris, on the street door of the Magnum Photos agency.

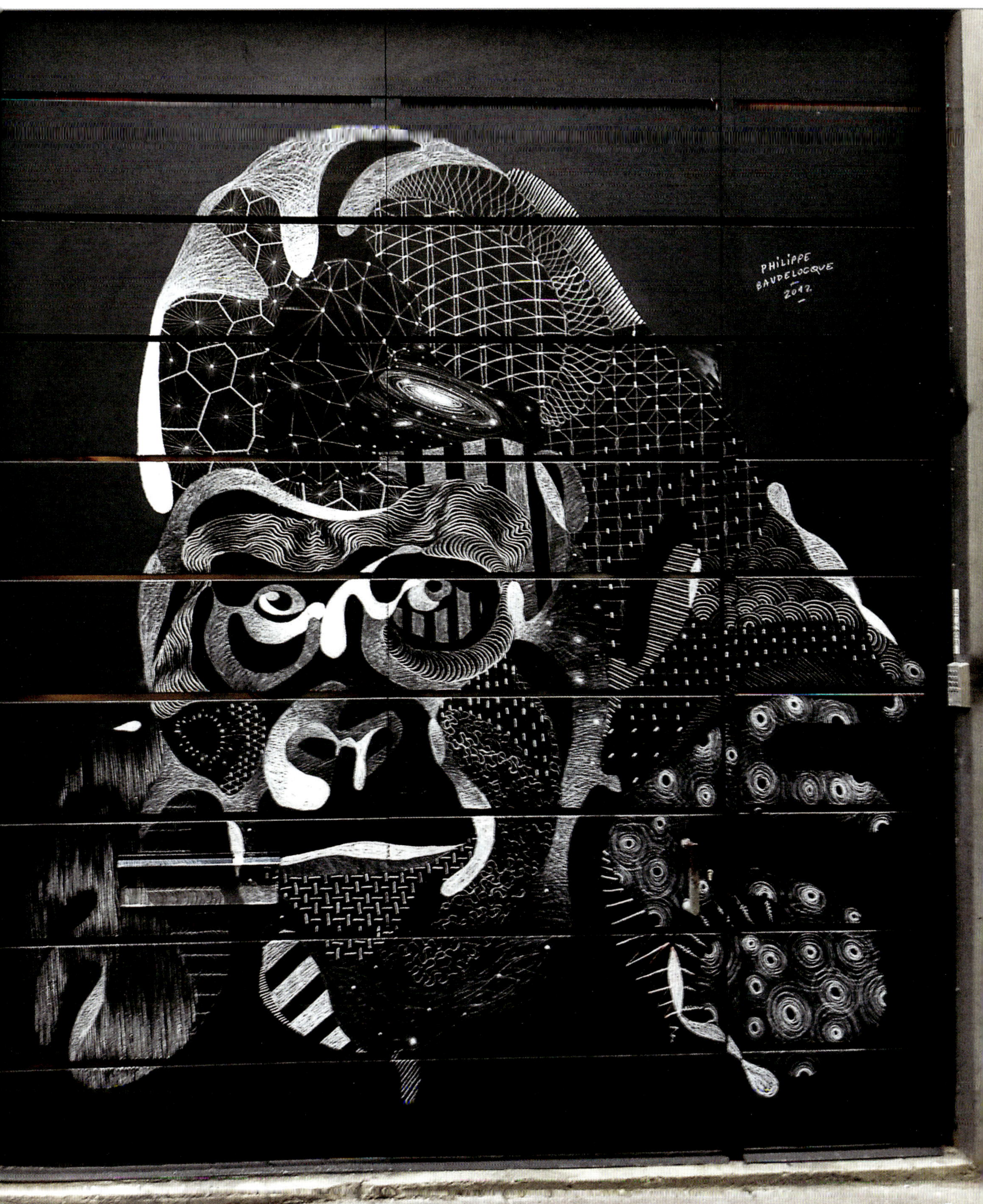

PHILIPPE
BAUDELOCQUE
2012.

He loves minimalist style: "I prefer big letters in silver and black, resembling architecture, huge block letters that are sometimes colorful. I even produced and presented some for my degree in 2002. It was inspired by design and architecture, very minimalist. Today I have kept the shape and dynamics of these letters and removed the meaning of the letters," he explains. There was one project that caused him several problems: "The most difficult . . . was the one that I didn't finish, a realistic character. It was a copy of one of Frank Frazetta's women. It was a long time ago!"

It is sometimes a little dangerous to do street art: "Of course, we would find ourselves in train stations, and the risk was primarily of being caught. There was a frightening episode once, being chased for some time in a small town in France after leaving the station . . . But there were also good times! Like when we went into the subway with my partner Nick, led by KET Ris-Aok, in New York. Before reaching the station itself we went through the underground interchange tunnels used by the railway workers. These tunnels were a real Hall of Fame! I saw tags by everyone: Seen, T-Kid, Skeme, Pjay . . . It was unbelievable! I saw most of the subway art guys." He goes on to describe a work that he'd still like to do, promising that it will happen soon. "Large chrome block letters, with some additional graphics that reflect me now. I'm going to do that soon!"

Many artists have inspired him, but he only wants to mention three: Jean Giraud, aka Moebius.

"My father had a subscription to an alternative comic anthology, *Métal hurlant*, in the 1980s. Moebius illustrated it and that's how I first encountered him. He's one of the masters, with his profusion of ideas, virtuosity of drawing, wealth of quirkiness, and his references to space and science fiction that I love."

James Turrell: "It's the same with him. He's a master and an example to me. He refers to things that I also refer to in my own way. Inner light, symbolic people like the Native American Hopi tribe, tradition, large internal and external spaces, and so on. In particular, I appreciate his sympathetic use of color."

Finally, Pablo Amaringo: "This now deceased Peruvian shaman depicted in his paintings the visions he encountered. I also occasionally represent these dimensions. I appreciate the naivety of the painting combined with the reality of the phenomena that we know exist."

Philippe then mentions other artists, like Tony Cragg, Utagawa Kuniyoshi, Fabrice Lacaze, Honet, Nicolas de Crécy, Richard Texier, Dondi, Bando, Hugo Pratt, Andy Goldsworthy, Os Gemeos, Margaret Kilgallen, Herzog & de Meuron, Josef Koudelka, and Bernard Plossu . . .

While he loves Paris, Philippe has no special preference for any place in the world. "I prefer first and foremost to feel connected with myself. When I'm connected, I feel comfortable everywhere. I recently discovered Hong Kong and I love it. It's like being in *Blade Runner*, the Ridley Scott film that I adore. I love to think about the future and as I see it, it's brilliant!" he confesses.

"I cannot speak for others, but for me I just want to play my own part to build a better world. If I play my part, I'll be fine, happy. I will have accomplished my work in this life," he concludes, his heart filled with infinite hope.

La Tour Paris 13, **2013** - On behalf of the Galerie Itinerrance, in 2013 Baudelocque participated with this work in *La Tour Paris 13*, a project that "repainted" a tower marked for demolition in the 13th arrondissement of Paris.

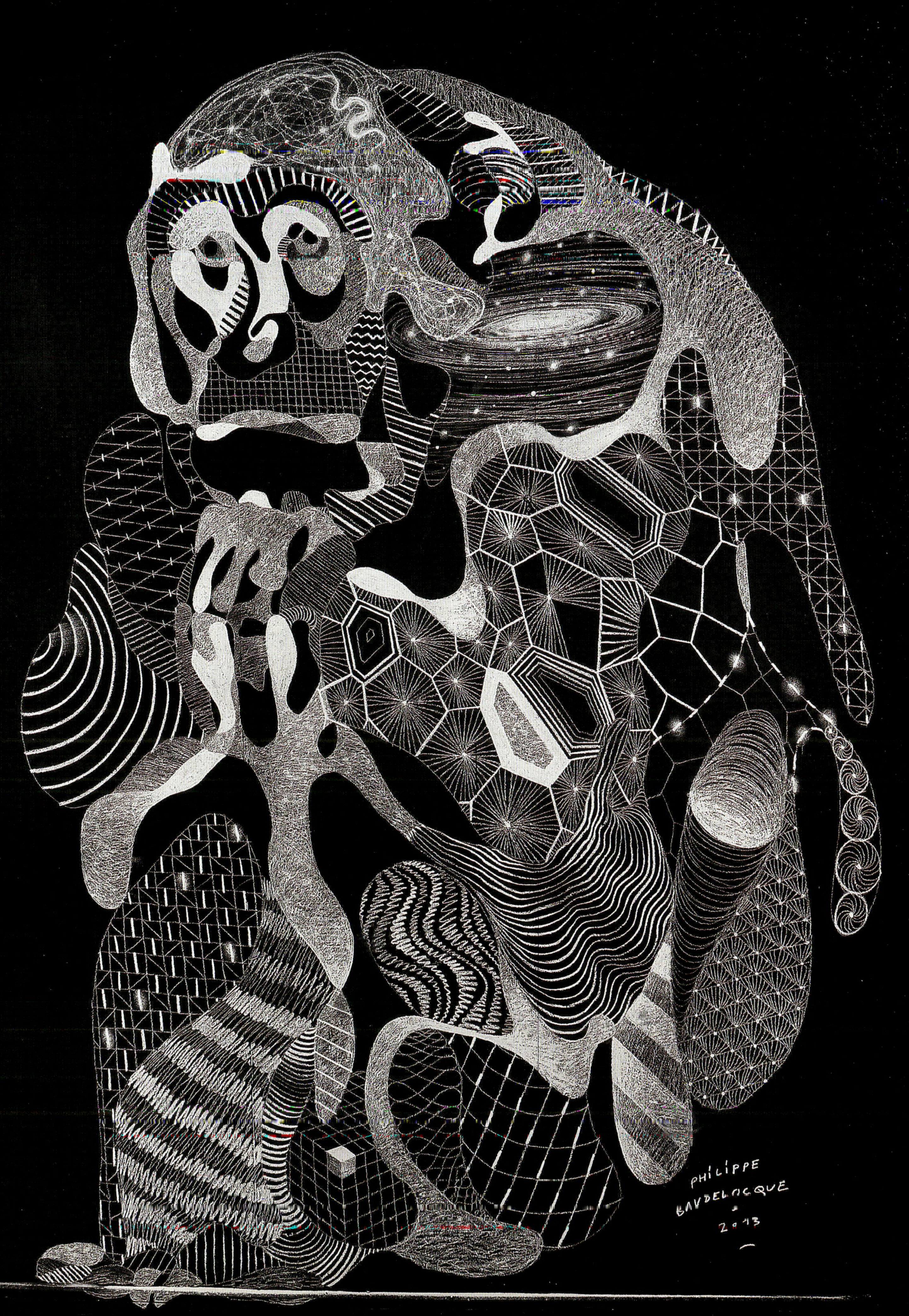

PHILIPPE
BAUDELOCQUE
2013

BECCA

Street Art Lady

Her touch is one of elegant and refined femininity. Her art conveys beauty and love, gentleness, courage, lightheartedness, and playfulness. If one considers that street art is a world dominated by men, it is nice to see her standing out for her sunnier works. Rebecca Midwood, better known as Becca, is simply expressing herself. "I like that my art is positive, that it feels good and it's beautiful to look at. I recently made a girl that I really like: she has a sword in her hand but holds it low, as if a form of protection, she is not aggressive and has her eyes pointed upwards, almost as if she is a visionary with a dream," she recalls from a farm in Austin, Texas, where she works and lives with her animals, a couple of cats and a dog, all very social, including the fawns who visit her from the nearby forest to eat corn on the cob.

Becca was born in Brooklyn; she earned her BFA from the Virginia Commonwealth University and MFA at the San Francisco Art Institute. She has been painting since she was a child, following in the footsteps of her mother, also a painter. "I lived for a while in Virginia to study art, but now I live in Austin, Texas, where my mother also now lives to stay close to her grandchildren. My mother is a native of Virginia, while my father was from New York, so I have always been back and forth. I also spent a period in Los Angeles after the riots, and many of my works can be found there: I was very active in the 1990s," she says. She was later selected by the LA Museum of Contemporary Art, but she had already created an unsolicited work on the door of the restroom of the museum. Today, her works are exhibited in galleries in Los Angeles, San Francisco, Austin, New York and at the Miami Art Basel. Some art collectors who own her work include actor Norman Reedus, from the TV series *The Walking Dead*, Leonardo DiCaprio, John Krasinski, Mike Tyson, as well as Balthazar and Aileen Getty.

> I decided to exhibit my works in the street hoping that someone would notice them. Fortunately, it worked and I found my first gallery.

"For Norman, I painted a wolf: he had seen one of my works, which he liked a lot, but I didn't have it anymore so I decided to make one specifically for him. It can be seen in a video on the Internet, which was taken while I was making it," she says.

"I made my first work of street art as a child, on a wall along the road that took me to school. They were letters. When I was sixteen, I invented a sort of alien figure with horns, which was inspired by a musical symbol and I put it under a bridge in Washington.

Rebecca Midwood, in art Becca, in her studio-farm in Austin, Texas, where all of her work is created.

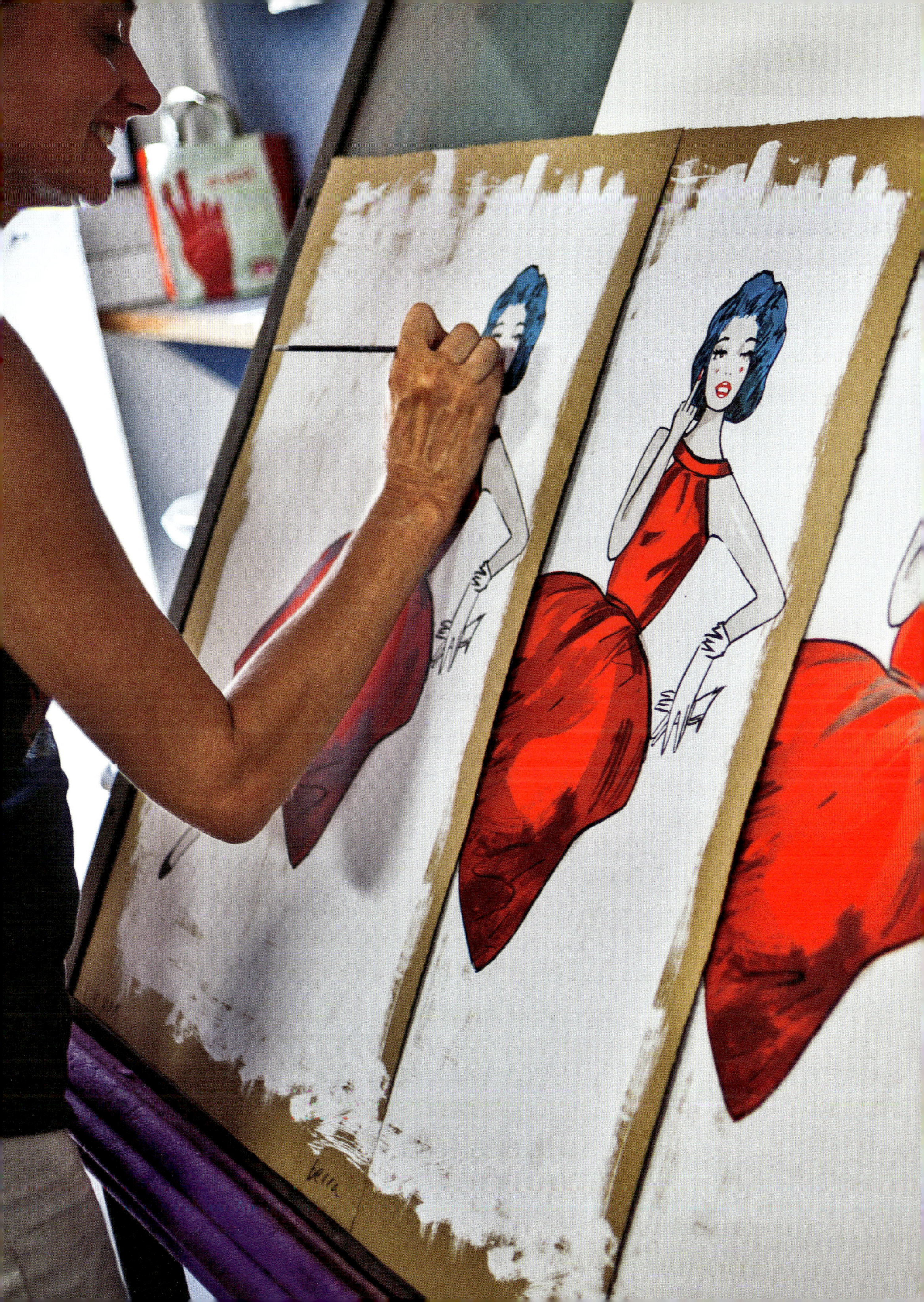

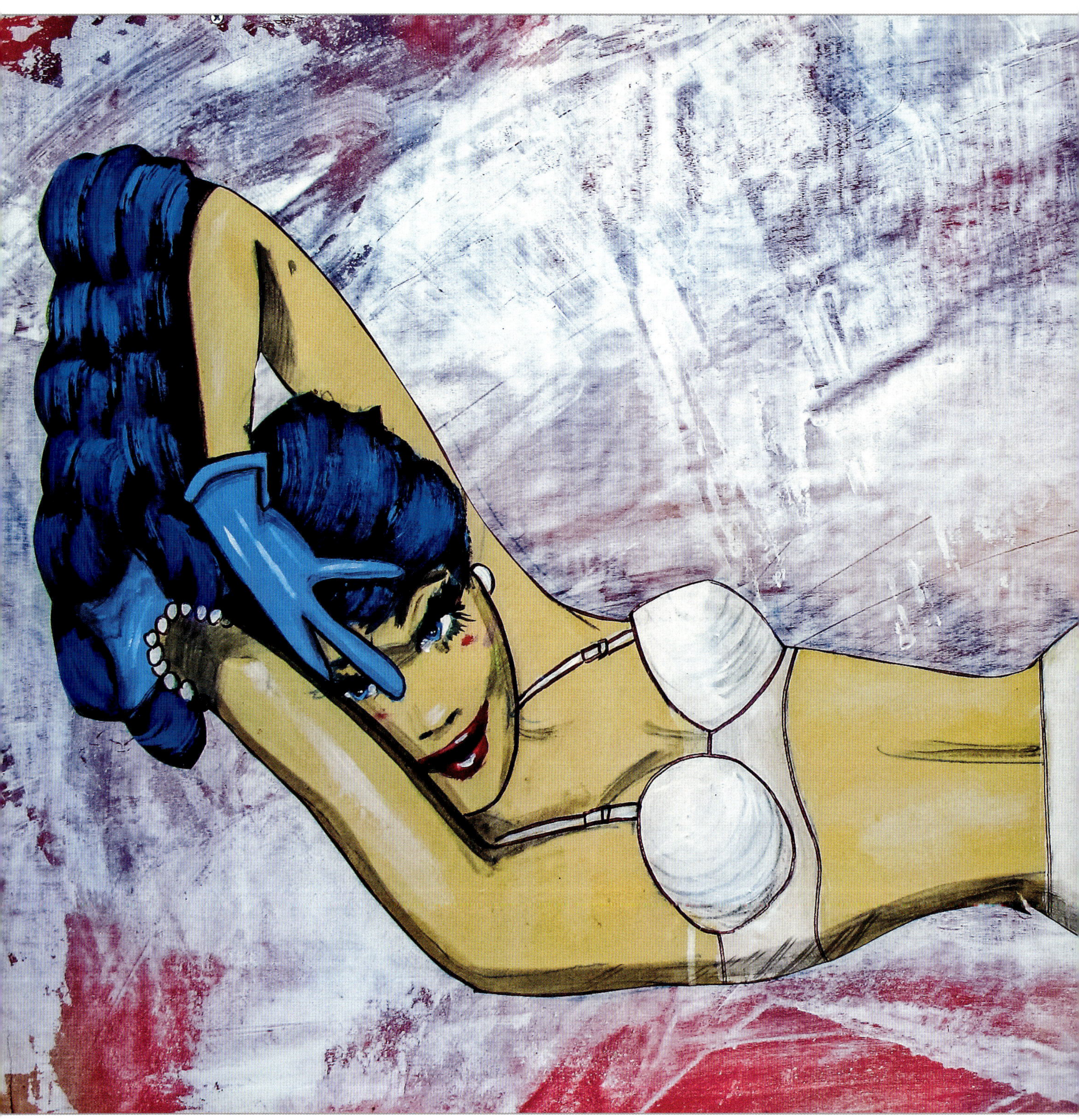

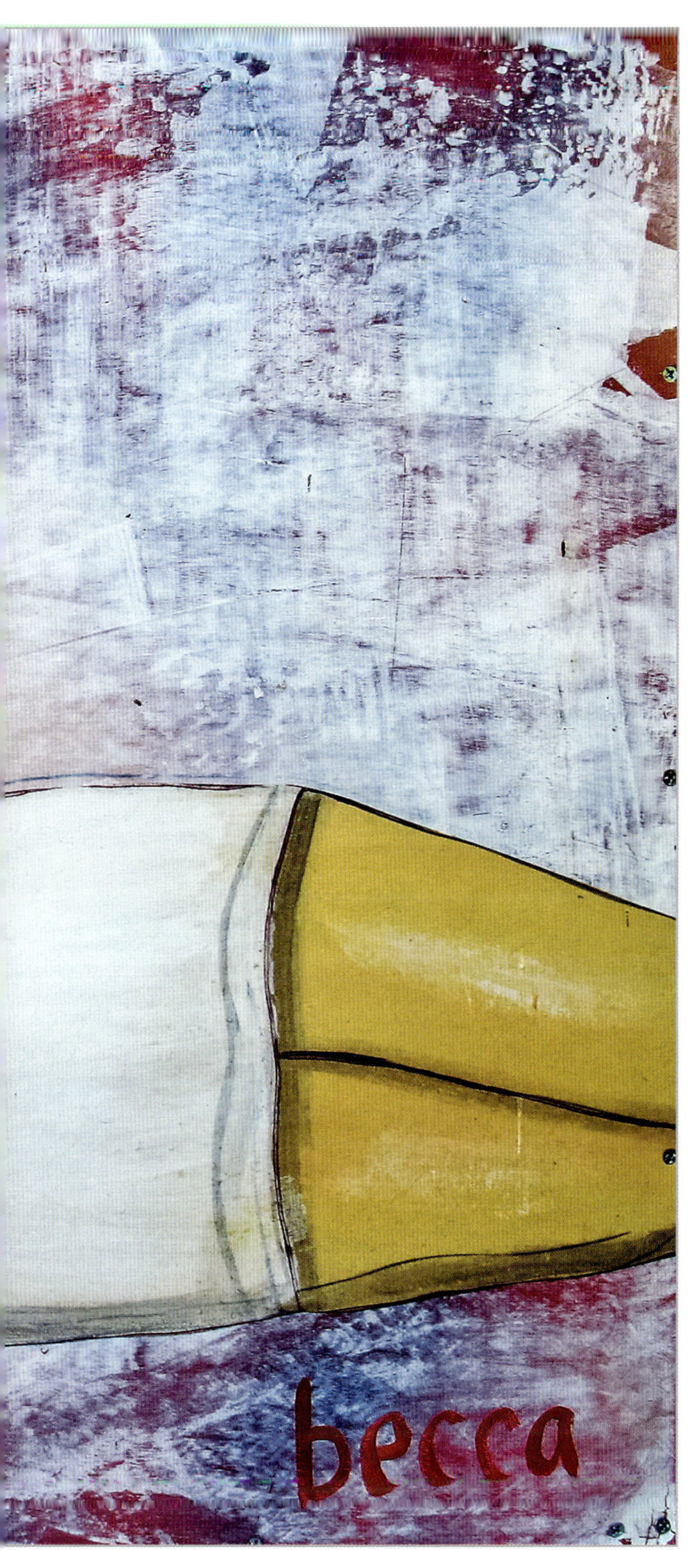

***Babes and Bears*, 2012**

For the *Babes and Bears* series, undertaken with Philip Lummang, Becca has often re-elaborated this subject that filters the classic iconography of Venus through American pop culture.

I made various works there and in Richmond, either alone or with my boyfriend from back then. That's how I got involved in street art and became passionate about it," she recalls, thinking back to the early days, almost thirty years ago. "I still want to create art and there are many things I want to do. I want to leave a memory of me," she says. "As for my subjects, I prefer female figures. Some look like me or like my friends, or people whom I see. All things inspire me. Even animals: wolves and coyotes, and more recently, fawns, perhaps because there are so many where I live," she adds. "Another character that I have always liked and represented in art is Hello Kitty, because I grew up with her and always found her interesting."

Becca's technique has evolved over the years. "Before I would put original works on walls, now I usually prefer to keep the originals and put prints in the streets. The reason is that many of my works have been destroyed and I do not have them anymore. I realized that they are precious to me and it's too big of a risk to expose the originals," she says with some regret. Indeed, several of her works, in the past, have been stolen: some by her fans, others just to be resold.

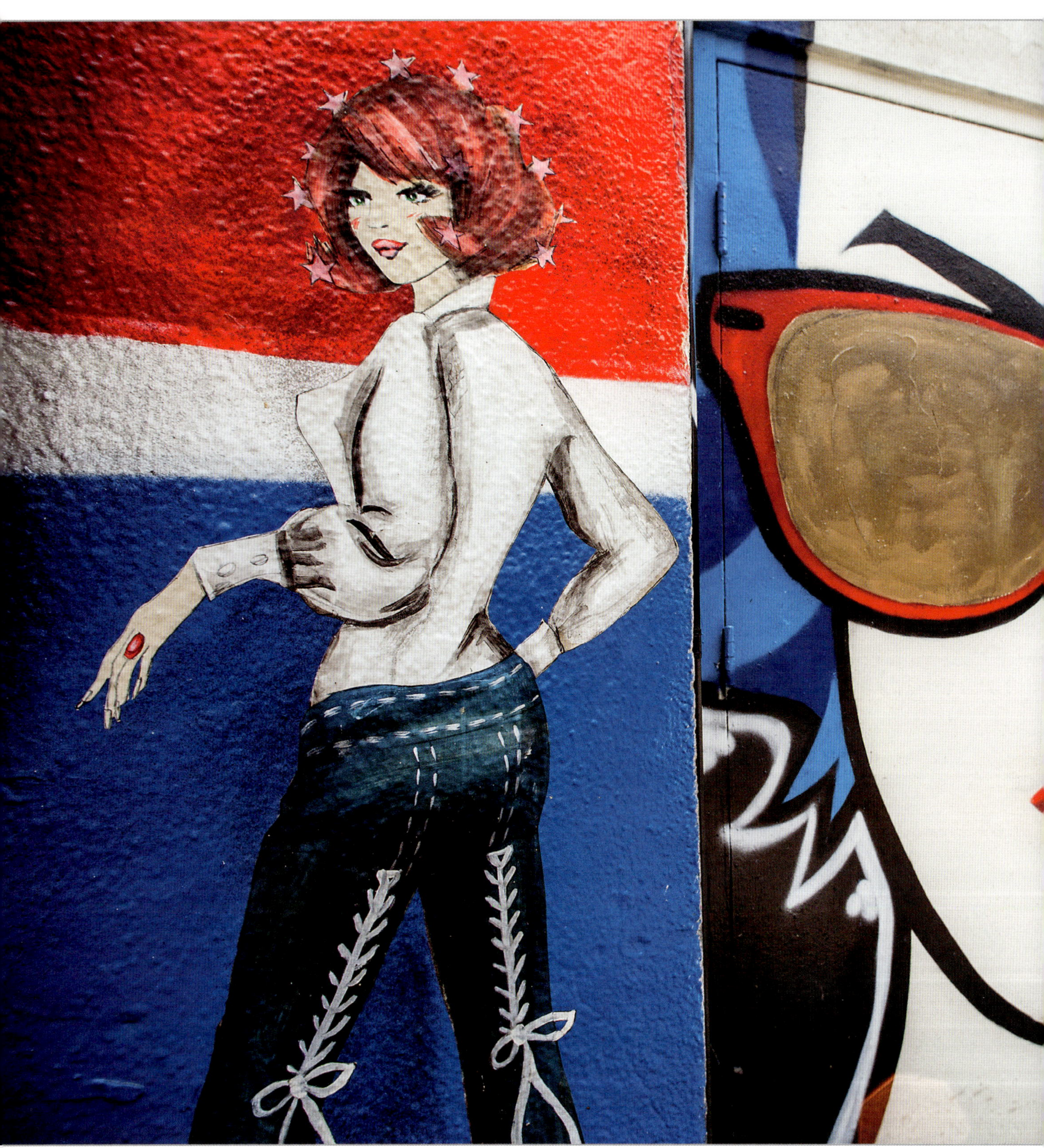

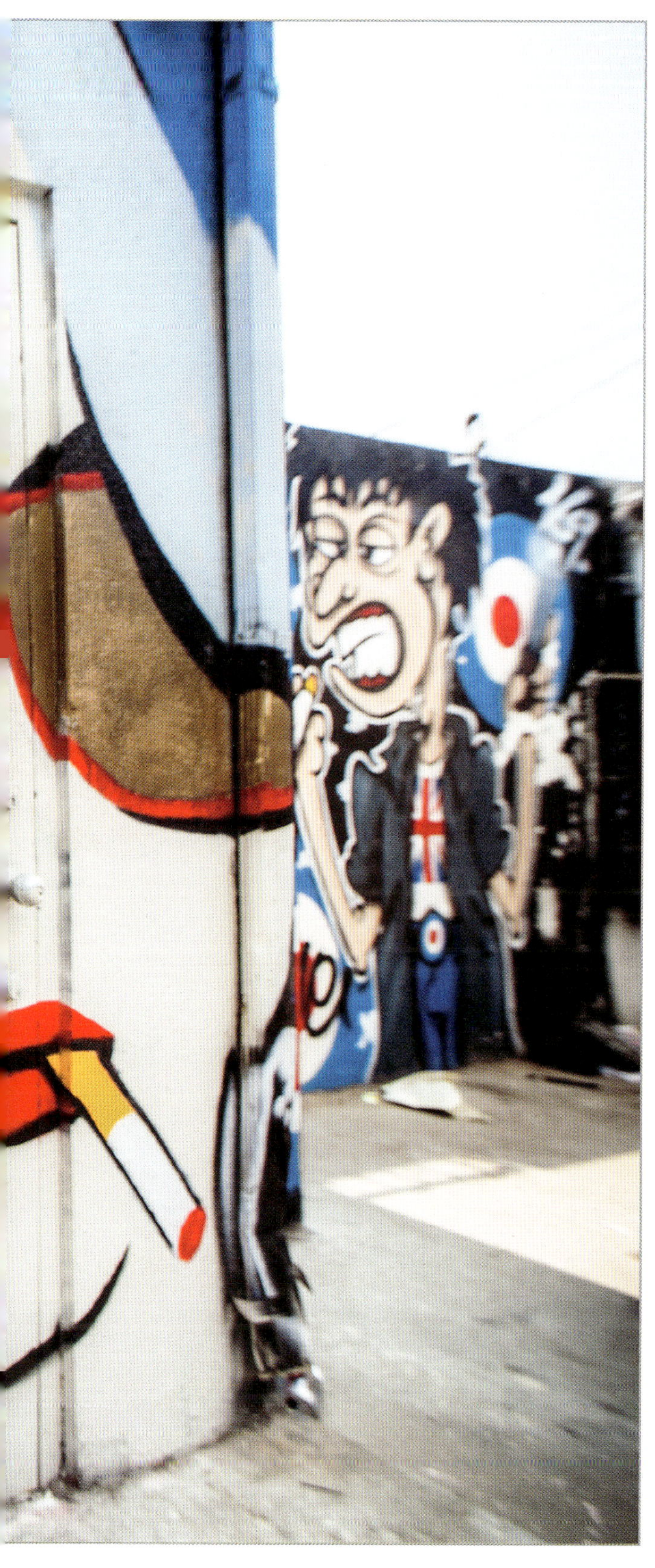

> "When I have an idea for a work, I don't think of anything else and never know what he outcome will be until the end."

"On the other hand, I love working in the street. When I came to Los Angeles, it was too expensive for me to prepare the slides of my work to show art galleries, so I decided to exhibit my works in the street hoping that someone would notice them. Fortunately, it worked and I found my first gallery. But the work process has remained the same: I usually paint everything in my home studio; then I crop it and prepare it to attach to walls. I've never had problems because I can attach them very quickly, it only takes me five or ten minutes," she explains.

"For me, art is a pleasure and a way to bring out emotions in others. When I have an idea for a work, I don't think of anything else and never know what he outcome will be until the end. Maybe I'd be better off choosing another type of job, like working in a shop or something, but I can't do anything but this. I am connected to art. I love all colors, but prefer them bright: hot pink, aqua blue, bright green, bright orange," explains Becca, who truly excels in her combinations of proportions, shapes and colors.

Los Angeles, 2014
The girls of Becca's world are all sensual and happy, self-determined and joyful, as the colors used in this piece seem to underline.

Becca believes she can work anywhere, she just needs to be in the right mood: "Most of my wolves are along the Indian Alley in Los Angeles: it is a special place.

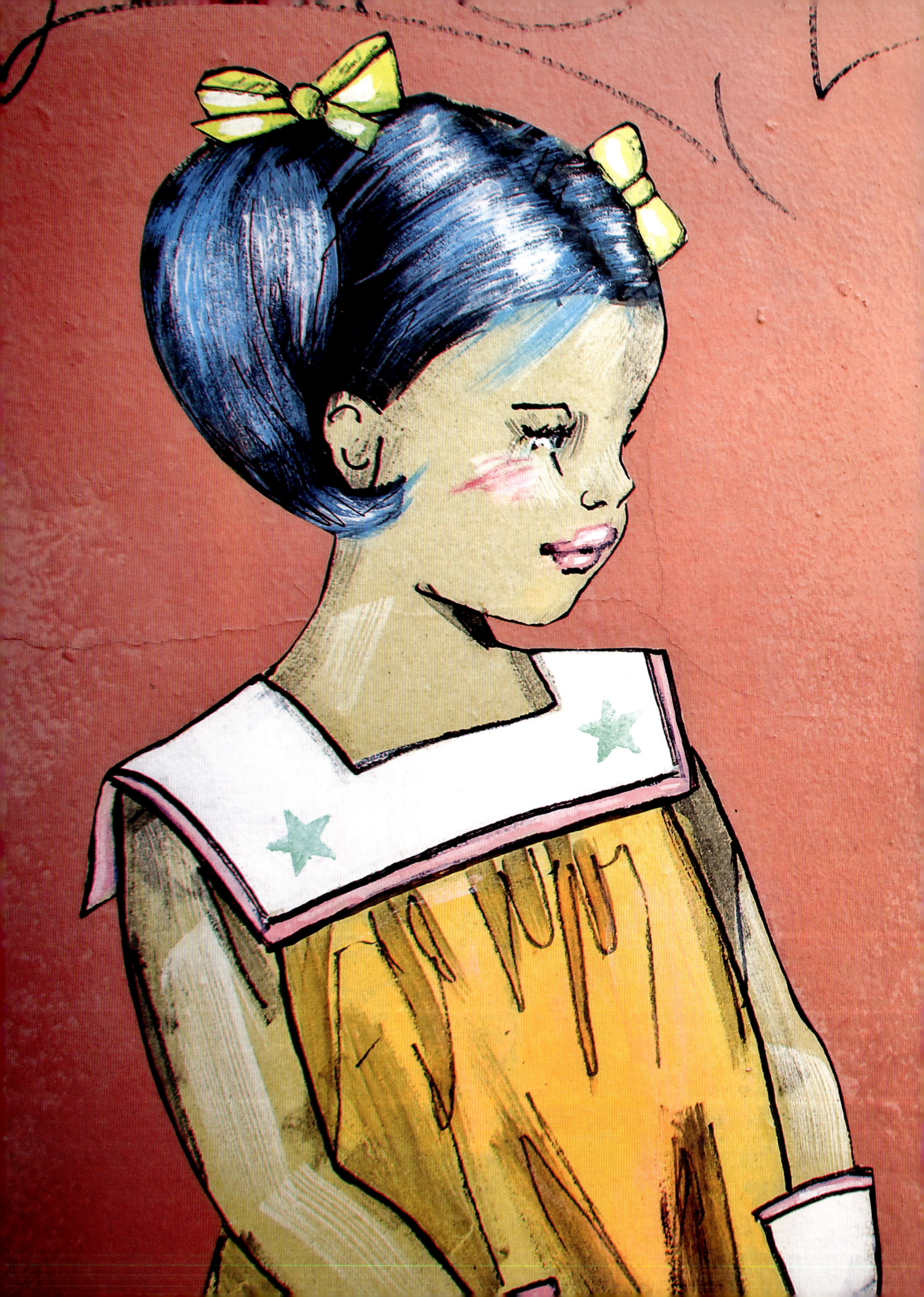

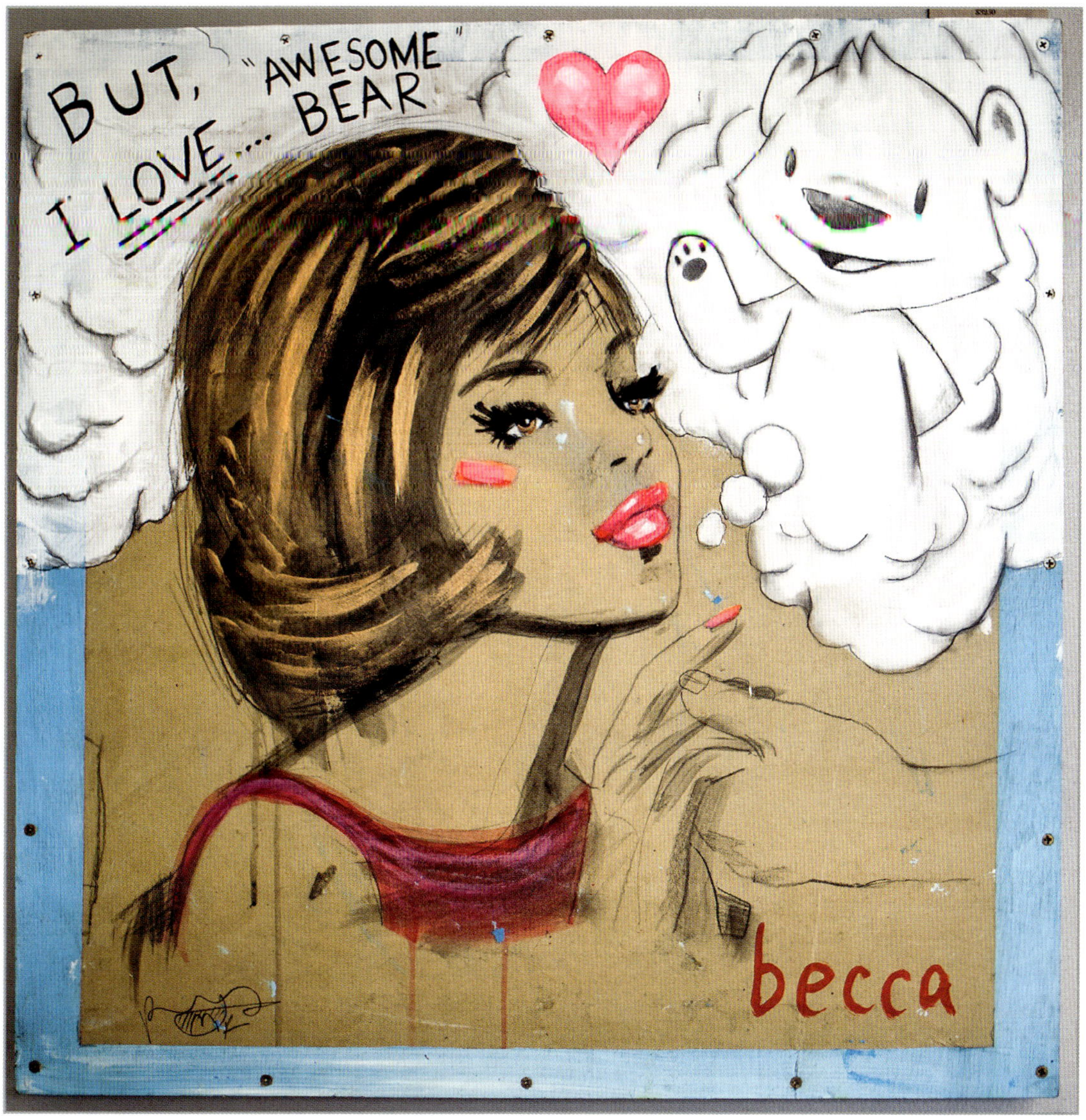

Orange Girl (Little Orange Dressed Girl), **2011** - Becca is a huge fan of the childlike imagination, as shown by this girl dressed in orange on a wall in Melrose, Los Angeles.

But I Love Awesome Bears, **2012** - The white bear – a symbol of tenderness – appears in this as in other pieces created by Becca in collaboration with Philip Lummang.

I'd like to do more also in New York, a city I know well and know how to move around, as well as in Italy, maybe. I have been there once, when I was a young girl; I would go back to Assisi, the town of Saint Francis, whom I admire, and install my works in churches and historical monuments," and then she confesses to having a very unusual dream: "One day I'd like to open my own casino, in which everything would have my brand on it, from the slot machine to the carpets, from T-shirts to accessories, lipstick and makeup. I know it's very ambitious, but, after all, dreams have to be big."

"I do not feel I have a particular belief in anything. I love animals because they are reliable, unlike people, who can change. Animals trust their instinct and do not have a creed; they are simply themselves. Because I knew I'd be asked this question, the other day I asked my dog what his creed was. He looked at me sweetly and I thought he said: 'To look nice and be cuddled and pet a lot.' Not bad, right?"

C215

Lover of Portraits, Cats, and Freedom

He is a specialist of the stencil, but with a style all his own. Christian Guémy, aka C215, confesses to being immensely attracted by faces, mostly of ordinary people and minorities, by the faces of beggars, street children, homeless men and women, old people, workers, and immigrants, but also by strange animals and free spirits, like cats. They are always strongly expressive faces. "Right from the beginning, I was attracted by portraits of people and animals drawn with stencils, and by contextual art. I made it a rule never to repeat myself, to work quickly, to create figures that evoke emotions," Guémy recounts from Paris, where he is at the moment. "And it's true, cats have always fascinated me. Moreover, for people on Internet they're a symbol, and so this seemed an excellent means to communicate on the web. But at the same time, they know how to live on the street, they may be stray cats, they're free and independent, and I identify very much with them. Human beings tend to compare themselves with animals. For me, the cat is a totem," he says, and adds: "It's important for me to create an art that relates to reality; I want to create a connection between the city and art. I hope for a new way to create art."

C215 was born in Bondy, France in 1973. He attended the Sorbonne University and completed a doctorate in research in Art History. He began to be successful in 2005. In 2007, he published his volume *Stencil History X*. "I began to paint in the streets at fourteen years old. I was influenced by my friends, by rap music, and by breakdance. I've drawn ever since I was child, and I developed a passion for various techniques. I began by 'writing my name,' in Orléans, a city not far from Paris. It's there that everything began." One amusing detail: "In the beginning, I had the idea of making my signature my yellow Vespa; I knew I was the only one to own one around there, and so it seemed natural to identify myself with it. At the same time, I thought it was something original. I created street art for pure enjoyment at that time," he says, laughing. "I was constantly looking for freedom, and I shunned conventional supports like canvas or paper. I wanted to live the moment of reality, to absorb the context. Freedom for me is a must," he explains.

> I was constantly looking for freedom, and I shunned conventional supports like canvas or paper. I wanted to live the moment of reality, to absorb the context.

Self-portrait of the artist created with stencils in Vitry-sur-Seine, based on a photo.

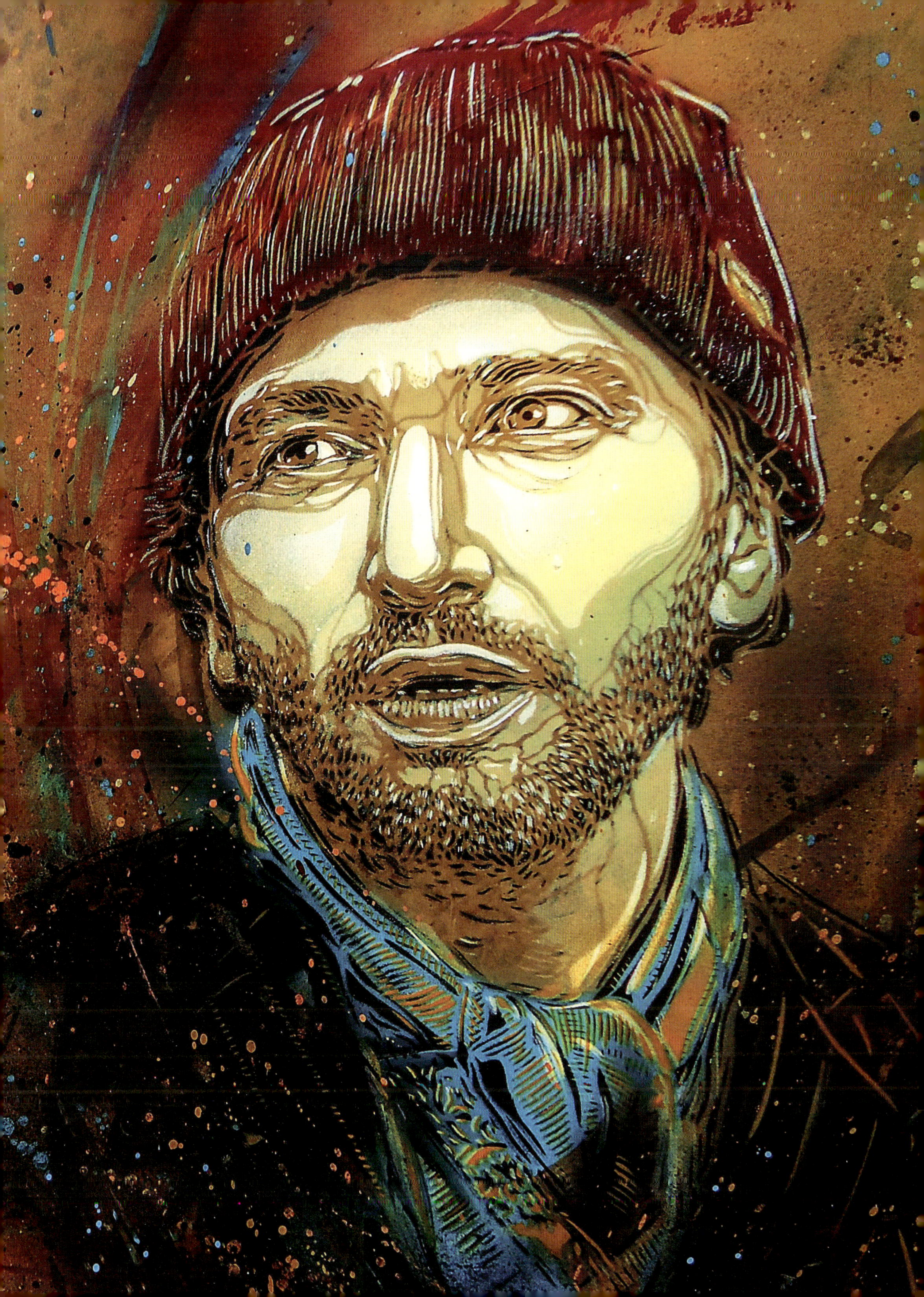

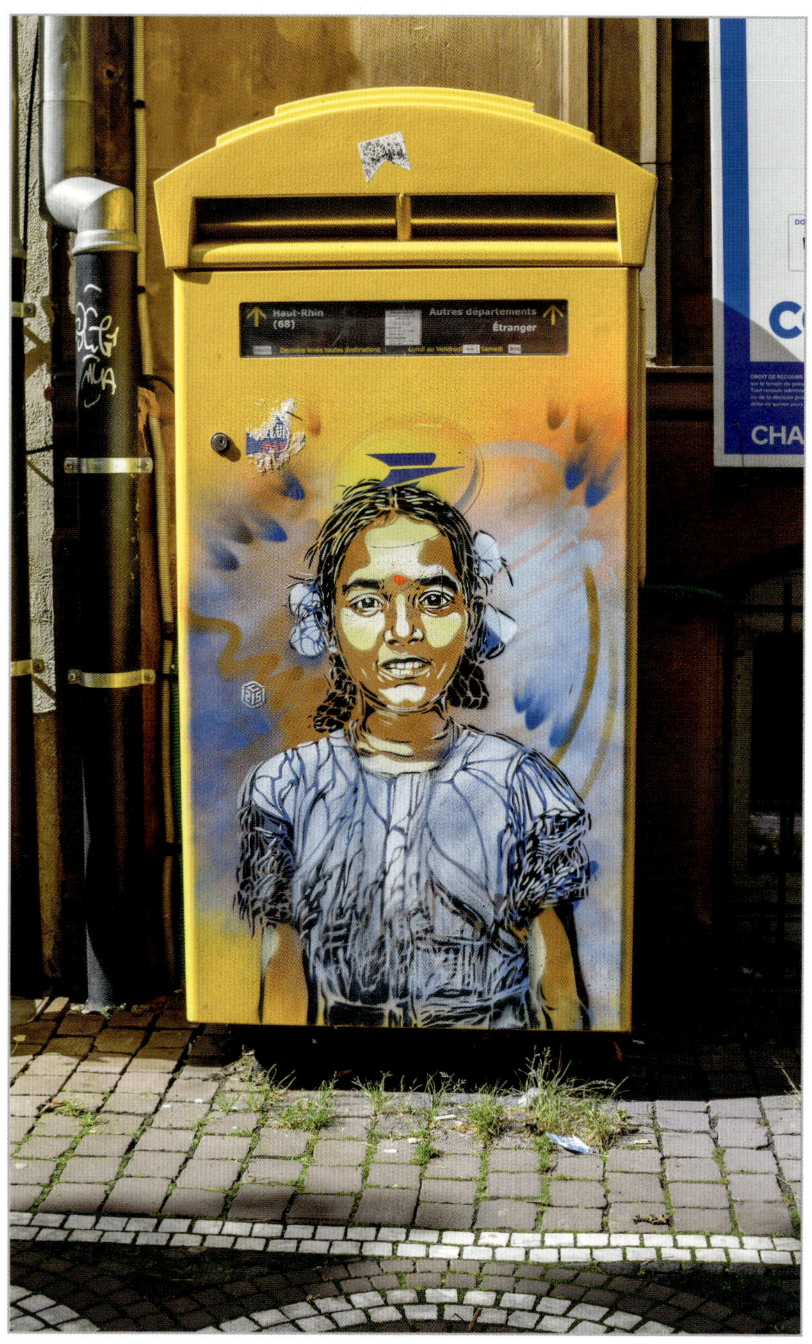

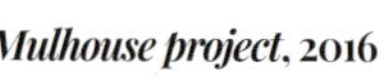

***Mulhouse project*, 2016**
In August, 2016, C215 created twenty or so stencils on mailboxes in the French town of Mulhouse, Alsace. This Hindu girl is in Rue de la Sinne.

***Mulhouse project*, 2016**
Also in the open-air museum in Mulhouse, a portrait of the French expressionist painter Bernard Buffet, who like C215 was fascinated by human variety.

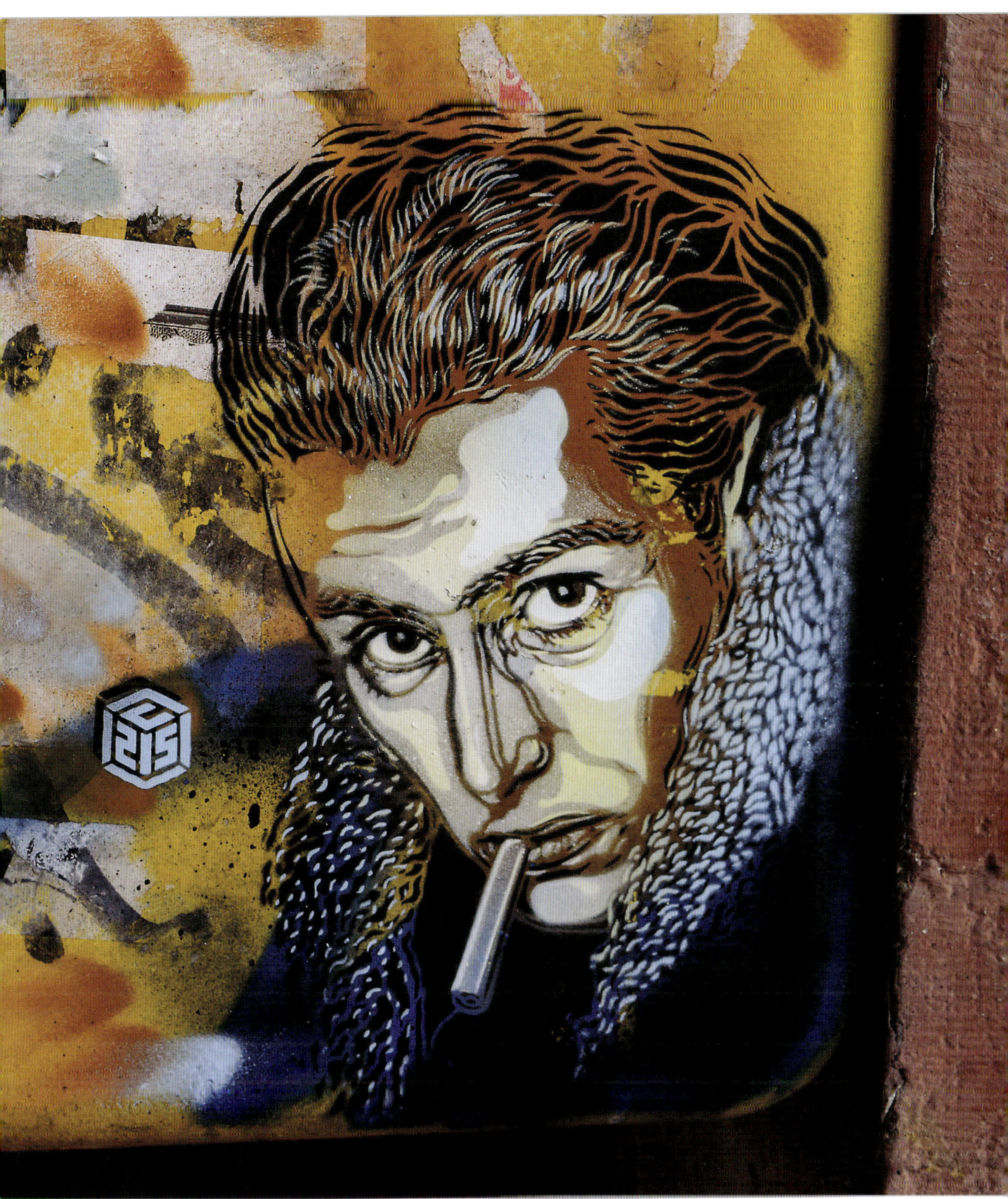

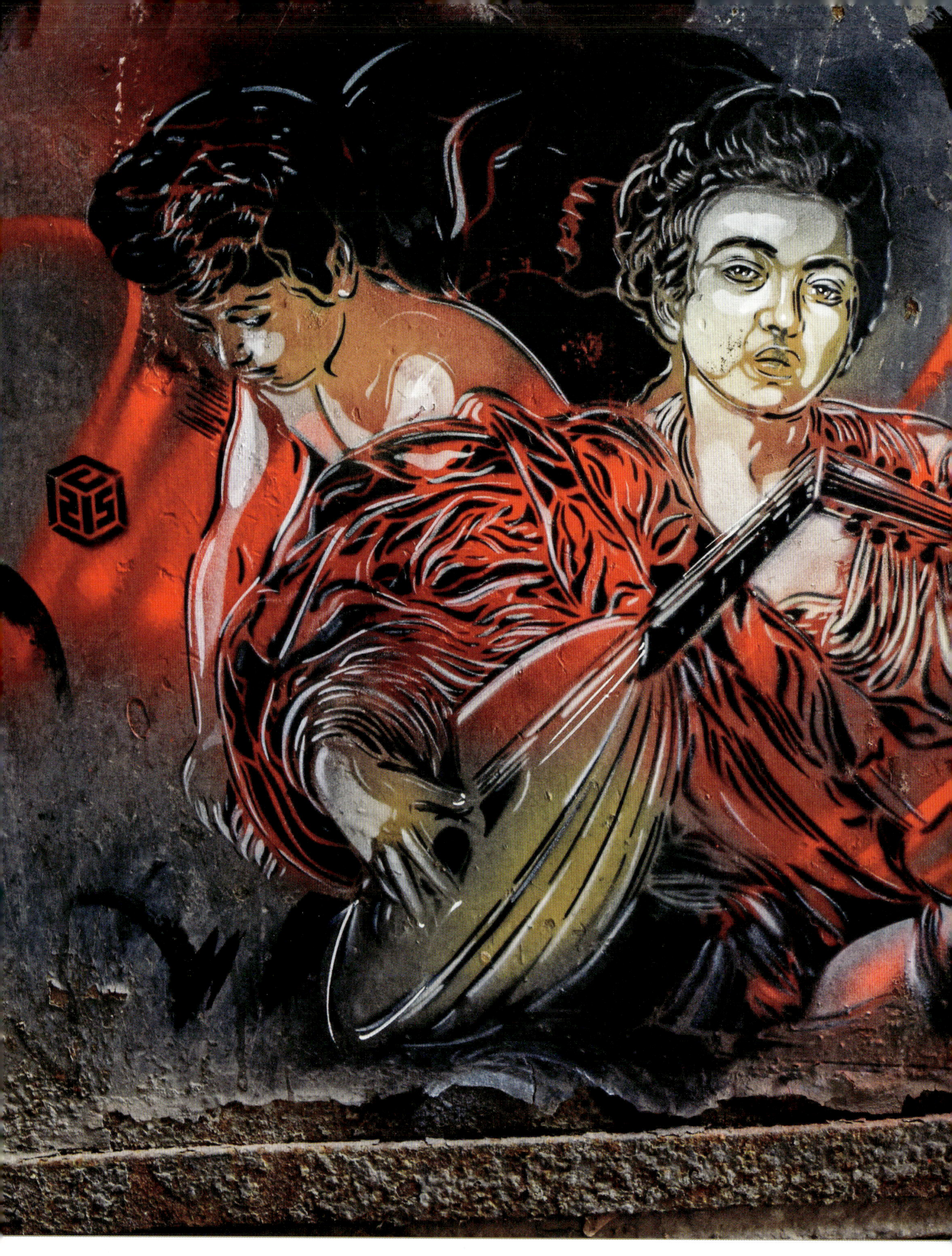

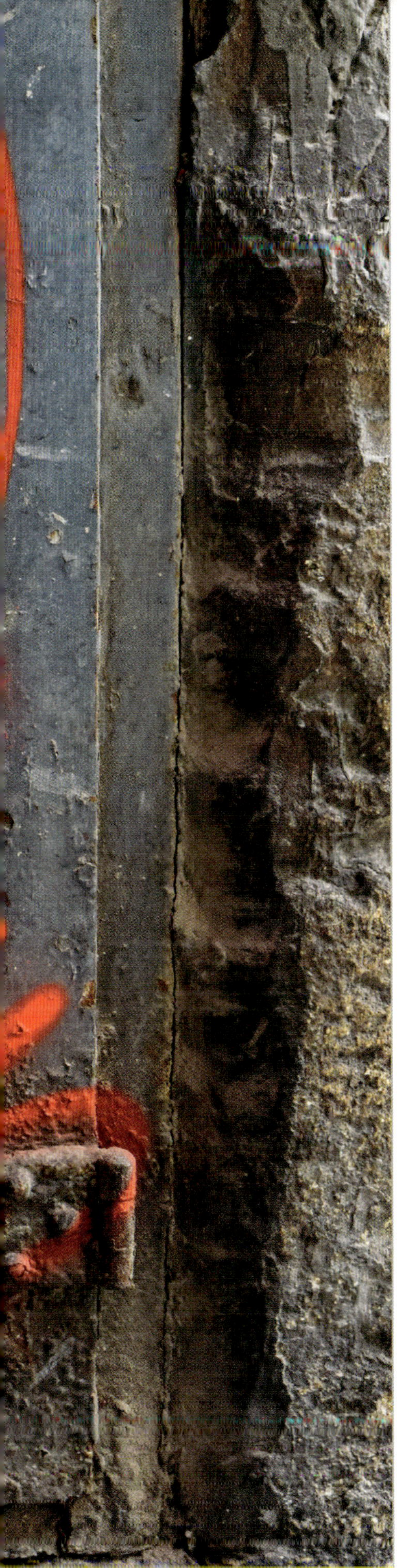

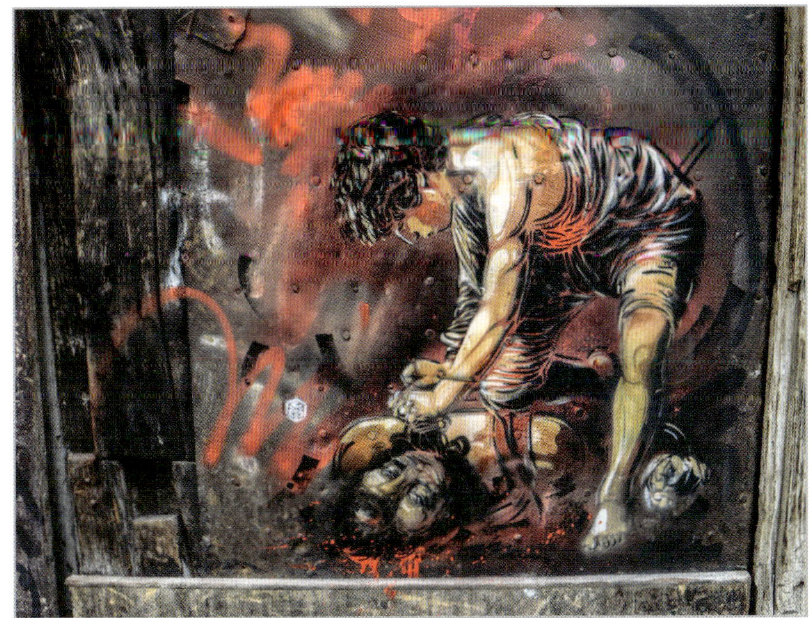

Now his works are all over the world: in Europe, Turkey, Israel, America, Africa. In the meantime, he continues to experiment with different techniques, and to create works on canvas or wood for art galleries. The book *Community Service* illustrates a great exhibition in Paris in 2010. "For me, above all else it is fundamental to reproduce and create emotions. From the technical point of view, I've tried to raise the stencil to a higher aesthetic form, even though I work fast, and to make it more cerebral, a way of perceiving reality. And sometimes even to offer an amusing point of view." Regarding the "message" that he wants to communicate through his art, he states: "I aim to struggle against the standardization produced by the city, to emphasize that people aren't numbers; I want to provoke emotions – I will never tire of repeating that – when and where people least expect them." He reflects on the political and social time we are living in, and adds: "At the moment, many immigrants are arriving all over Europe, people are tense and nervous and don't understand that these immigrants are the solution, not the problem. So with my art, through the choice of some of my subjects, I try to make them feel welcome, to promote the values of freedom, equality, and antiracism." One of the artists he loves the most is Caravaggio: "I have tried to work like him on *chiaroscuro*, because I think he had a really modern way of painting.

The Musicians, 2015 - The stencil technique chosen by C215 is based on the use of a *chiaroscuro* evoking Caravaggio. In 2015, in Palermo, the French artist dedicated a series of works to the great master.

Davide and Golia, 2015 - Six of the twelve works created by C215 in Palermo have been stolen, but *Davide and Golia*, an homage to Caravaggio representing the eternal struggle between strength and weakness, remains in place.

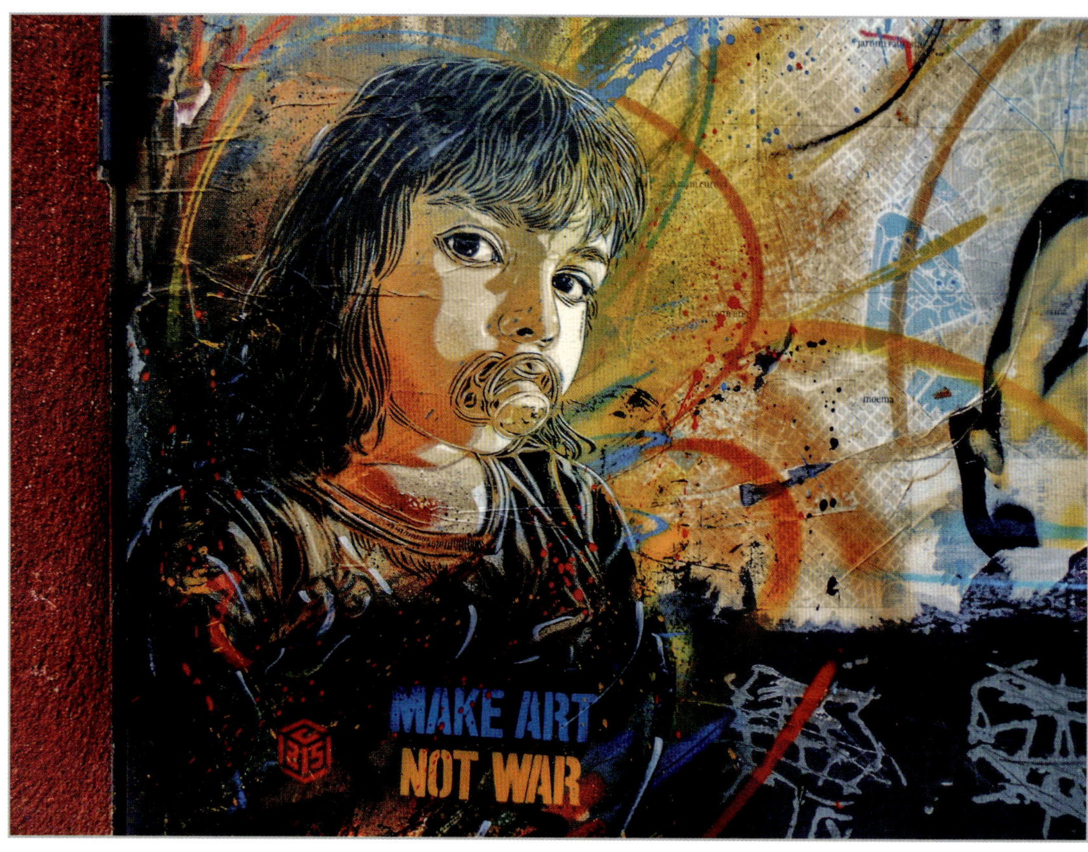

***Nina (Make Art Not War)**, 2012* - The innocent face of a little girl like Nina, the artist's daughter, here portrayed in Vitry-sur-Seine, embodies and communicates a message of peace.

***Chat**, 2012* - The cat, like the one depicted on an Enel energy box in Rome, is technically a very difficult subject to represent.

And then I'm a great fan of Banksy, a great master of communication, and I admire very much Ernest Pignon-Ernest, who, like me, feels close to Caravaggio – also because of his special relationship with Naples. He is also attracted by classical figures, by socialist subjects, by portraits, by prisoners . . . his art is rich in humanism. I also love poetry, I have a preference for Guillaume Apollinaire, I, too have composed and published poems. I believe a strong connection exists between poetry and figurative art. One of the greats in communication through painting is, in my view, Albrecht Dürer."

C215's daughter, Nina, is just as passionate about stencils, even if he makes it clear that she has other interests: "She is very committed to school, she isn't a street artist, she has her own plans. We don't know what she'll choose – at the moment she wants to become a scientist. I'm an artist, her mother is a dancer and my daughter wants to make her own way. She's thirteen years old, about the age when I began to produce street art, but she is calmer than me. And I'm happy that she is," he says candidly. However, Nina, is the subject of various works he has created. "I'm really inspired by her, and I've done many portraits of her. I'm an orphan, and for me it's fundamental to have a strong bond with my daughter.

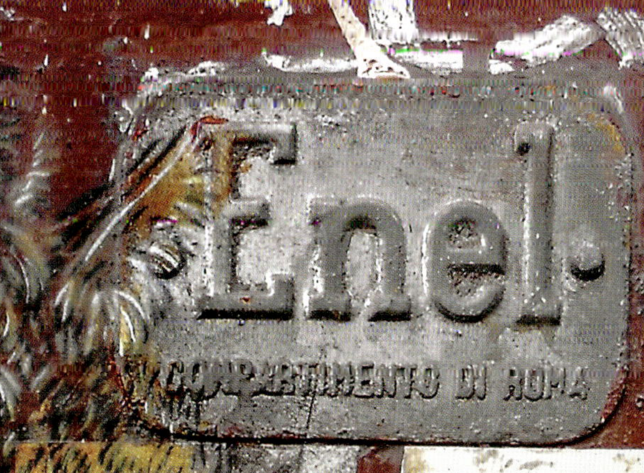

Enel
COMPARTIMENTO DI ROMA

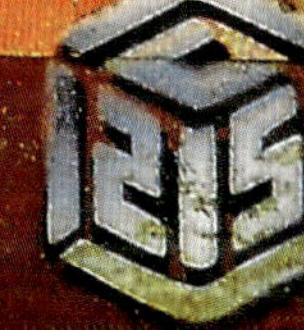

SGOMBERI
SLOCHI
e GRANDI
PORTI
nti - Uffici
ntine - Giardini...
ESTIVI E FUORI ROMA
VENTIVI GRATUITI P.I.V.A.
333.65 846

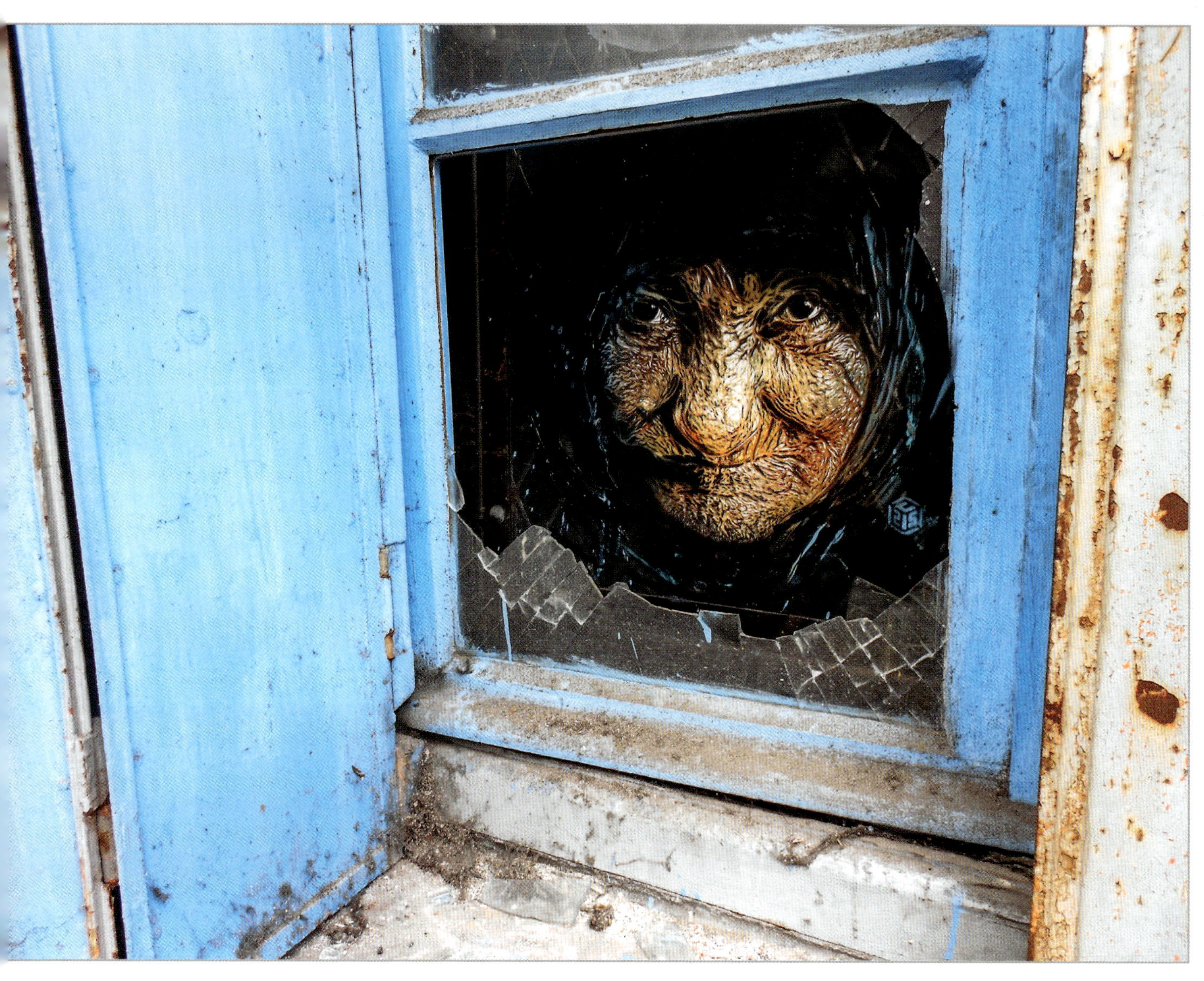

They Are only Made of Clay, 2012 - The positioning of the work behind a broken window, in Vitry-sur-Seine, gives greater depth to the face of the woman, which is already particularly intense.

"If everyone could be happy
in the place where they lived
and could live there without fear,
it would be a better world."

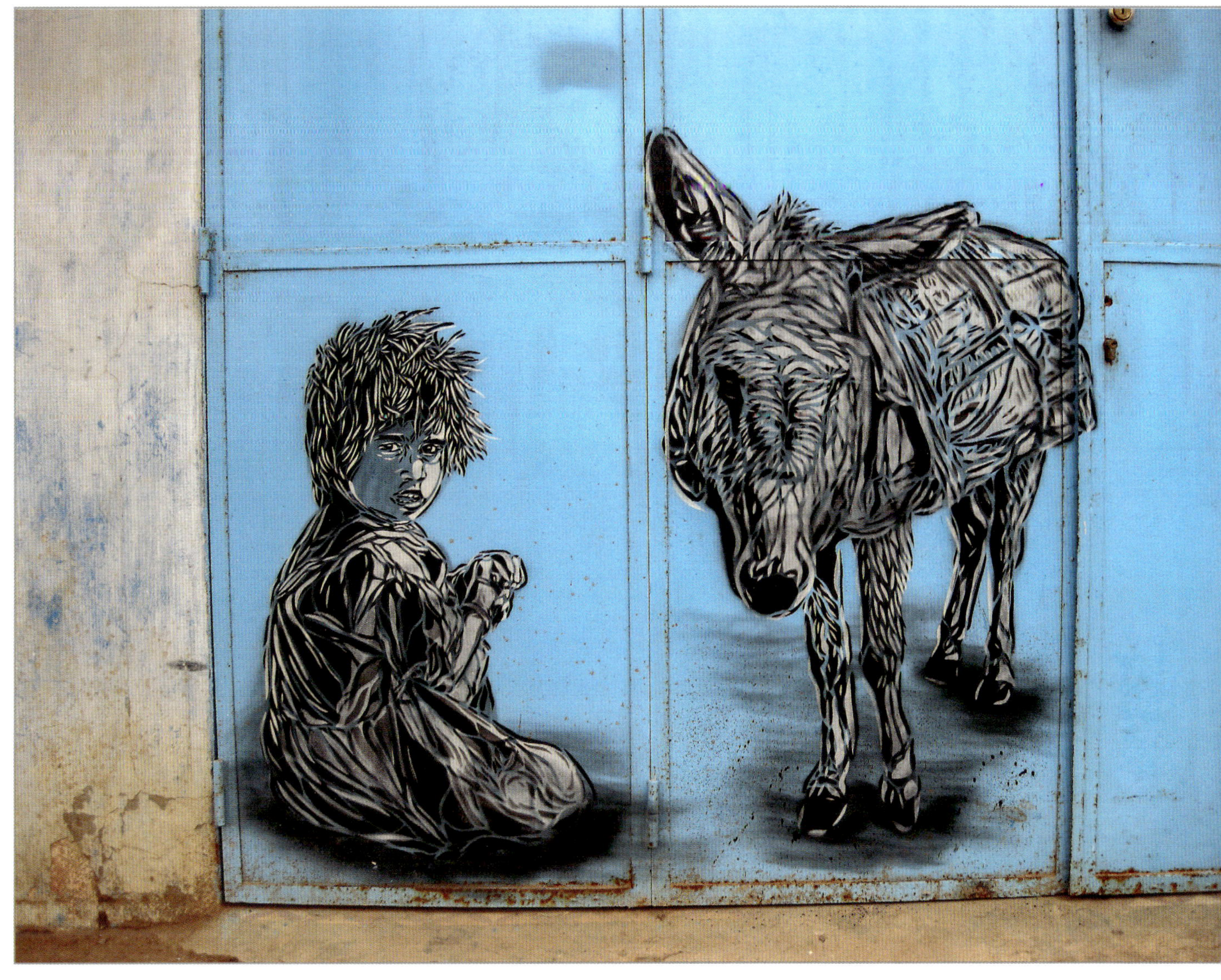

2008 - This little Indian girl, alone and sad with her donkey, can be interpreted as accusing the Western world of hypocrisy.

I lost my mother when I was only five years old and grew up with my grandparents, since I didn't have a father," he confesses with a tinge of sadness in his voice.

The mural he considers most important is the one he painted in Rouanda: it depicts some Tutsi youth saving Hutus, and is a symbol of the terrible genocidal period which afflicted the country and which so fiercely pitted the two peoples against one another. "It was important to take risks to give a sign of life to other people," he says, reflecting on that period. Other works he is attached to are those created in the slums of Haiti and Jamaica. "I've never had problems with the police, because I'm careful not to ruin buildings. In this sense I'm very respectful. I want people to appreciate my art and it's important not to annoy people or damage things," he explains, regarding his way of relating to others. He'd like to visit North Korea and create art there.

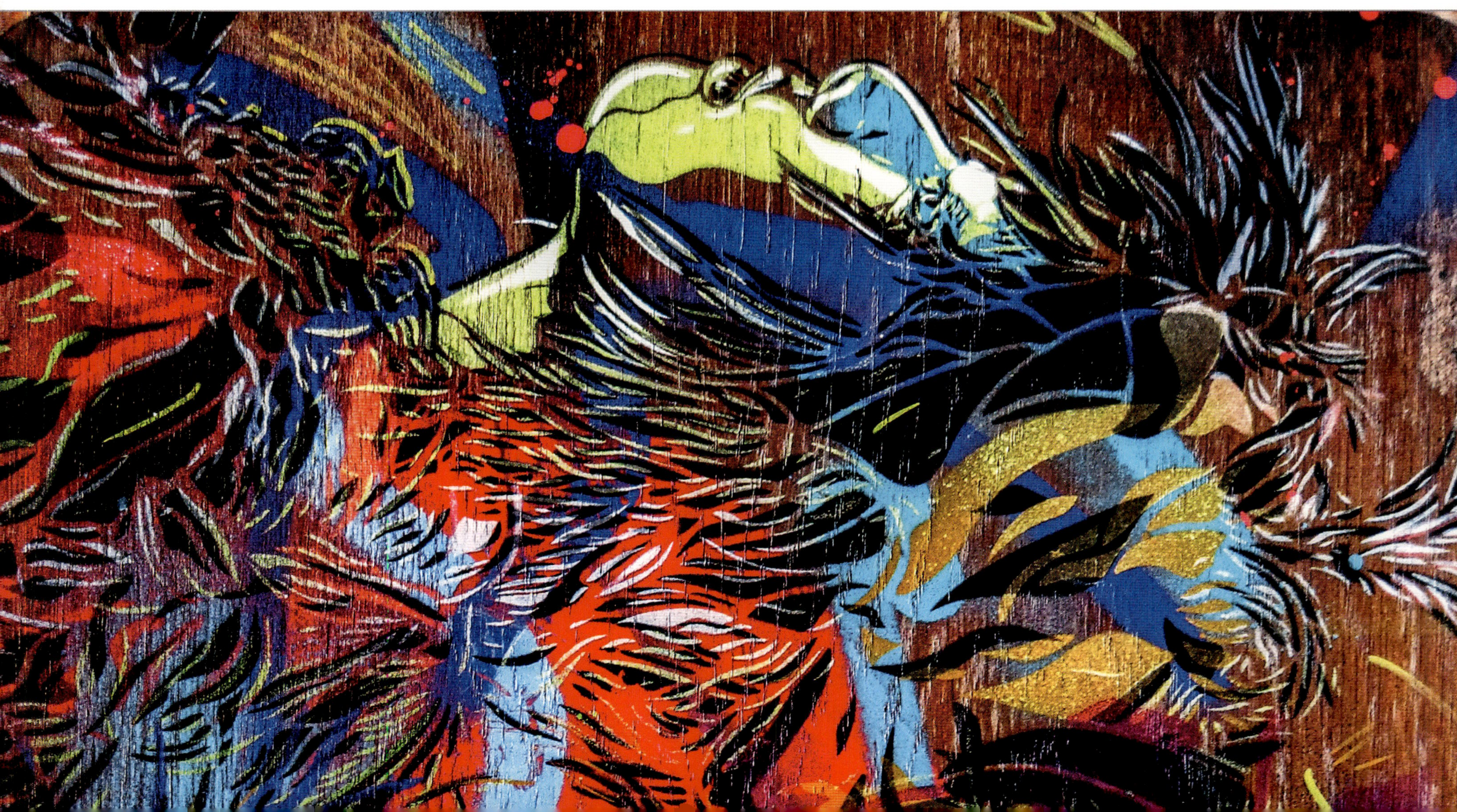

Midnight Dreams, 2010 – C215's talent is also expressed in the depth of the gaze of his subjects, like these inspired by *A Midsummer Night's Dream*.

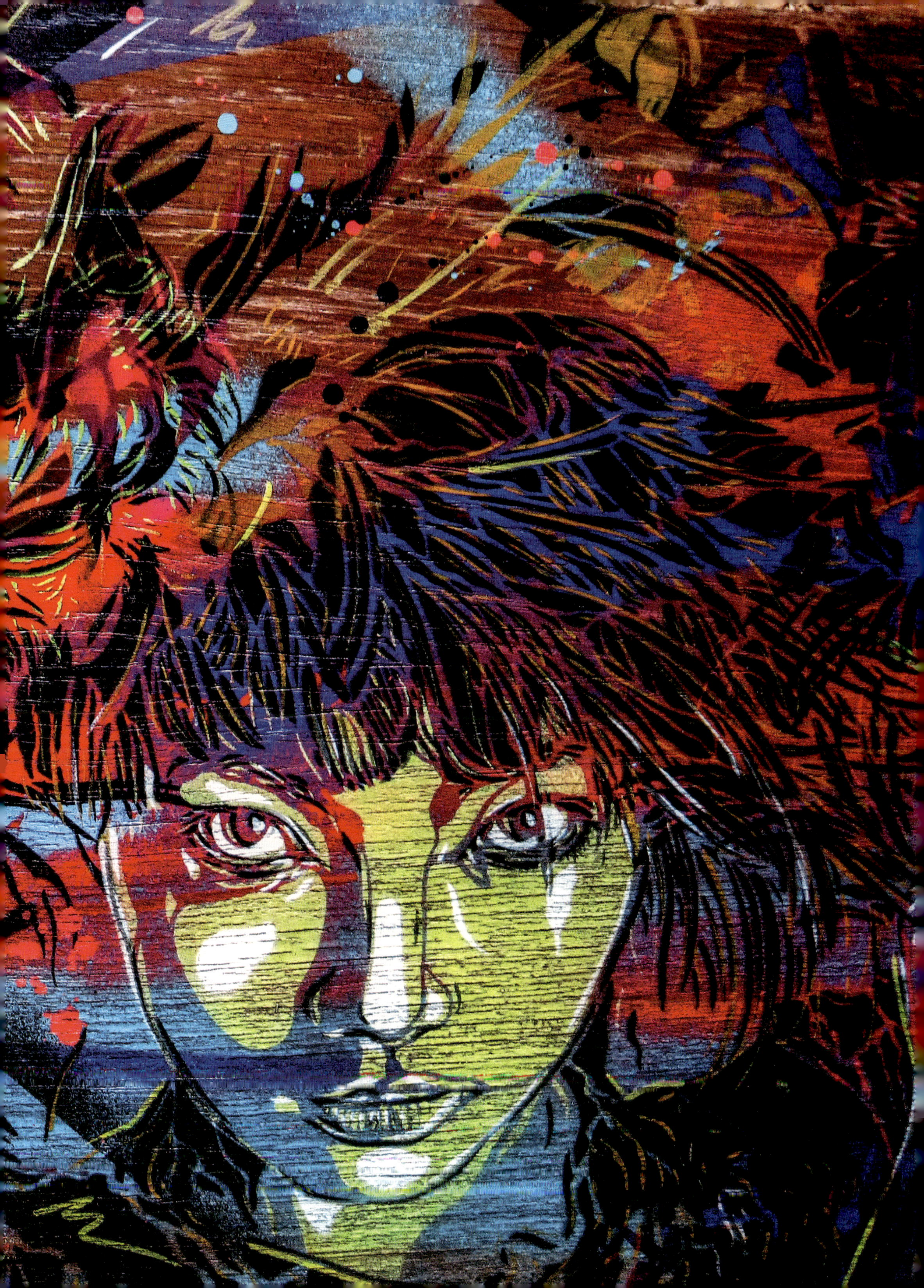

Furthermore, he'd work in Naples and Rome, whose historic centers he loves and describes as "very evocative places, full of character."

However, C215 cannot hide his love for Paris: "It is the world street art capital, its walls are full of it and I invite everyone to see them. I love Paris very much because it has so many places to discover or rediscover. It's practically impossible not to be active here!" And he adds, full of hope: "If everyone could be happy in the place where they lived and could live there without fear, it would be a better world."

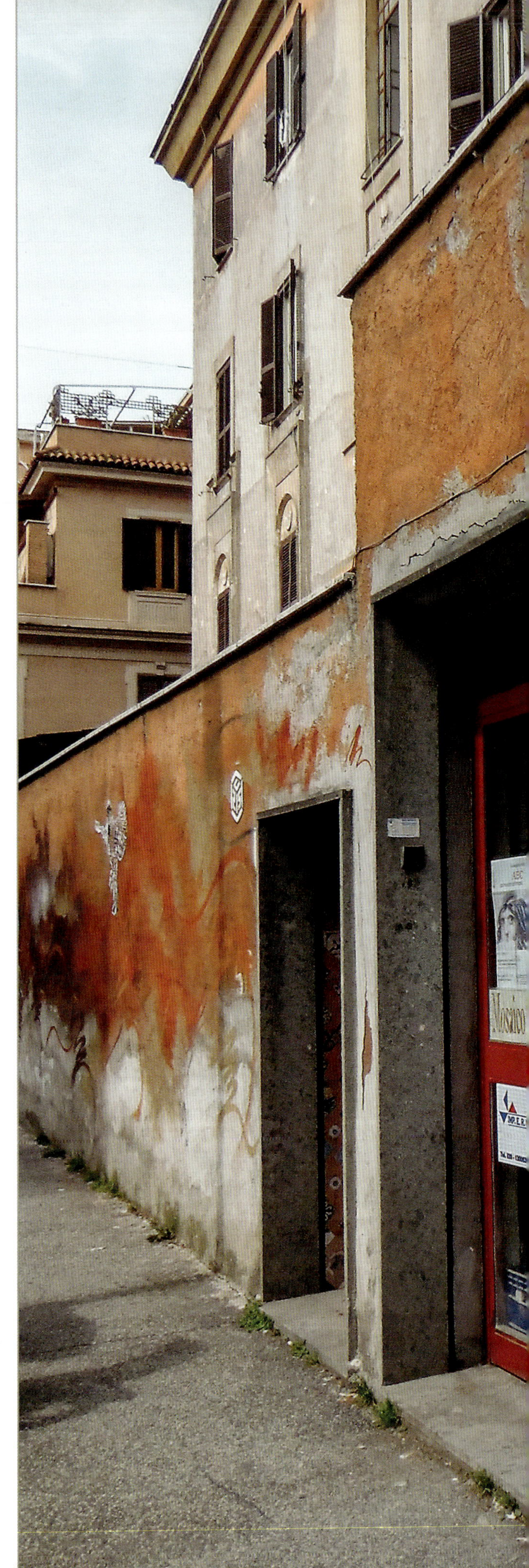

Rome, 2014
The theme of migration and welcome for migrants is deeply felt by C215, who chose a multi-ethnic quarter like Torpignattara in Rome to create a large-scale work.

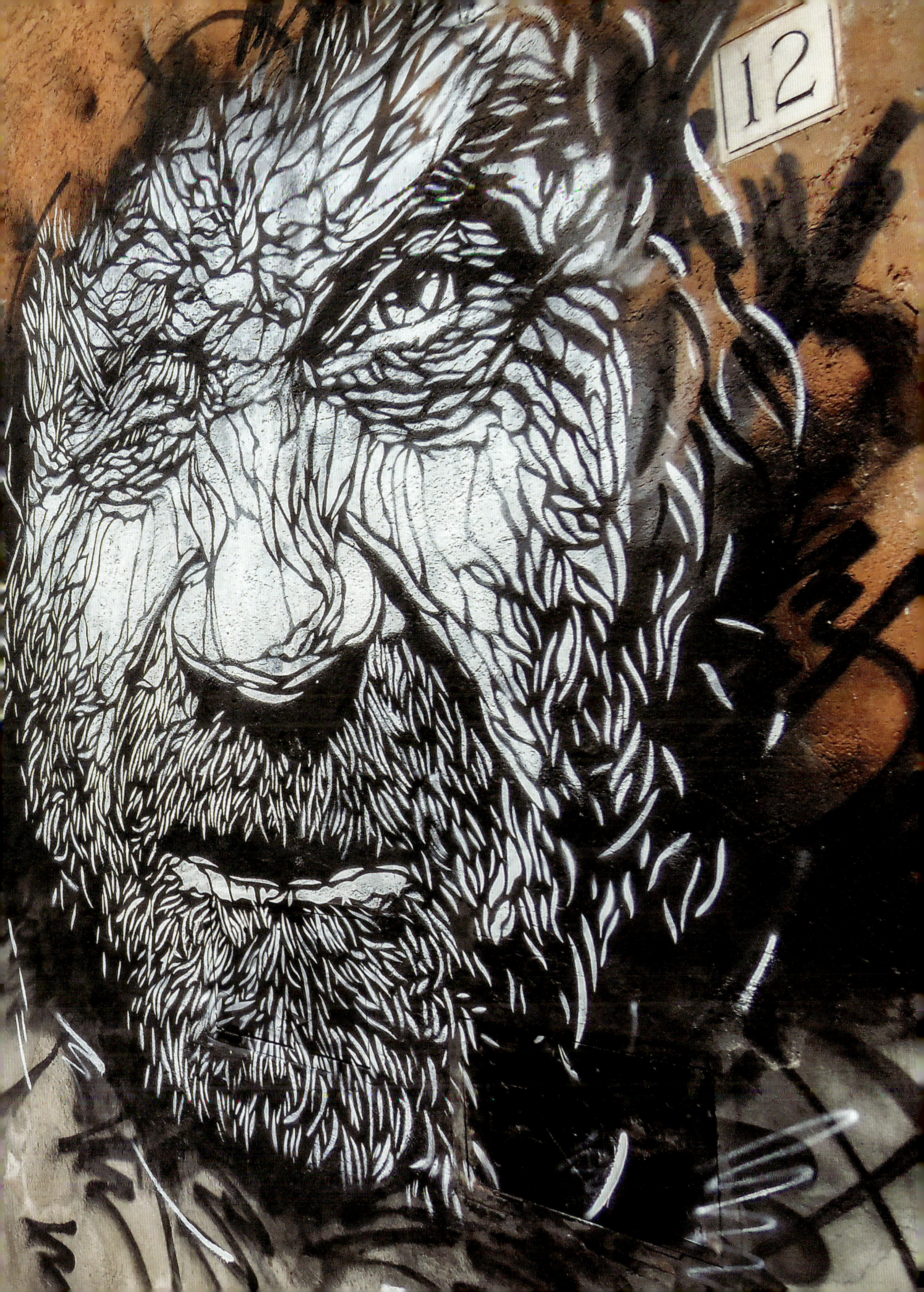

Paris, 2008 – Homeless, musicians, misfits: elaborate stencils recreate a forgotten humanity, surprising the observer along the streets of the Paris banlieues.

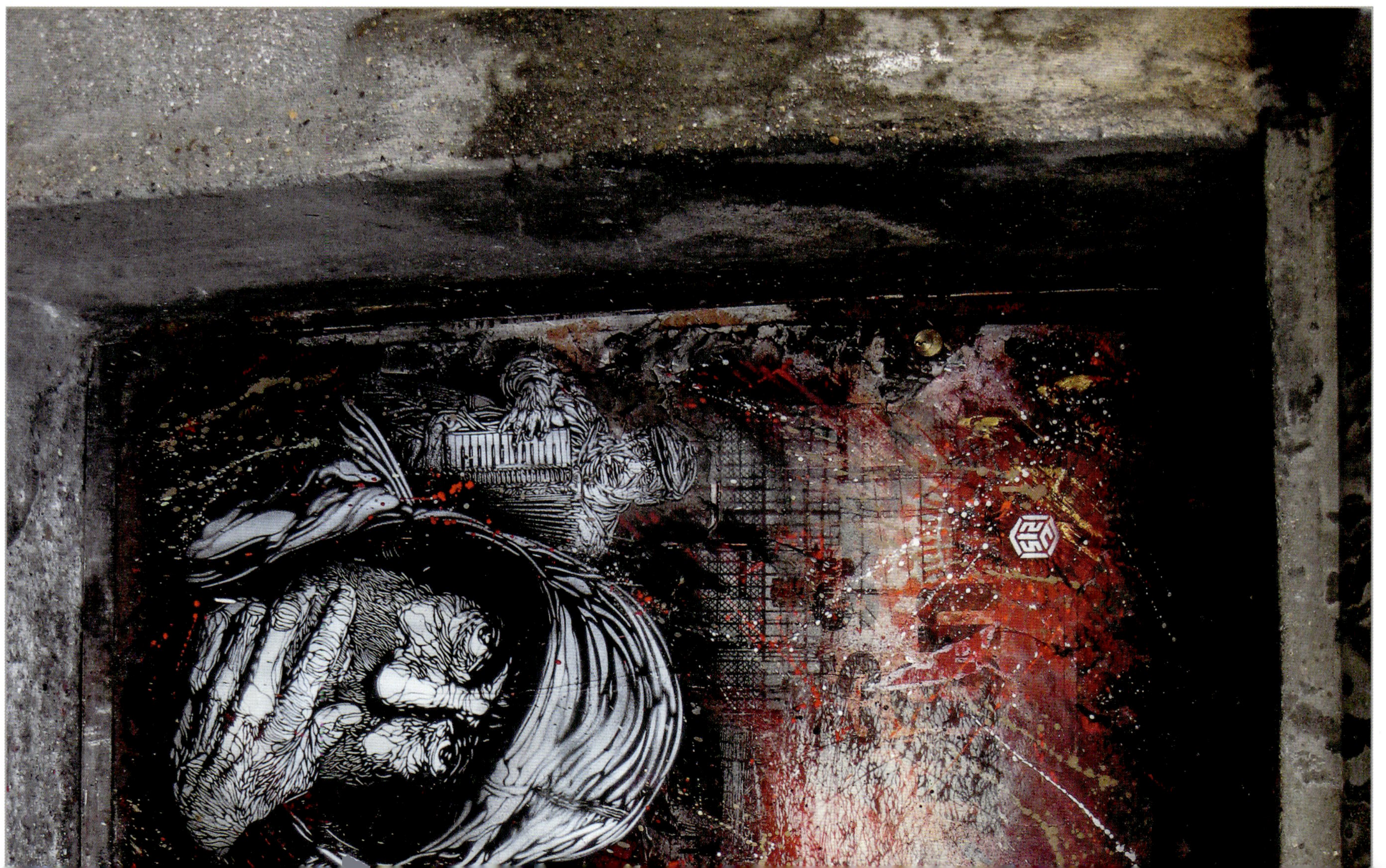

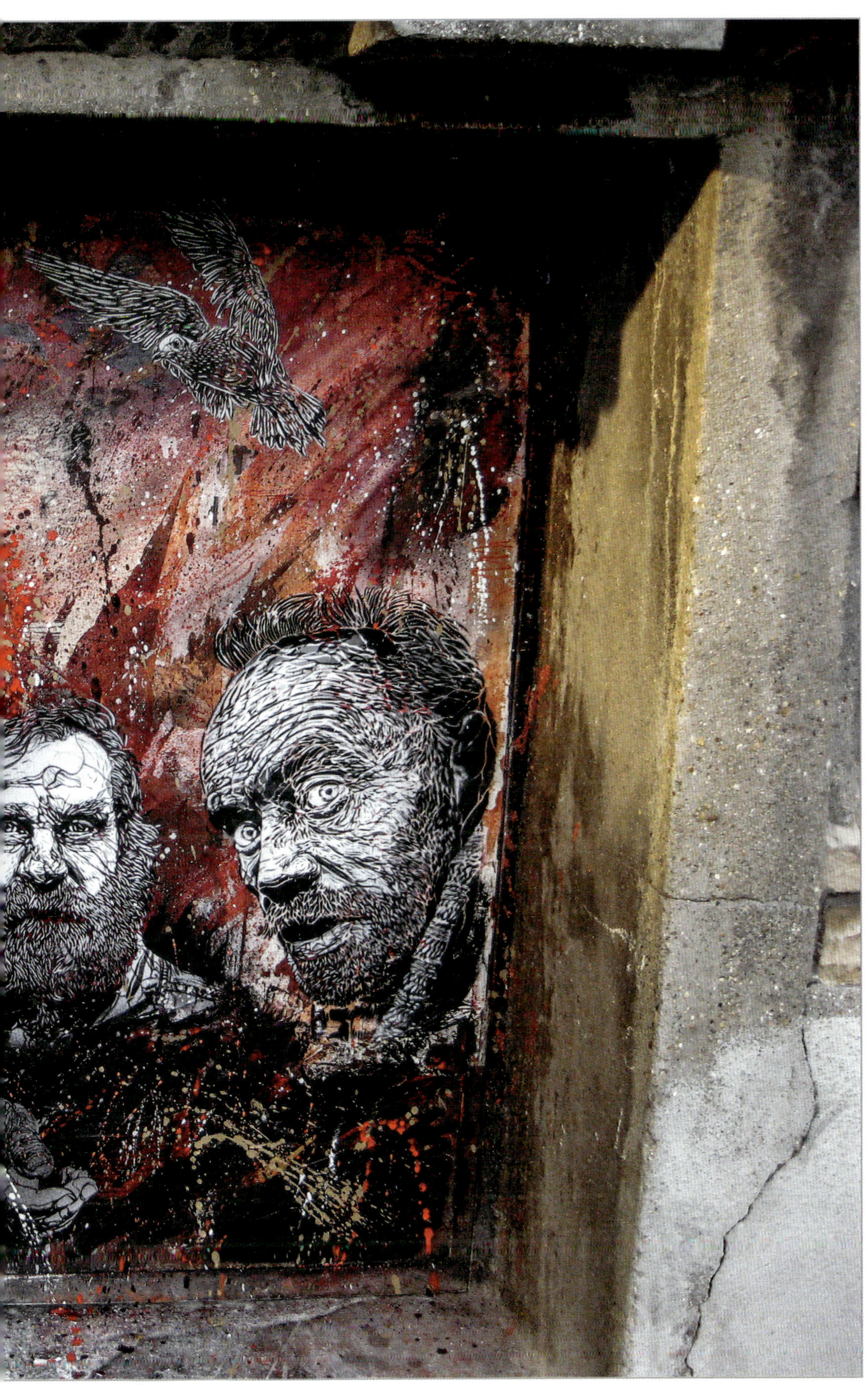

DAVID CHOE
Wild and Creative Rebel

He is like his art: wild and free. There are no limits to his creative provocations, which, at times, border on pornography. Born on April 21st, 1976 to parents of Korean descent, David Choe grew up in Koreatown, Los Angeles. One of the world's greatest contemporary artists, he is a graffiti artist and muralist, a painter, a cartoonist and musician. His works are erotic and sensual, moving between degradation and exaltation, and, at times, science fiction, in a style that he himself has termed: 'dirty style.' He started working as a boy with spray paints in the streets, preferring to draw faces and characters like cartoons rather than write tags with his signature. He soon became famous for his bucktoothed whale. He has confessed that he began drawing because he was inspired by *Star Wars*, *G.I. Joe* and *Robotech*, but it is said that his first graffiti was inspired by a verse from the Bible. At sixteen, he participated in the 1992 Los Angeles Riots, the uprising that followed the beating of Rodney King, an African American taxi driver, which lasted several days. Shortly after that, he left school to travel, hitchhiking his way across the United States, Europe, the Middle East and Africa.

He returned to Los Angeles at twenty-one wanting to become an artist and, for a few years, he attended the California College of Arts & Crafts in Oakland, in the San Francisco Bay Area. After being jailed for one week for one of his graffiti works, he returned to Los Angeles. There, he started to draw and wrote for several pop-culture magazines, including *Hustler*, *Ray Gun*, *Vice* and the Asian cult magazine, *Giant Robot*; in 1999, he made a graphic novel, called *Slow Jams* (self-published and distributed at the *San Diego Comic Con*), which was followed by another novel that soon gained cult status: *Bruised Fruit* (2002). After being snubbed by several art galleries, as well as continuing his work on the street, he exhibited his work at the Double Rainbow ice cream shop, located on Melrose Avenue in Los Angeles. The exhibition was a great success: having sold all of his works on show, David Choe had to replace them with new ones he had just made. In 2003, he traveled to Tokyo, where he is highly regarded, but following a misunderstanding in which he punched an undercover security guard, he ended up in prison again, that time for three months.

> Don't be scared, don't judge. Make every decision, every stroke and every mark, guided by passion and freedom, and not based on fear.

David Choe in his New York studio, based in Chinatown.

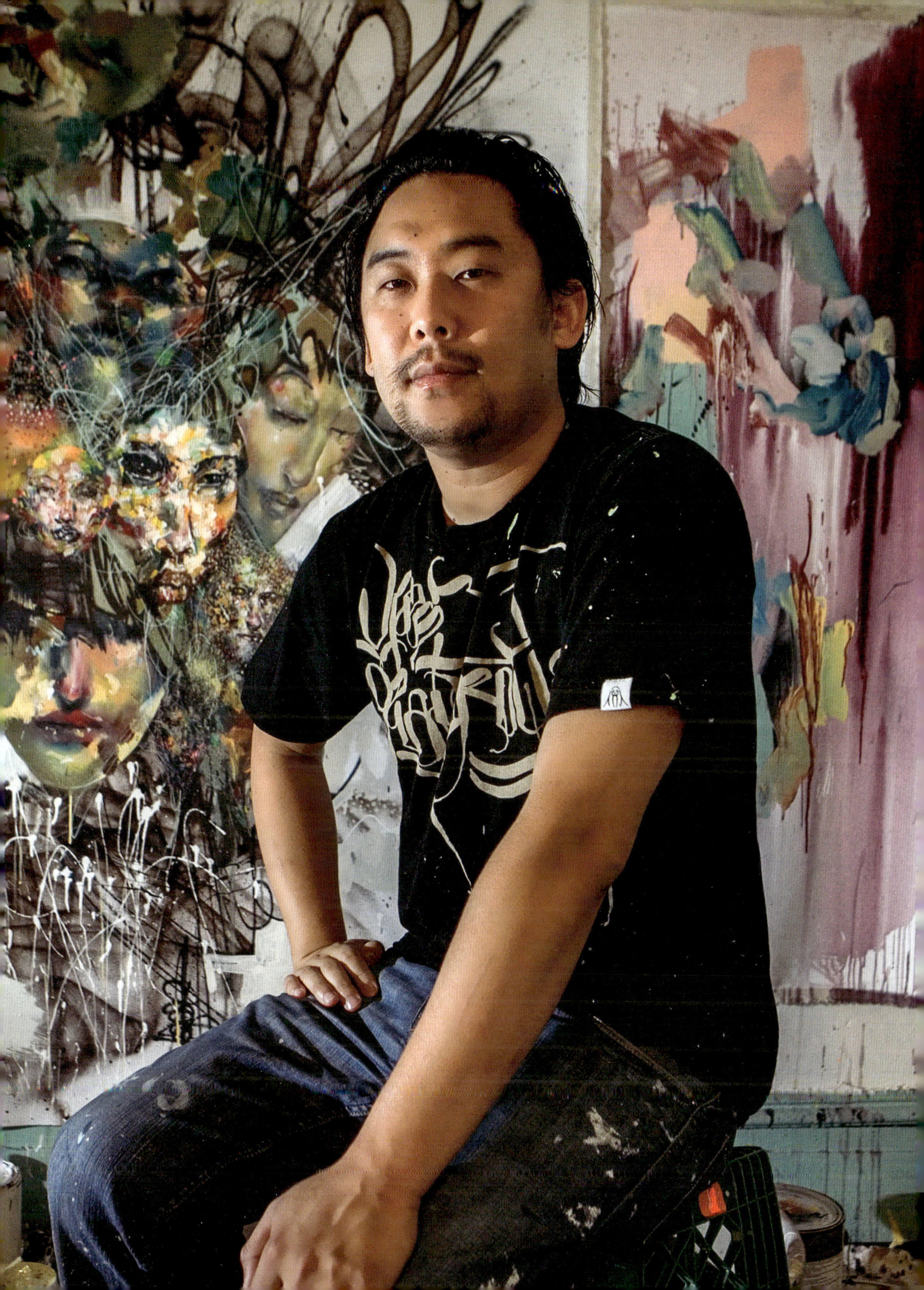

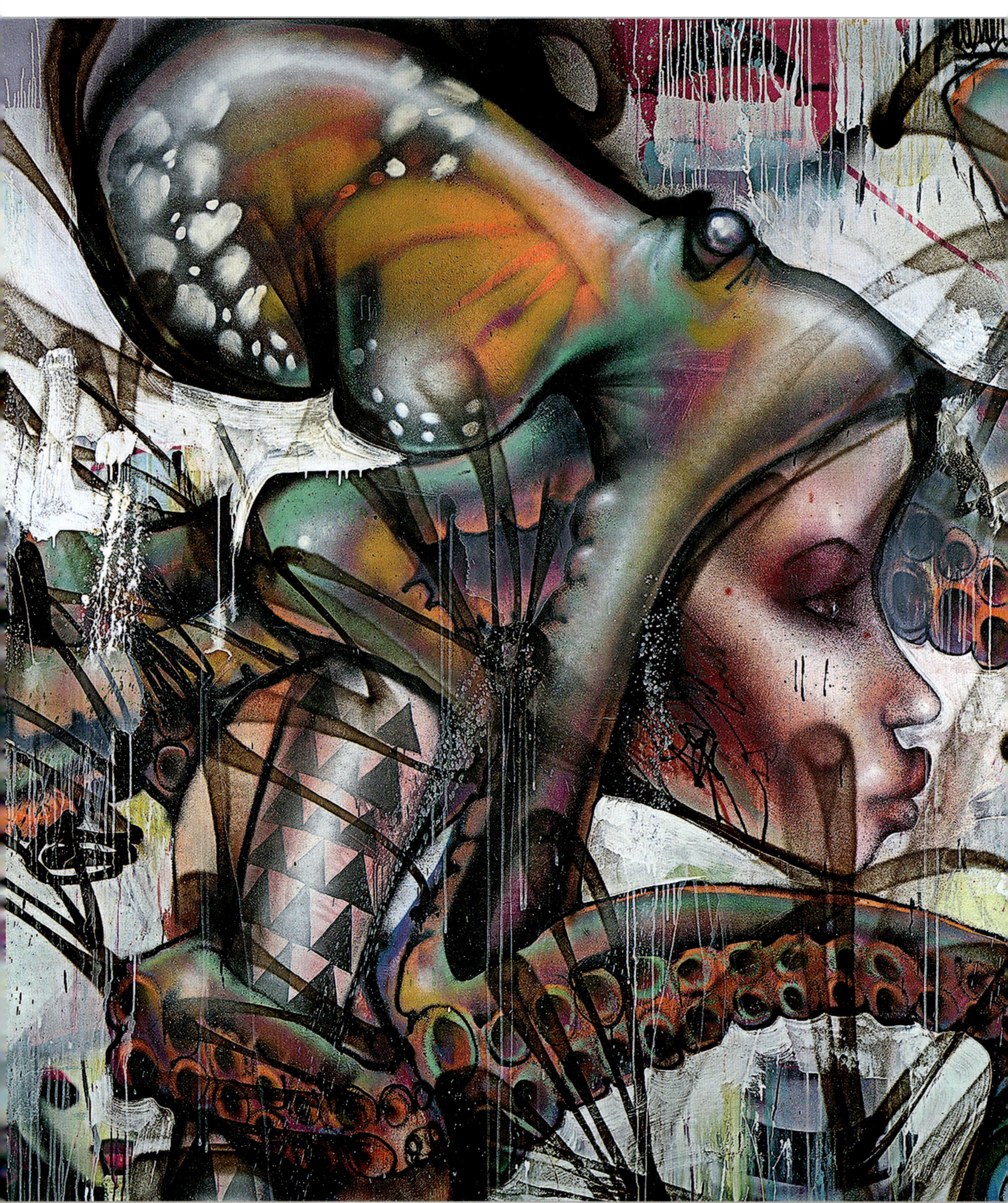

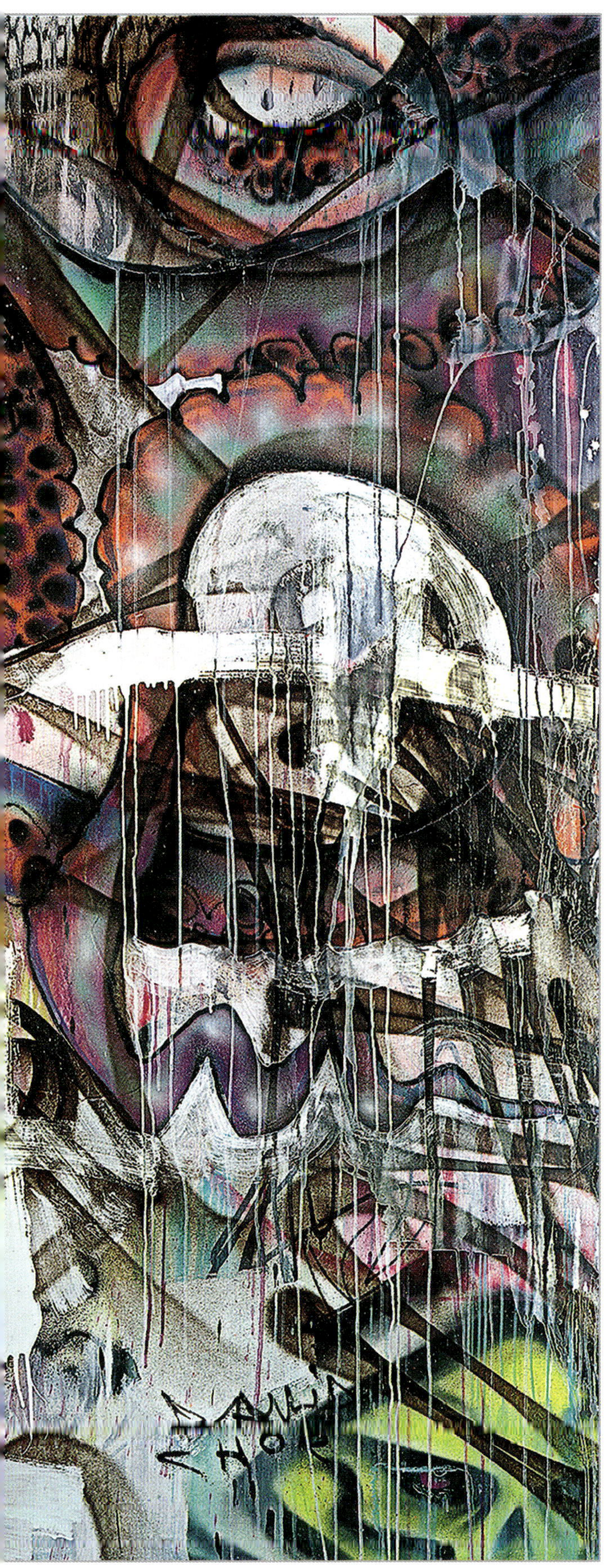

Despite suffering from anxiety and loneliness, in that period he completed over 600 drawings, many of which were portraits of his fellow jail-cell mates; he even used tea, soya sauce, his own blood and urine to finish a series of erotic paintings.

Upon release from prison, he returned to San José, California, where he accepted a commission from Heidi Fleiss as well as from some stars and businessmen; in the meantime, several museums and galleries started to invite him to exhibit his work. Jobs then started coming thick and fast: designs for movie sets, like *The Glass House* (2001) and *Juno* (2007), and the realization of the album cover, *Collision Course* (2004) for Jay-Z and Linkin Park. But the opportunity that effectively launched his career worldwide was offered up by one of Choe's fans, Internet entrepreneur Sean Parker (co-founder of the sites Napster, Plaxo and Causes), who, in 2005, commissioned the artist to paint graphic, sexual murals for Facebook's first head office in Silicon Valley, when Parker was president of the company. The success of the mural was such that, later in 2007, new President and CEO of Facebook, Mark Zuckerberg, commissioned Choe for the decoration of the company's new headquarters. At that time, Choe wasn't a firm believer in the so-called "new economy," but being an avid (and lucky) gambler, he agreed to be paid, not in cash, but in company shares – shares which are today valued at around 200 million dollars. Those same murals were then re-created by a couple of his friends, Rob Sato and Joe To, for the set of the film, *The Social Network*.

2012 – An octopus enveloping a female profile with turgid lips: it is a subject to which Choe returns several times, made famous by a mural created in 2012 in Kona, Hawaii, which was erased a few days later.

In the 2008 presidential elections, Choe painted a portrait of the then-senator and future-president, Barack Obama. Choe's image was used for the campaign and the original was then exhibited at the White House. Among other activities, provocations and projects, it is also worth mentioning his web series, *Thumbs Up!* in which he hitchhikes around the world with his friend, Harry Kim. In 2013, he began conducting the online lifestyle podcasts, *DVDASA* (Double Vag Double Anal Sensitive Artist), with the porn star Asa Akira.

I met him at SOB's, at 204 Varick Street in New York, during a concert with his band MANGCHi, in which Dylan Fujioka, Money Mark and others also performed: after some initial chit-chats, a few dances and a light show, David took the stage, dressed like a lobster and wearing a monkey mask, and he bewitched everyone with his music.

"*MANGCHi* means 'hammer' in Korean and *Mangucci* means 'critter': we are filled with love and light, and I'm honored and grateful to be in the best band in the known universe, with the most beautiful and talented artistic creative free-thinking mutant misfits, exploding black rainbows out of our heads, hearts, hands and booty holes into the souls of all mankind. Art is the gateway drug to freedom.

Recognize." This is how David Choe explains the philosophy of the band as well as his own personal vision. He then begged me, stressing his request with PEACE AND LOVE, that we reproduce his exact words, without censuring them or eliminating them from the text. And sometimes he expressed himself with drawings as well as with his voice. When I ask him to tell me about his passion for graffiti, this is how he starts to reply:

```
          ))  _______  ((
           .-" " " " " "-.
        /^\/  _.    _.  \/^\
        \(  /__\  /__\   )/
         \, \o_/_\o_/   ,/
          \   ( _ )    /
           - . === . -
            __) - (__
           /   ~~~    \
          /   /   \    \
         /   :     :    \
         \| ==(*)== |/
          :   \ | /   :
         ____)=|=(____
        {____/ \____}
```

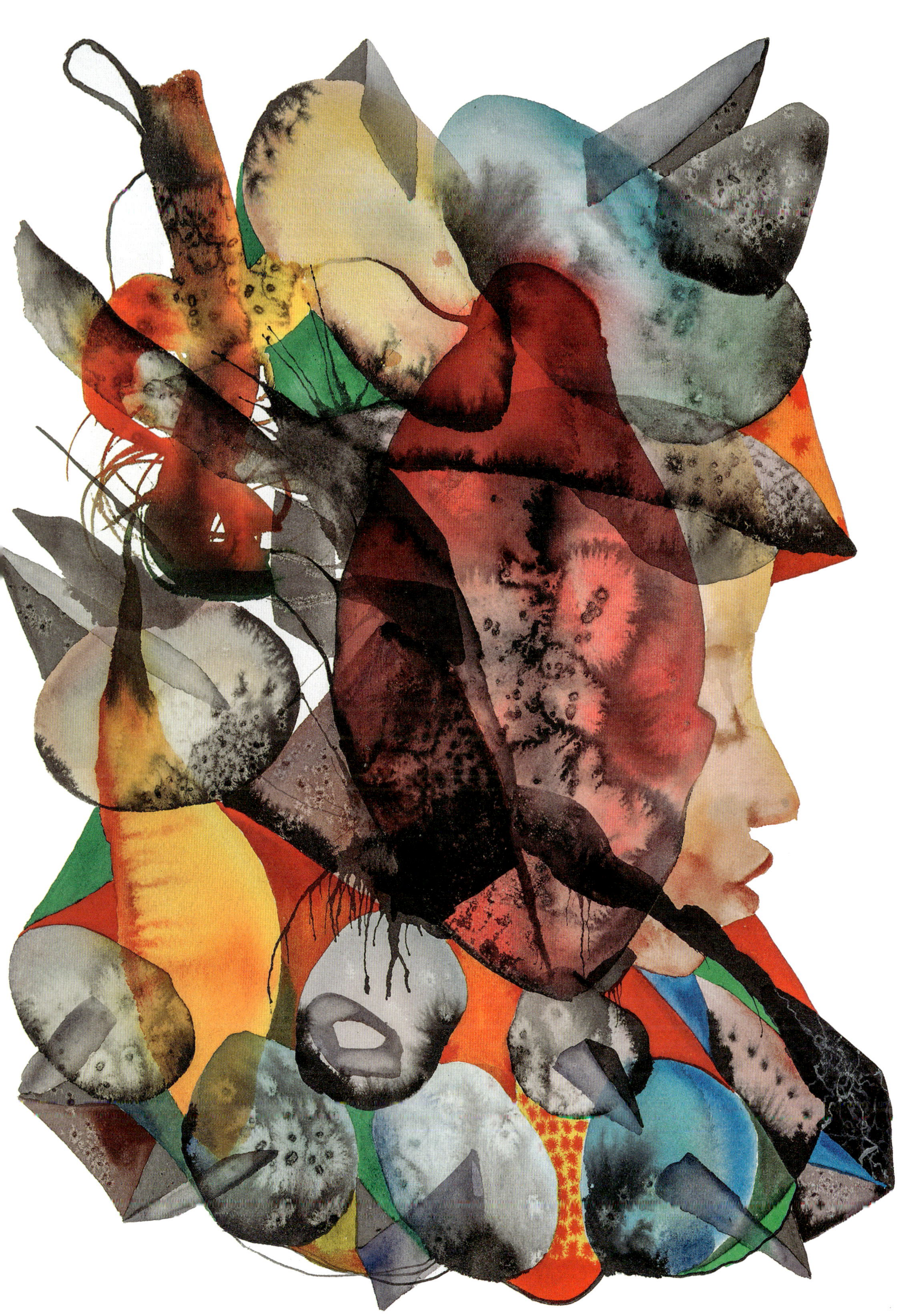

He describes his passion for music and comics as follows:

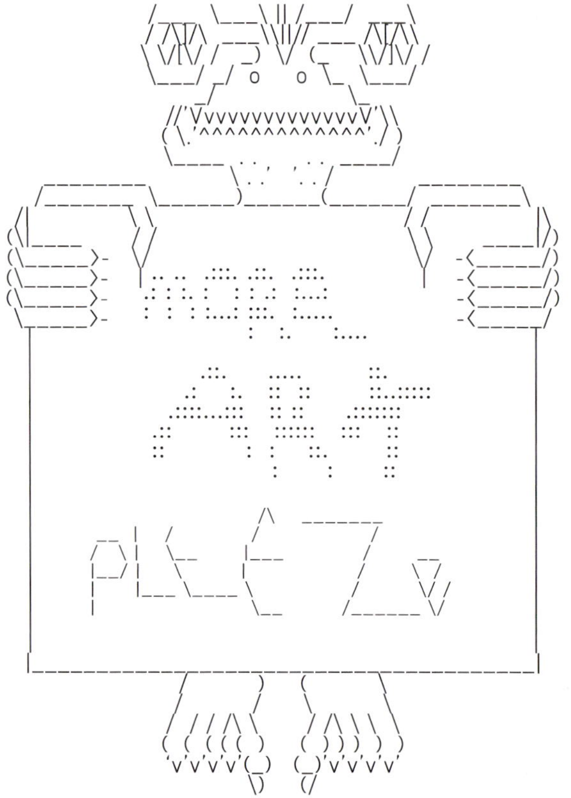

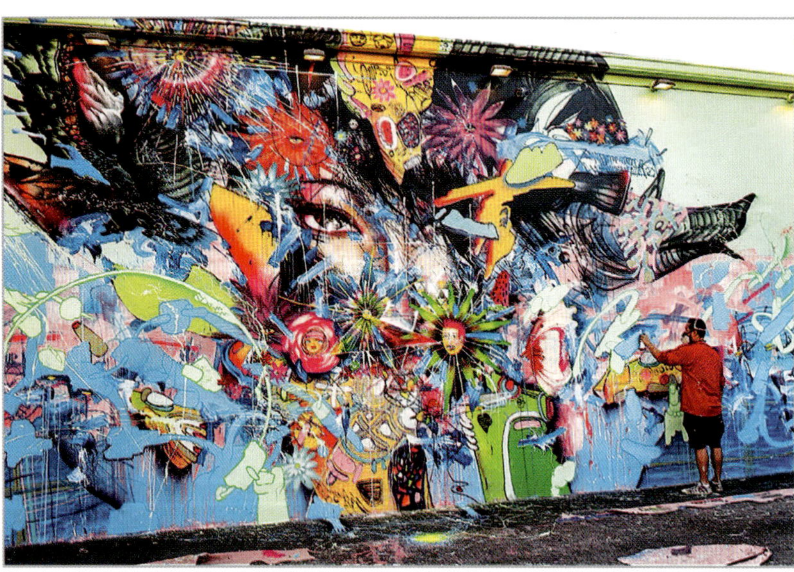

Nothing Lasts Forever, **2016** - For *FearLessWalls* 2016 Choe created a large mural
in Wynwood, a district of Miami. The face of a woman blends into an explosion of
colors in which you can barely distinguish other eyes and faces.

Pho Paw, **2013** - In 2013 Choe was protagonist of *Snowman Monkey BBQ*,
a large exhibition set up in Mexico City: among the works presented there
was this female face.

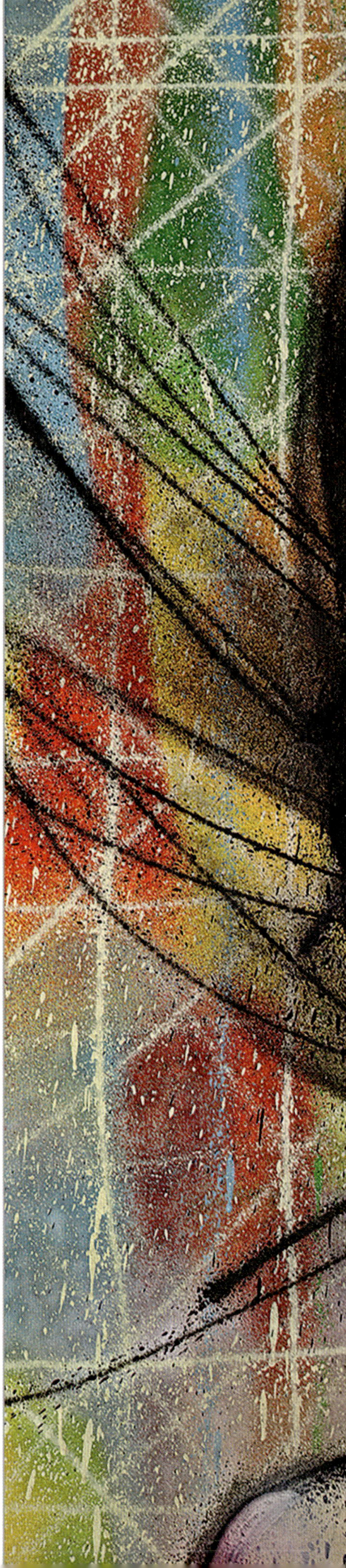

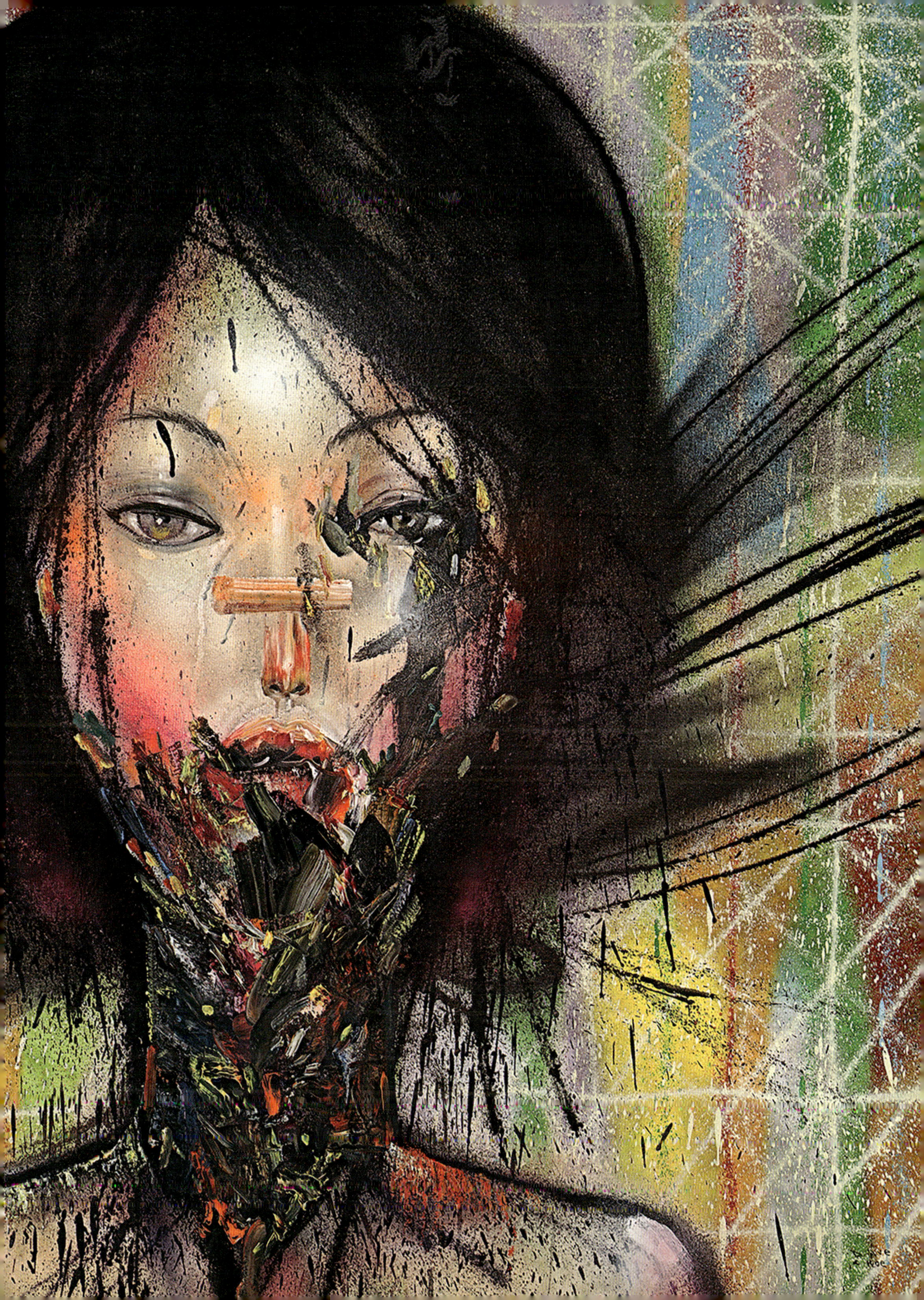

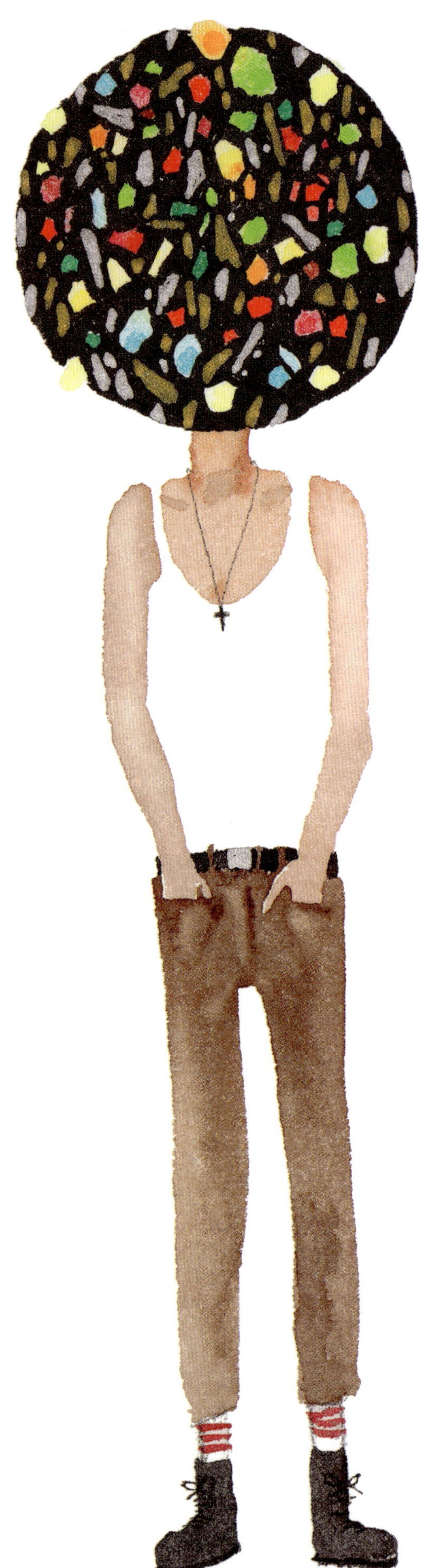

What he wants to achieve with his art is: "Hurt people, hurt people. So as to transform the hurt and trauma that we all have into love and compassion; don't be scared, don't judge.

Make every decision, every stroke and every mark, guided by passion and freedom, and not based on fear. When I can do that in my art, in a painting, in a drawing, then it builds confidence to express myself fully and not make fear-based decisions in all areas of my life."

Even his relationship with sexuality is very special: it emerges, for example, from the curvy women with lots of make-up who populate his art: "I learned about sex from reading articles in my cousin Susan's *Cosmopolitan* magazines when I was a teenager, before the Internet."

He jokes about his artwork: "My inspiration comes from my bipolar medication." And he adds: "Regarding my New York show, I have three words: TOO MUCH SWAG. Actually, last night I had dream that a gorilla with a heart-shaped nose and bat-wing ears, wearing a shiny red suit and big snapping lobster claws, came out and played the timbales and cowbell over all our punk songs and that ended up happening. And the most ridiculous part is that I'm not even lying right now and I'm known in many respected circles as a pretty big liar. Burn." He then reveals how important music is to him and how every place corresponds to a particular sound track: "LA – blasting out in my car at max volume, singing (screaming) at the top of my lungs, *What's going on* by 4 Non Blondes. NY – headphones on, walking over the Brooklyn bridge, while listening to P.O.D.'s song *BOOM*; it makes me walk with swag, like I'm a tough guy, like I'm in an action movie with giant fireball explosions going off behind me in slow motion, like I'm getting so juiced and gunked up right now just even thinking about it. Respect." And his favorite place in the world to make art: "Jail."

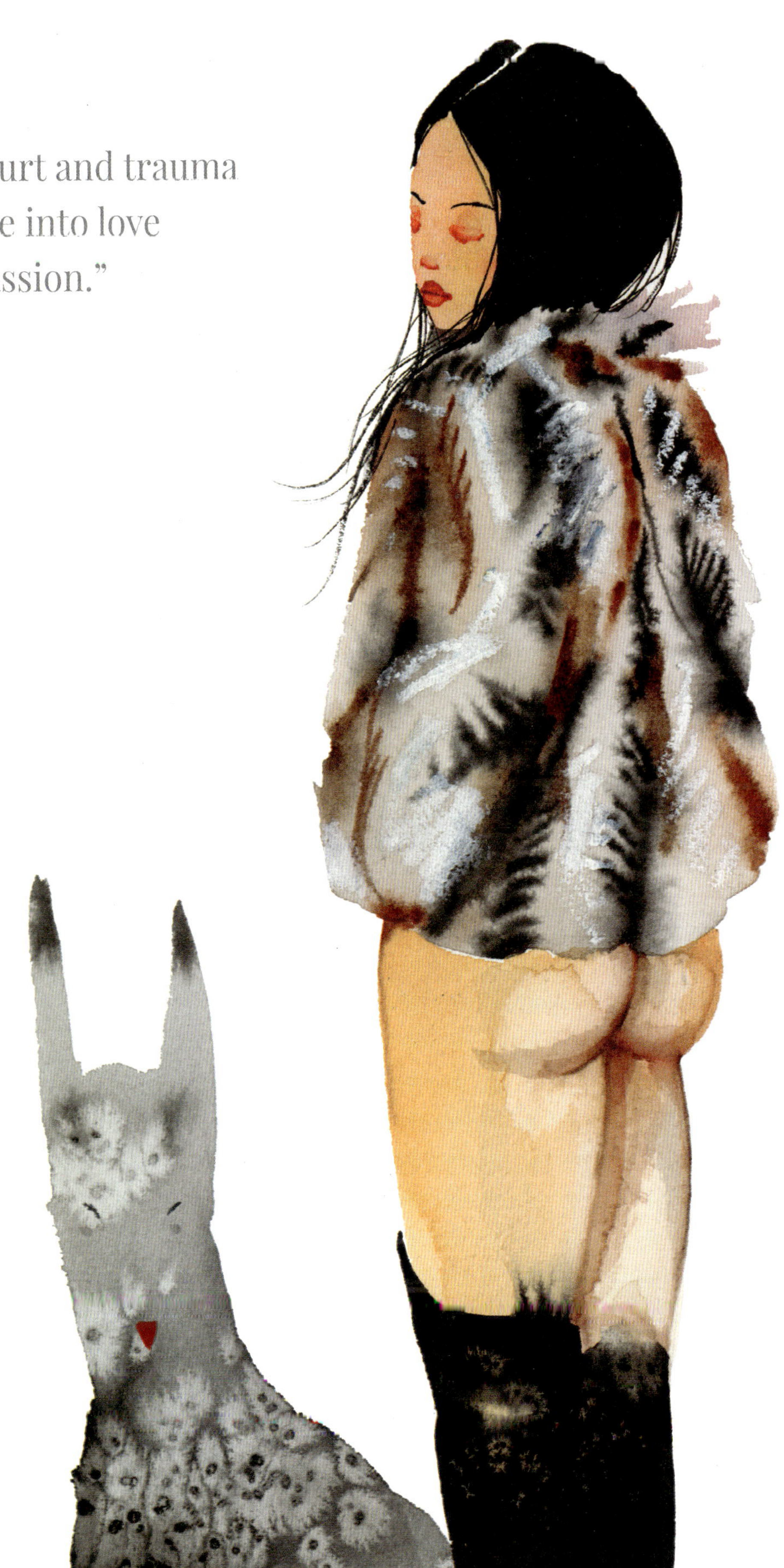

Flooding, 2013
Choe greatly appreci-
ates watercolor paint-
ing, which he special-
ly uses to represent
human figures. In this
case, the artist sur-
prises us by "hiding"
the face of his subject
behind a kaleidoscope
of colors.

Watercolor furs, 2016
Eros is a recurring
theme in David Choe's
art: sometimes it is
declined in an explicit
and even brutal way,
and at others – as in
this case – in prints
and watercolors of a
refined elegance.

BEN EINE

Master of Letters

"My art? Fun and freehand. Colors look random but I spend a lot of time mixing colors that wouldn't normally fit together. I don't ever project my art onto buildings or have a final set concept for a piece until I'm at the wall or location, sometimes I'll have an idea and then change my mind, it really depends on whether something has inspired me while I'm there," British artist Ben Eine tells us from Dubai where he is currently working on a new project. "My art is trying to take a boring space and make it fun and exciting and something people can and will enjoy now and forever. The messages of typefaces and words are powerful," he states with a certain determination, one that has characterized his entire artistic development.

Born in London in 1970, Ben started painting on trains and walls when he was fourteen years old and was arrested several times as a youngster. At that time, which he describes as a period of transition towards adulthood, he worked for a bit for Lloyd's of London, in the insurance market, but continued with his true passion, street art, content to paint during his lunch hour.

He only stopped for a while when some of his friends were arrested and ended up in prison, but he was unable to contain his irresistible "creative fever."

He does however admit that today he prefers to ask for permission, in order to avoid problems or have his creative freedom limited in any way. "I got involved in the early days of graffiti, I was a cheeky little shit, couldn't breakdance, had a vague interest in art. I started seeing the NY and American subway trains painted in the 1980s in magazines and hip-hop videos and started knocking about with a crew of graffiti artists in London." Eine soon realized that he wanted to invent something a bit different from the other graffiti artists that he saw around, who were all quite similar and in the end rather uninteresting.

"Basically if I continued doing graffiti I was going to go to prison, street art seemed a way to continue painting illegally but in a way that people thought was legal. I was painting the streets with Banksy for many years and there was a small group of us each with our own different style, the time and places just seemed to work.

> I don't ever project my art or have a final set concept until I'm at the wall or location, sometimes I'll have an idea and then change my mind, it really depends on whether something has inspired me while I'm there.

Ben Eine engaged in the creation of a stencil for the *Alphabet House* in Middlesex Street, London.

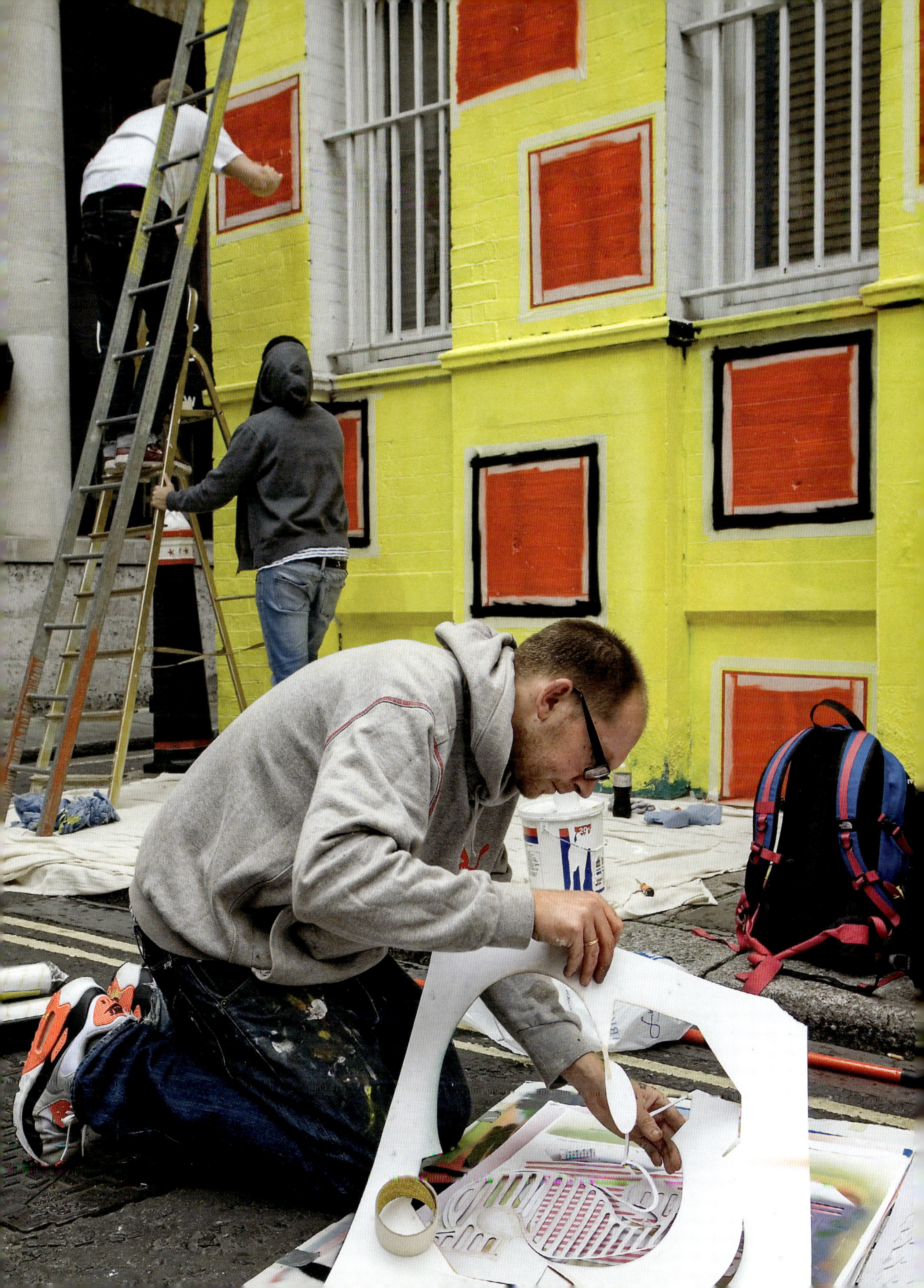

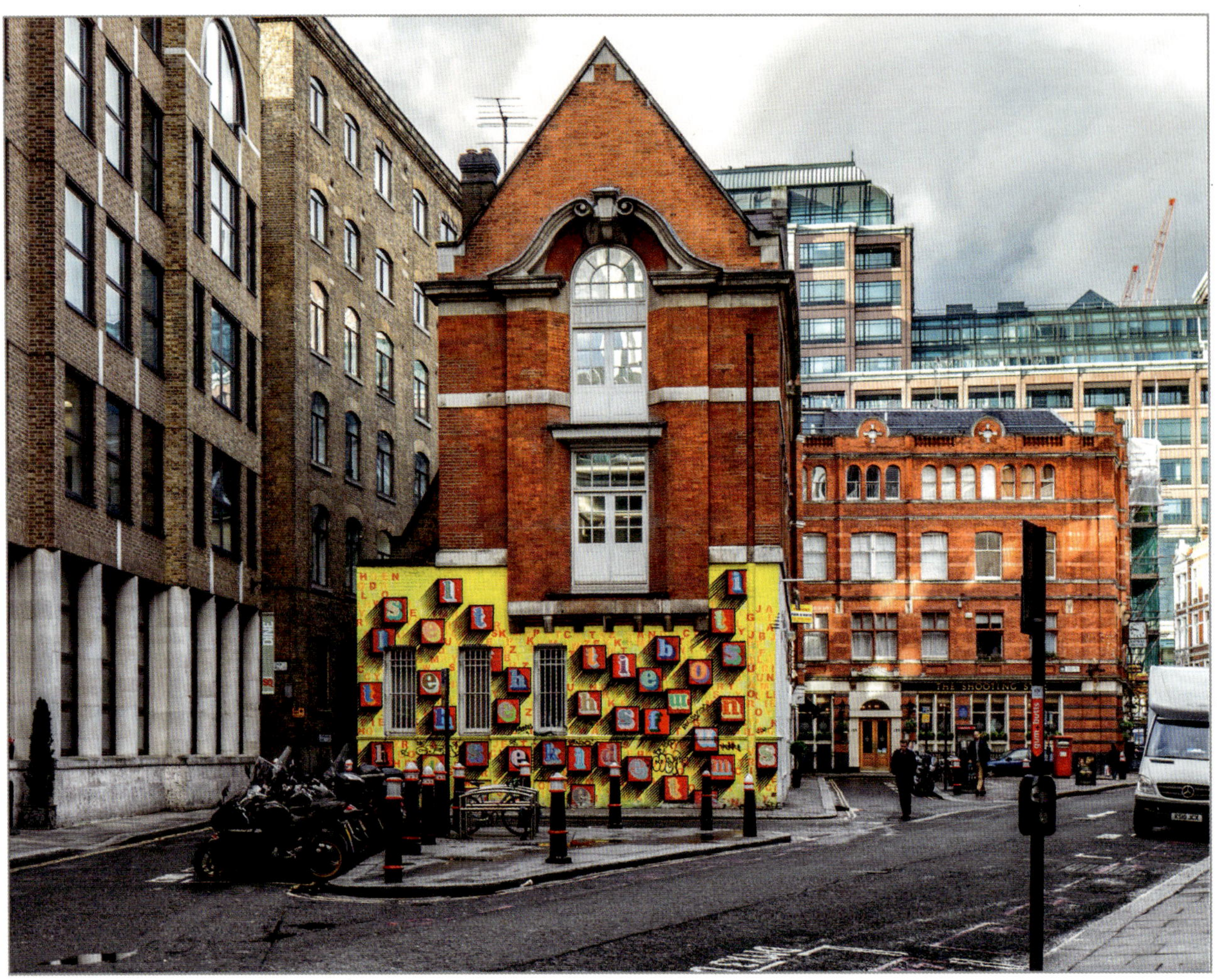

Alphabet House, 2010 - One of the best known and most demanding works by Ben Eine: a rainbow of mobile characters on a yellow wall, in the London district of Spitalfields. The street has been renamed "Alphabet Street" by many residents.

Street art didn't have a name for a long time so I was taking the raw elements of graffiti, the spraying, the colors, the urban locations but refining graffiti letters into typefaces and fonts.

I was really able to develop my distinct style of letter forms over the years from the early 2000s and put my art on storefront shutters, large buildings and in prominent city locations."

He adds that among the works he has created the one he is most tied to is *SCARY*; it is in London, along Rivington Street in Shoreditch, and dates back a dozen or so years but every so often Ben returns to touch it up and repaint it. "It's been in many films and TV shows, the public responded amazingly to the piece and it's one of the reasons I painted so many pieces in and around the area of Shoreditch in London."

But his art has moved way beyond London: Europe, America, Japan, South Africa, on the streets and art galleries and in the most prestigious museums; and it was a very proud moment when the then British Prime Minister David Cameron gave the then President of the United States Barack Obama his piece *TWENTYFIRSTCENTURYCITY*.

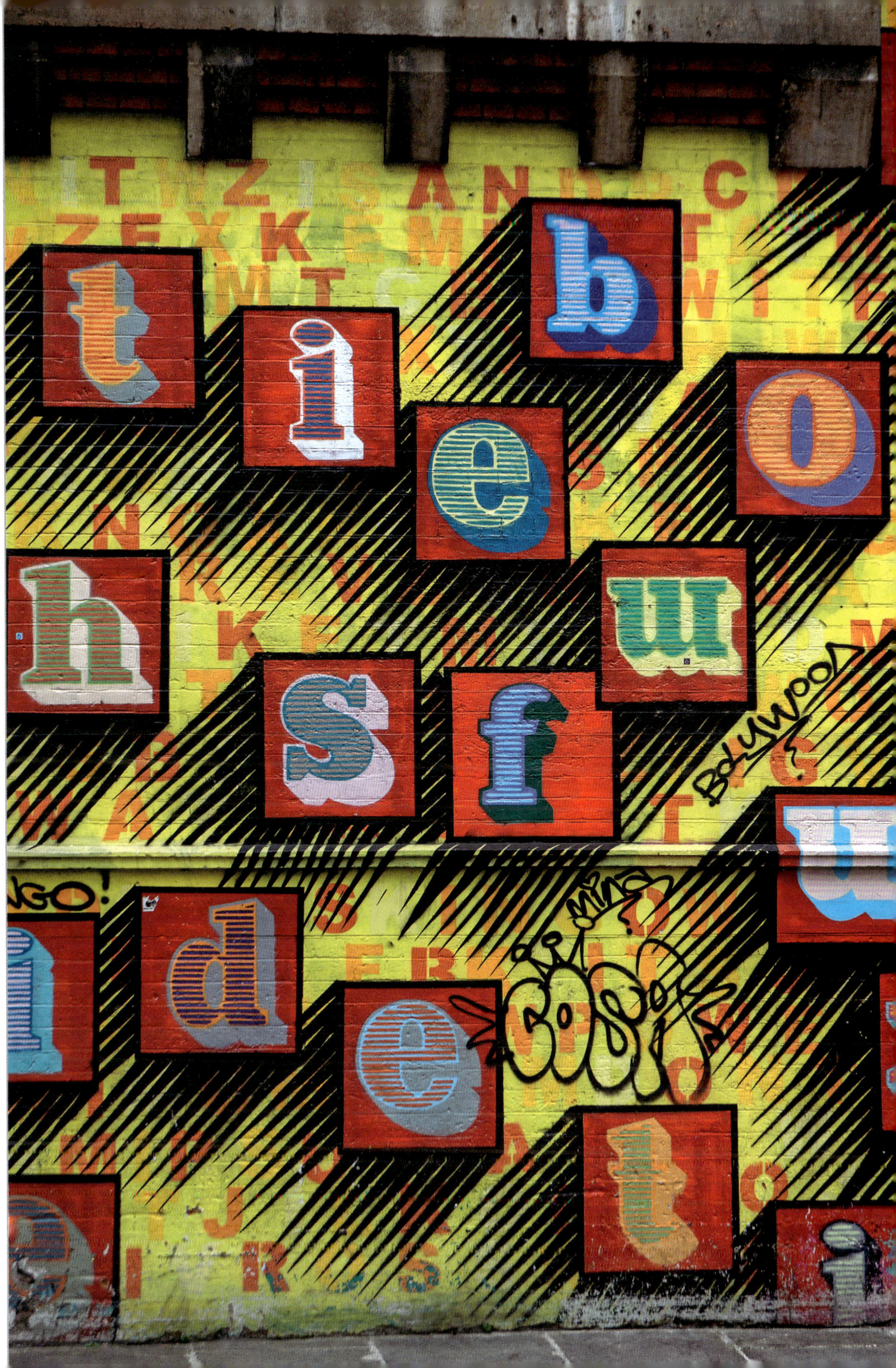

Alphabet House, 2010 – The letters are painted in brightly-colored paint on a red-brick wall. Ben Eine has stated that he derives great satisfaction from watching children close to his works scanning the letters.

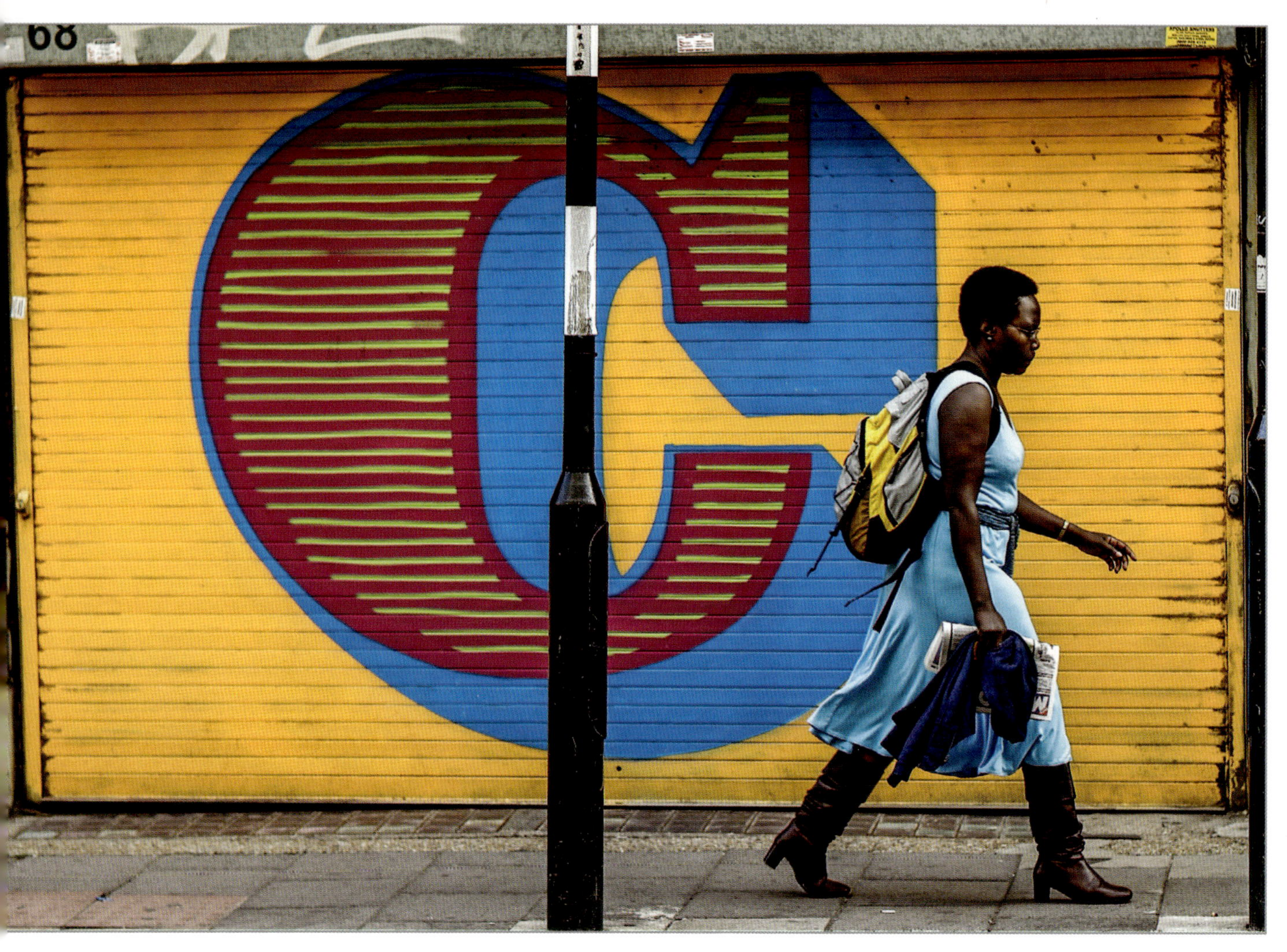

C, **2010** - A great C on a shutter in London. In 2010, the then Prime Minister, David Cameron, gave Obama a work by Eine, inviting him to visit the places where his murals can be found.

"I've been illegally painting a few walls
in and around London when the police
have come up to me and asked what I'm doing,
because it's not your typical graffiti,
they don't see it as vandalism."

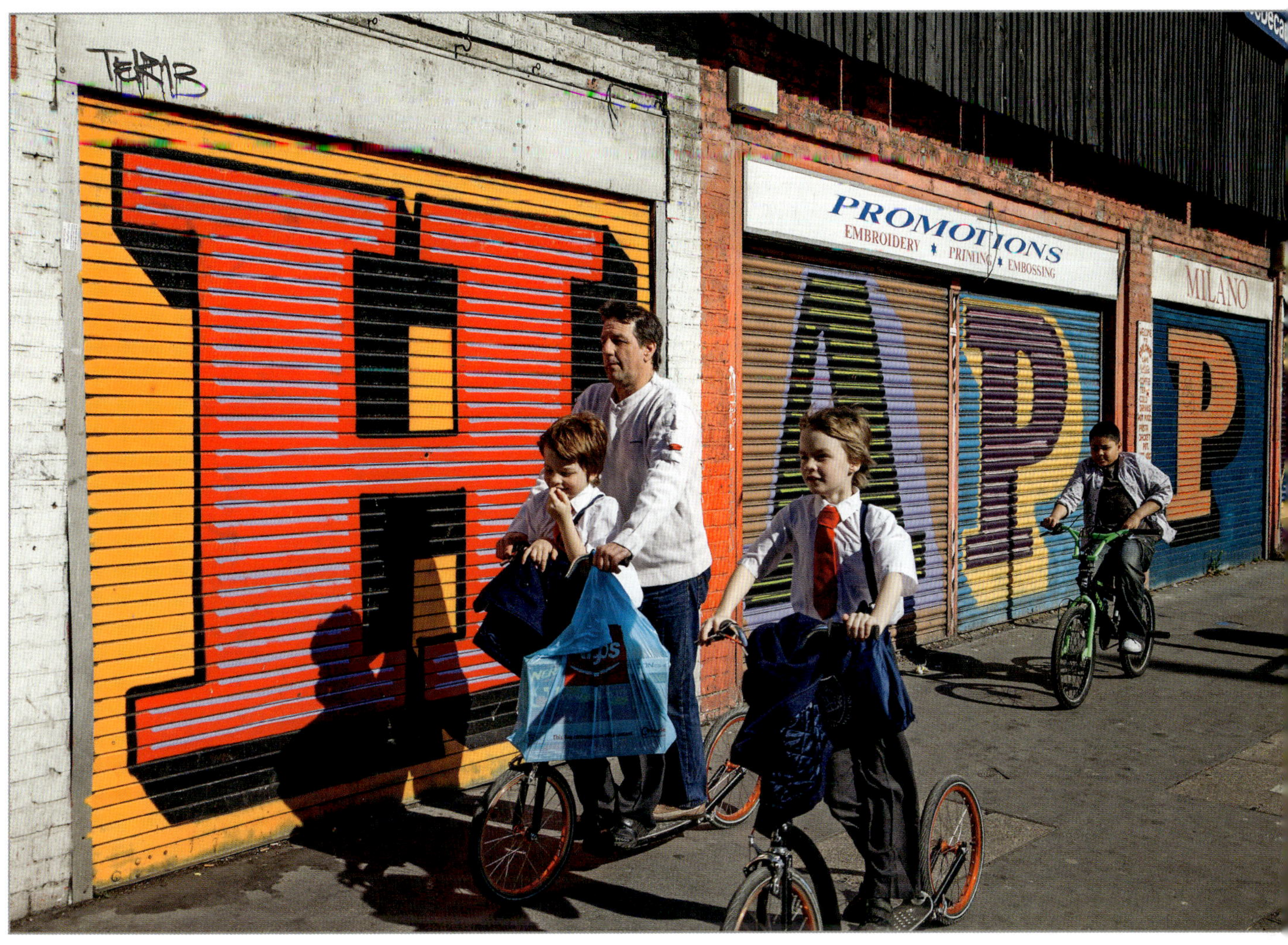

***HAPPY*, 2010** - Happiness doesn't last forever: if a shutter is raised, or if one of the letters is deleted or covered, the word HAPPY disappears. The work is located in Middlesex Street, in London.

In 2011, Eine was invited by Amnesty International to design their 50th anniversary poster, an honor awarded to other great artists such as Picasso and Miró. His works have also been used by the pop group Alphabeat and in a number of music videos, including Stepping Stone by Duffy.

There are a number of artists that inspire him: "How & Nosm, KAWS, Delta, Keith Haring, Retna. All of these artists have such a wide range of styles but have all started their art careers by painting on the streets."

"I've been illegally painting a few walls in and around London when the police have come up to me and asked what I'm doing, because it's not your typical graffiti, they don't see it as vandalism, and I'll tell them 'yeah I have permission to paint here by the building owners.' You can't do that with tagging or traditional graffiti," he adds, thinking back to his past experiences. Another unusual event happened a few years ago in Mexico City. "We knocked on this guy's door and asked if we could paint his wall, he walked outside looked at the wall, looked at us and said 'yeah I don't care, do it.'

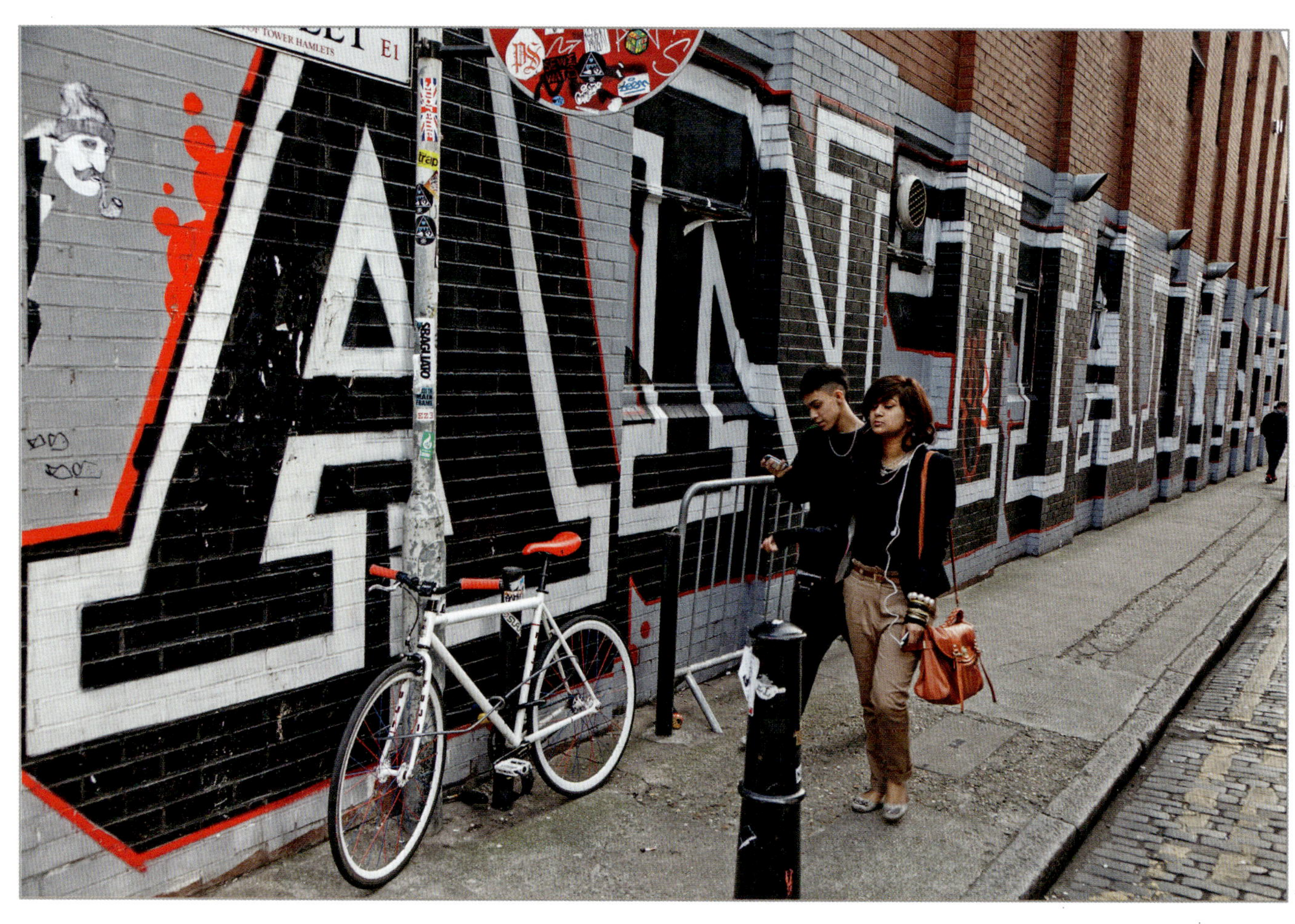

ANTI ANTI ANTI, **2010** - The thrice-painted word "Anti" in black and white is created for the Anti Design Festival, organized in the district of Shoreditch, in London.

"My art? Fun and freehand.
Colors look random
but I spend a lot of time mixing colors
that wouldn't normally fit together."

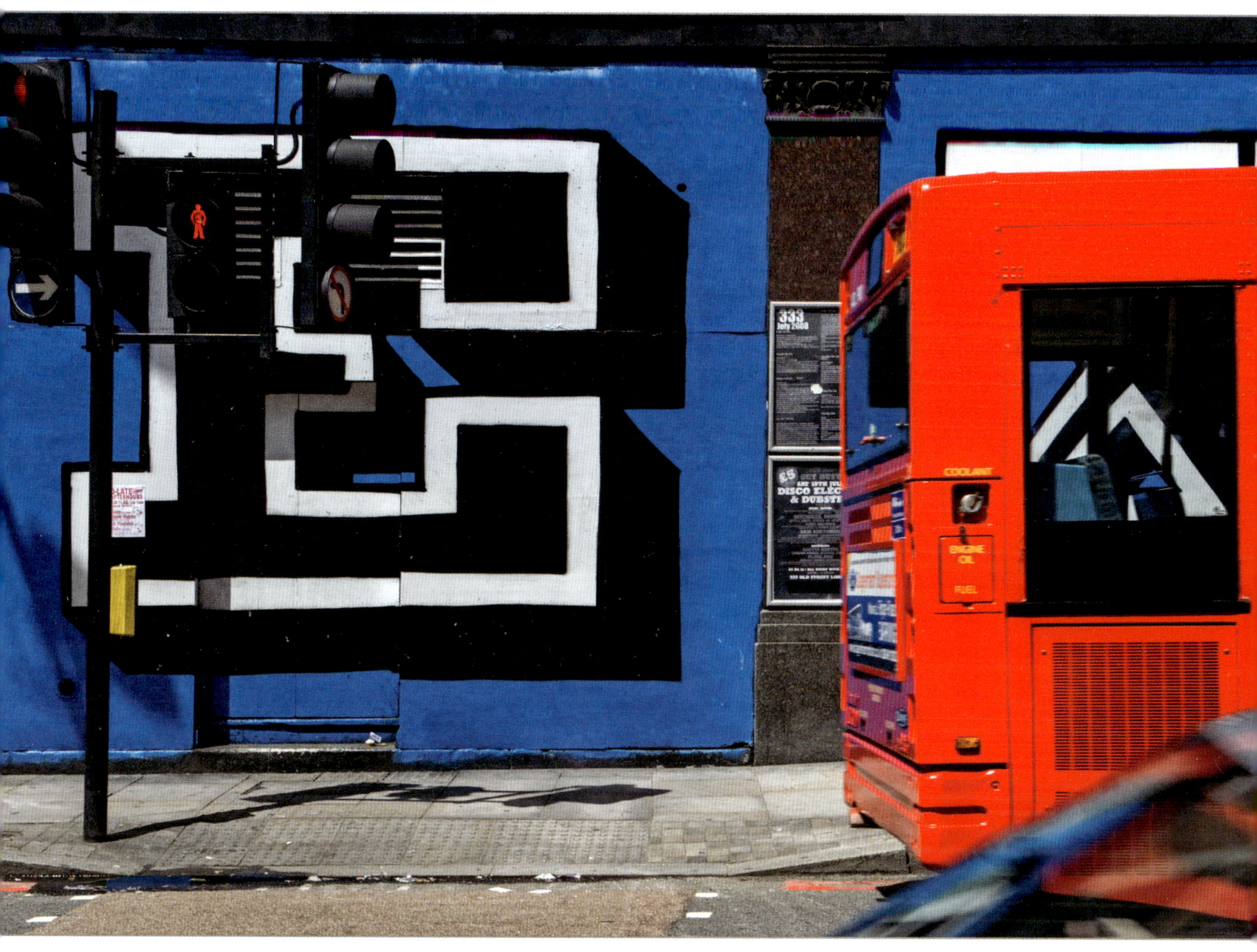

E - A huge E in the district of Hoxton. It is one of Ben Eine's favorite letters; many of the first words (Exciting or Express) created by him on the walls of London begin with this vowel.

Two days later just as we are finishing this lady comes over to us shouting and screaming at us, we tell her the guy in the house said it was okay to paint and she tells us it's her wall and has nothing to do with him, apparently they were neighbors that really hated each other . . . she had been away all week."

Today Ben Eine lives in Hastings, England, with his wife and three children, though he travels a lot for work. Hastings has the honor of being home to many of his pieces. Nonetheless he loves Mexico City, "Mexico City is lawless and fun, the art is explosive on the streets and it's everywhere, the people are fun and so welcoming.

Though London is my hometown so when I paint anywhere there it feels very special!"

EL MAC

Realist of Faces and of the Human Figure

"Do to others as you would have them do to you": this is El Mac's motto. Also known as Miles MacGregor, he was born in 1980 in Los Angeles, where he still lives and works despite frequent travels to carry out projects around the world. He has left his unmistakable mark in Mexico, Sweden, Denmark, Canada, South Korea, Italy, Belgium, France, Germany, Ireland, England, Cuba, Vietnam . . . He divides his time between murals and paintings. "I would like to consider my art perfectionist realism with soul. I try to create the most perfect, beautiful images that I possibly can. Much of it I would consider as part of the tradition of social realism, with a focus on the marginalized, poor or working-class people. I also have always taken on the challenge of trying to portray feminine beauty as timelessly and uniquely as possible." El Mac began in the mid-1990s with acrylic painting and graffiti art, mainly devoting himself to the representation of human faces and figures: his artistic vocation is almost innate. "I was serious about making art from an early age, thanks largely to the influence of my mother, who is a talented painter, and raised me to see art as a way of life. Making art was seen as almost a sort of religious activity. Then, when I was around fourteen, I became interested in graffiti, thanks to some of my friends and the book *Subway Art.* Graffiti was a way to overcome my introversion, by creating art publicly with friends," he explains. He also speaks of another motivation that has inspired him a lot: "It was also a way to introduce adrenaline to the art-making process, which is addictive. As my abilities improved, I came to value and respect the impact that public art could have in reaching a wide audience, and started seeing it as a social service. I felt that, in my own small way, I could make a positive difference by putting art in places that lacked it."

He has vague memories of his earlier projects, but several adventures are unforgettable. "I do remember one of the first times; I was painting faces on freight trains in the mid-1990s while living in New Mexico. Despite the weight on my conscience for sneaking around at night doing something illegal, it was exhilarating!" he recalls with emotion.

"I've never really had a favorite color, but I've been partial to Vermilion red for a while now.

> I hope to inspire
> in the same way
> I was inspired
> at a young age
> by the classic works
> of great artists
> of the past.

Miles MacGregor, nicknamed El Mac, in a moment of reflection. The artist loves exploring new places and cities: travel is for him an infinite source of inspiration.

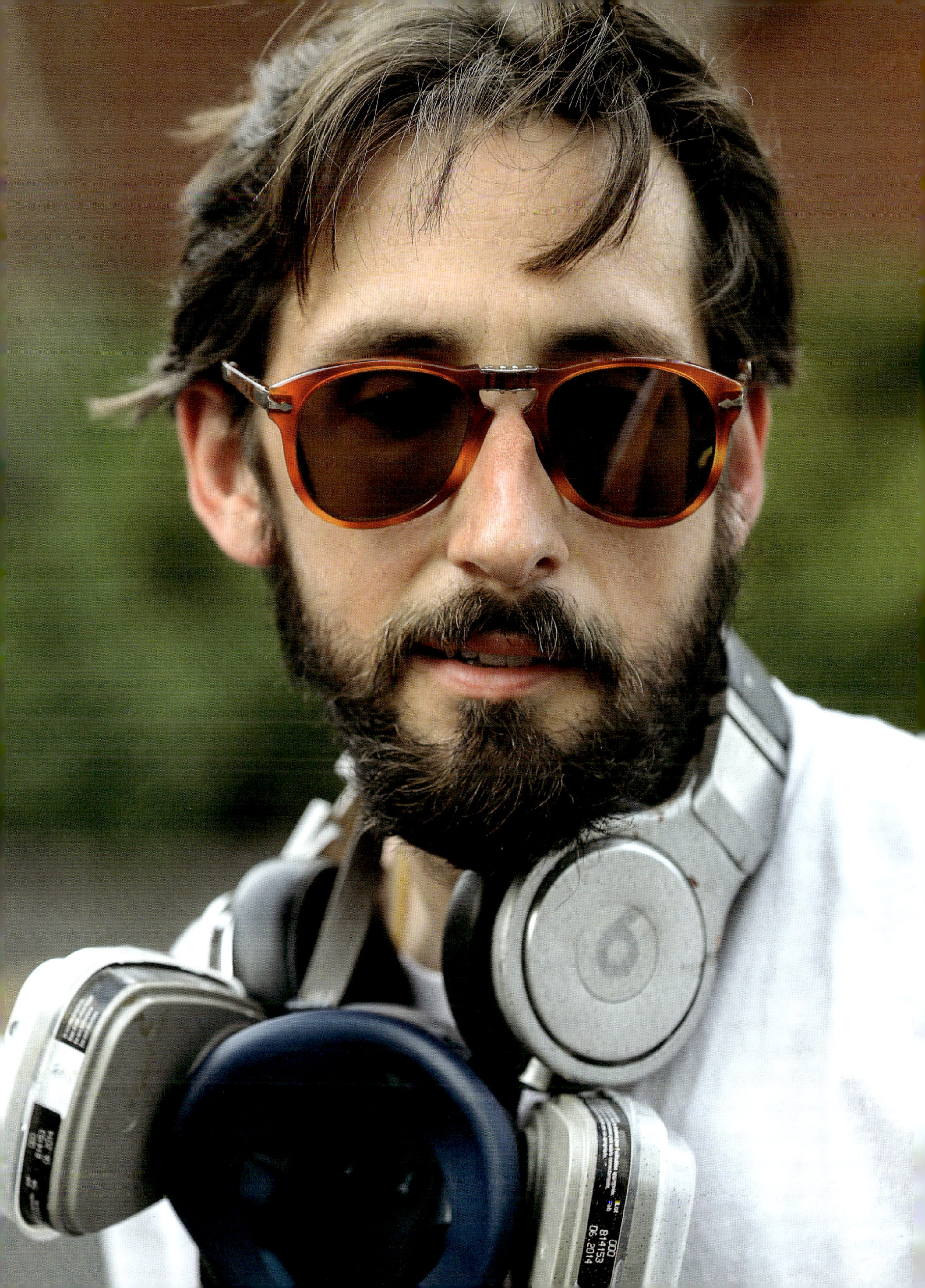

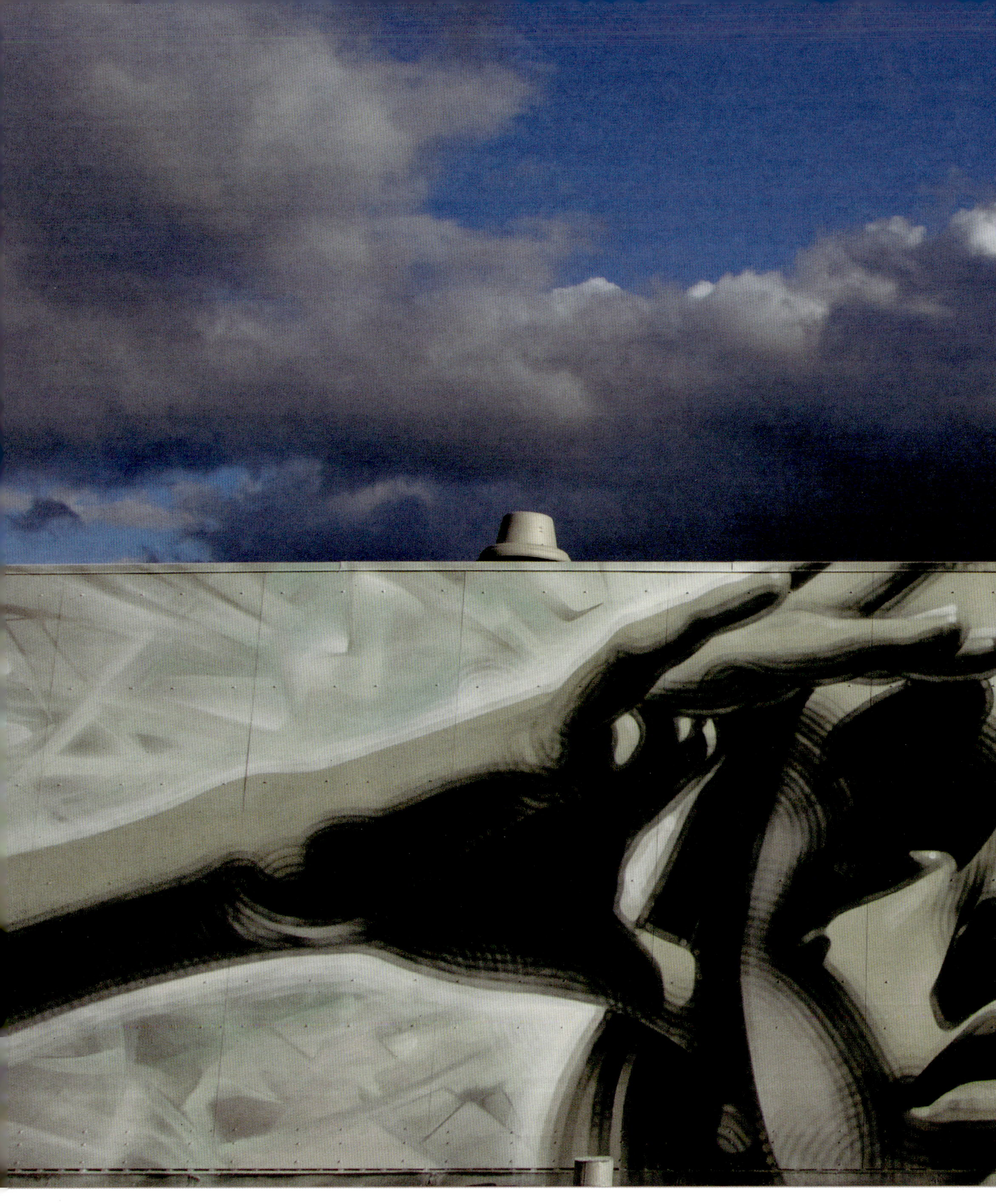

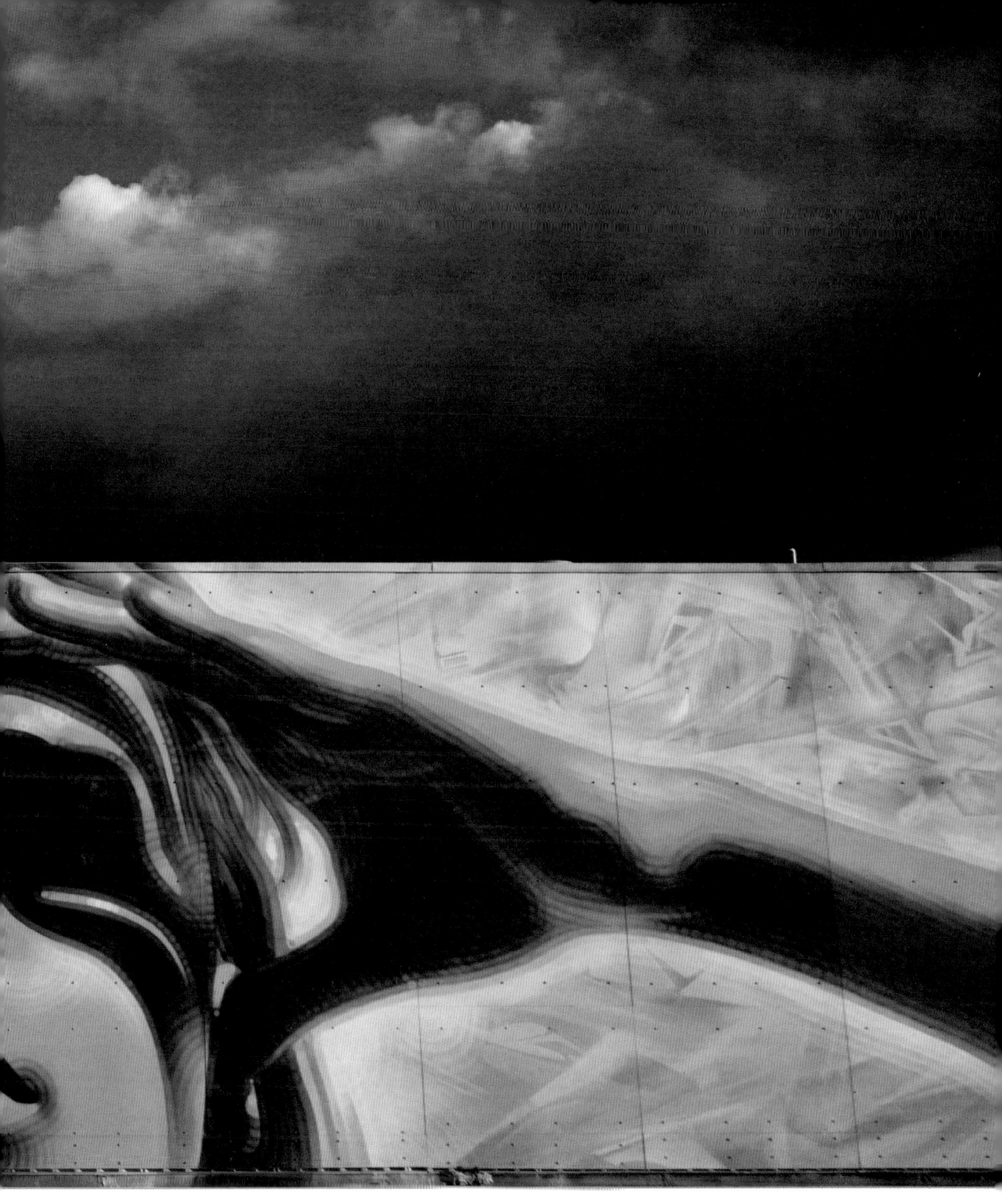

To the Future, 2013   El Mac was entrusted by Eventscape with the realization of this striking mural located in Toronto, Canada;
it was created in collaboration with Canadian artists Kwest and Stare, who mainly worked on the background.

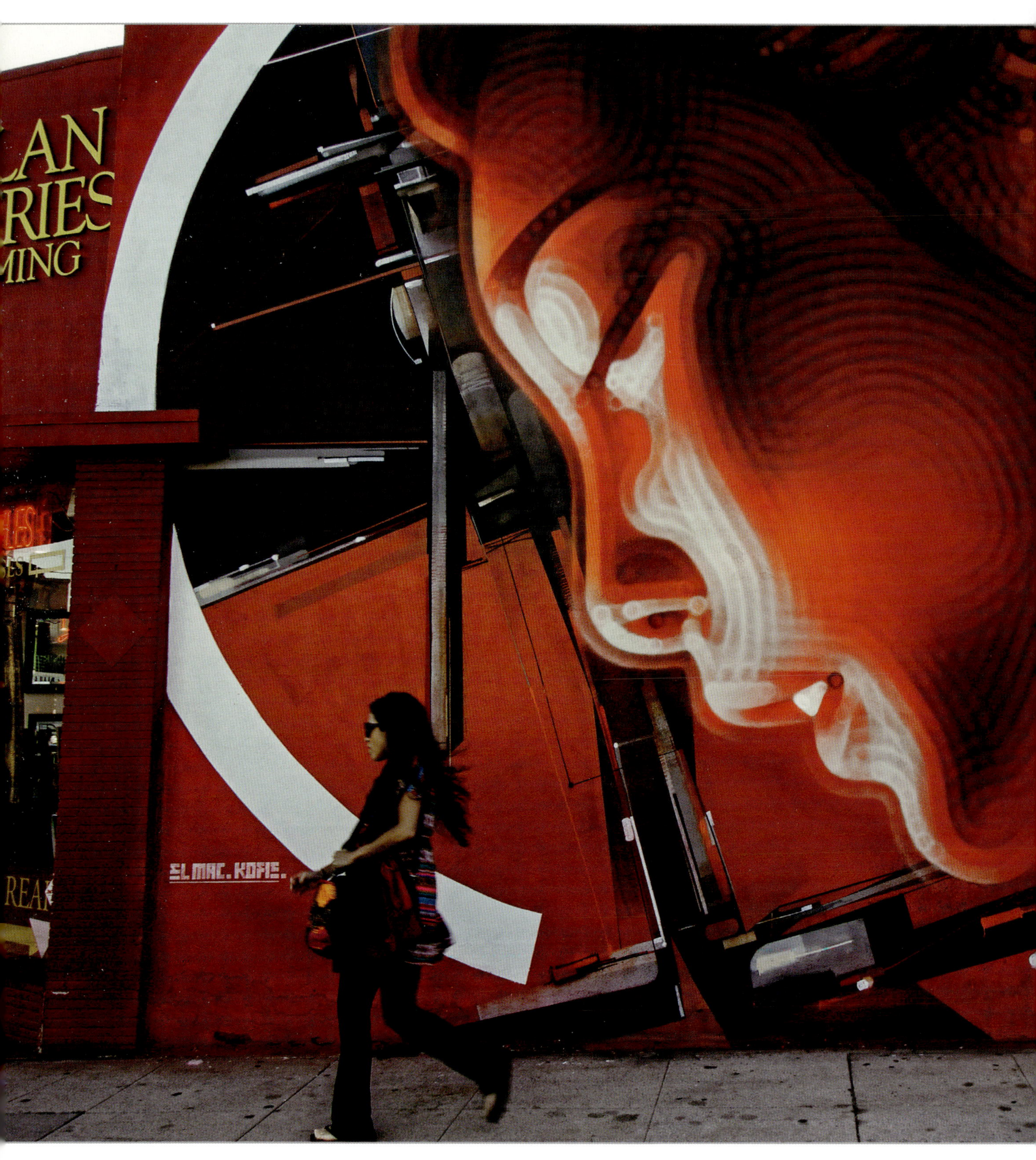

Icarian Flight, 2016 - A fiery red, like the heat that burnt Icarus' wings, characterizes this spectacular mural in Los Angeles, created in collaboration with Augustine Kofie.

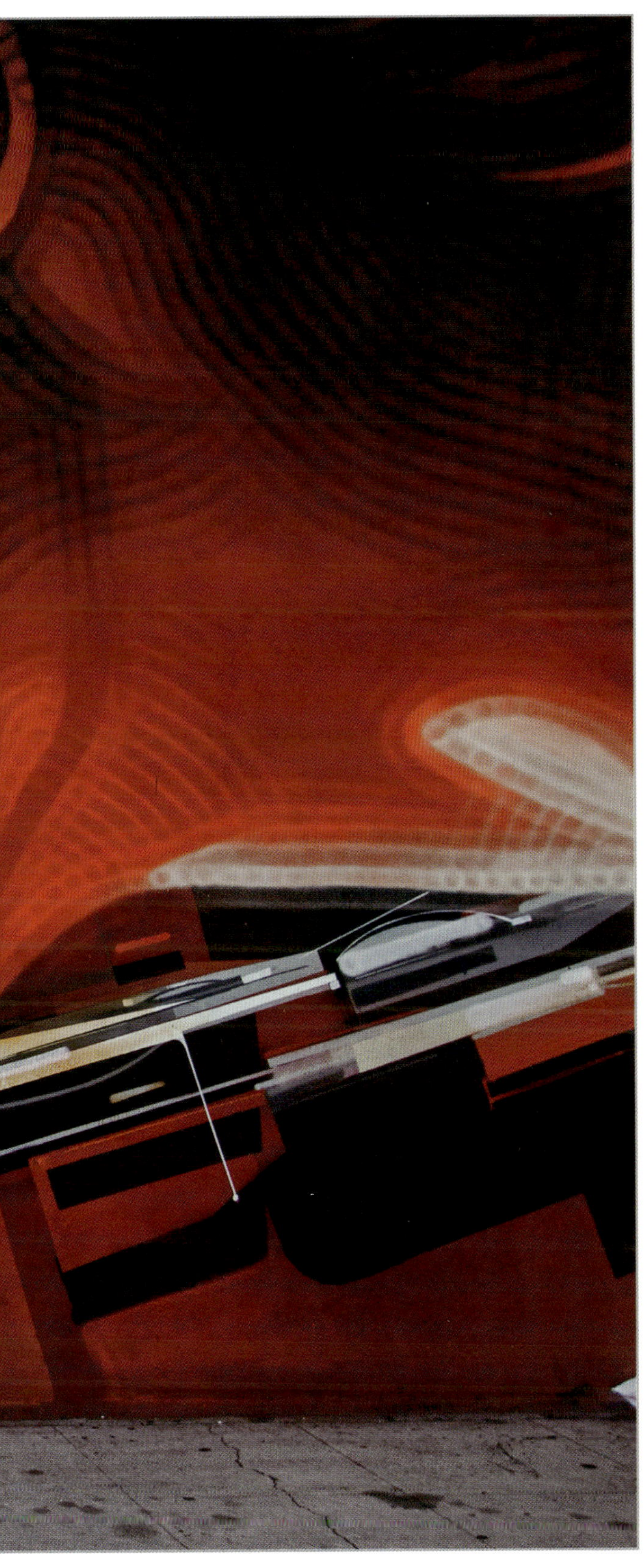

It has really taken me my whole life so far to develop my technique, which has evolved organically over many years. Whether working with pencil, brush or spray paint, much of my work involves careful, precise rendering using repeating patterns. My paintings and murals are normally based on my own photographic references, in order to maintain a consistency with subject matter, lighting, angles, etc. An important part of my artistic practice involves active observation of and drawing from life, something I've done regularly since childhood. I enjoy it and I think it improves one's understanding of anatomy and nature, which shows through in the finished work."

Through his art, El Mac aims high: "I usually hope to convey a message of upliftment. I hope to impart a little bit of my soul and humanity with my work, even if it's just through a subtle expression of a simple portrait. I hope to inspire in the same way I was inspired at a young age by the classic works of great artists of the past."

He has several sources of inspiration, some which have been more important than others. "My mother, certainly, for obvious reasons. Alphonse Mucha has always been a huge artistic inspiration and influence for me, since childhood; his drawings, his posters, his amazing Slav Epic series of mural-sized paintings. He has produced so much beautiful work that speaks to me. Also Gustav Klimt, for the way he portrayed beauty; Vermeer for his technical perfection; Caravaggio for his boldness and the way he would paint poor people and prostitutes as biblical figures. The great Mexican muralists, like Jorge González Camarena and Diego Rivera, for all their contributions to muralism. Moebius for his mastery of line and color; Chuck Close for his innovations in portraiture. The pioneers of the modern graffiti movement as well, like Dondi, Blade, Futura, Lee, Daze, Phase II, Haring and so on. There are so many more out there."

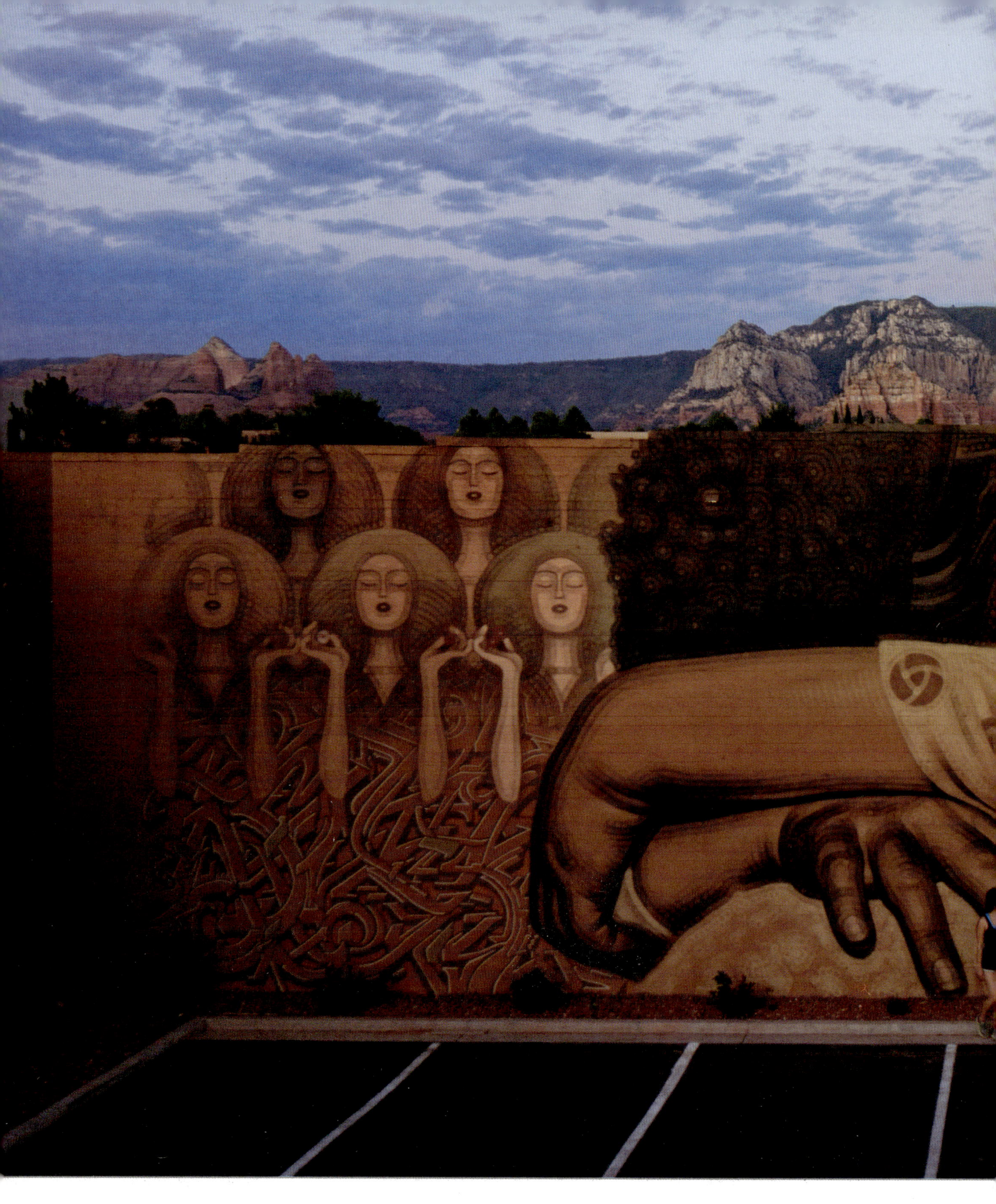

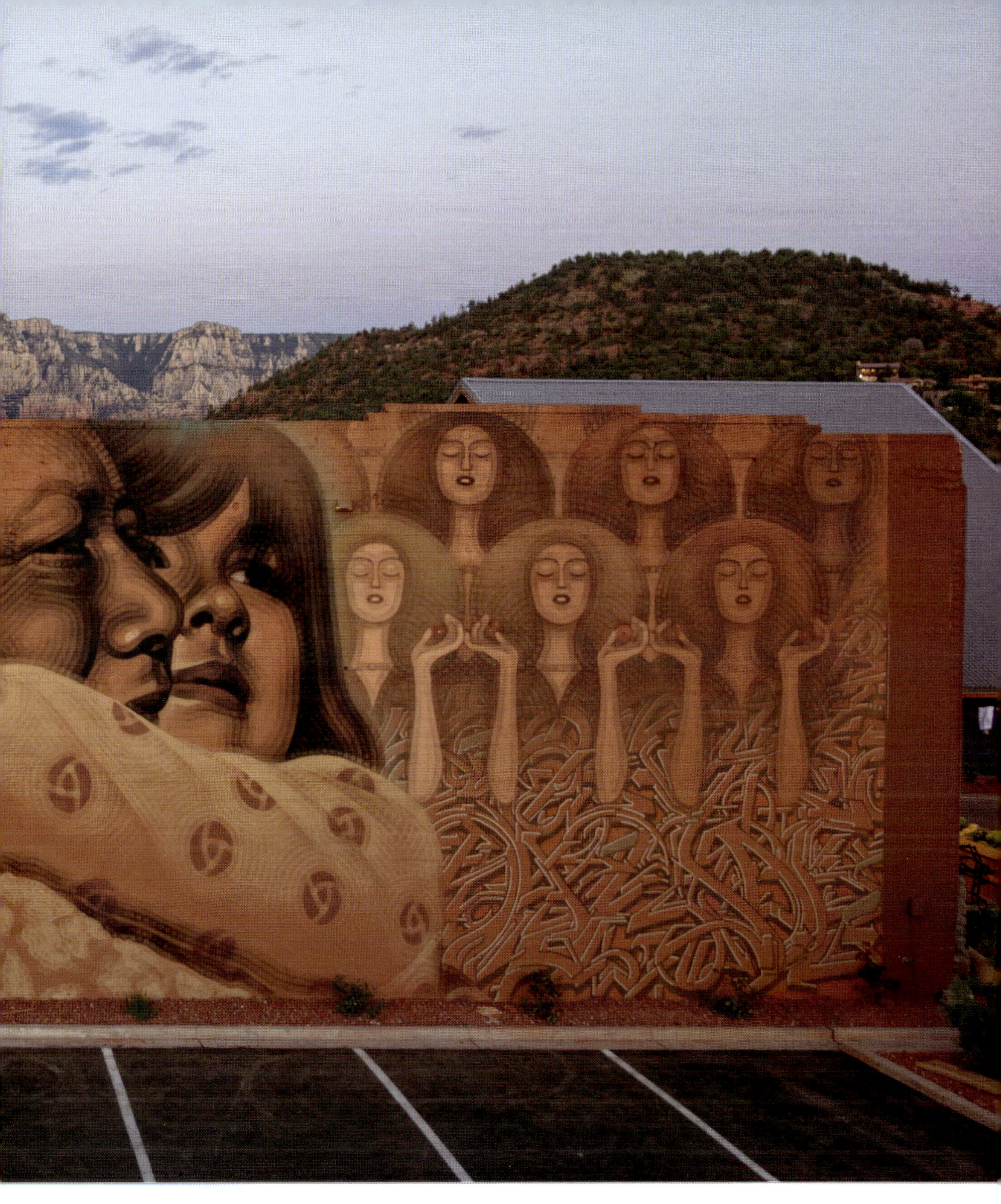

***Spark of Divinity**, 2016* – Commissioned by Whole Foods in Sedona, Arizona, this work pays homage to Gustav Klimt, who had a fundamental influence on El Mac's aesthetics: in fact, the background reminds us of the great Austrian master's *Beethoven Frieze*.

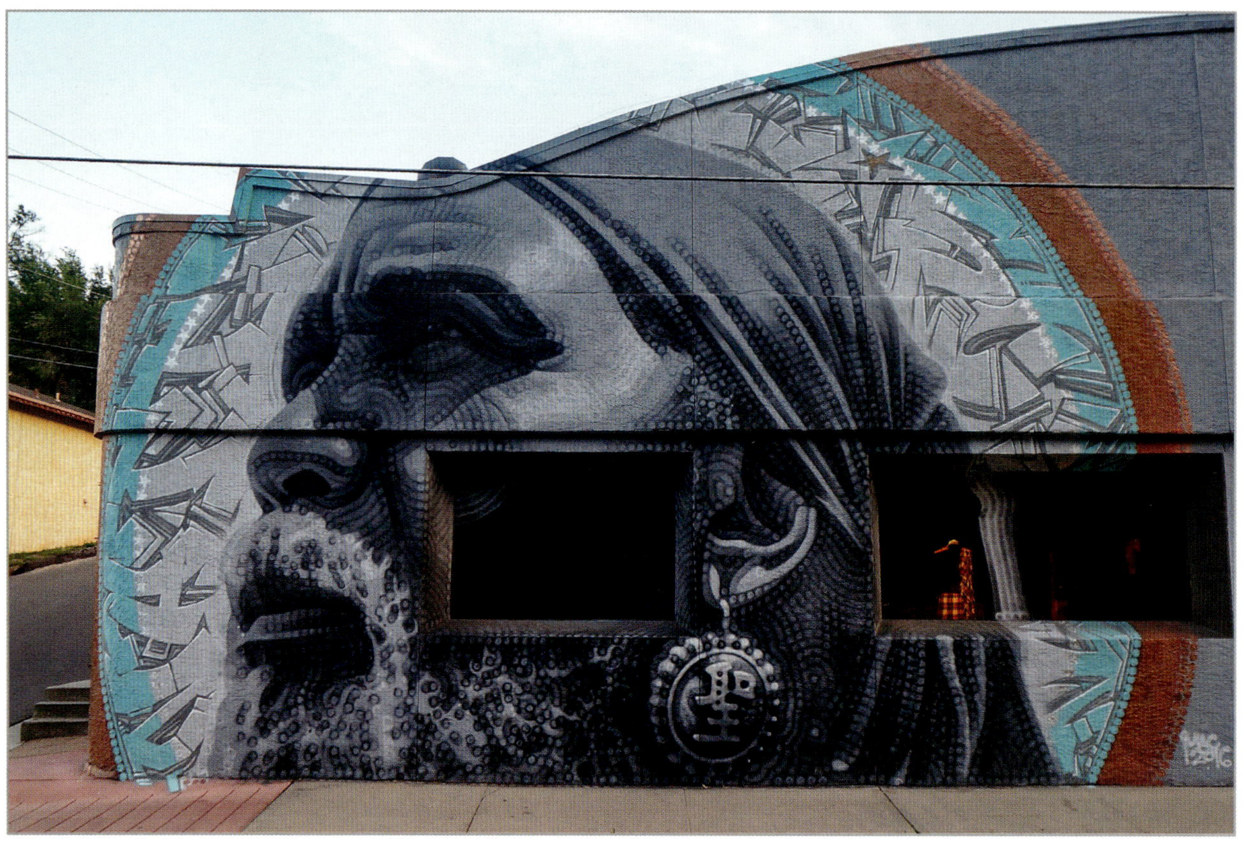

***Native Son (The Saint Flyod)*, 2016** - For the Manitou Art Center in Manitou Spring, Colorado, El Mac depicted the legendary local artist Floyd Tunson (1947).

***Hssain Ahnana*, 2016** - Portrait of Sahrawi nomad Hssain Ahnana in Merzouga, Morocco. The work was realized in the ambit of the *Igloo Hong Art Project*, an initiative set up by David Choe.

To those who do not consider street art a true art form, he responds: "The term 'street art' encompasses so much and can be used so broadly. I avoid using the term because of this. 'Street art' could include anything from illegal letter-based graffiti to a legal public mural that took an artist months of work to paint with brushes to a photocopy that was pasted on a wall. Some work involves more artistry and originality than others. I'd like to think that real art is ultimately recognizable regardless of its context."

Among all of the works he has created, some have a special value. "I painted some pieces for a museum exhibition in Bruges, Belgium in 2003 – that was a life-changing experience for me. I also remember painting a wall in a poor neighborhood in Mexico City in 2006, with Retna, and I remember it started raining and getting dark, and the local guys with us were so generous about trying to secure lanterns and a makeshift cover to protect from the rain. There have been so many memorable painting experiences around the world; some glamorous, many not so glamorous, and I value all of them." Some projects have definitely been more adventurous than others: "My wife and I were attacked once in Milan while I was fixing one of my old damaged murals by people who thought we were vandals. I have also painted in some pretty rough, sketchy areas before, and have had some issues with police before, but for the most part I try and stay out of trouble and not bother anyone. Live and let live."

"There are still so many parts of the world I haven't visited or painted in yet such as Asia, South America and Africa. Los Angeles and Phoenix will always be my home-cities, and to a broader extent, much of the American southwest feels familiar and

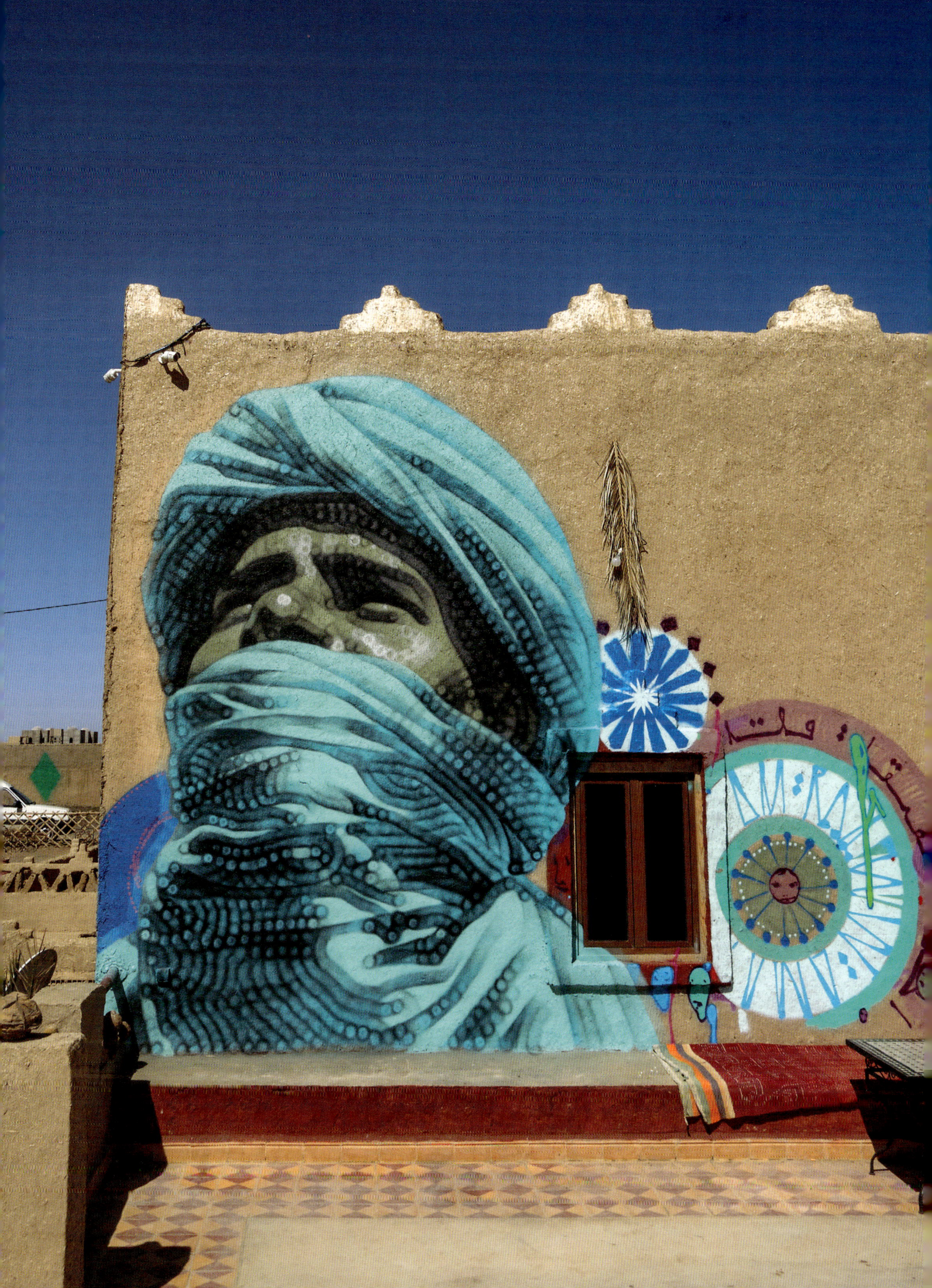

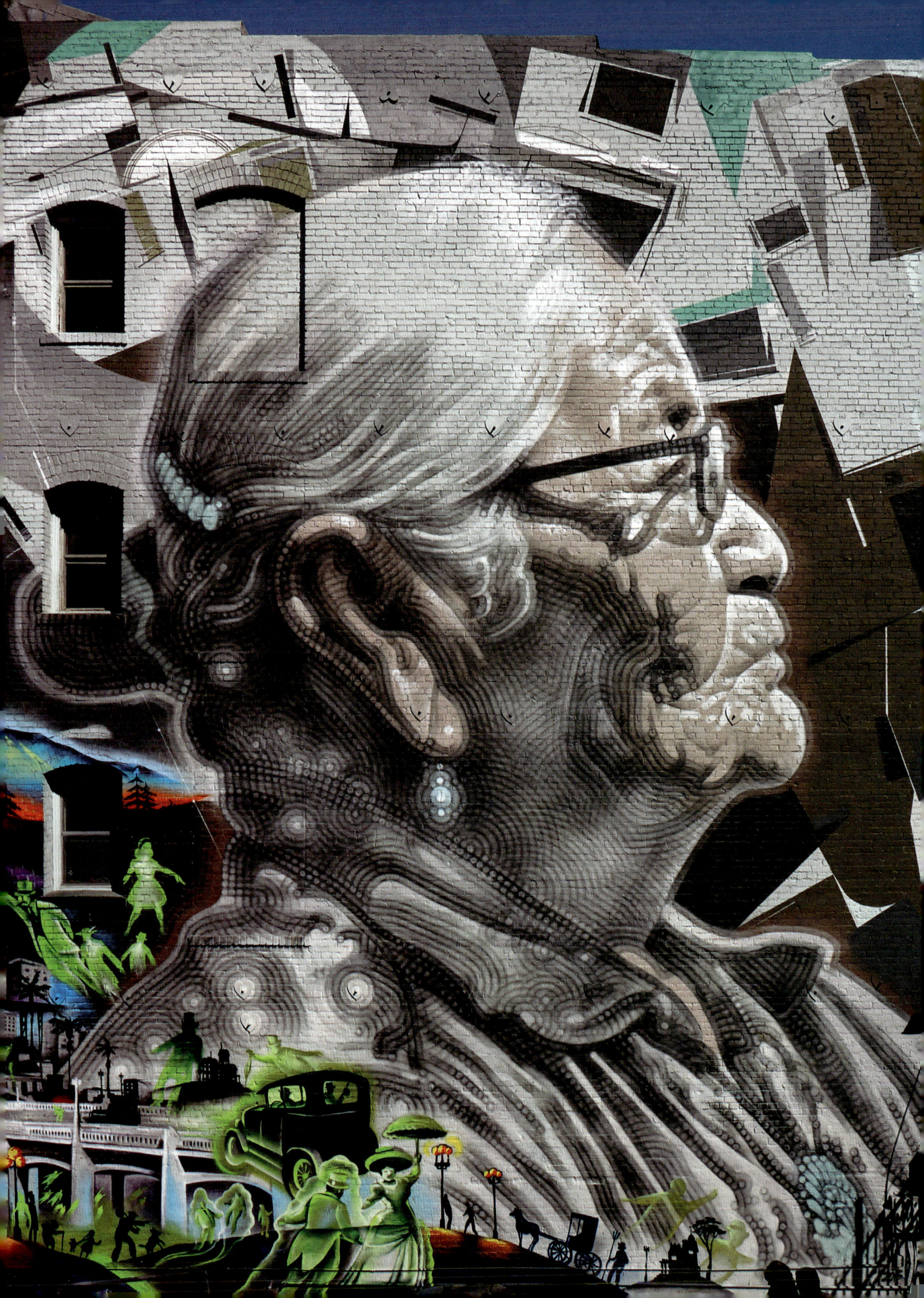

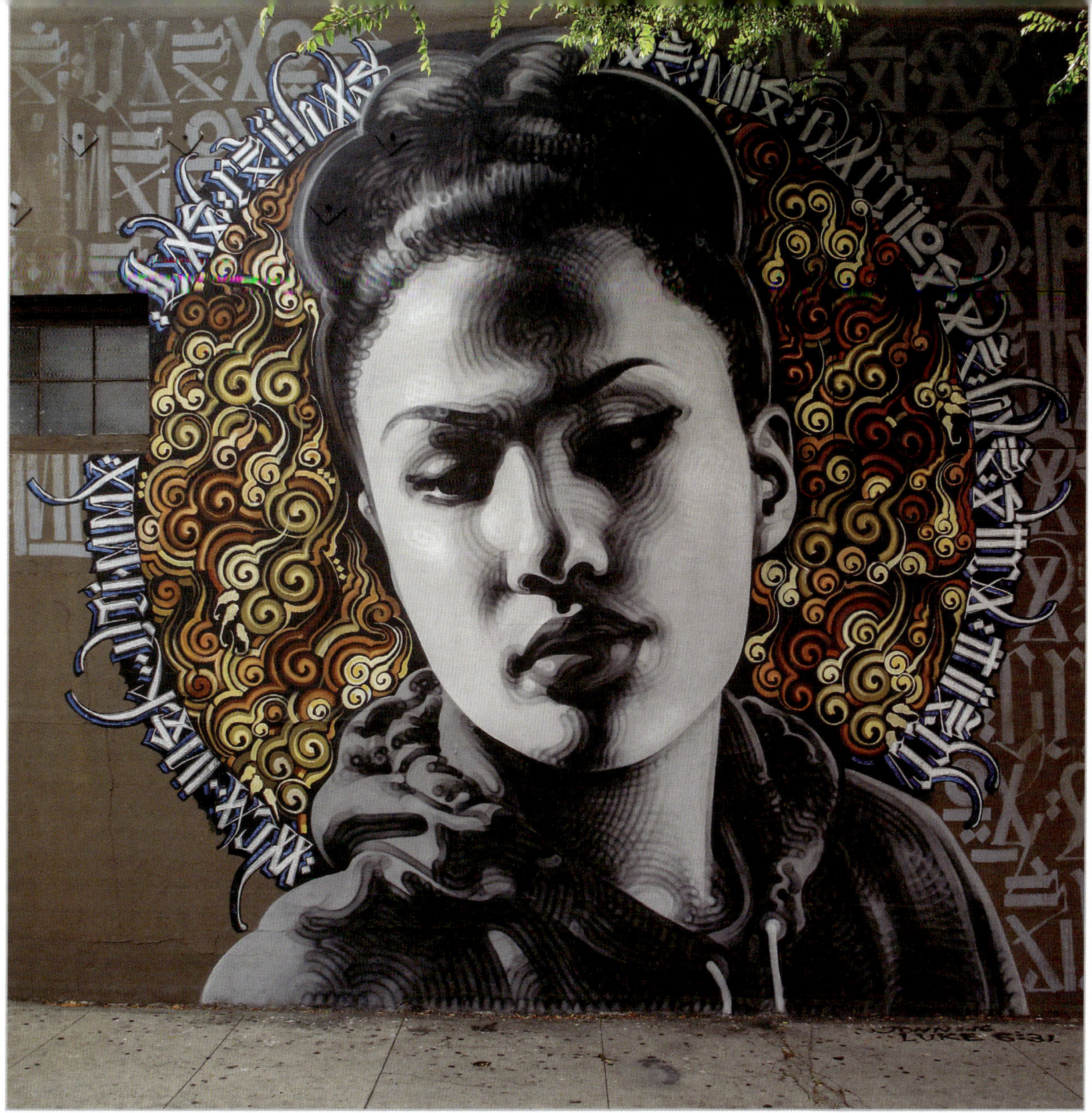

La Abuelita/Mà'sàní, 2015 - A grandmother painted in collaboration with Kofie and Nuke on the façade of the American Hotel in Los Angeles. For the picture sat Martha Gorman Schultz, a Navajo blanket weaver.

Summer Madness, 2010 - This work, used for the cover of *The World Atlas of Street Art and Graffiti* (Yale University, 2013) and located in Hollywood, was painted in collaboration with Retna for the Ruger tattoo shop.

informs my work, and so I enjoy creating art there," he says. "I also derive a lot inspiration from traveling and experiencing other parts of the world, as I imagine most of us do. I have always experienced exceptional support for public art in Mexico, so painting there is always something I appreciate. The same goes for Europe," he continues.

"I think there is much shared anxiety around the world for what will happen in the future. There are so many dangers, tragedies and injustices happening around the planet to be worried about, it is difficult to maintain optimism. As the old saying goes, artists have an ability to comfort the afflicted or afflict the comfortable. Not sure which would be more helpful now, but I will always try and make the most beautiful, powerful art that I possibly can. For the world, I wish more peace, equity, sustainability, compassion and justice, and less xenophobia, ignorance, and violence," he says, adding: "I am endlessly grateful for being able to share my art with the world and to have had such a supportive audience."

EVOL

Transforming the Urban Landscape

His urban environment is transformed by installations representing crumbling miniature apartment blocks, Soviet-style mini-districts, and small desolated architectural complexes. "Judging from the traces on the inner sleeves of my dad's records or in all kinds of books, you can tell I started drawing on everything available from a young age," Tore Rinkveld – aka Evol - admits, smiling, from his home in Berlin. He was born in Heilbrom, in Germany in 1972. "But perhaps all kids do this," he adds. "As a kid my dad often took me to race tracks, a fascinating atmosphere for a small kid. I loved the design and graphics on those cars. Record covers were also a constant source of joy and inspiration. Anyway, I really enjoyed drawing or painting. I preferred working in black and white as I get bored mixing colors and cleaning brushes," he recalls.

He studied at the HfG Schwäbisch Gmünd, in Germany, and at the Kuopio Academy of Arts and Crafts, in Finland. "I never really did 'classical' graffiti, I mean besides scribbling on school desks and things like that. I didn't even really notice it until the beginning of the 1990s," he says. Until one day, "One of my best friends told me that a record shop owner wanted to commission some graffiti artists to create a mural for him. My friend told him he would do it and asked me to help. We went to buy some spray paint, we practiced a while in my basement, painted the shop, got paid, bought a bottle of champagne and celebrated in the bathtub," he continues, laughing.

"But the important thing is that thanks to this experience I discovered the features and benefits of working with spray paints: you can create big pieces, quickly and on almost all surfaces. The colors are ready, well made and easy to carry. And the best thing is you can choose where you want to create your piece and the next morning everyone who walks past it will see it," he reflects.

So it was by mere coincidence that Evol marked this turning point in his existence: "With what was left of the spray cans, I created my first open-air piece. As I wasn't too bothered about letters, I made something that looked more like large cartoon characters. I didn't know how to sign my piece off, and I didn't care. I wanted to tell stories.

> There is a certain thrill in spending the whole night in front of a wall... But I prefer the feeling of the day after, when I can see what I have created by the light of the sun.

Evol at work in the Palais de Tokyo in Paris during the *Lasco Project #3* exhibition.

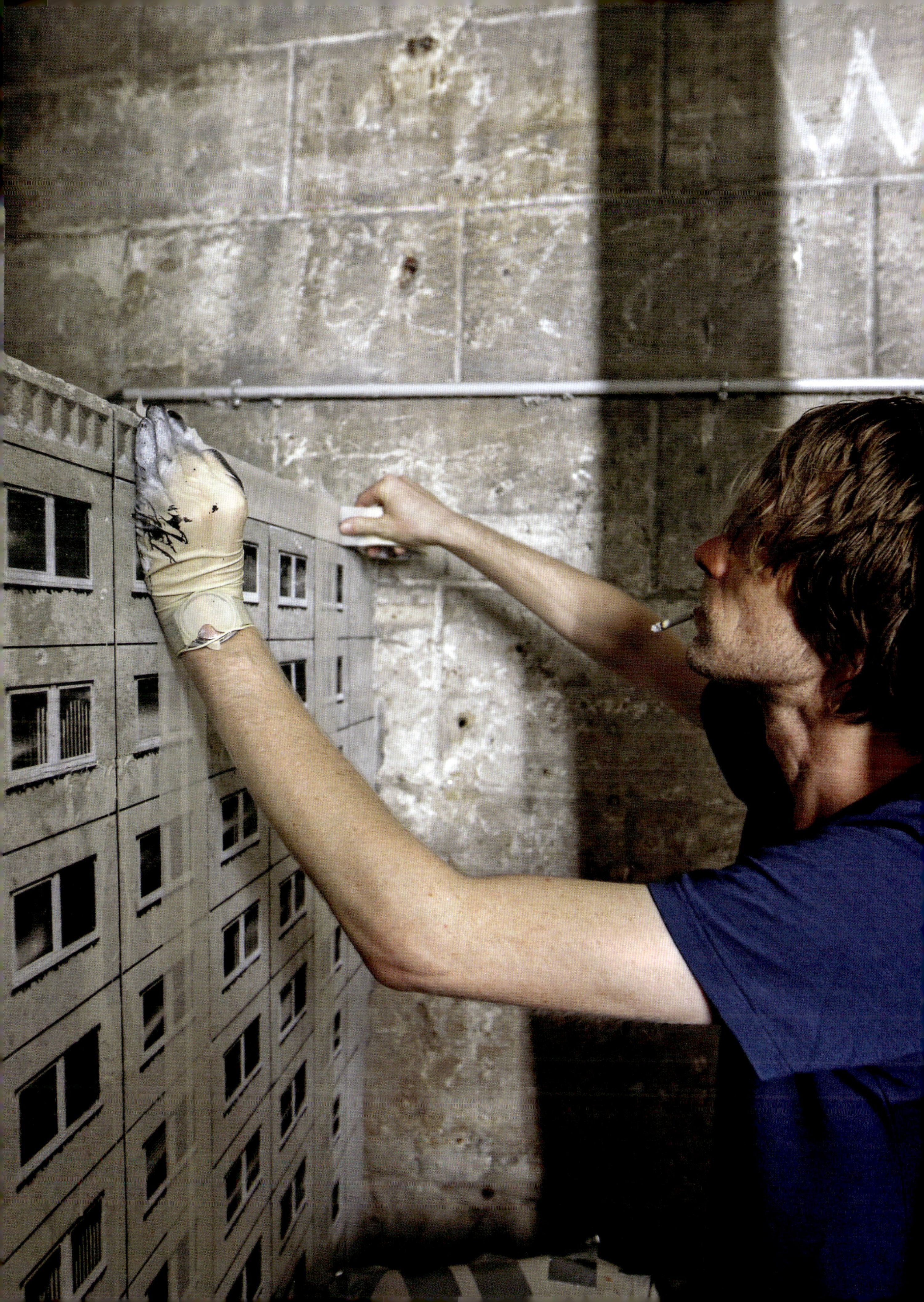

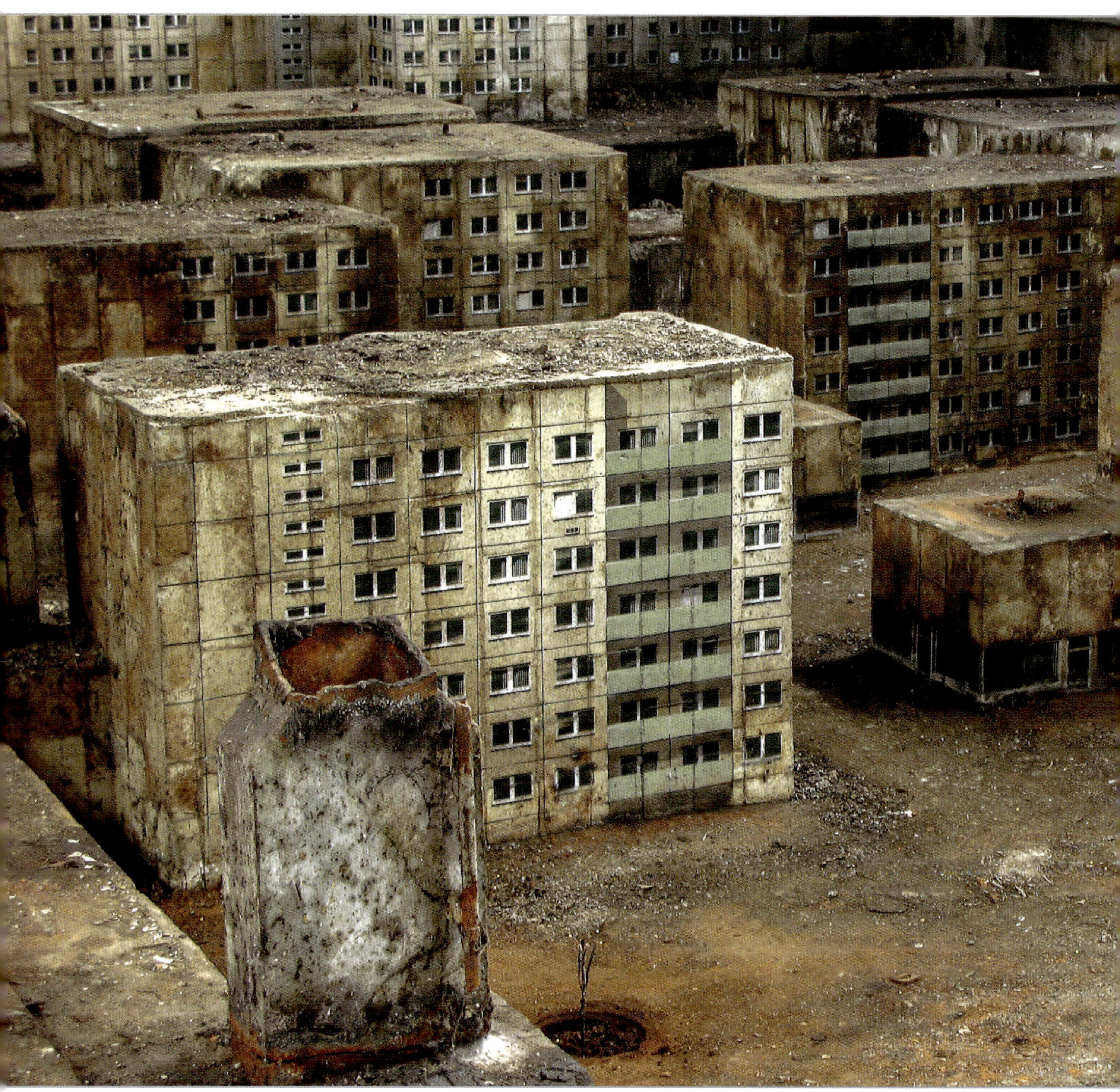

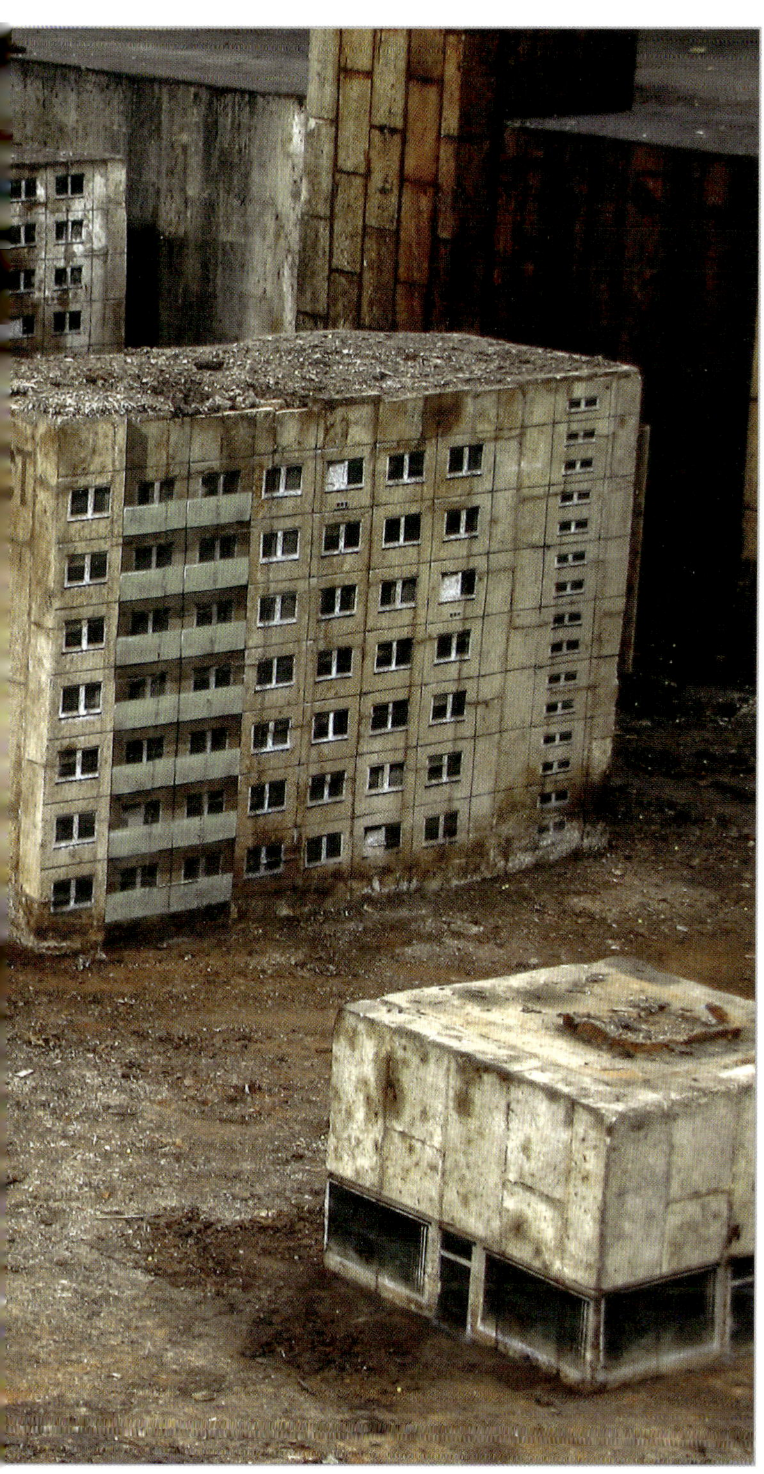

Caspar-David-Friedrich-Stadt, 2009
A real socialist city "built" in a former slaughterhouse in Dresden, once East German city. In Dresden lived for more than forty years Germany's most romantic artist, Friedrich, to whom Evol's installation is dedicated.

I got better quickly and not long afterwards I met the local street artists. That is how I started out in this universe and discovered this subculture." The emotions came straight away. "There is a certain thrill in spending the whole night in front of a wall . . . But I prefer the feeling of the day after, when I can see what I have created by the light of the sun."

Evol has developed a variety of techniques for his work both on the streets and in the studio: "Regarding my stencils, I use a lot of the photos I take wandering around; just architectural situations that interest me. Based on these, I draw a sketch, separate the colors I want to use, and create an order in which I want to layer them. This is quite a long process, also because I don't want the typical bridges (that are necessary to keep a stencil together) to be visible. So I try' to cover them with follow-up layers. And then there are the various layers of transparent shades that build up. It somehow works like a complicated screen print, but with the advantage that I can also cover uneven surfaces."

To Evol, surfaces are very important, "perhaps even the most important element," he says. "I love using leftover materials and I have a weakness for rough sketches and signs. If I find a piece of cardboard I work with its own characteristics, using the folds and imprints.

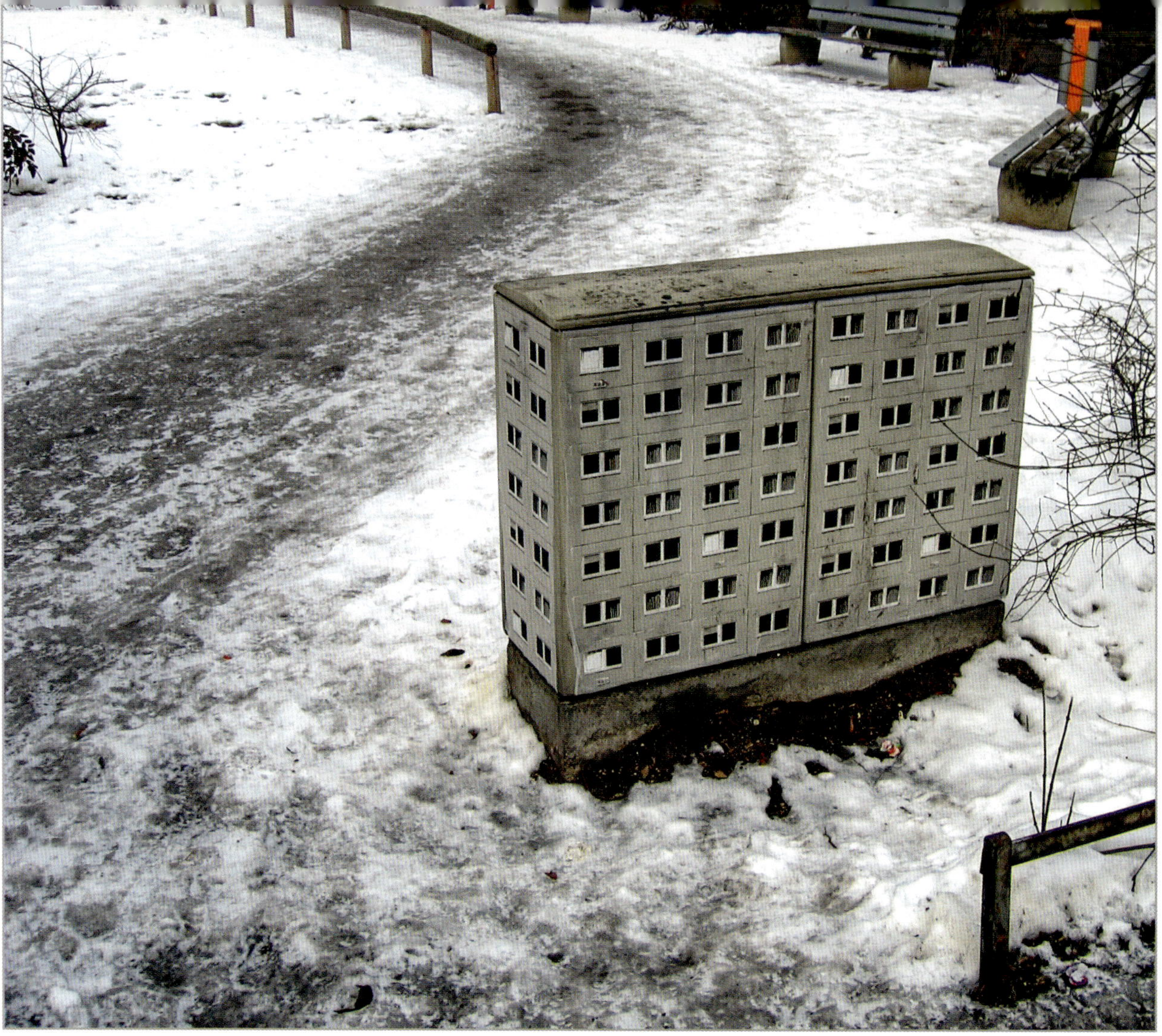

Nuremberg, 2005 - A classical intervention by Evol in snow-covered Nuremberg: the artist transformed humble items of street furniture into opportunities for reflection on the landscape identity of the city.

Since the aim of my work is to obtain a realistic effect, deteriorated materials, dirt and residues are fundamental. I must confess that it is anything but a spontaneous process: on the contrary, each element is thought out in advance. And the challenge is to respect the initial project," he explains, further describing his technique. "But I don't like describing my art too much; I'd rather leave that up to others . . ."

"I'm not even a great fan of the 'message': I don't like it when someone tells me I have to think of something in particular. For me, a good piece of work must only offer potential points for reflection, preferably on a number of different levels, and let the observer interpret them. Everyone has their own personal perception. I likc it when art triggers a strong impression without having to understand the entire background. I prefer art that has an immediate impact."

Evol draws inspiration from almost everything and has been influenced by a number of different artists, for a number of different reasons: the list is endless. "My friends are vital for my work, some of them are artists themselves with whom I can discuss and challenge myself. It is important to get feedback. Another great element is music: I doubt I could work without it," he reflects.

"I reckon my favorite color is a spray paint transparent black: the best invention after

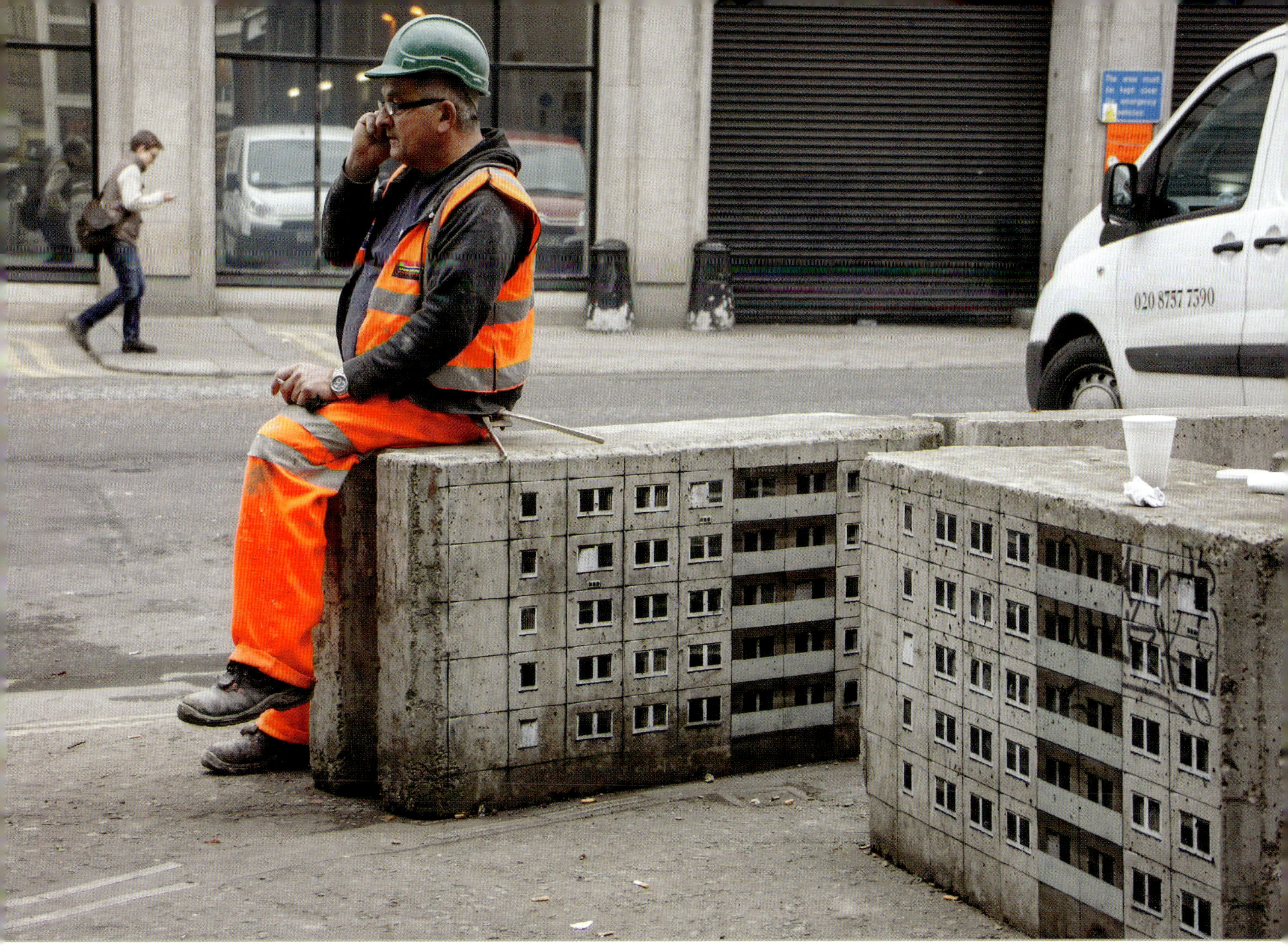

London, 2011 - The works "live" with the city and die with it. It is one of the features of street art, which is still more evident in Evol, an artist fascinated by the evolution of buildings through time.

the spray paint itself!" he says smiling. To those who believe that street art is not real art he replies: "Perhaps they're the neighbors of those people who think that their cat could paint like Picasso! There's no sense in discussing it: there's a lot of controversial art and a lot of bad art. On the other hand, I think that when street art is exhibited in a museum it's no longer street art." Evol himself finds it hard to describe himself exclusively as a street artist: "I never planned to become a street artist and I wonder if I really have become one. I'd rather consider myself an artist who occasionally works in a studio, and other times on the street. I simply do what I like and what feels right to me. And

this includes a whole load of trial and error: in the end it's like trying to grow a plant from a seed."

He loves some of his works more than others. "Each new piece is my favorite, and some remain so even later on. Sometimes it depends on the luck of finding the perfect location, like the abandoned slaughterhouse that I transformed on Caspar-David-Friedrich-Stadt. It was a truly disgusting place, covered with grease and burned fat and a repugnant smell of burned horn. It was hard to stay there for more than five minutes without a mask. But all of this disgust contributed to the beauty of the piece," he explains, citing other examples: "Nordkreuz was the

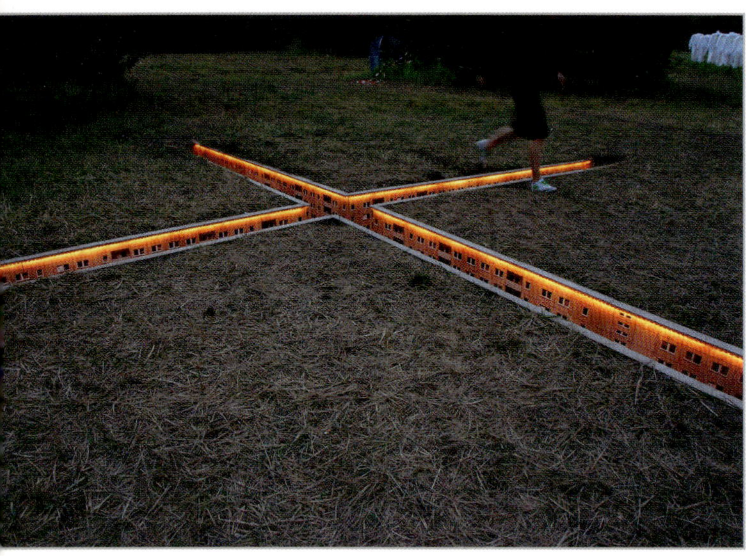

complete opposite: initially, there seemed nothing to valorize in the location, nothing to use: just green pastures and a blue sky. So I decided to 'cut the idyll open' to show the disgust below. It was easy on paper but hard to put into practice. I was happy though to see that you can also work on land that you don't know," and continues to speak of another challenge. "I created an installation in the corridor of an art-hotel that a friend was setting up in an occupied house: the Flamingo Beach Lotel. It was the first time that I created entire scenery and it was a fantastic experience turning on the lights. Since the ownership situation was rather difficult, she had to close this wonderful place all too soon and unfortunately very few people were able to see it. But two years later by a strange coincidence we decided to build a replica of that corridor for an exhibition, only I didn't know where to build it as my studio was too small. And a few days later I received a request from a film troupe who had stayed in the hotel and who wanted to film a scene in that corridor. When I explained that I

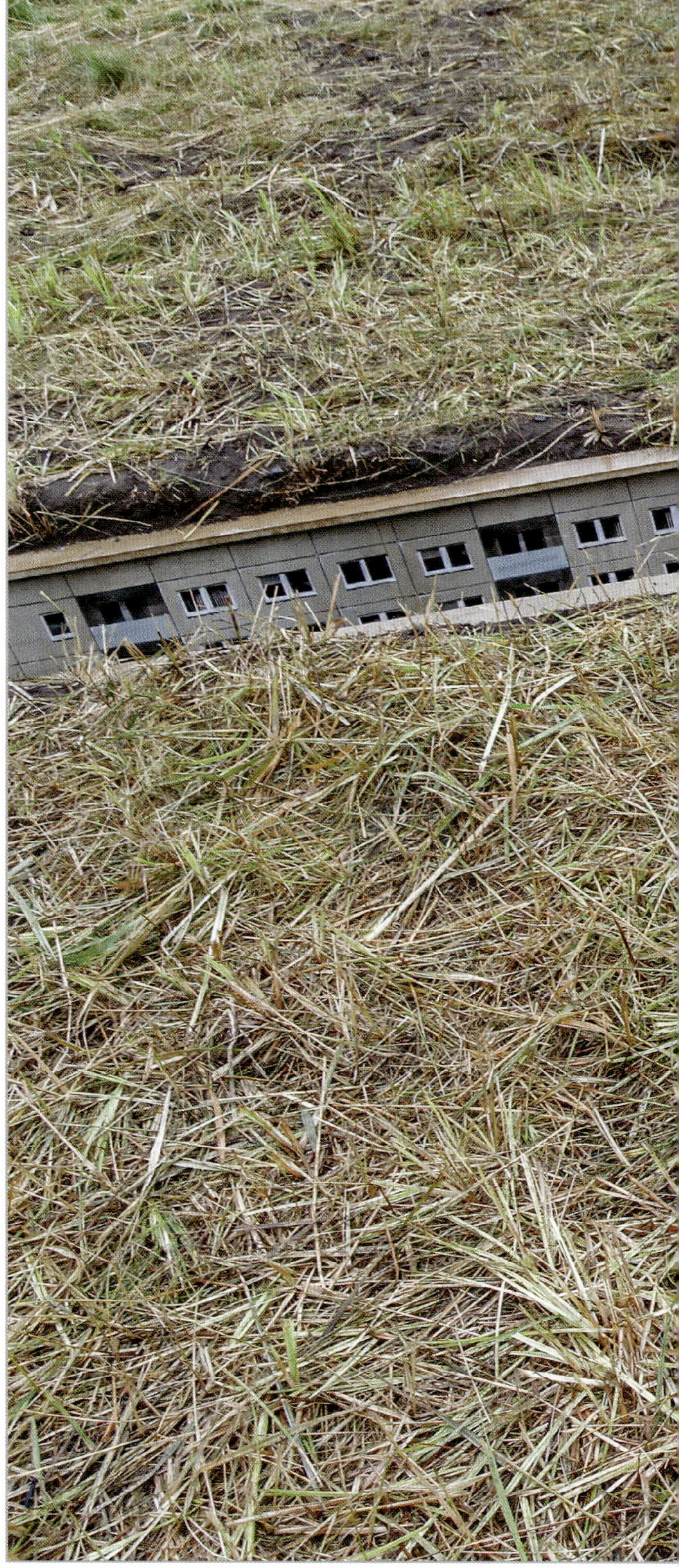

Nordkreuz, **2011** - This 5 feet deep cross was cut into the ground; its arms are 29,5 feet across. It represents Evol's solution to paint in the absence of pre-existing supports, in the Dockville Festival of Hamburg.

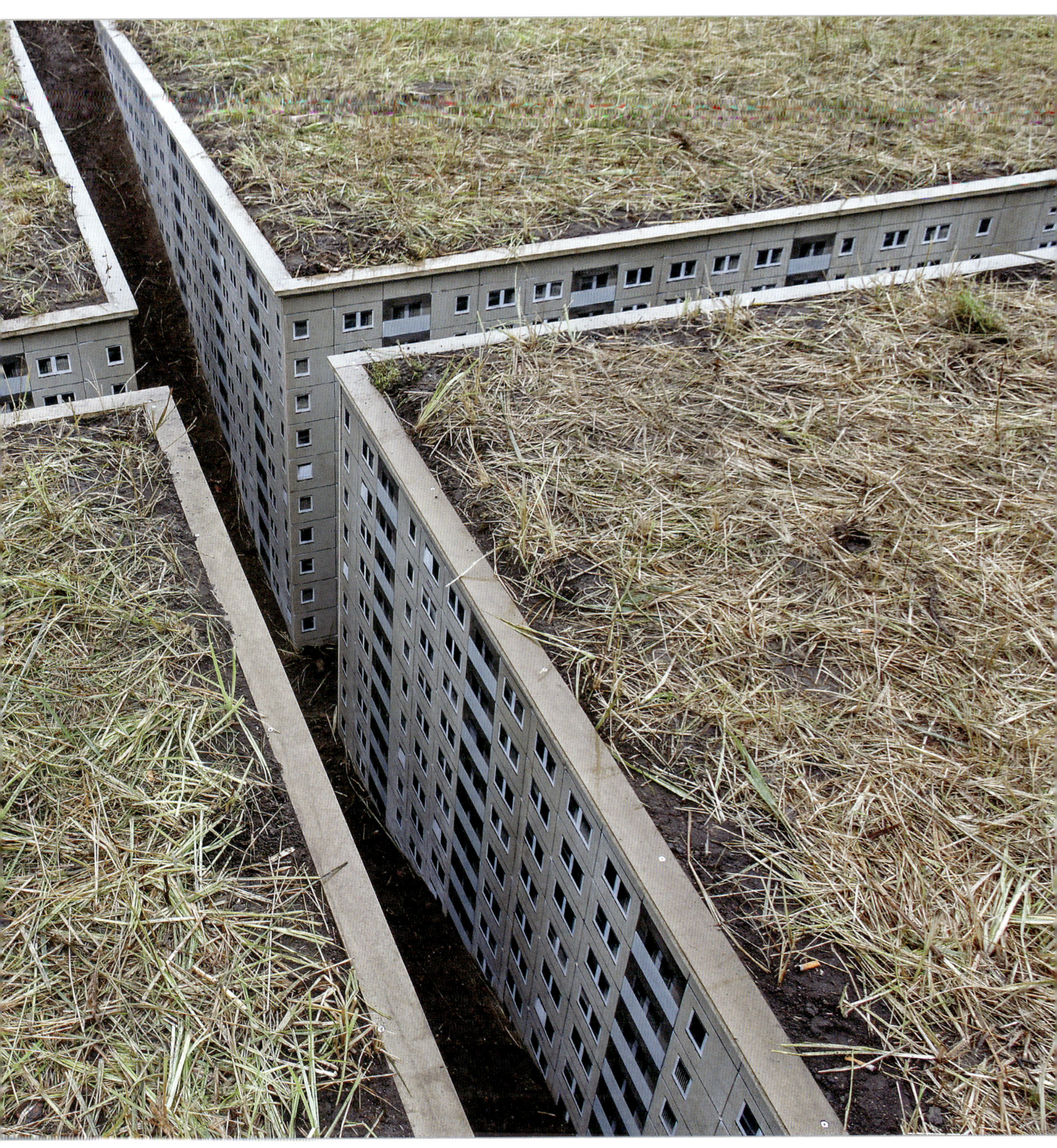

Nordkreuz, 2011 – A lawn becomes the roof garden of Soviet-style buildings leading to an alienating effect. This piece, somewhere between land and street art, was born from Evol's collaboration with Matthias Hübner and Brad Downey.

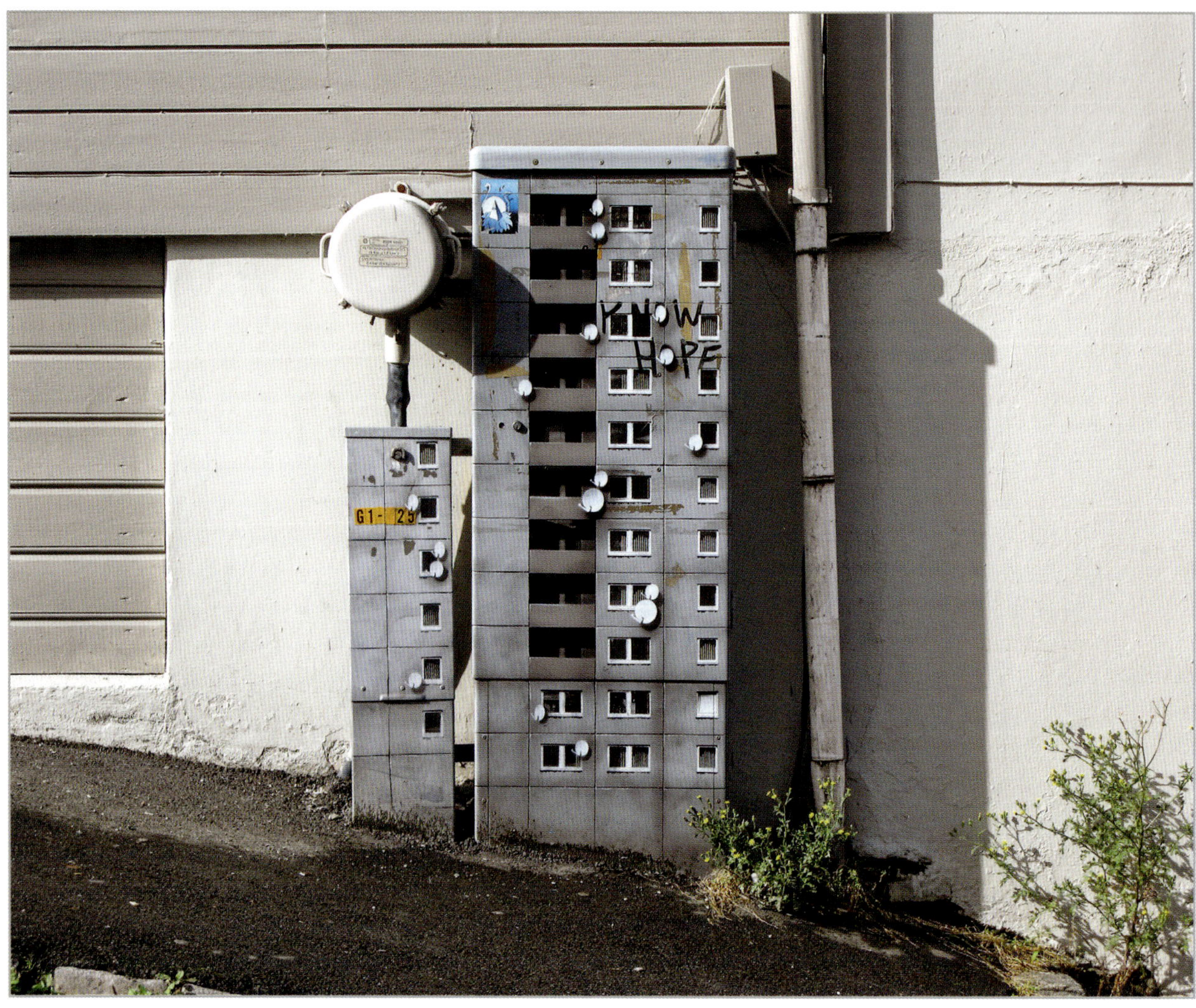

Stavanger, 2010 - Evol derives inspiration from surfaces and places. Here the satellite dishes depicted on the balconies evoke the round shape of the structure on the smaller box.

wanted to reconstruct it but I didn't have the space, they told me I could do it in their studio. In this way I recreated this piece quite close to its original location. I love it when things like this happen, but also more banal coincidences. Like when you find out that the postbox you have decided to decorate is in front of a card shop whose display window is lit by an ultraviolet light at night. This allowed me to transform the postbox into an apartment block with windows that lit up at night, thanks to the light that came from the display window. In a certain way it was a site-specific piece," he goes on. "I am more interested in the result than in the risk I may run in completing a piece. Of course there have been a few dangerous situations, but I am not proud of them, and with hindsight I think it was stupid," he admits with sincerity.

Asked if he has a favorite city, he answers, "Of course there is this one place, this vibrant rough and elegant city, impressive culture

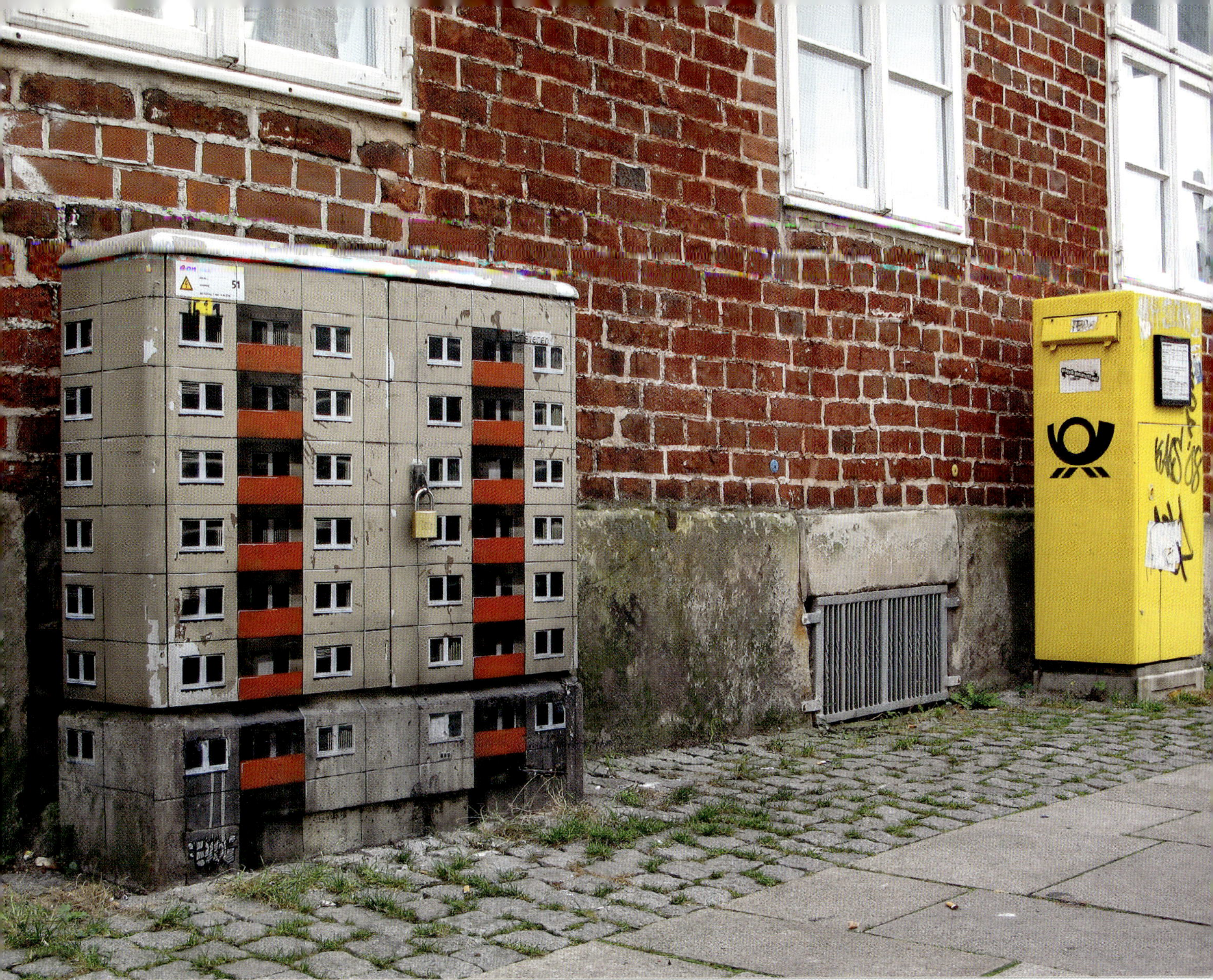

Lüneburg, 2009 - On the occasion of ARTotale 2009, Evol scattered site-specific interventions through Lüneburg. The red stripes seem to evoke the brick facades featured in many buildings in the city.

present at every corner, with the nicest sand on the beach and the most beautiful mountain trails, where the lakes are refreshing in summer and the fall has incredible colors, where people have humor and dignity, and I finally managed to speak the language. But to prevent the rents from going up even further and the streets from getting too crowded, I'll answer your question with: Bielefeld."

The truth is, he adds, that he feels a particular connection with Berlin, even though it doesn't have all the characteristics listed above and has its own pros and cons.

Evol doesn't have a particularly positive vision for the future. "I am rather pessimistic. To resort to a stereotype: there are too many old men with high education and low testosterone and young men with low education and high testosterone. That's one hell of a challenge," he muses. What we need for a better world is "for people to overcome their motherfucking greed."

SHEPARD FAIREY

Great Visionary

Sometimes an image can fly to far-off places and conquer the world. That is what has happened with several works by Shepard Fairey: when he speaks, he seems to gaze off into the distance. His words are full of that intelligence that only a great visionary can possess. He was born on February 15th, 1970 in Charleston, South Carolina; and besides being one of the greatest contemporary artists, he is also a designer, activist, and illustrator as well as the founder of Obey Clothing. "I got inspiration from the skateboard scene. I began to do drawings for skateboards and T-shirts in 1984," he recounts: it is an interesting sector for him because it is democratic, for everyone and open to everyone.

Fairey became famous when he was still attending the Rhode Island School of Design, thanks to the sticker *André the Giant Has a Posse*, based on the face of the professional wrestler André the Giant. The stickers were taken to many cities in the United States by the skater community and a large group of alternative artists, in the context of a street art campaign in 1989; and they immediately stood out because of their original, innovative design. "In the beginning, it was only supposed to be a phenomenological experiment. But what has always stimulated me is provoking, asking questions about everything, wondering about the meaning of things . . . Above all, I want to arouse curiosity with my works, to get a reaction. I also want to reach the widest audience possible. To do this, I use every means to communicate and spread my ideas," Fairey comments.

Then the first drawing of *André the Giant Has a Posse* was modified stylistically and semantically to become the *Obey Giant*, who appears on walls in every form, often illegally. "But Obey was born more as a symbolic face than a propaganda icon."

Fairey achieved even more fame in 2008 during Barack Obama's election campaign when he created the *Hope* poster for the future president. Since then, he has officially been considered one of the most famous contemporary artists, and his works can be found in important museums like the Smithsonian and the National Portrait Gallery in Washington, the MoMA in New York, the Los Angeles County Museum of Art, and the Victoria and Albert Museum in London. His first exhibit, *Supply & Demand*, was held at the Institute of Contemporary Art in Boston in 2009, and included works in different media, such as prints, drawings, stencils, stickers, illustrations, and collages, and with various materials, such as wood and metal, in addition to canvas.

> I want to create valuable art, which at the same time is political and can contribute to a better world.

Shepard Fairey works on a wall of the P.S. 19 Asher Levy School in East Village, New York, in September 2016.

Hope, 2009 - The face of Barack Obama, at the time the new President of the United States, on a poster along 14th Street, in Washington D.C.

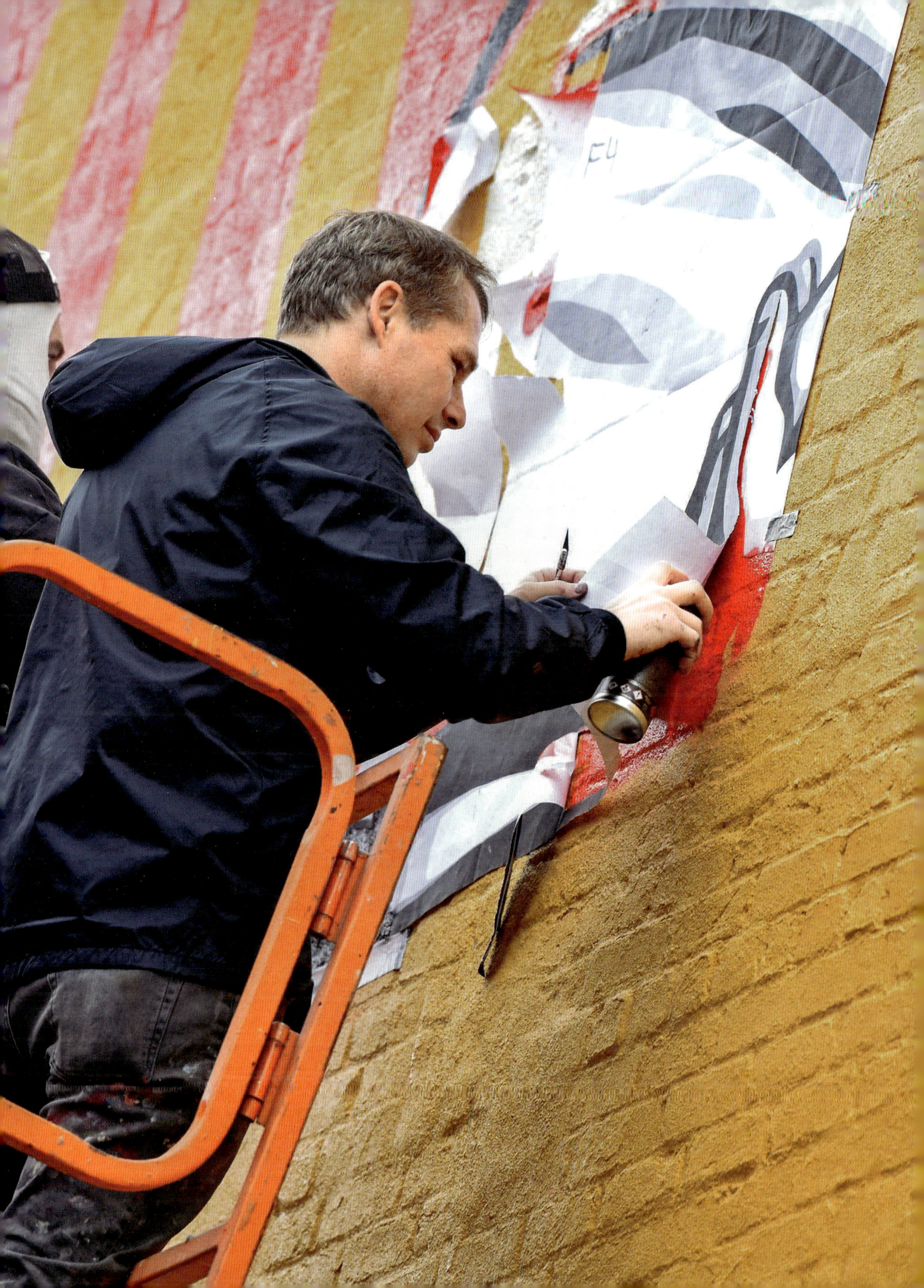

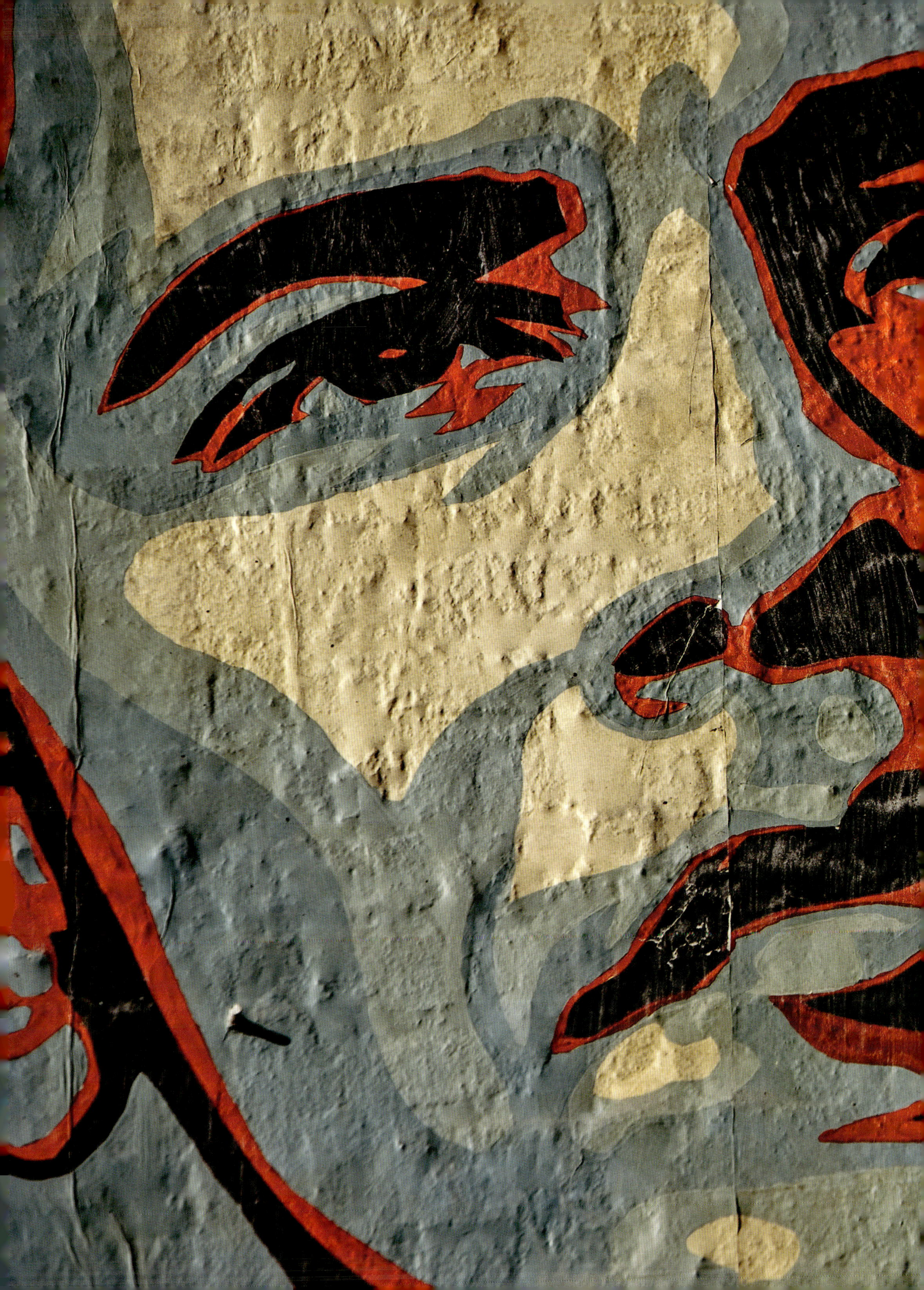

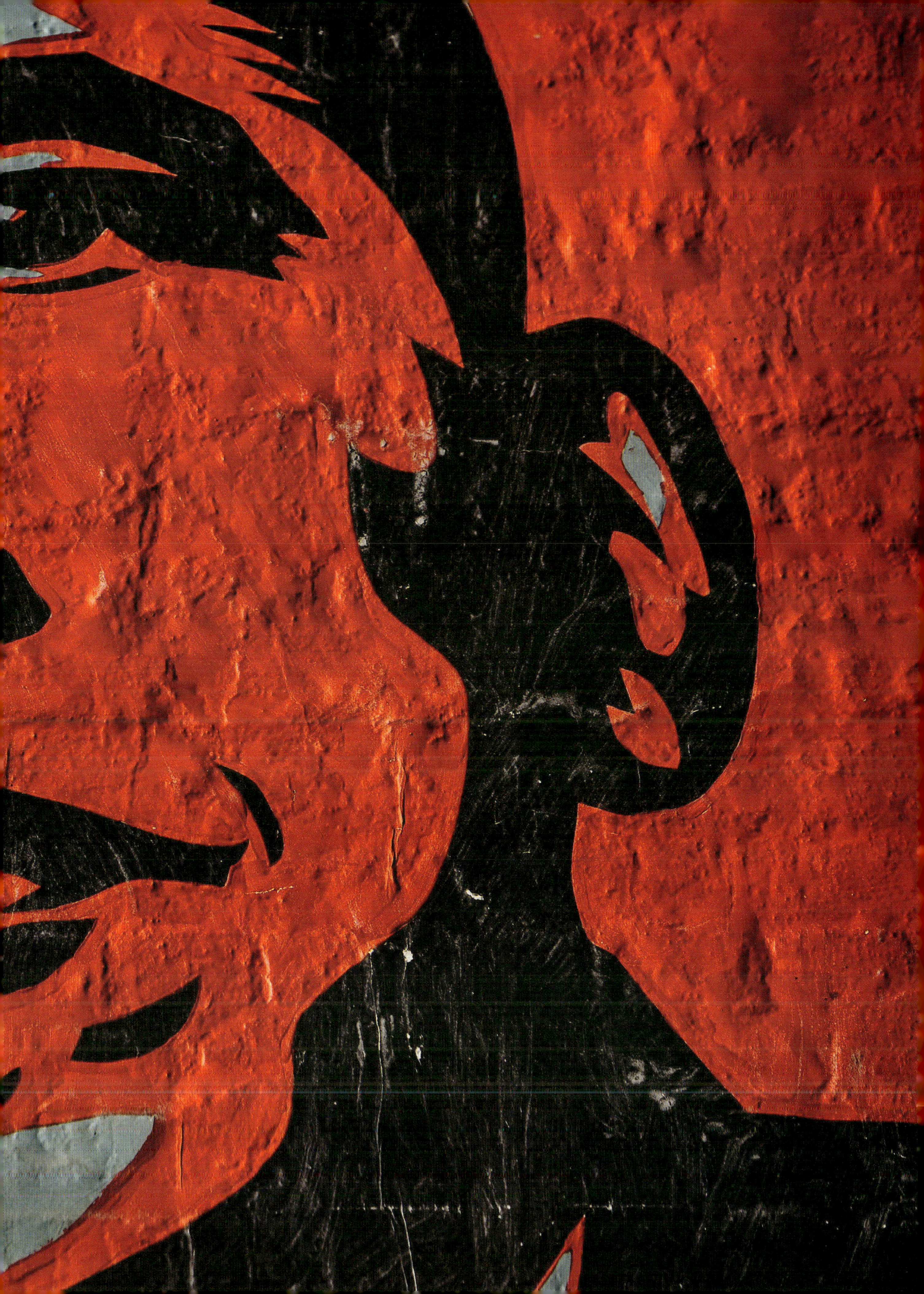

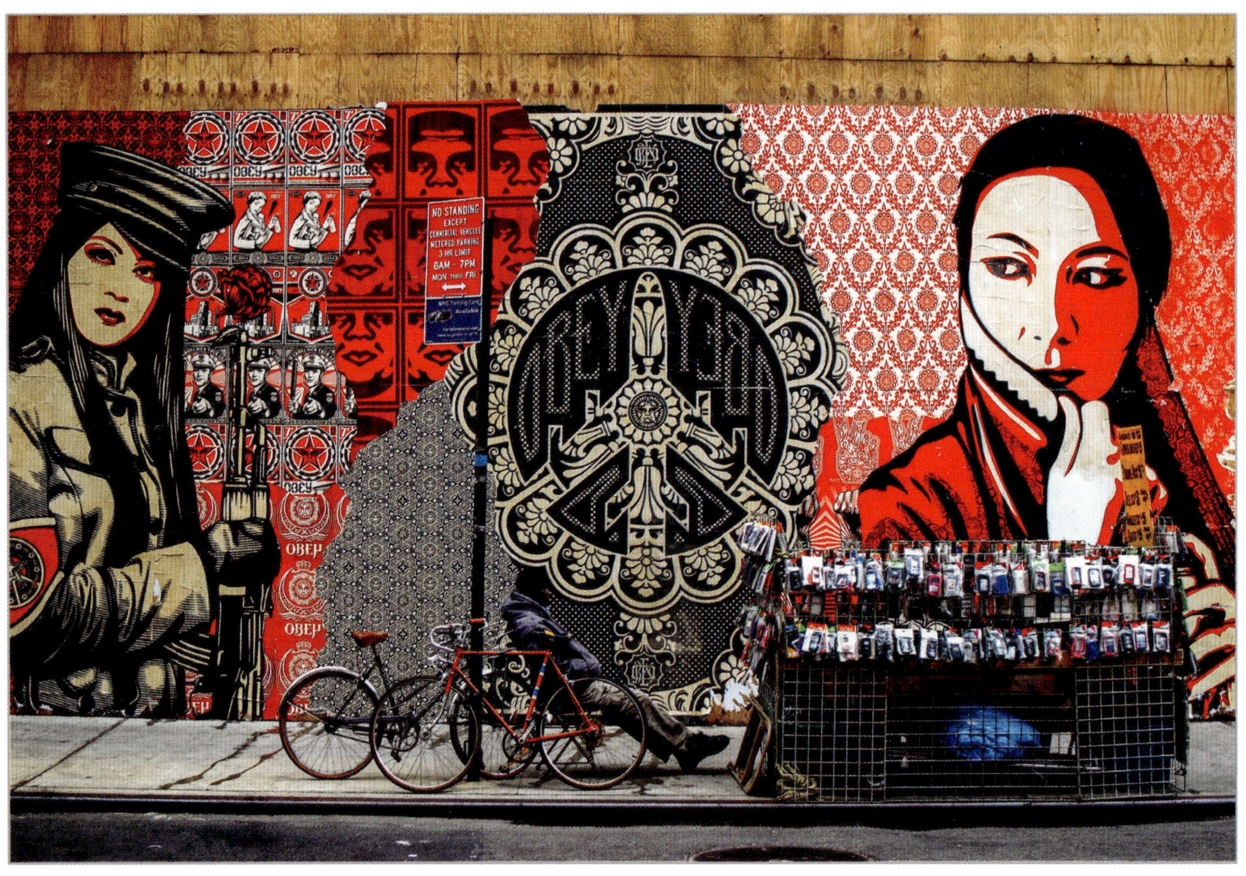

New York, 2012 - On this red collage along 31st Street in New York the image of two female figures with a strong presence superimpose on recurring themes in Fairey's art, like the face of the wrestler André The Giant.

Nelson Mandela, **2014** - In 2014 Fairey depicted the face of Nelson Mandela, both on the occasion of Art Basel Miami Beach and, in a giant version, on a building in Johannesburg, South Africa.

Fairey has always collaborated with various non-profit associations and organizations like the Music is Revolution Foundation to support talented young people: his project, the Obey Awareness Program, enables him to collect funds for numerous causes. He has also founded Alternate Graphics, to print drawings on T-shirts and stickers; the design studio BLK/MRKT Inc. (existing from 1997 to 2003) specializing in guerrilla marketing and high-impact campaigns for Pepsi, Hasbro, and Netscape; and the design agency Studio Number One with his wife Amanda.

There have been numerous other collaborations: he created the covers for the Smashing Pumpkins' album *Zeitgeist* and the Led Zeppelin compilation *Mothership*, the "anti-war" and "anti-Bush" posters for the street art campaign *Be the Revolution* with the artists Robbie Conal and Mear One, and a poster for the film *Walk the Line* about the musician, Johnny Cash. Among his murals, one of the most significant is *The Nelson Mandela Mural*, in Johannesburg. Nevertheless, Fairey has been arrested several times for vandalism and damage to public property during his artistic career.

Fairey also participated in the documentary *Let Fury Have the Hour*, which was presented at the Tribeca Film Festival in New York in 2012. "I got involved because the writer and visual artist Antonino D'Ambrosio, who was debuting as a director, has been a close friend of mine for many years.

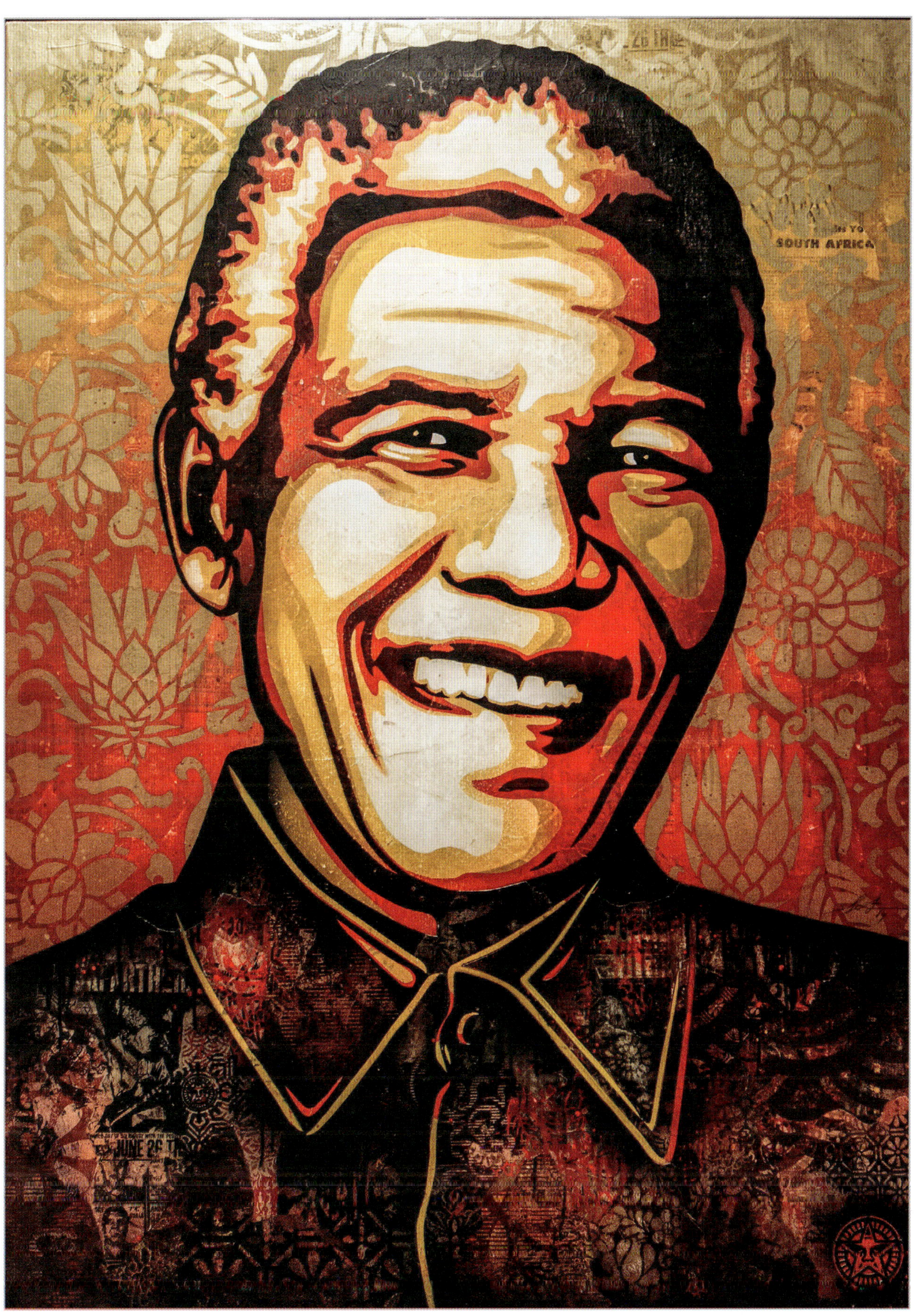

SOUTH AFRICA
APARTHEID
JUNE 26 T

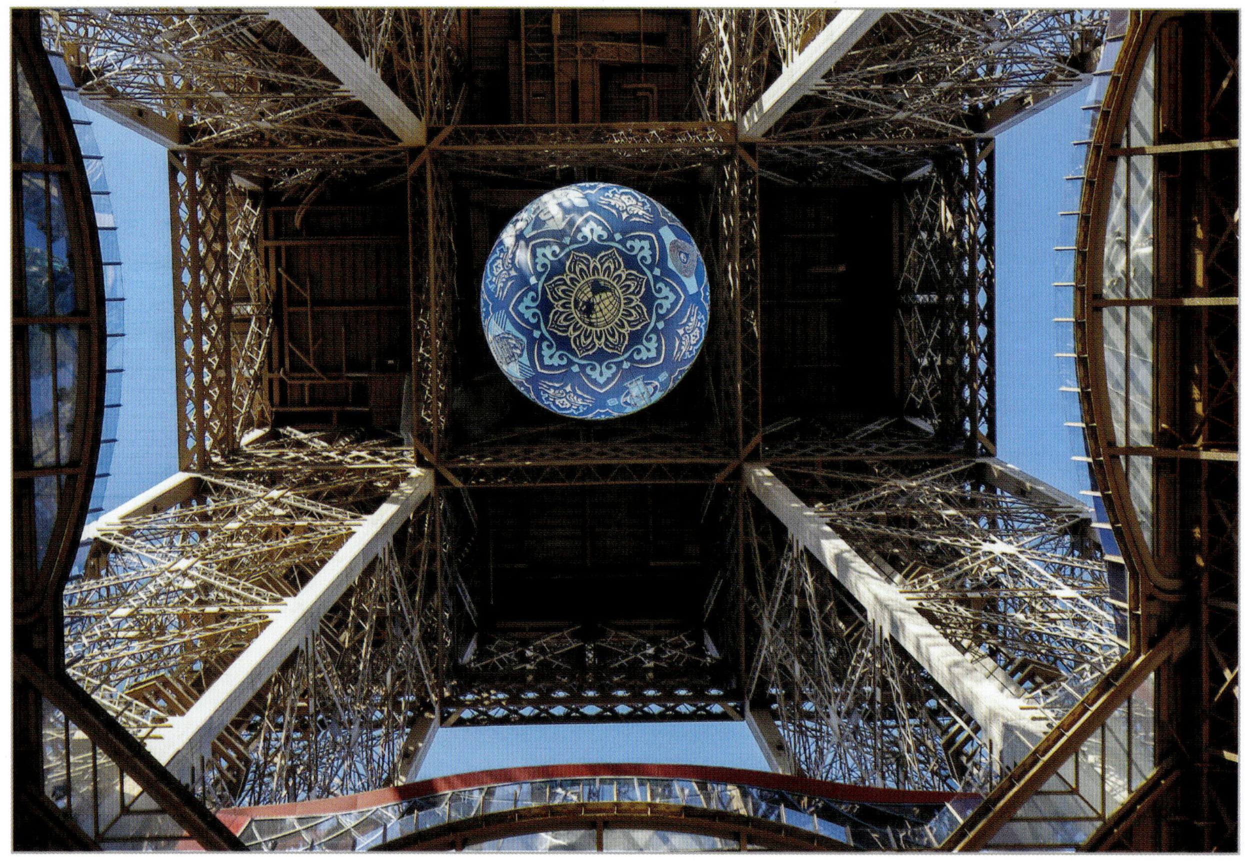

***Earth Crisis*, 2015** - A globe, a contribution to the environmentalist cause, hanging under the Eiffel Tower for the Conference on Climate Change COP21 in Paris, in November 2015.

***Earth Crisis*, 2016** - Six months after the COP21, Fairey returned to Paris for a personal exhibition on the same theme at the Galerie Itinerrance.

Antonino describes himself as belonging to a generation of thinkers, activists, and artists who had channeled their creativity into opposition to the political and social influence of American culture in the 1980s. It's also my history. Besides the interview with me, there are ones with Eve Ensler, Wayne Kramer, Edwidge Danticat, John Sayles, Chuck D., Tom Morello, and Lewis Black. It is a hymn to artistic power and expression," he explains.

"I want to create valuable art, which at the same time is political and can contribute to a better world. I love music, and in particular I'm very much inspired by Bob Dylan's songs, Public Enemy's hip-hop, Bob Marley's reggae, and many others . . . for me, any kind of art which poses questions is important, as I never tire of repeating. Art must question the status quo: it must be sublime and rebellious, beyond the control of the institutions. I think it is fundamental for an artist constantly to reconsider his life, to allow him/herself to be challenged," he continues. But it is a commitment that involves everyone: "Voting is only part of this process. Another part is expressing your point of view, considering how and where to spend your money, thinking what you are buying before you buy it.

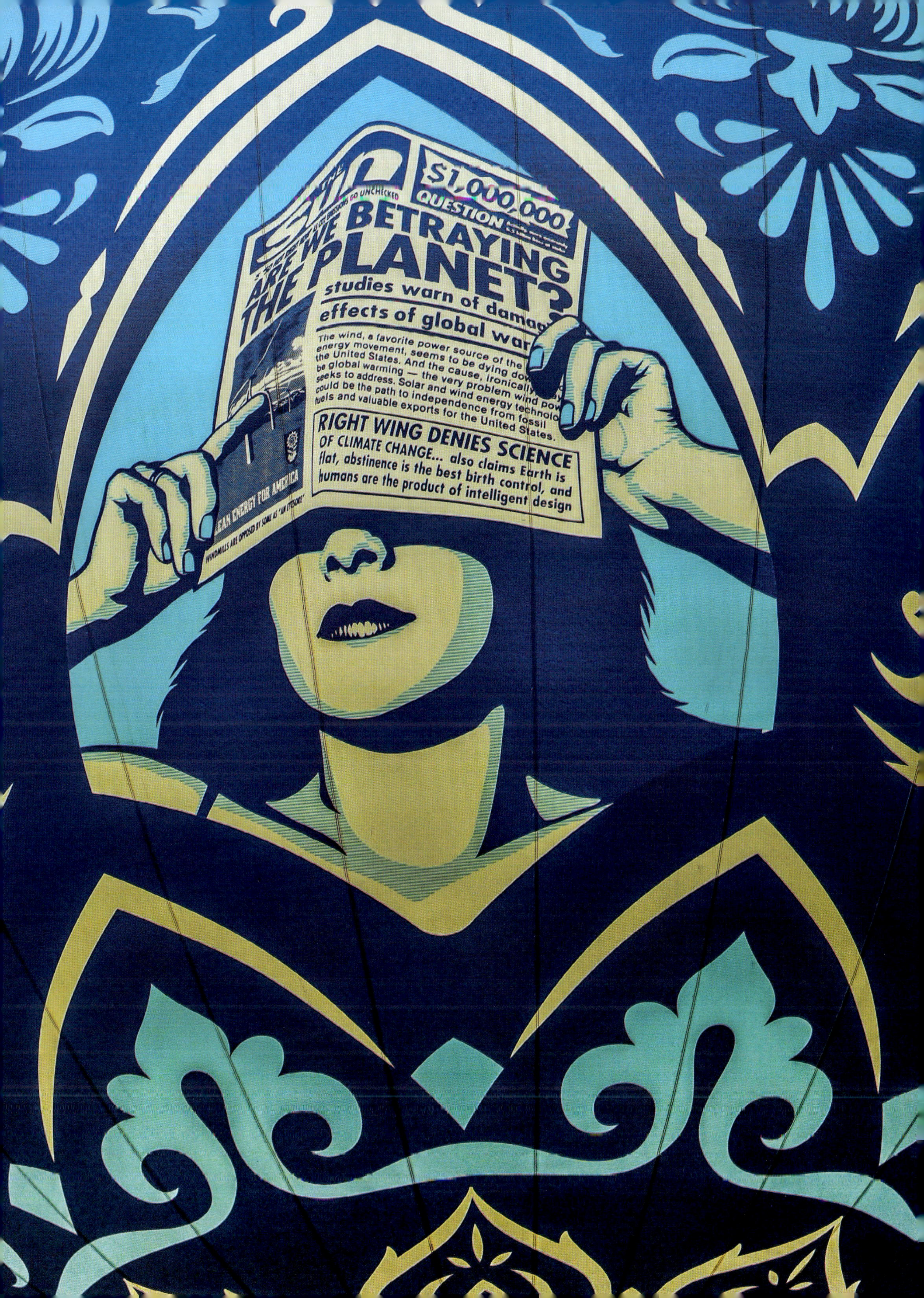
THE SUN
$1,000,000 QUESTION
ARE WE BETRAYING THE PLANET?
studies warn of damage
effects of global war
The wind, a favorite power source of the
energy movement, seems to be dying dow
the United States. And the cause, ironically
be global warming — the very problem wind pow
seeks to address. Solar and wind energy technolo
could be the path to independence from fossil
fuels and valuable exports for the United States.
RIGHT WING DENIES SCIENCE
OF CLIMATE CHANGE... also claims Earth is
flat, abstinence is the best birth control, and
humans are the product of intelligent design
CLEAN ENERGY FOR AMERICA
WINDMILLS ARE OPPOSED BY SOME AS "AN EYESORE"

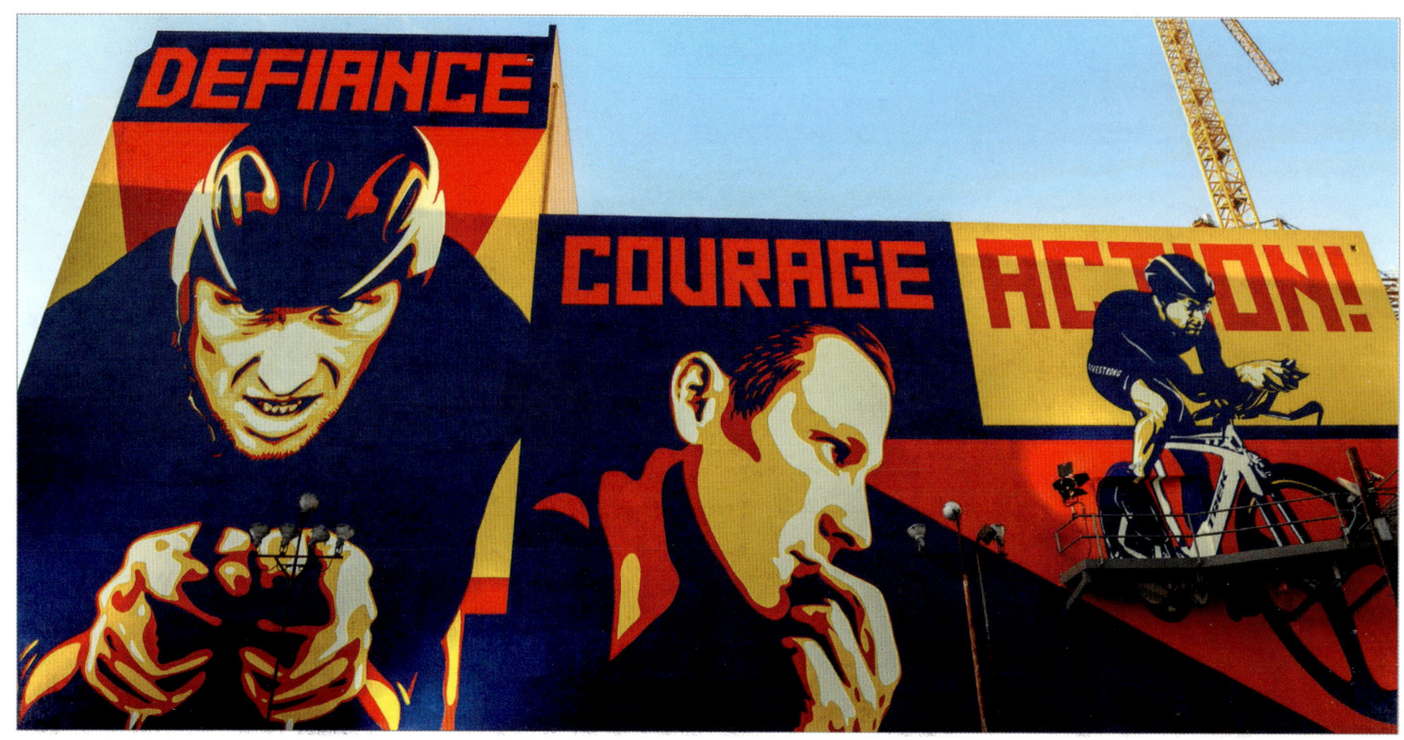

Defiance, Courage, Action, **2009** - In March, 2009 Fairey celebrated with this mural the return to racing of Lance Armstrong (later disqualified for life for doping) on the Montalban Theatre in Hollywood, on the occasion of an event sponsored by Nike.

For my part, I've tried to use my art to highlight or provoke opinions and raise money to support causes," he reflects. "I do it with my art, and I can only say who I am. Anyway, I'm convinced that everyone, in their own way, must play their part".

When he reflects on the future, he cannot but remember his role as Madeline and Vivienne's father. "I've taught them to draw, I try to play and have them listen to good music. And I'm committed to explaining what's happening in the world, the events we're confronted with, to instilling kindness and humanity, compassion, social justice, and the struggle against every type of prejudice. I've always thought children intuitively had an instinct to assimilate things from a very early age," he says, and adds that, since his daughters were born, the protection of the environment has been one of the causes closest to his heart. "I've supported several fundraising campaigns for the problem of climate change, but since I became a father I've become still more concerned, because I want my daughters to be able to live in an eco-sustainable world."

Although he's American, Shepard Fairey has a very particular passion: "I was born in South Carolina, for a time I lived in San Diego, and for a long time I've lived in Los Angeles. My first trip to Italy was when I was fifteen, with my art teacher: I went to Milan and Lake Como; I later executed a big project in Venice, which is a unique city. There is so much beauty in Italy, and as an artist it's simply wonderful to look around, walk in the street, and admire the urban landscape, where I can create, but also simply discuss philosophy and life over a coffee."

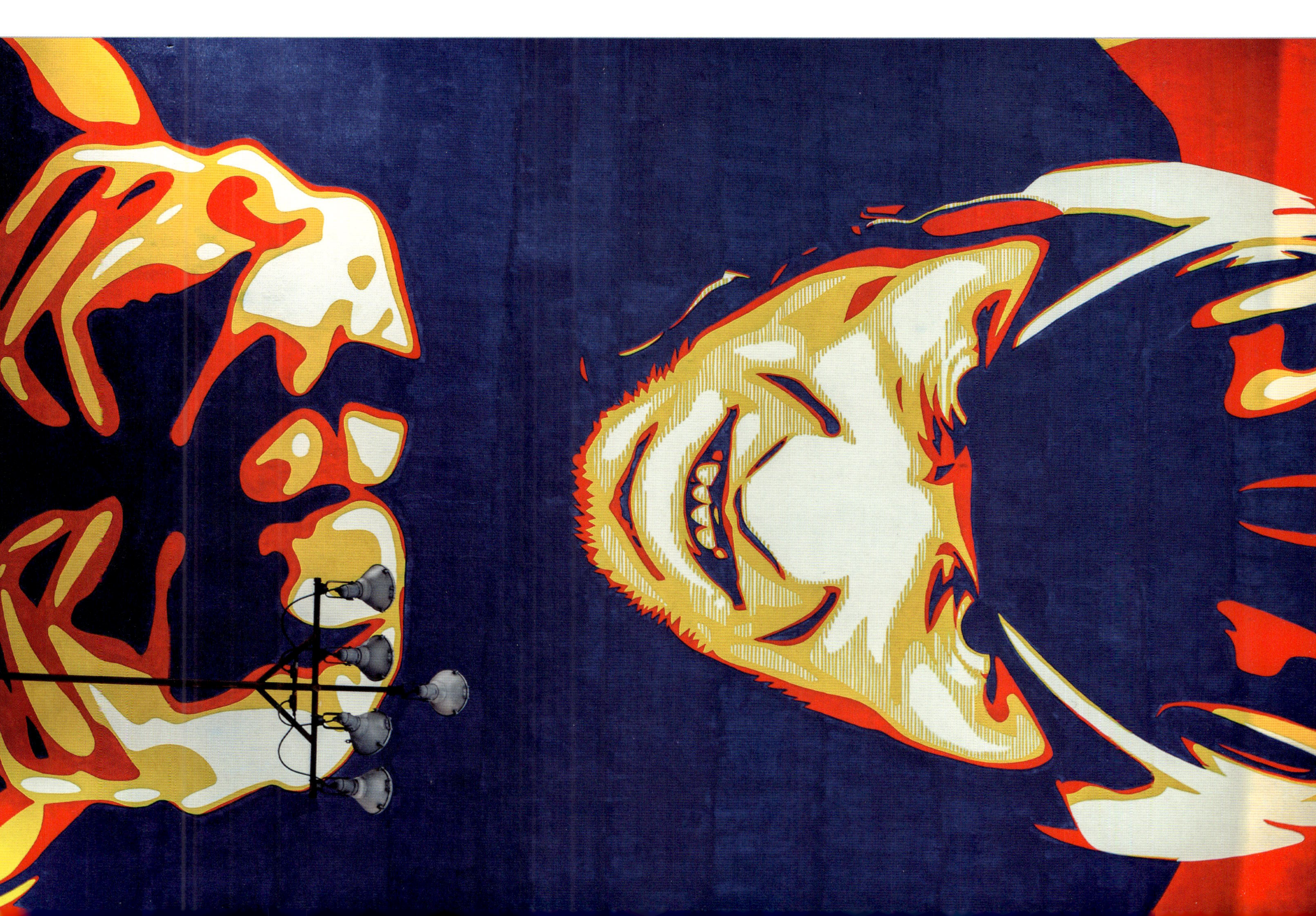

Defiance, Courage, Action. **2009** – Detail from the great work dedicated to Armstrong. Fairey had also decorated the cycle that the champion used in the Giro d'Italia 2009; it was then auctioned for 110,000 dollars.

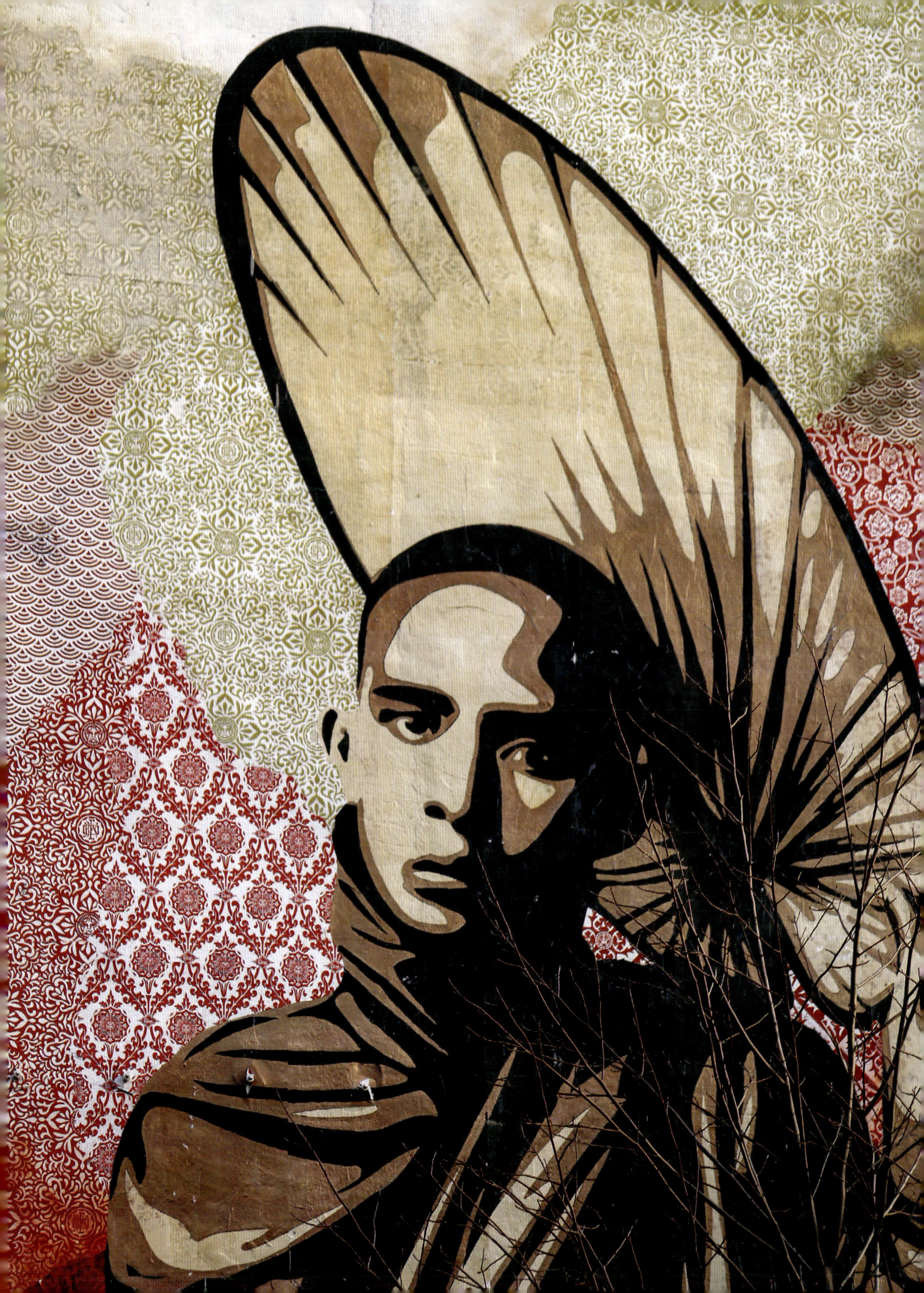

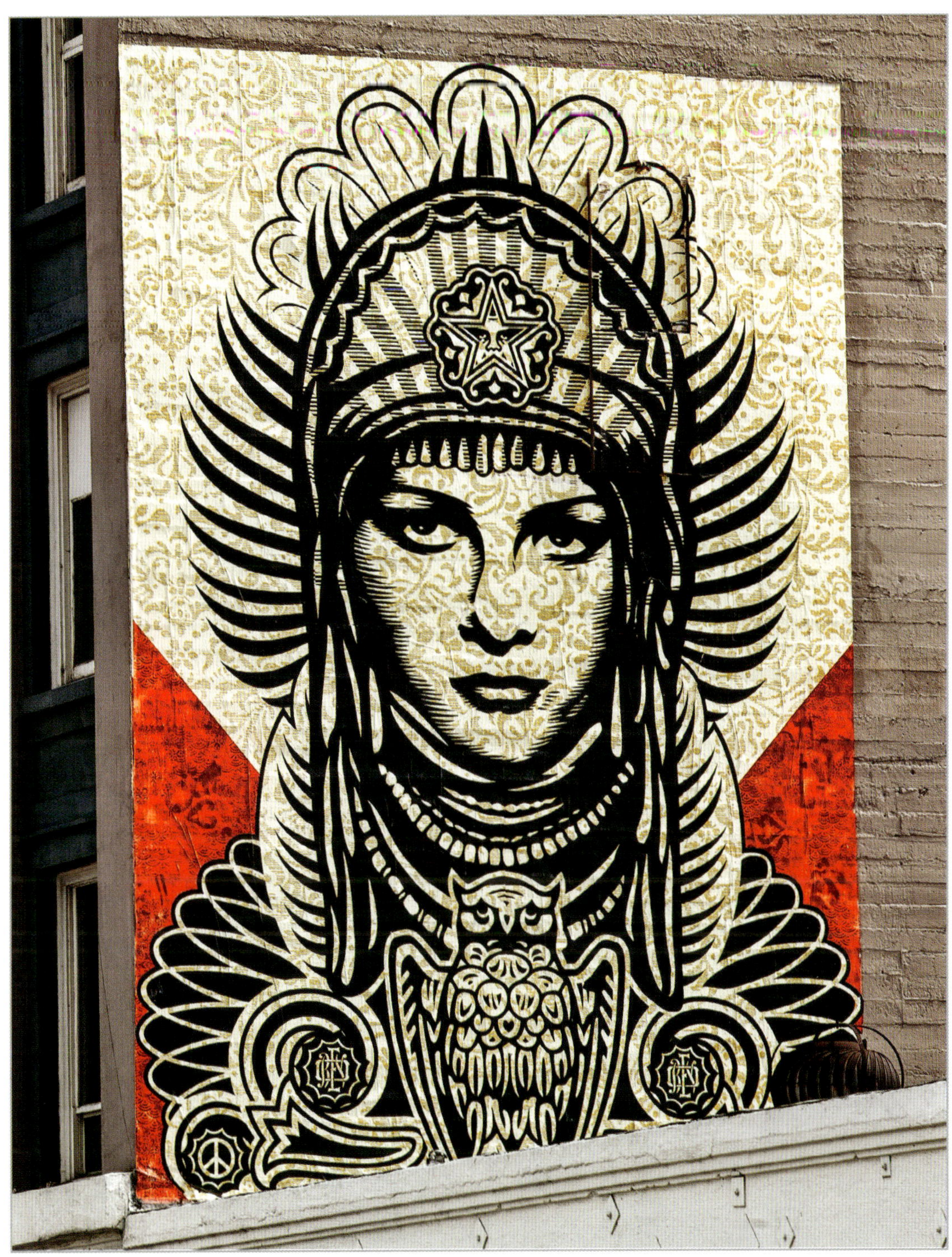

Burmese Buddhist Monk, 2010 - This monk's face is a detail from the mural created by Fairey in Cooper Square, New York, to support the non-violent resistance of the Burmese people.

Peace Goddess, 2009 - A face that is magnetic, fascinating, timeless; this is the interpretation that Fairey gives to the peace goddess, on the Poketo Flagship Store in East 3rd Street in Los Angeles.

FAUXREEL

Evolution Lover

He's become famous for the large photographs he pastes onto walls, but he considers it just a phase: "It is important to change your expressive and aesthetic method. I think art is based on ideas and it is especially effective when you use different materials and techniques, as there is always something new to learn. As an artist I get bored using the same things," Dan Bergeron, in art Fauxreel, from Toronto explains. "I am hugely close to my city. It has changed a lot recently: it has become more international, it hosts a number of globally-important exhibitions such as the Toronto Film Festival and people are starting to realize that Toronto and Canada in general are wonderful places. When doing public art, it is important to establish a strong connection with the surrounding area, with its people and its architecture. Toronto is home to Graffiti Alley, made up of twisting alleyways full of loads of works by local and international street artists, but I enjoy discovering new areas, where nothing has yet been created and which don't tend to draw attention. I want to create something innovative. As well as Toronto, I also love Paris and New York, for their strong energy. I feel especially at home in Paris, it is just so special and magic, it is unique." But Toronto is where everything started: "Yes, this is where I first got into street art. Then in London, where I had some friends, I found some pieces that looked like what I was creating and which interested me. We used different materials and techniques, we were moving away from the traditional graffiti methods. And seeing all of this really opened my eyes."

How he developed his art is very deeply linked to another of his passions: "I think that my love of skateboarding is what got me into open-air art. I started as a kid and discovered the city in a completely different way to move around and interact with your surroundings through different eyes. Skateboarding showed me that you can be anti-conventional, it taught me to have an open mind, to be creative, to use the world around me as a canvas." This is how Fauxreel explains why he feels so close to the urban context and the community in which he grew up.

> Art is simply
> the person that I am,
> it is not a job,
> I need it simply to exist.

In Hazel's Eye, 2015 - For the Toronto 2015 Pan-Am Games Fauxreel and Specter created under a bridge a mural to commemorate Hurricane Hazel (1954).

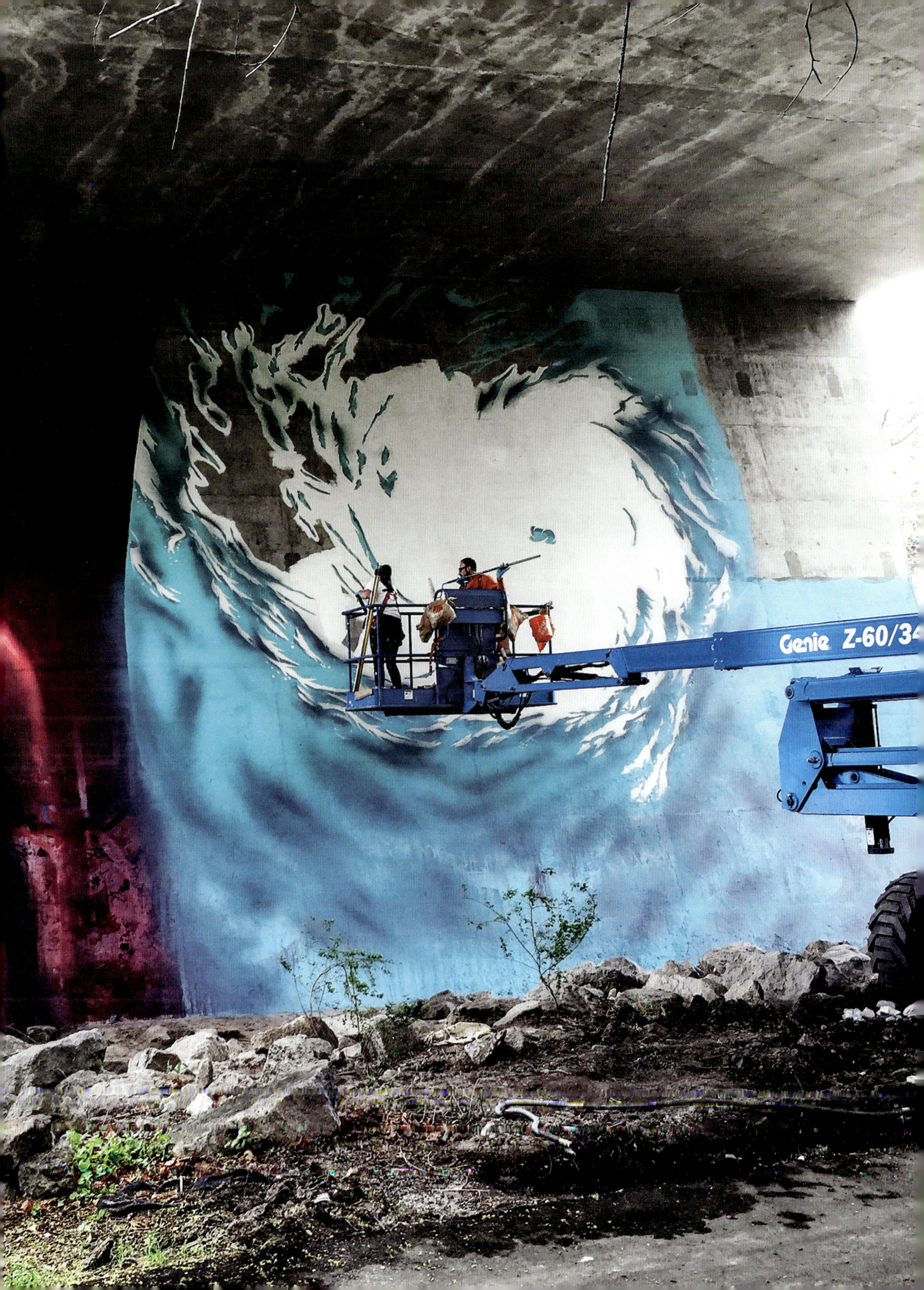

Genie Z-60/34

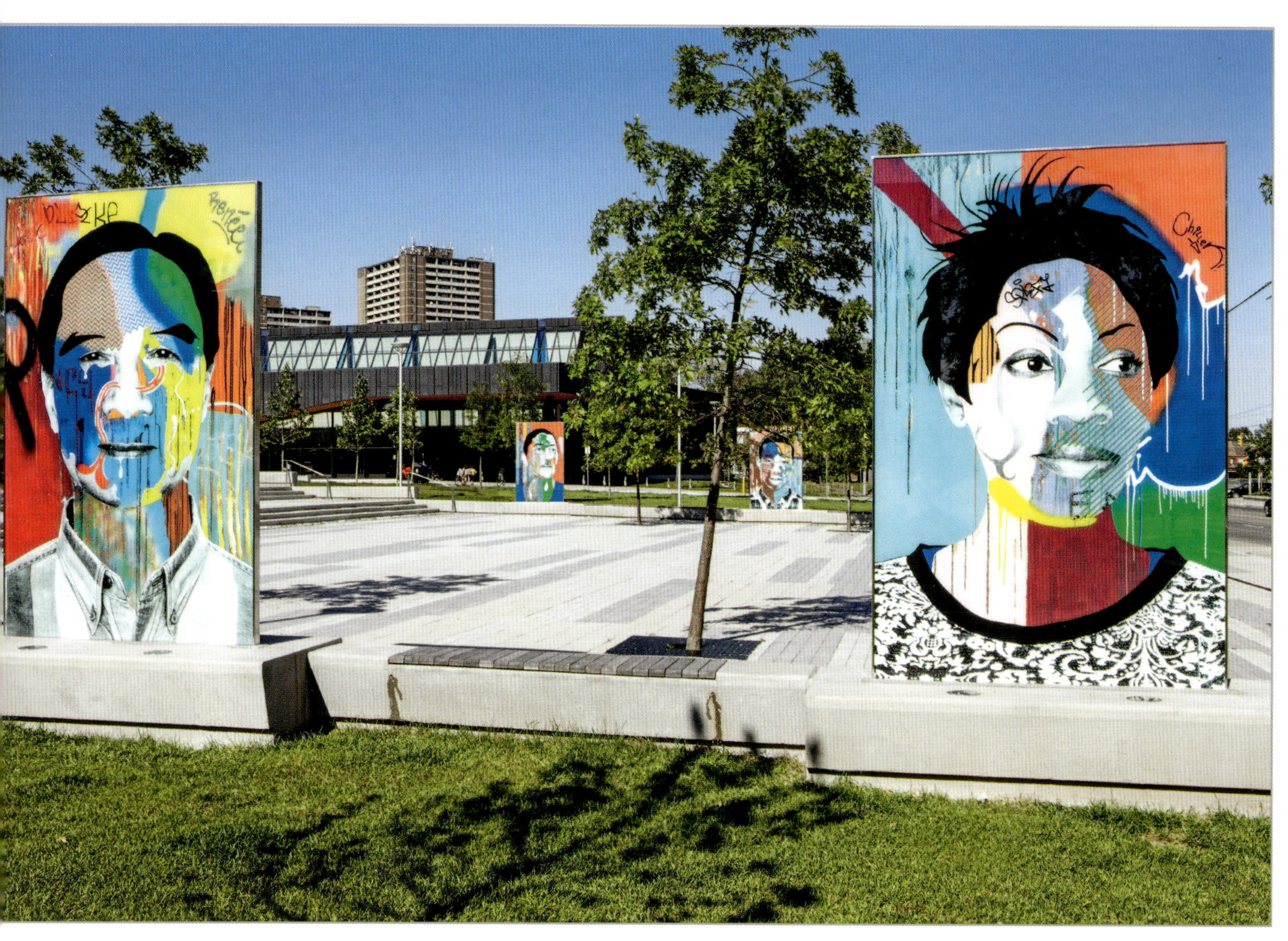

Faces of Regent Park, **2015** – Commissioned by the City of Toronto, the large laminated panels in Regent Park –
which are adapted to the architecture of the context – show the faces of 12 local inhabitants.

"I started when I was about twenty. Some of my friends were graffiti artists and I enjoyed watching them, but I still knew I wanted to do something else. I started by placing large black and white photographs that I developed in the dark room, and experimenting with professional architectural prints. Even the images I photographed were more artistic than classic, they looked more like paintings. In the beginning I only applied them to metal, but then I experimented with other surfaces and I started using a sort of glue that I made myself out of flour and water which gave me greater range."

Fauxreel studied Film and Sonic Design in Carleton University in Ottawa, but he considers himself self-taught as his interest in photography started after he had finished studying. "In the beginning, I just thought it was the best way to get my work noticed in the city. My first piece of street art dates back to 2002, photos I'd taken in London, of architecture but still artistic. In time, I started really thinking about what I was doing, the reason why I was so dedicated to a particular subject, what the message behind it was supposed to be. And I realized I was particularly interested in portraits, in people: being human I analyzed myself and others, I wanted to hear their stories."

He started accepting commissions and in the meantime dedicated himself to his projects, be-

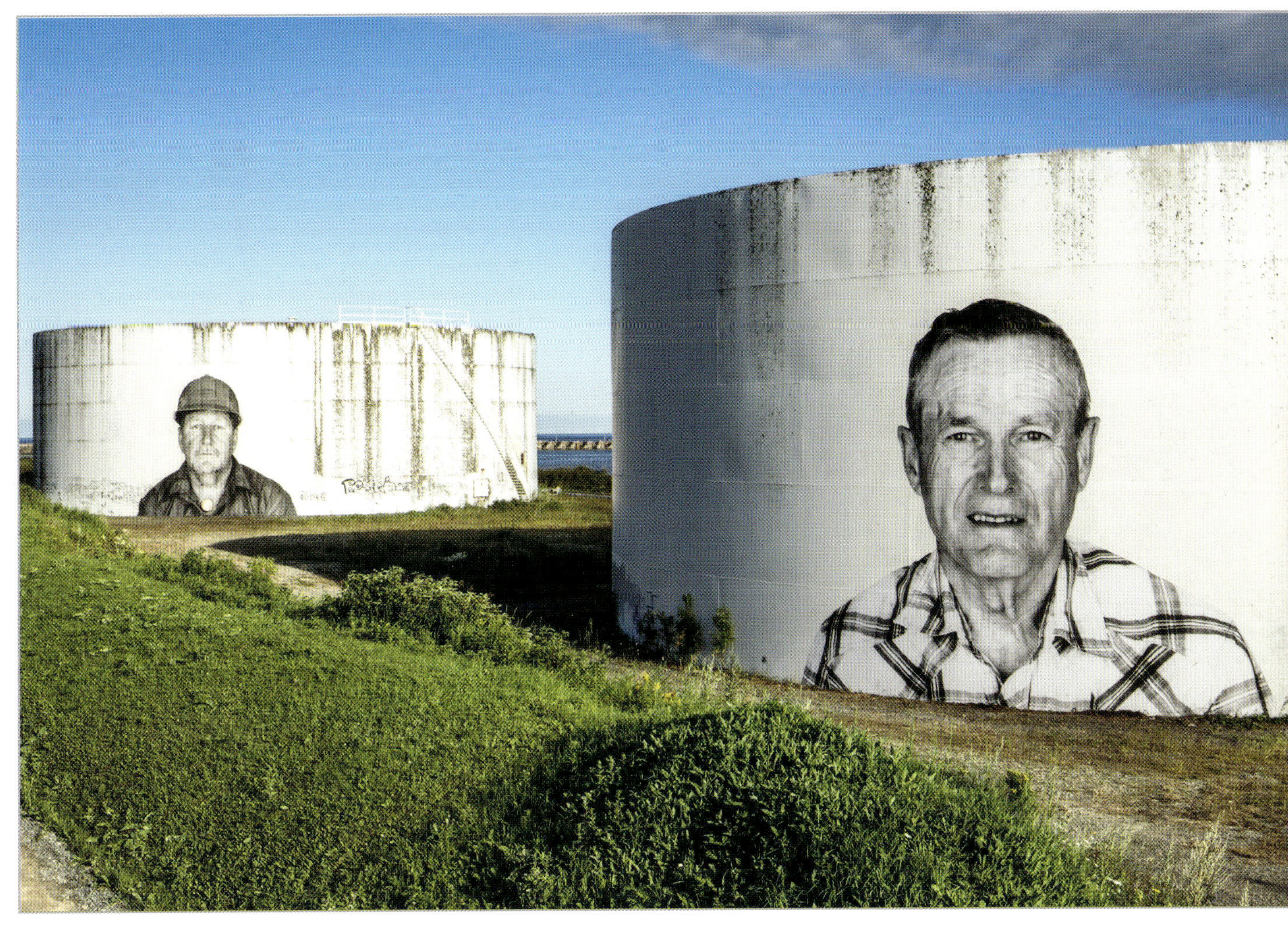

Gaspesia: Les portraits en papier, 2011 - These two portraits are part of an imposing photographic project in solidarity with the workers of the Gaspesia paper mills (Chandler, Quebec), all of whom were laid off when production was moved to Vietnam.

coming increasingly interested in public art and furthering his own vision. "I was fascinated by those people who are rarely represented. Advertising is king and, especially in North America, is dominated by white faces. I wanted to explore the more unusual characters, those whose faces had hidden meanings, who would get others interested in who they were. At the same time, working on advertising billboards further changed my methods: I started creating street art that would make passersby wonder if it was advertising or not. I basically wanted to play with people's perceptions, push limits, go over the top." This is even how the *Vespa Squareheads* project was born, with four guys whose heads have

been replaced by handles of the Vespa S, a revival of the 50 Special launched by Piaggio and interpreted by the artist in a decidedly original way.

His work is aimed at the community, as well as setting new challenges. Like the *Unaddressed* project, dedicated to the homeless. "I am not sure that there is always a political message in what I do, but there is certainly a reflection on what is going on, something extremely contemporary. The project I did with some homeless people who I photographed and shared in various districts of the city was a way to give them a voice, through written phrases that represented what they thought: I wanted people to share their experiences.

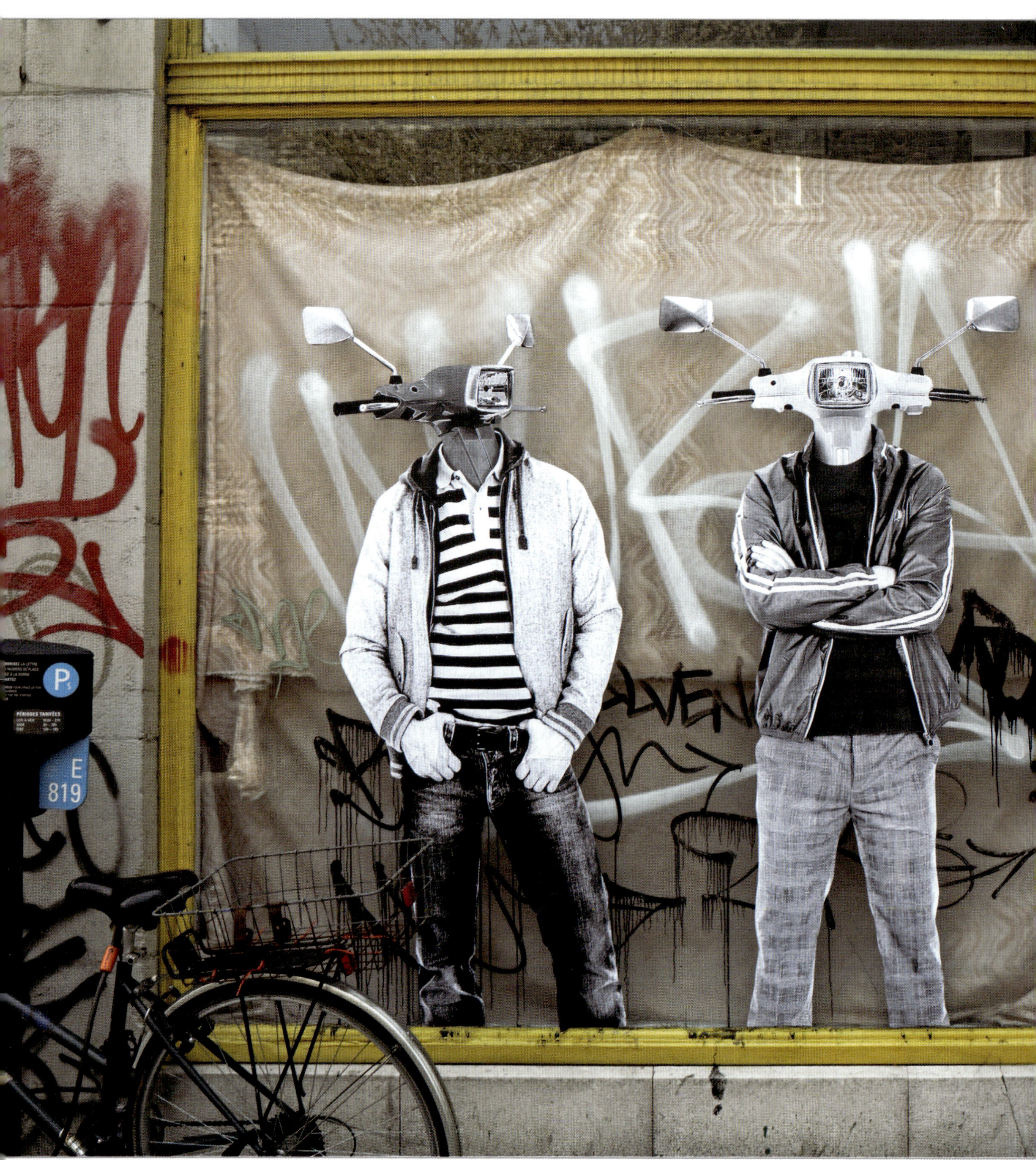
P
PÉRIODES TARIFÉES
E
819

I hoped that people would therefore understand, feel empathy, want to help them. I wanted to make a difference, however small, hoping that it would have a ripple effect throughout the world."

Another important experience was in Quebec for *Gaspesia: Les portraits en papier.* "These enormous portraits are of men who used to live in a paper mill that was closed, leaving the town devastated and with a huge unemployment rate. I placed these gigantic images on the buildings of the abandoned paper mill and all around the city. People came to me and were so moved they were crying and thanking me for having immortalized them. It was a very important project for that community, which, despite its despair for the closing of the factory (which reopened in Vietnam), felt at least that years of work weren't simply forgotten. Subsequently this piece triggered a number of interpretative routes, such as the problem of globalization and of toxic chemical pollution as in Chandler they carried out controls on the chemical materials used, while in Vietnam they don't. And beyond this, there is the fact that people living in remote areas had never before seen this kind of art."

One in Four was another project that had great impact: "In Toronto, loads of black youths are stopped by police officers questioning them who they are, what they're doing. This is illegal in our country and yet the percentage of black men stopped is phenomenal. So we are basically dealing with a racial problem here. This is why I wanted to bring together the faces and stories of people who have been stopped and exhibit them on the streets of the places where they had been questioned."

Fauxreel seems to favor large-scale works. He is quick to stress, "You can paint a huge canvas in a studio, but when it is hanging on the wall of a large building it will seem tiny in comparison.

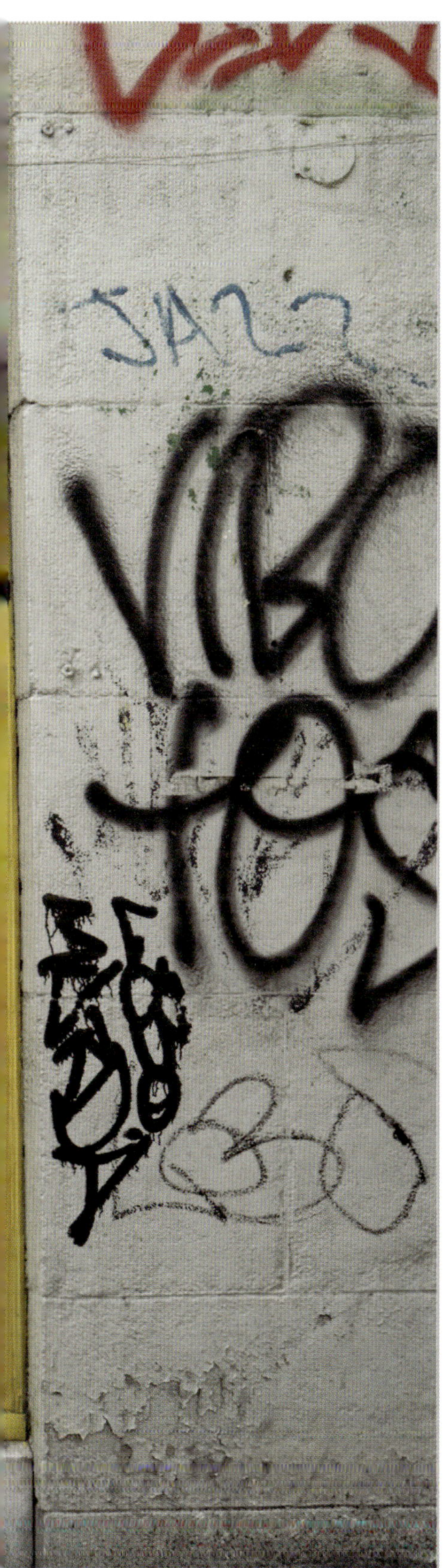

Vespa Squareheads, 2008
Hybrid characters between youngsters and handles in Montréal, Canada. Fauxreel chooses the Vespa Piaggio to reflect the relationship between street, street art and advertising.

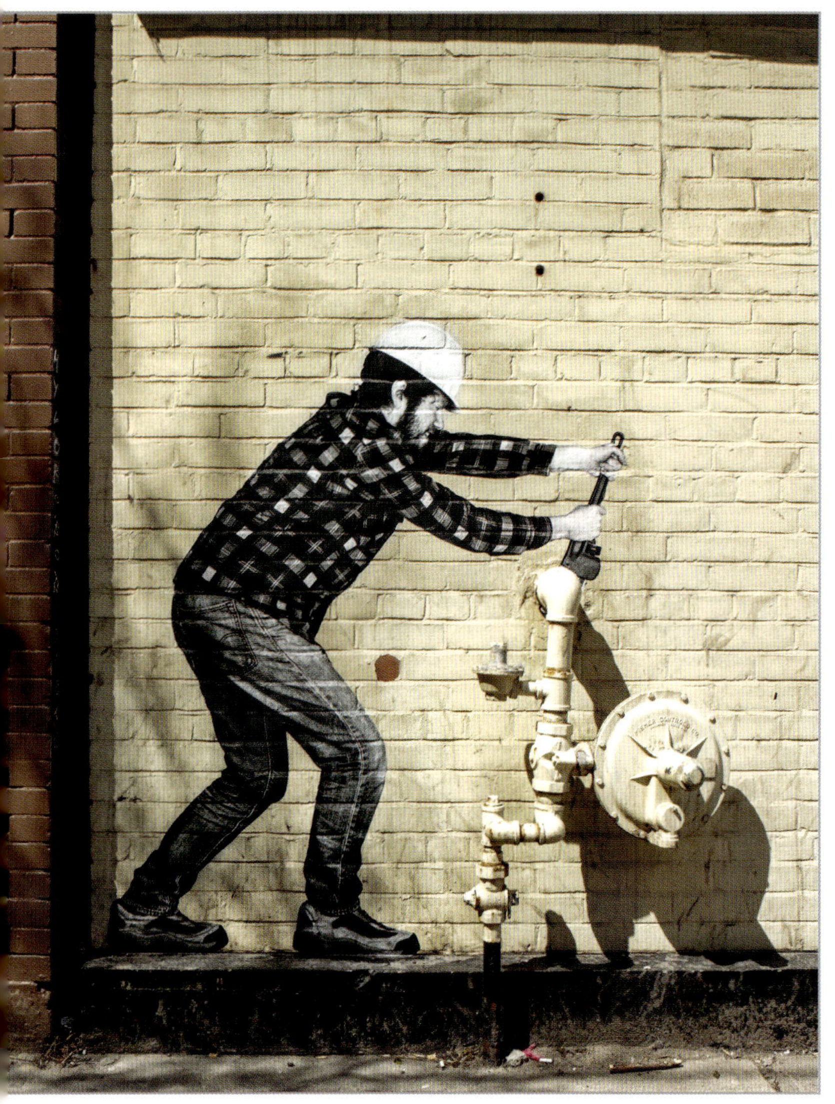

Men At Work -
The Pipe Wrencher, 2010
The *Wall Impressions* project shows everyday people in everyday activities, such as this factory worker depicted in Toronto.

Men At Work -
The Measurer, 2008
Another piece, this time in Vancouver, from the huge *Wall Impressions* project, expressing solidarity with factory workers and jobless.

This is why the size of the pieces has to suit the surrounding area: they often have to be huge to be visible within the context."

He has recently moved towards colors and abstract paintings. "My photographs have always been in color, even though architecture printers printed them in black and white. In the beginning I adapted myself to this, but I enjoy working with color. Abstract art serves as a break from my social work which is extremely intense. I need to alternate to distance myself. The 'abstract world' allows me more freedom in the rhythm and form of the lines and colors; I blend a range of styles. As I said, change is vital for me otherwise I feel pigeonholed, like in a commercial production, and I'm afraid then that people would only commission me for a certain type of piece. But for the moment I receive commissions based on my ideas: they give me the chance to develop and I see this as a challenge, even if it can sometimes be exhausting.

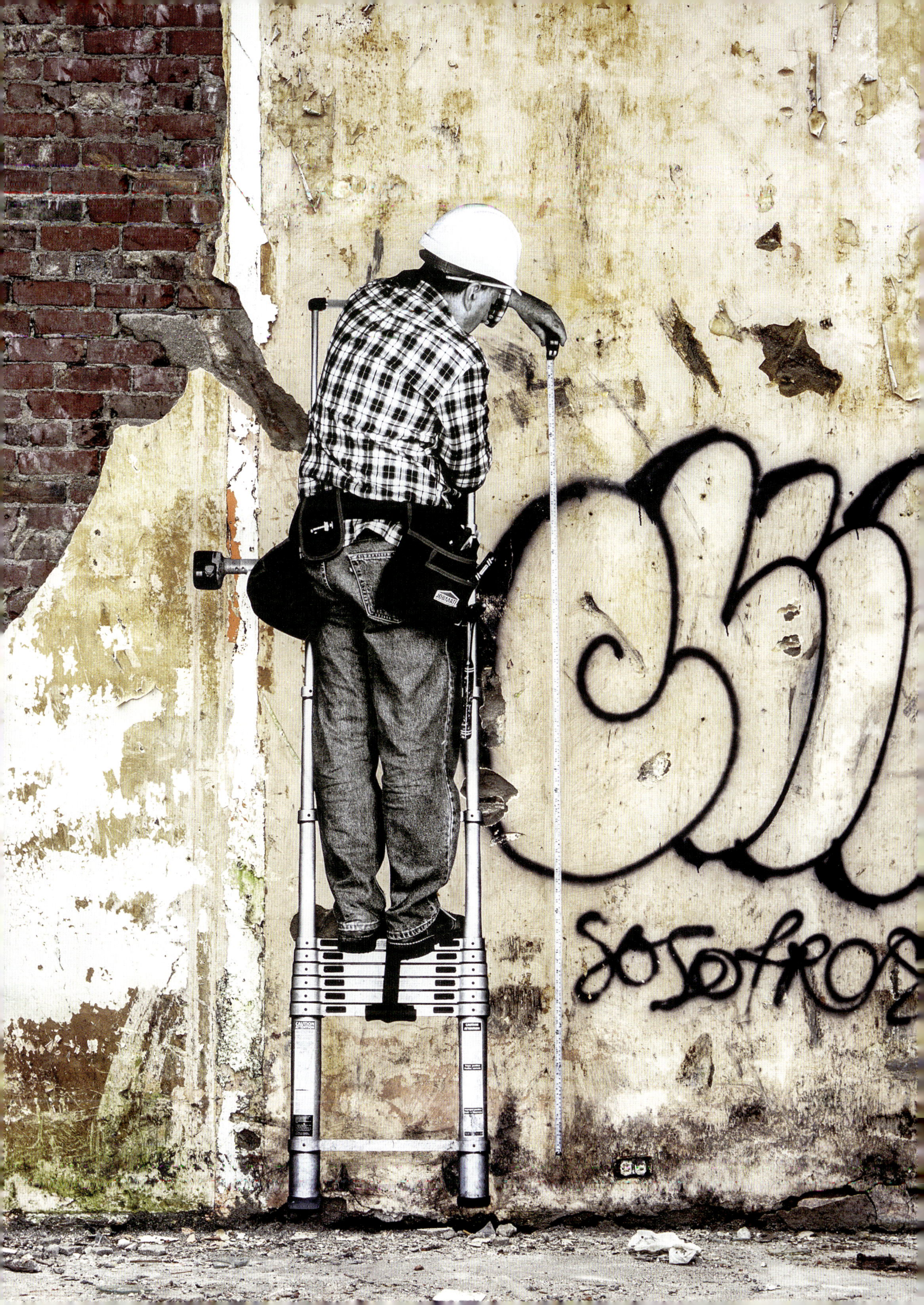

SOSOFROS

No one knows this better than my wife, and the mom of my two kids, who used to work in the Art Gallery of Ontario. She helps me find the right direction for all the ideas I get," he admits.

His hope for the future is better solidarity. "I hope that one day we will understand each other, or that we will at least try, in the name of equality. It is important that people work hard, but following their own vocation, that everyone can do what they love, that we all have opportunities, and that we are all willing to help others with compassion. I don't want my art to 'hit like hammer blows', but I do aim to trigger small differences that in turn may inspire other larger ones." And he is quick to clarify that he is not looking for celebrity: "I don't want my career to simply shoot to the stars; I would prefer it more like walk up the mountains, when you maybe descend to the valleys for a while or stop to look at the landscape. I know I want to live a long life and I feel my career is just starting out, I'm not looking to retire but hope to continue with my projects until I'm seventy-five or even older. Some artists achieved fame at really young ages and now have disappeared from the scenes. For me, art is simply the person that I am, it is not a job, I need it simply to exist."

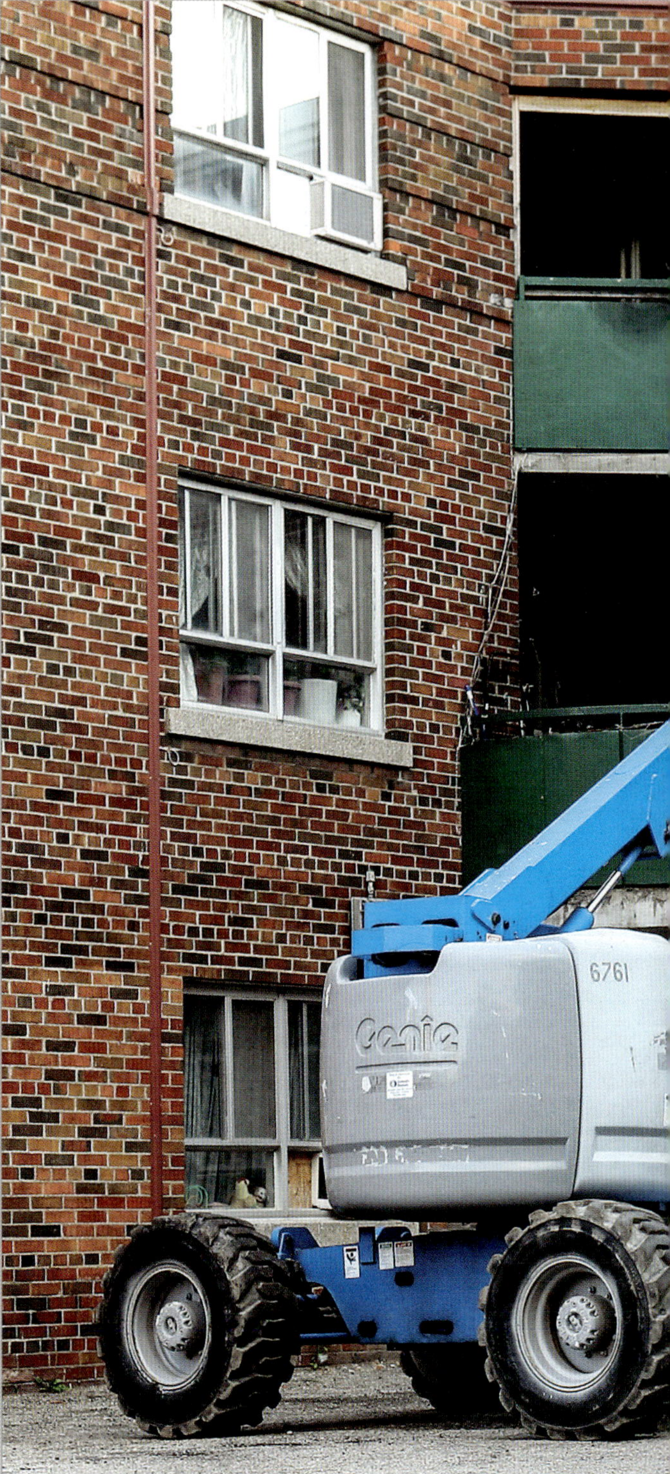

Regent Park Portraits, 2008
Little Inez can admire her own gigantic photo in black and white on the walls, as can other inhabitants of Regent Park, Toronto.

Face of the City, 2010
The familiarity of the human face, like that of Joe in Paris, is adapted by Fauxreel to the layered surfaces of the buildings, full of tags, graffiti and posters.

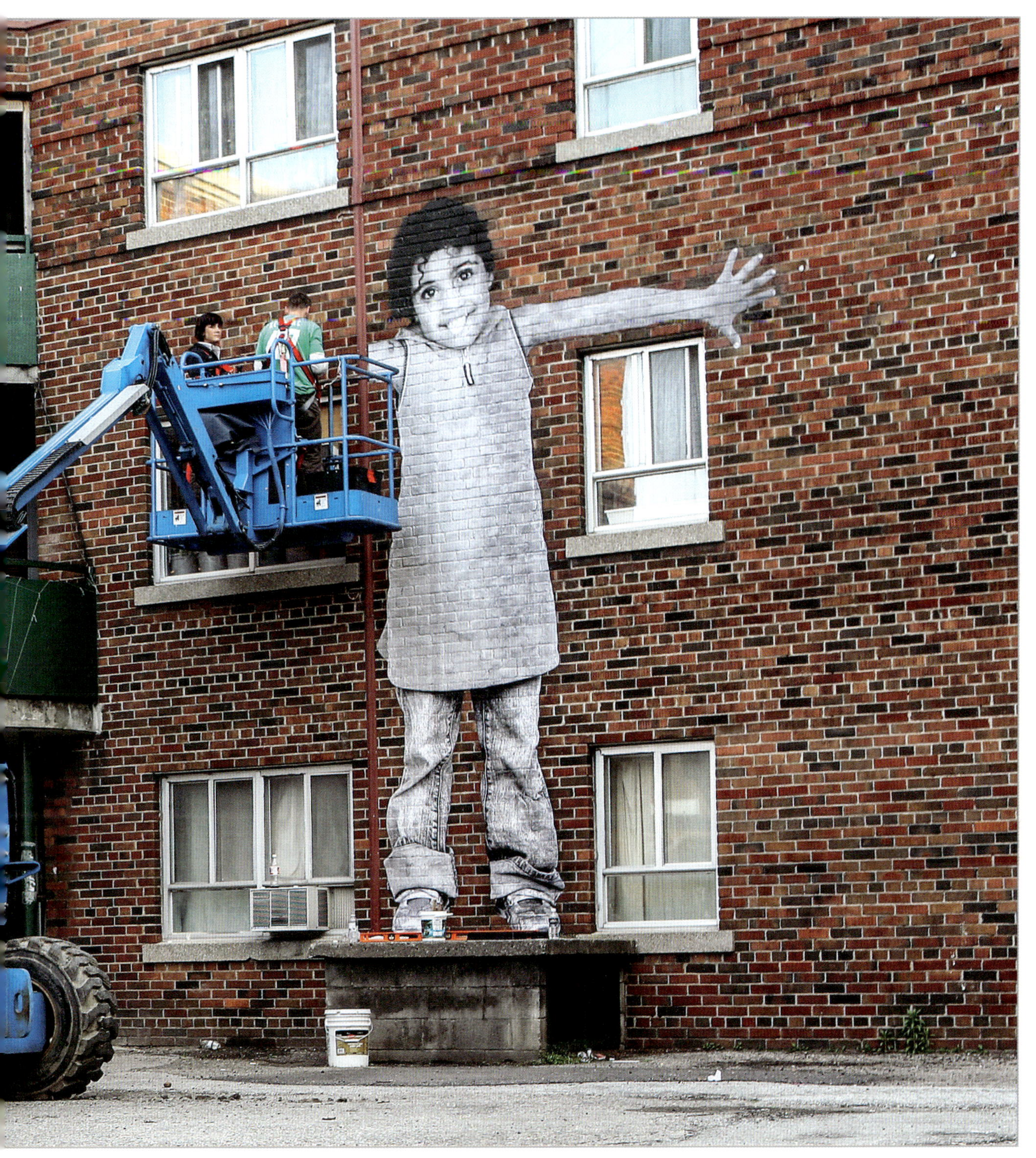

"You can paint a huge canvas in a studio,
but when it is hanging on the wall of a large building
it will seem tiny in comparison."

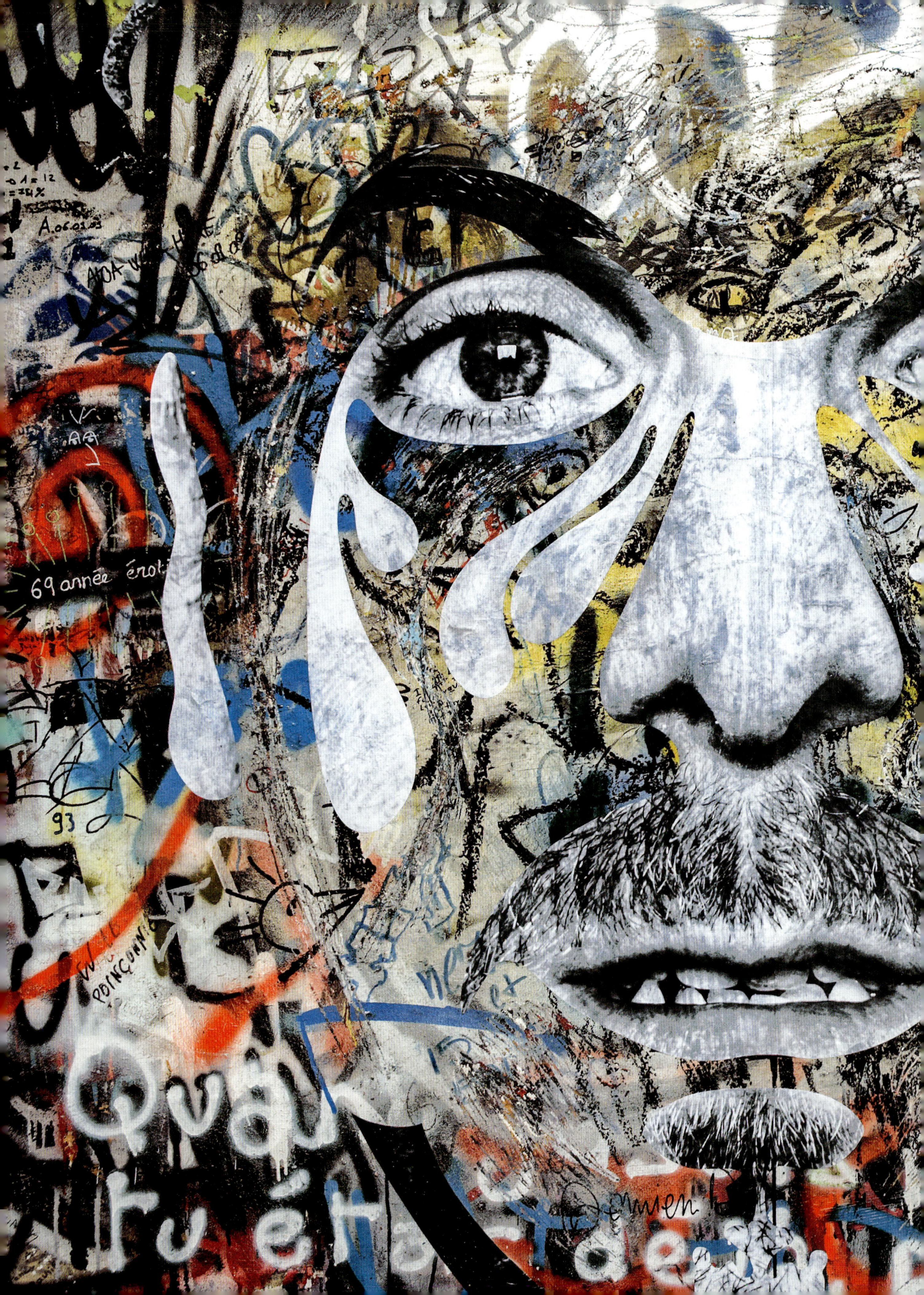

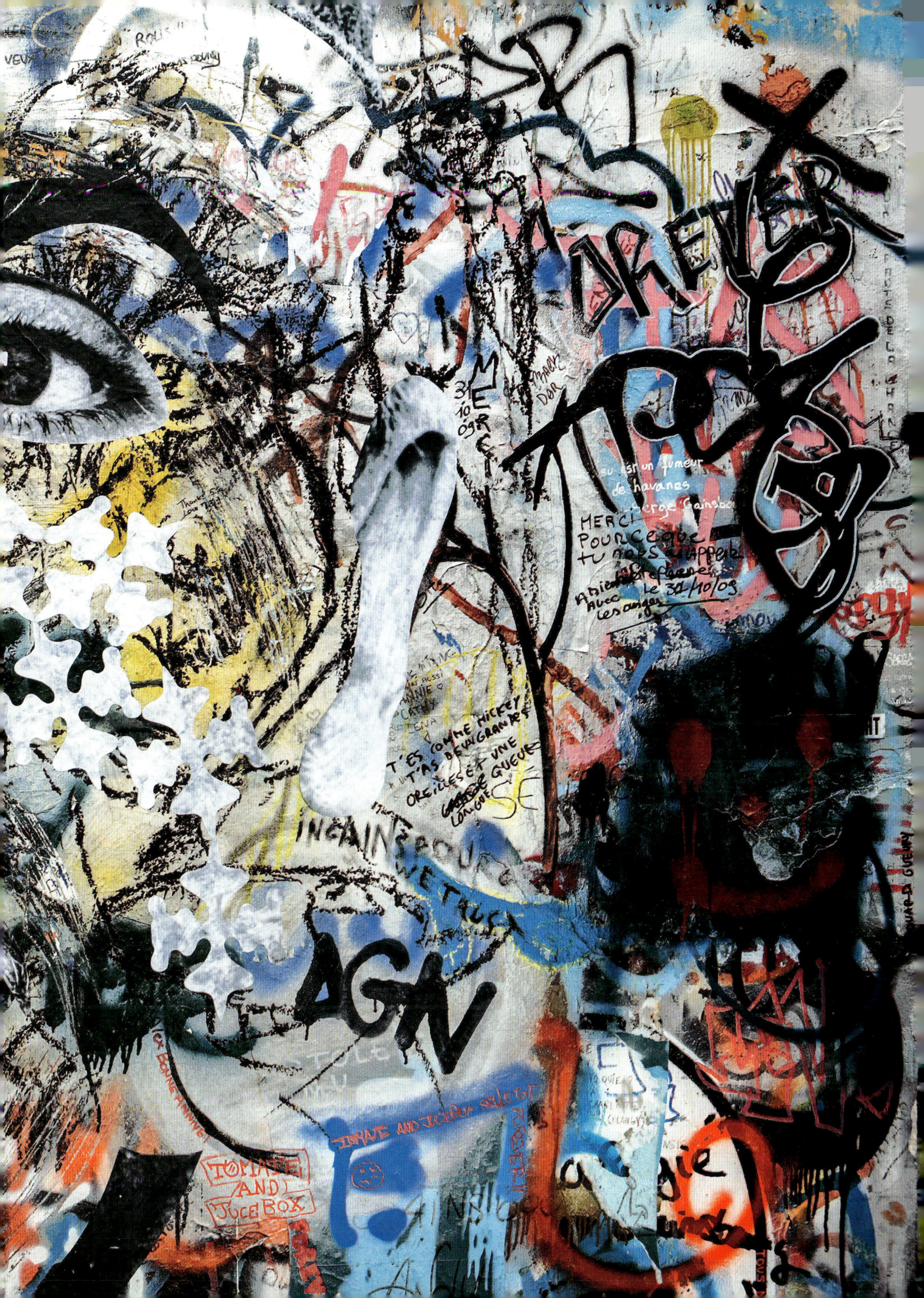

INTERESNI KAZKI, AEC
Mythological Dreamer

His graffiti exude a strength of color and a magic of images similar to those of mythology. They are composed of fantastical, adventurous creatures, sometimes dense with exoticism, sometimes more playful and carefree, in a mixture of humans and animals which lead to universes of stories and adventures, in magnificent dream-journeys, profound spiritual connections. By means of his words, these images acquire still more meanings and impressions, emotions and memories, and symbols. For example, he advises us to look at his creations from different perspectives, as when one peeks into a phantasmagoric kaleidoscope, which is able to change images in a moment with every single movement, and to make a deep impression, which can mark the soul.

"Art should be selfless," states AEC from Kiev, in his native Ukraine. His words immediately tell us how his temperament is full of passion and generosity, of authenticity and directness, just like his works.

Interesni Kazki (IK) is the name that identified the duo comprising the Ukrainians Aleksei Bordusov and Vladimir Manzhos, who used the names of AEC and WAONE. They began to work together in 1999, becoming the pioneers of the graffiti movement in Eastern Europe and taking their art to the whole world, besides Ukraine and Russia: Mexico, Croatia, Spain, Portugal, India, South Africa, and the United States.

It has been said of them that they have been inspired by themes like religion, science, history, cosmology, and also social and cultural elements. However, the artists themselves have stated that they prefer those who look at their art to be absolutely free to decipher it, rather than relying on predetermined interpretations or the judgments of art critics or other experts.

Since they became famous, they have increasingly begun to work separately, to the point of breaking up their historic partnership.

AEC is considered the more surrealist of the two. Besides relating their adventure, he reveals the universe that led him to become a star in street art. He promises to continue alone on the existentialist path, with bright, vibrant colors, but also to use black and white.

> The creative process is a mystical path for me, connected with self-improvement.

AEC looks at just completed work in the suburbs of Cancún, Mexico. The painting pays homage to the great tradition of Mexican murals and celebrates the importance of education and culture.

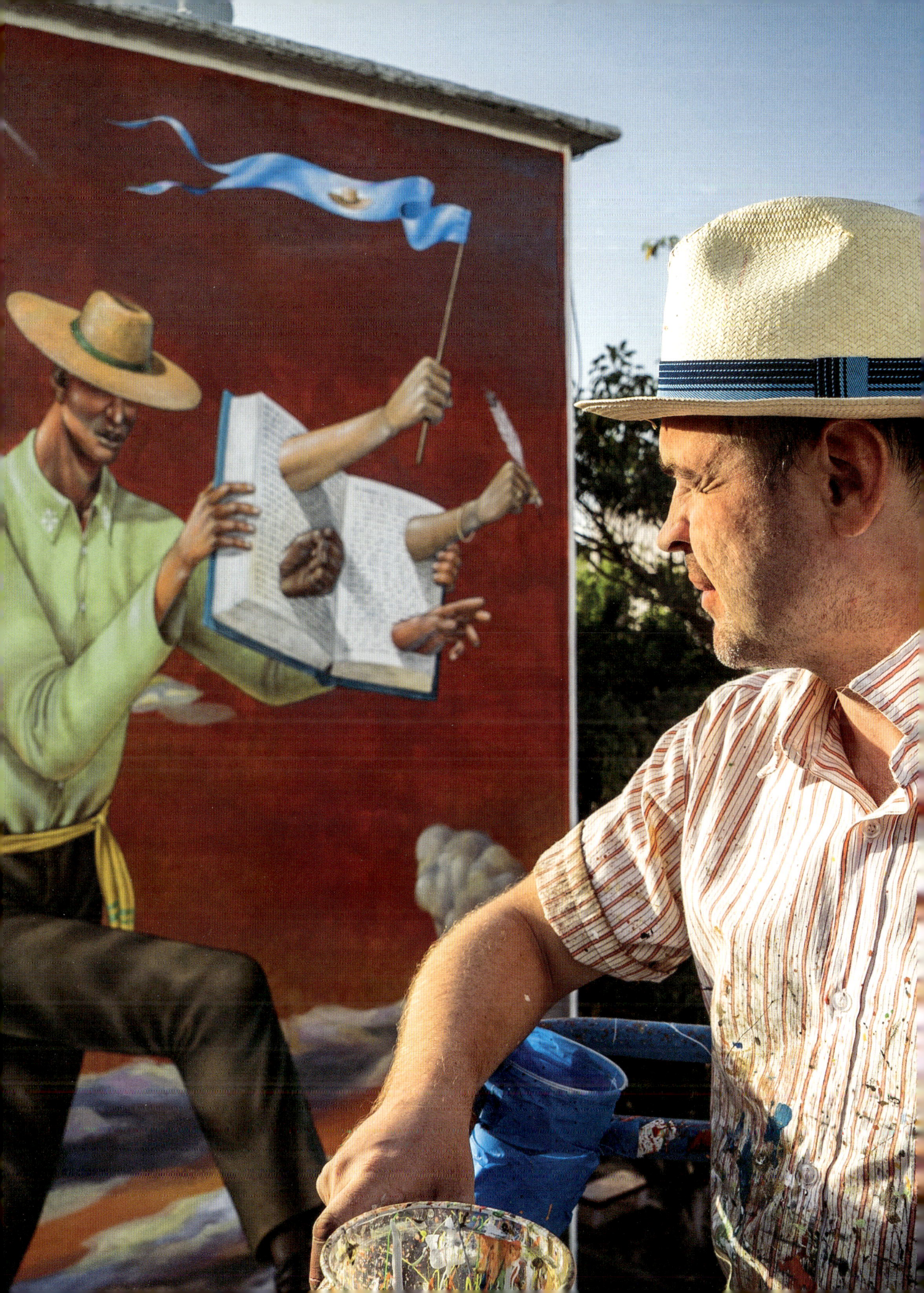

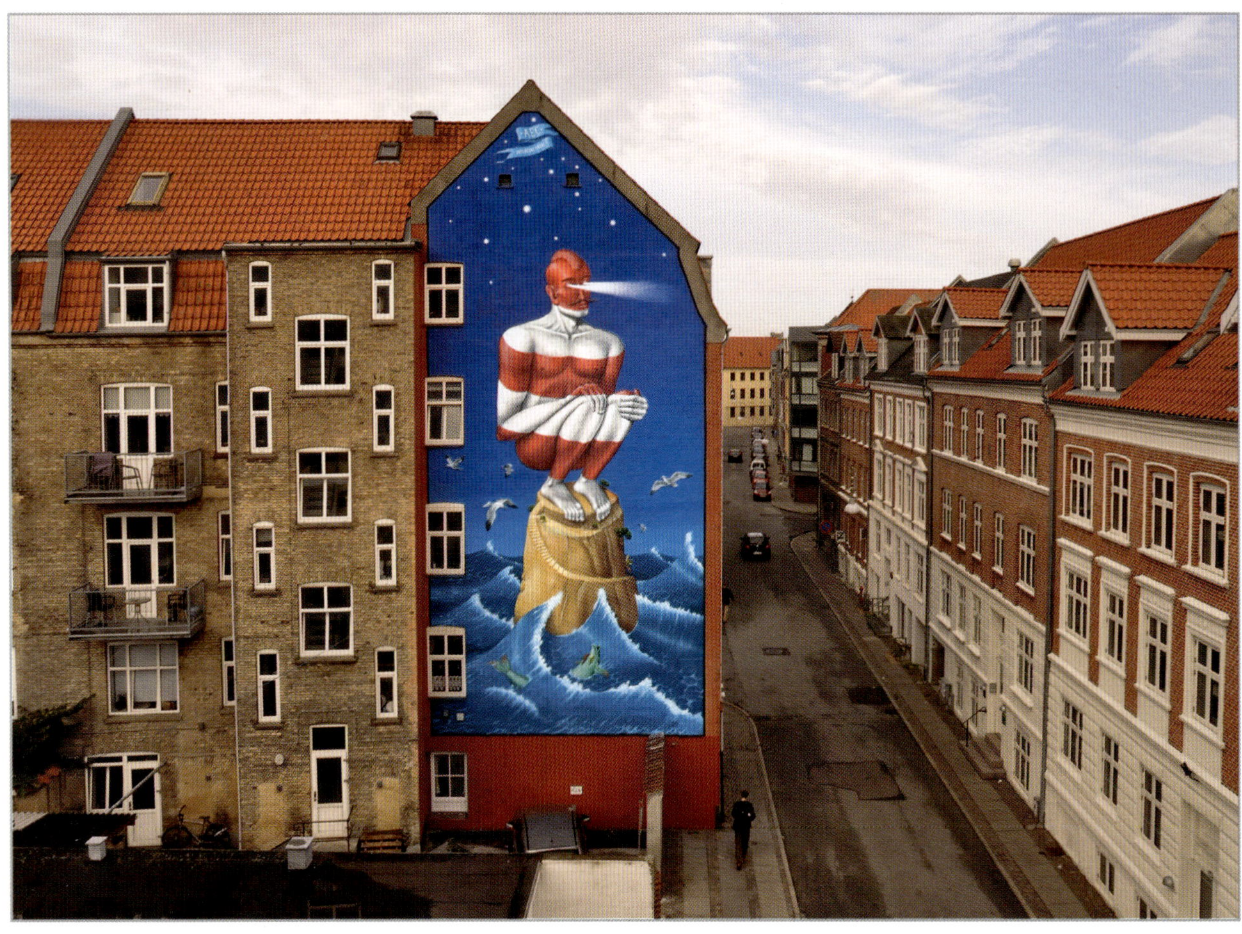

The Lighthouse, **2014** - In September, 2014 AEC takes part in the *WE AArt Project*, an initiative organized at Aalborg, Denmark. His mural on a façade in Holbergsgade, the former harbor area, shows a lighthouse-man with a red and white body and eyes emitting rays of light. Prints with the same subject have been offered for sale to support the foundation PangeaSeed, which has chosen art to convey its message of defense of the sea.

WAONE has announced that he will continue to explore and develop monochromatic painting, as he has already done in one of his latest murals, *Matter: Changing States*. At the moment, however, he has decided not to release further comments.

On the other hand, it is AEC who relates their adventure together and his present journey alone. "My mother told me that I started to draw at four years old, and I haven't been able to stop since then. I started with traditional graffiti-writing on the streets in the late 1990s. I was a member of a big graffiti crew, in which we communicated and painted together. Also that time I met Vladimir (WAONE) and we started to paint together, developing our own direction in painting – inventing more characters and ceasing to create letters and words . . ." he explains.

Then, around 2005, I invented a new name – *Interesni Kazki*, which in Ukrainian means "interesting stories" or "interesting fairy tales." This name united us both as a duo for ten years. What I am doing now is a kind of 'neo-muralism,' I guess, a completely different movement to traditional graffiti, from which we started. Although we were a duo, I always worked more on solo pieces, especially in the last two-three years.

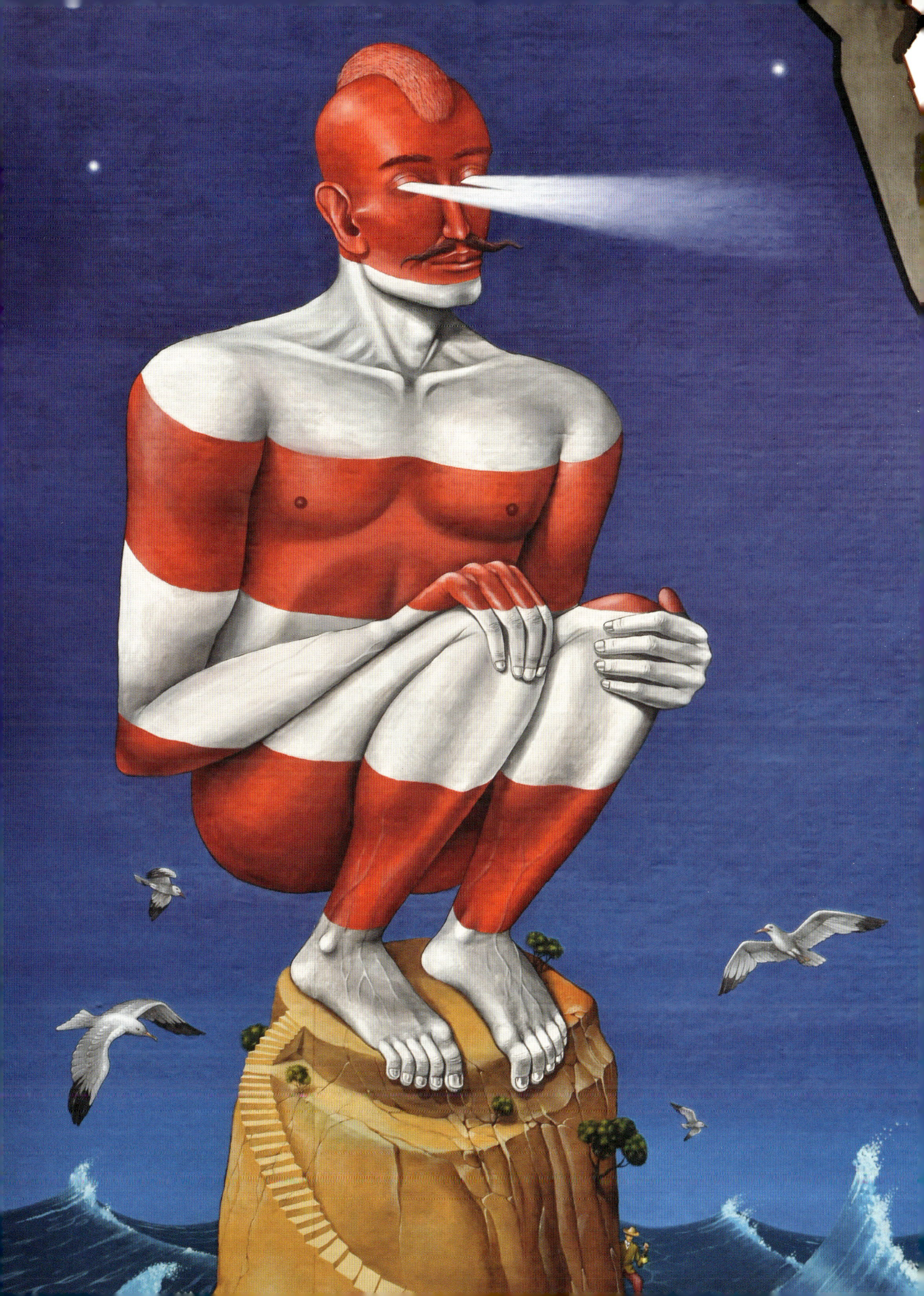

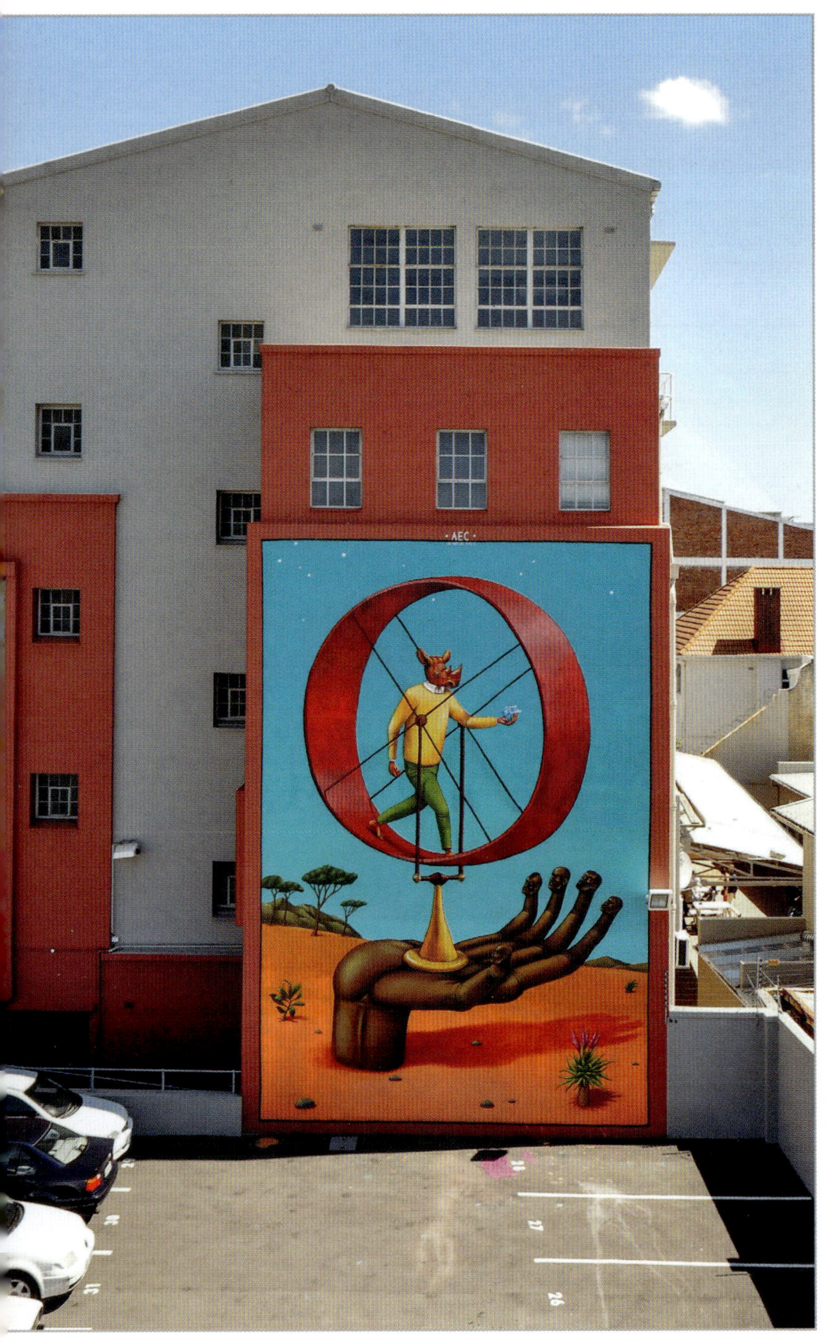

Treasure of Africa, 2013
Part man and part rhinoceros, the protagonist of this mural, created during an artist-in-residence program in Cape Town, South Africa, seems to be chasing the great diamond he is holding in his right hand. It seems sure to lead him nowhere, since the figure is inside a wheel. Everything is supported – and watched – by a great hand that evokes the idea of a suffering, plundered Africa.

Finally, we decided to take different paths and not work together any more.

On their separation, he adds, "The decision was made at the beginning of 2016," and at the same time he shows some images of his most recent works, immortalized with the camera. His characters can be various, unexpected, surprising. In one work a colored woman triumphs, half leopard and half human, emerging from the jungle holding a stone head in her hand. In another, we see a man in a zebra costume taking off his mask to show his human face. In a third work, we see a fascinating female creature with the face of a flower riding a mythological horse with the head of a being similar to a divinity.

His enthusiasm is the same as when he began, and now that AEC is a successful artist he is even more open to experimentation.

"The first time was 1998, and I was very excited by this kind of crime art. At that time, I was studying architecture at university and graffiti was something new and fresh, a protest against everything I had seen and knew about art," he confesses, smiling.

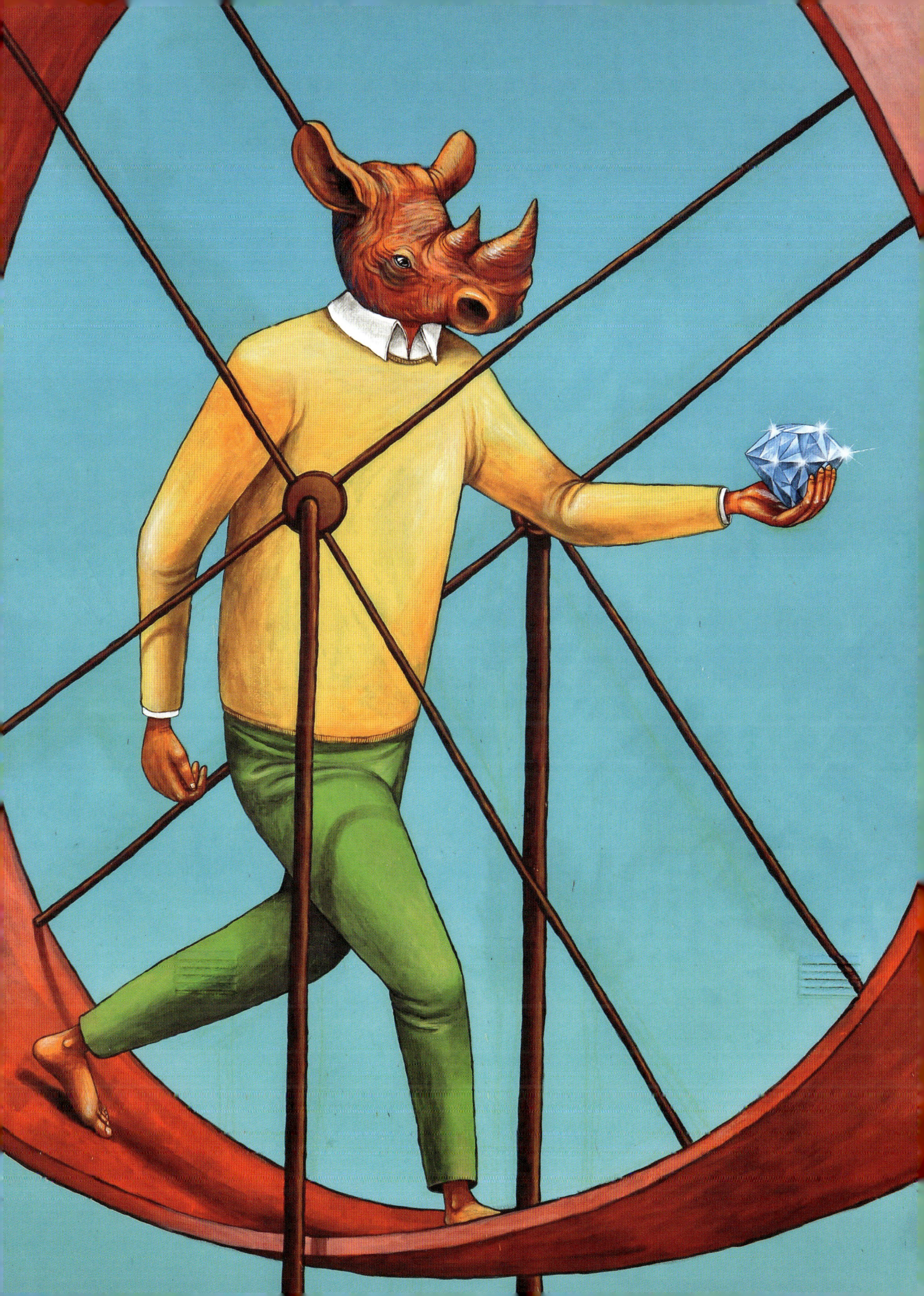

His technique played a fundamental role. "At the beginning, I used spray paints – the traditional tool of graffiti artists. Around 2012, I visited Mexico, where I discovered for myself the tradition of Mexican muralism, which flipped my understanding of painting on the wall . . . I saw works by Siqueiros, Riveira, Orozko, Makarena, and many others. I saw different concepts, technique, scales: everything was very impressive. The most important thing for me was content and technique – social topics and a kind of folk, magic realism. As regards technique, they used brushes and acrylic, water paints. Since that time I have started to use acrylic paints and brushes, gradually abandoning spray paints, so in the last four years I've used only acrylic paint and brushes for the walls and for working on canvases, and I really enjoy it. Also, I do ink drawings on paper; sometimes I color them in watercolors."

"Now I can call what I am doing a mixture of symbolism, mysticism, and surrealism. Different people compare my works to works by Bosch, Goya, Dali, Riveira, and Moebius. It is not really important for me what they are called. Instead, I can say that I'm keen on mythology, history, religious topics, mysticism, and science and that I use all these topics in my work."

In contrast to many street artists, AEC does not desire to leave a particular meaning, but is more interested in tracing a global vision. "I would not want to generalize about a special message of all my art, but I can say that what I am doing is discovering the Universe and myself through art creation. The creative process is a mystical path for me, connected with self-improvement. The message of the piece can be pretty clear for someone and hard to understand for others. Everything depends on a person's sensibility to art, because most of the works I do allow for a free interpretation. Even for me, the result of the work can be a mystery and doesn't have a final meaning," states AEC, reaffirming the total independence of his work.

He also thinks about the artists of the past who have inspired his works and his ideas: "I have already mentioned some of them . . . I've always admired Bosch, for his imagination and his courageous ideas, especially if we consider the age he lived in, Bruegel, Beato Angelico, Dalí, Goya, Michelangelo.

***Odysseus Escape from Polyphemus*, 2015** - In the port of Catania – a city built near the place where, according to legend, Polyphemus lived – AEC has dedicated a work to the myth of Ulysses and the blinded Cyclops, reinterpreting it from a contemporary perspective.

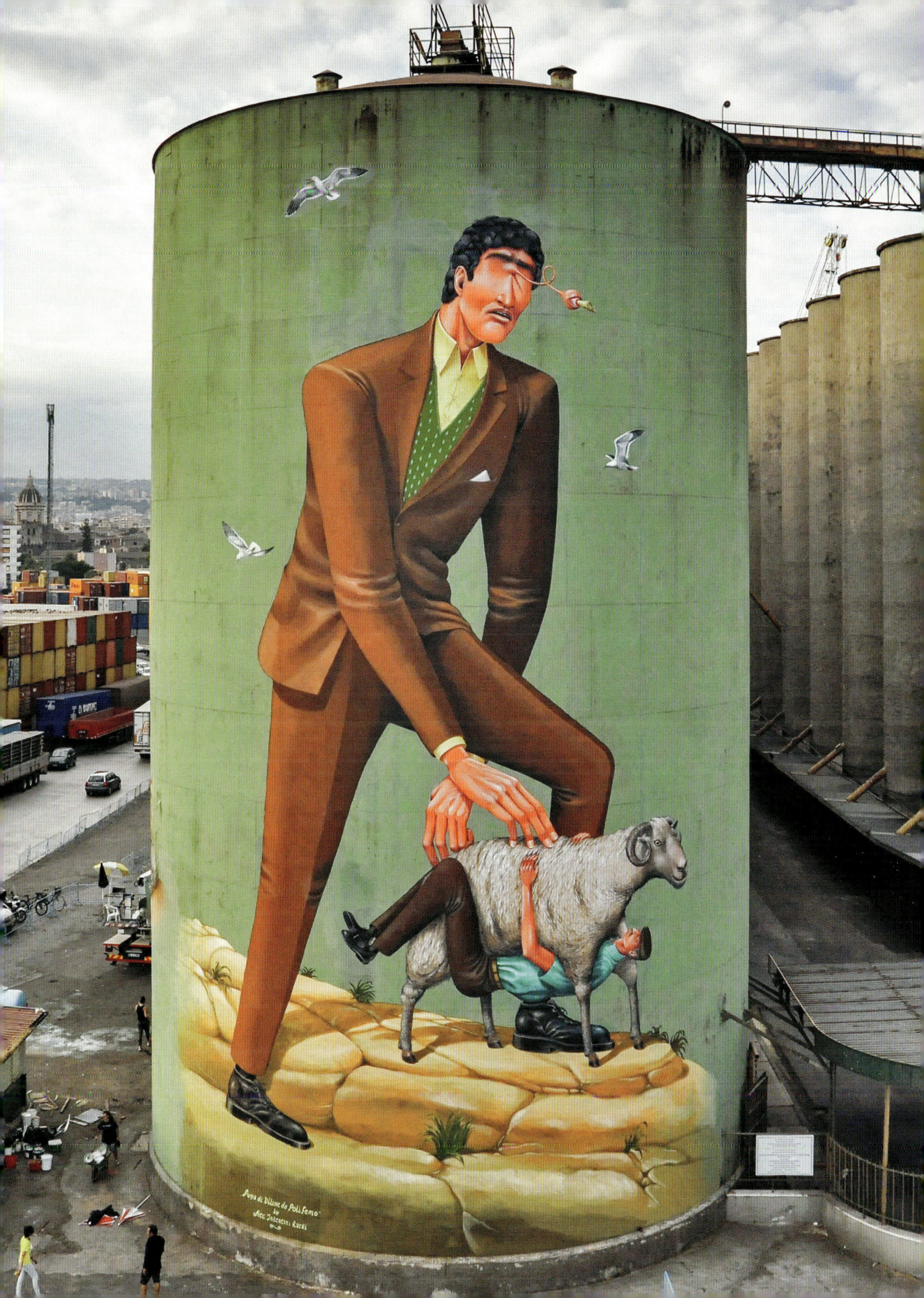

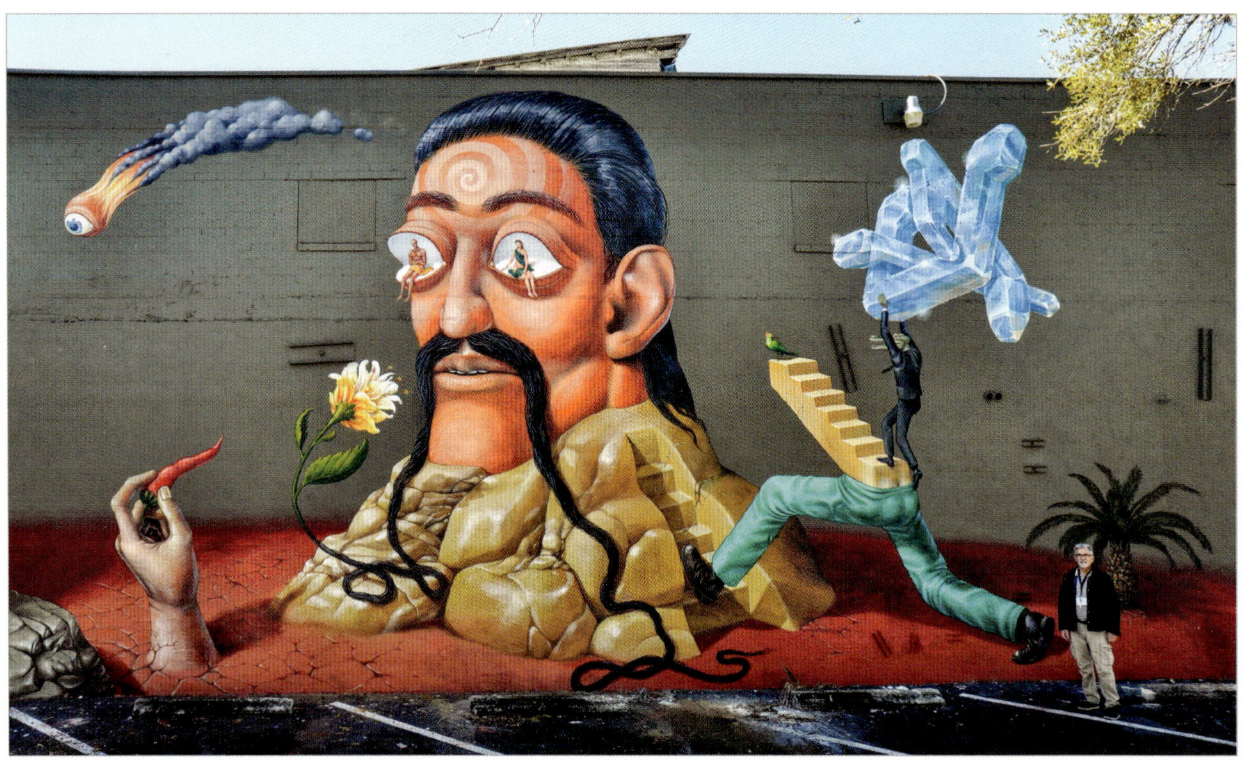

Intuition or Sixth Sense of Pedro, 2016 - AEC created this work in Gainesville, Florida, in collaboration with WAONE. There are evident references to the greats of surrealism, from Delvaux to Magritte and Dalí.

The Hatching of Humanity, 2016 - To rise above the Earth, little more than an empty shell, to follow one's dreams, led by intuition: this is the invitation that AEC makes to those who see this mural in Heerlen, in the Netherlands.

Among the more modern ones, I've been influenced by the Mexican school with its very expressive composition and the combination of color and light, the wonderful images connected with native history and culture, and the magical atmospheres; by Moebius (Jean Giraud), with his incredible imagination linked to the power and the supernatural ability to draw; by the director Alejandro Jodorowsky, and by Jean-Michel Basquiat." He follows and respects various artists, also among his contemporaries: "Robert Crumb; Julio Larraz for the irony, humor and incredible colors of his paintings; Stelios Faitakis; Blu, for his strong ideas and the context of his work as well as his great drawing ability; Jaz (Franco Fasoli); Momo; Zio Ziegler; Escif; Ericailcane; Liqen; Eversiempre; Saner; Nev-er 2501; Elian, for that incredible mixture of colors, great pieces; NUNCA; 3ttman; Vhils; El Mac; Alexis Diaz; Gaia; Teo Moneyless Pirisi; Sego; Aryz; Os Gemeos, for their imagination and because they inspired me so much when I started to paint on walls in the streets, Okuda; Maya Hayuk; Martha Cooper; Fintan Magee; Fikos Antonios; Speto; Vitche." He gives a list that could continue.

The primary source of his art is, more than anything, mythology, myths and legends: "I love them so much that when I travel I like to discover the places I go to, and particularly to listen to the people who live there, not simply read about them in books." Regarding colors, which have so much impact on his work, he states: "I prefer intense turquoise, melon yellow, warm and intense green.

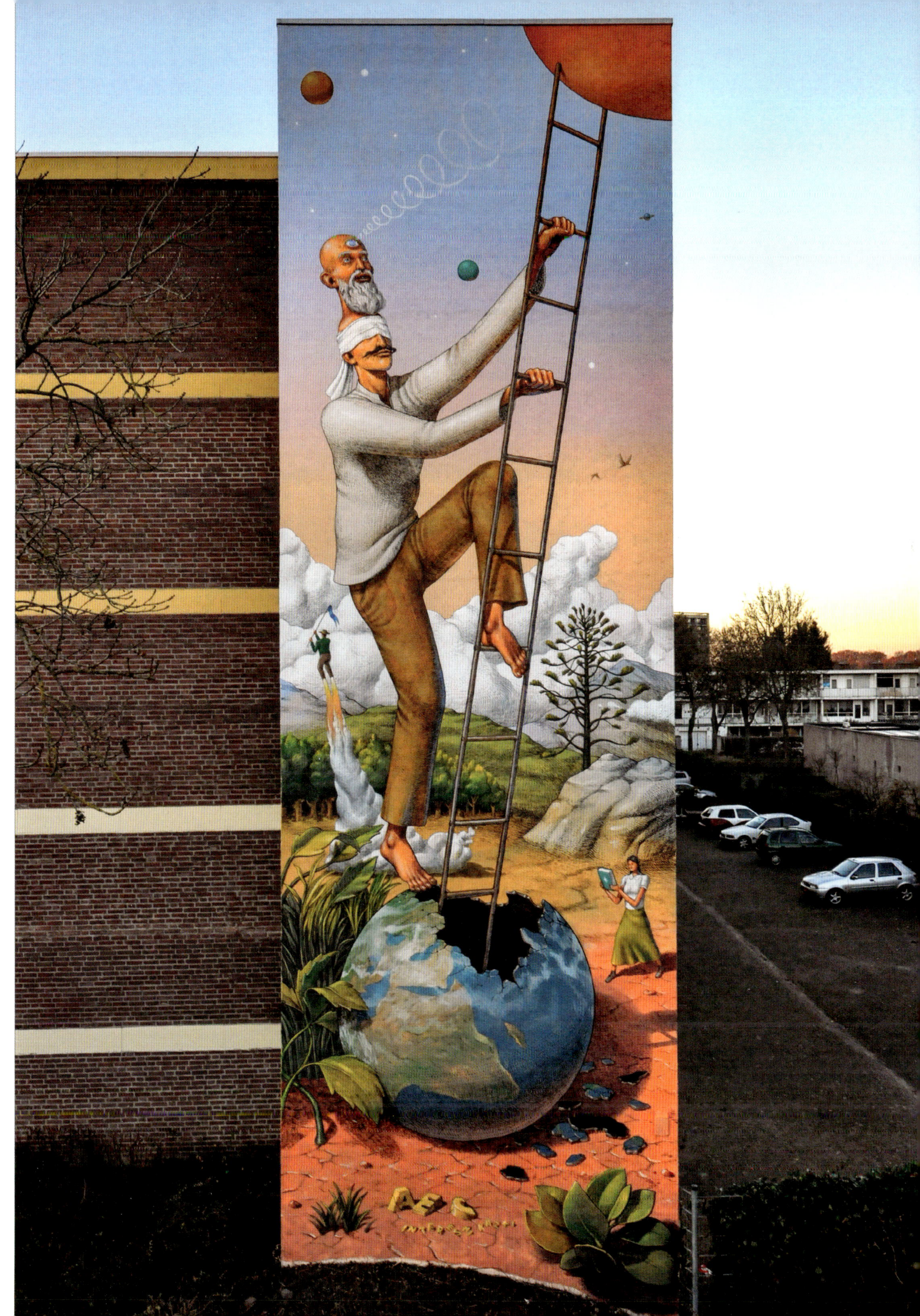

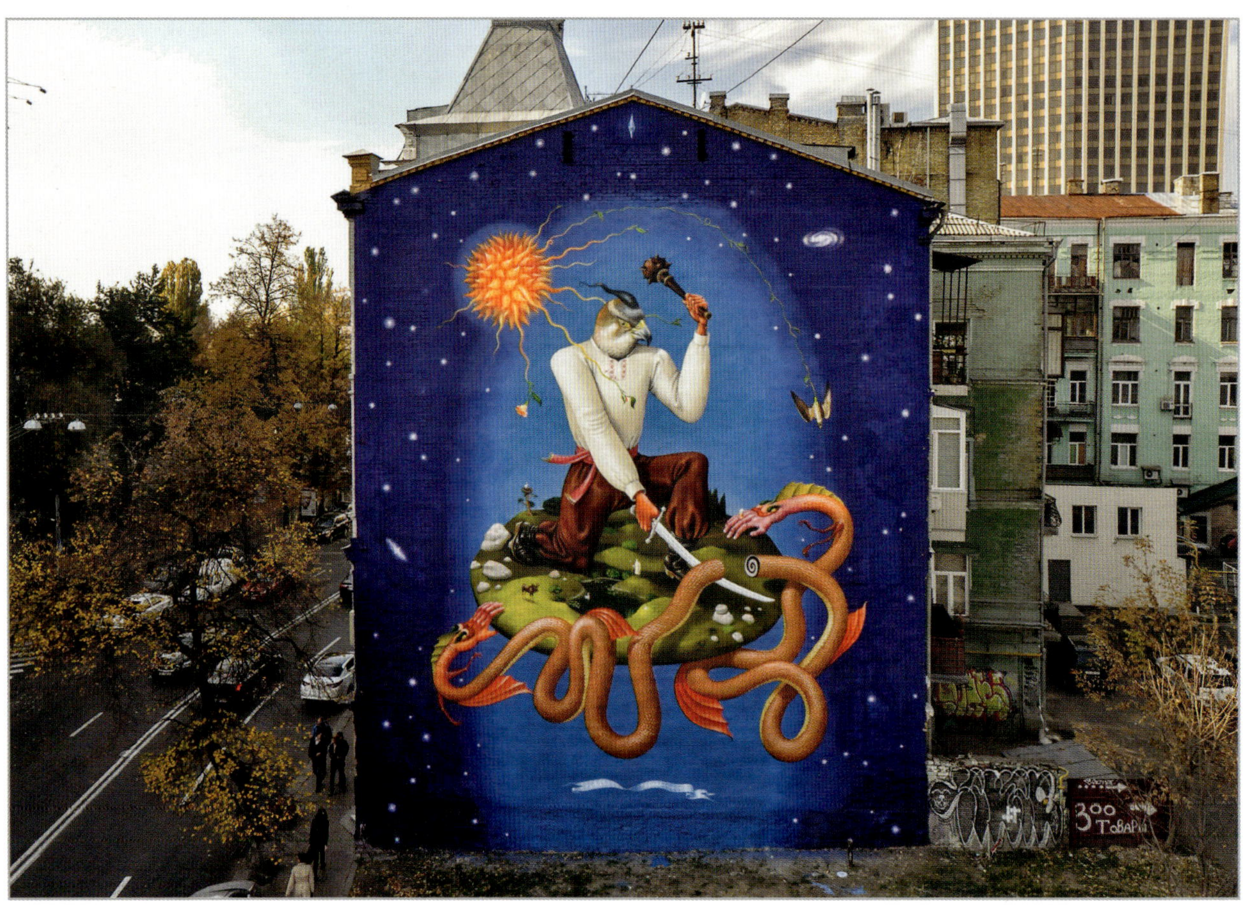

The Ukrainian Saint George, 2014 - In Kiev, in his Ukraine, AEC tackles one of the most significant subjects in the Orthodox Christian artistic tradition: Saint George killing the dragon, a scene symbolizing the triumph of spirituality over the snares of the flesh and matter. The artist upsets the traditional iconography by transforming the saint into Cossack bird in traditional Ukrainian dress defending an idyllic world.

But I love all colors and shades; everything depends on how they combine. Sometimes it can be beautiful, sometimes not."

Regarding his art, he emphasizes: "As I said, I prefer not to call what I am doing now graffiti, but murals. My favorite, and the most difficult mural I've done, is the recent one I painted in Ibiza, Spain, in the town Sant Antoni De Portmany. I worked on it every day for three weeks from early morning till late, in the sizzling summer sun, and it was really hard, I even got sunstroke. The main story of the mural is the removing of one head and the applying of a new one onto a large pile of stones which form the body. The stone head represents the government and the pile of stones/body is the society and structure of the country. The monkey on the top of the pile of stones/body is burning the book *On the Origin of Species*, by Charles Darwin. It is a symbol of revolution because it is the negation of the idea of evolution as revolution. In some ways, to create this piece I was inspired by what is happening in my country, Ukraine, where revolution has already happened twice in the past twelve years.

The Ukrainian Saint George, 2014 - Saint George also has a patriotic significance which is evident if one considers that it was painted in 2014, the year of the Ukrainian Revolution and the Russian occupation of the Crimea.

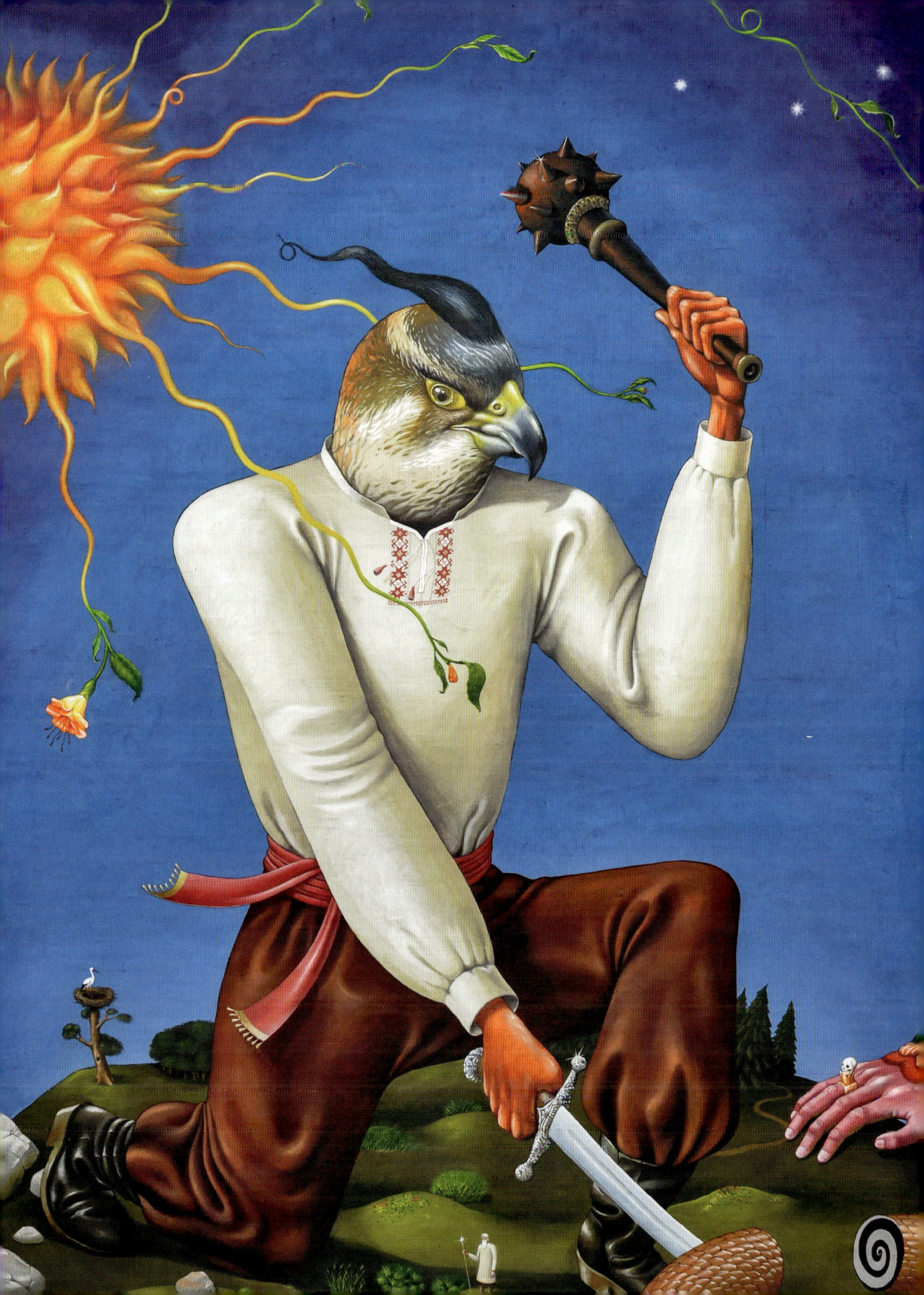

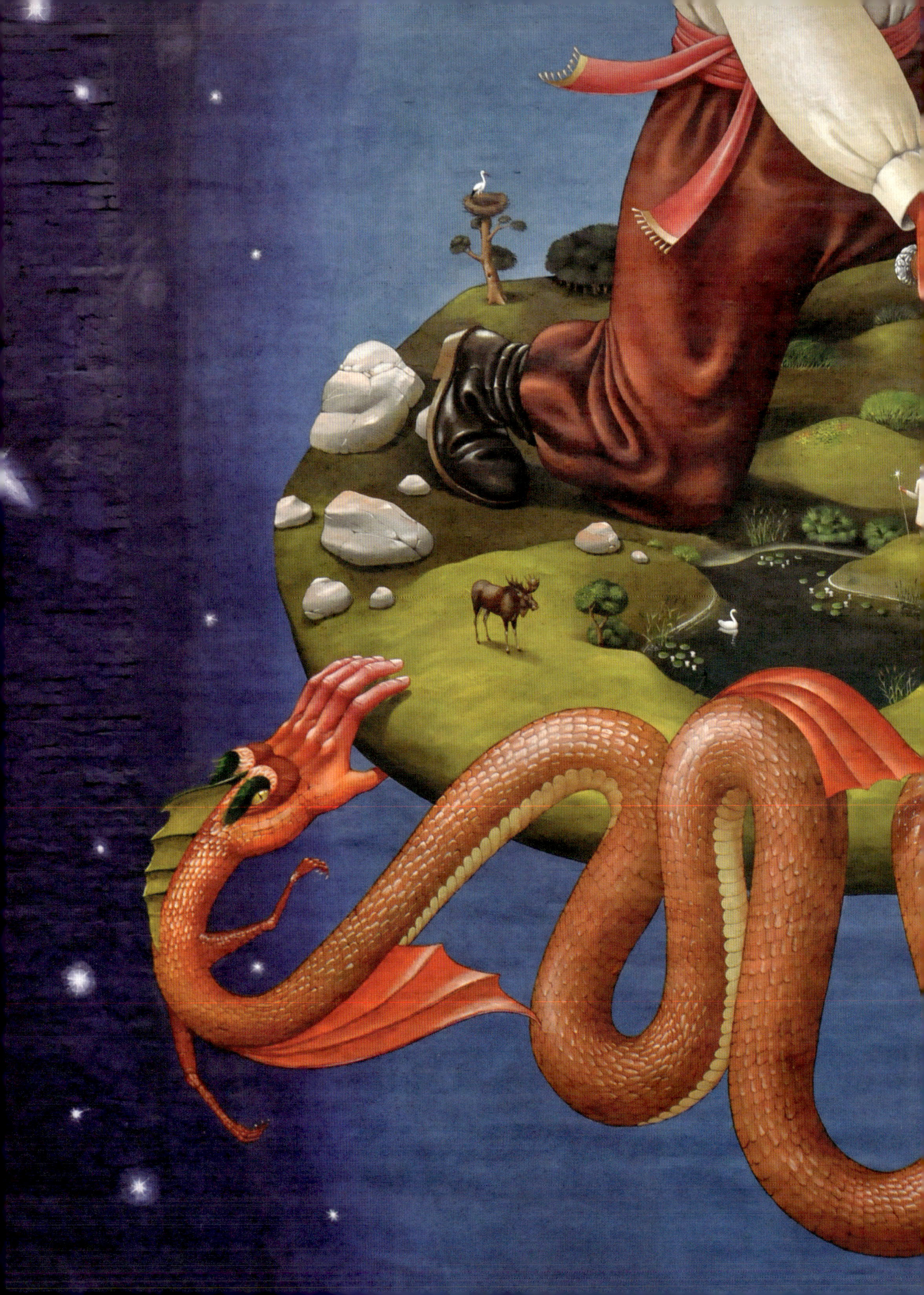

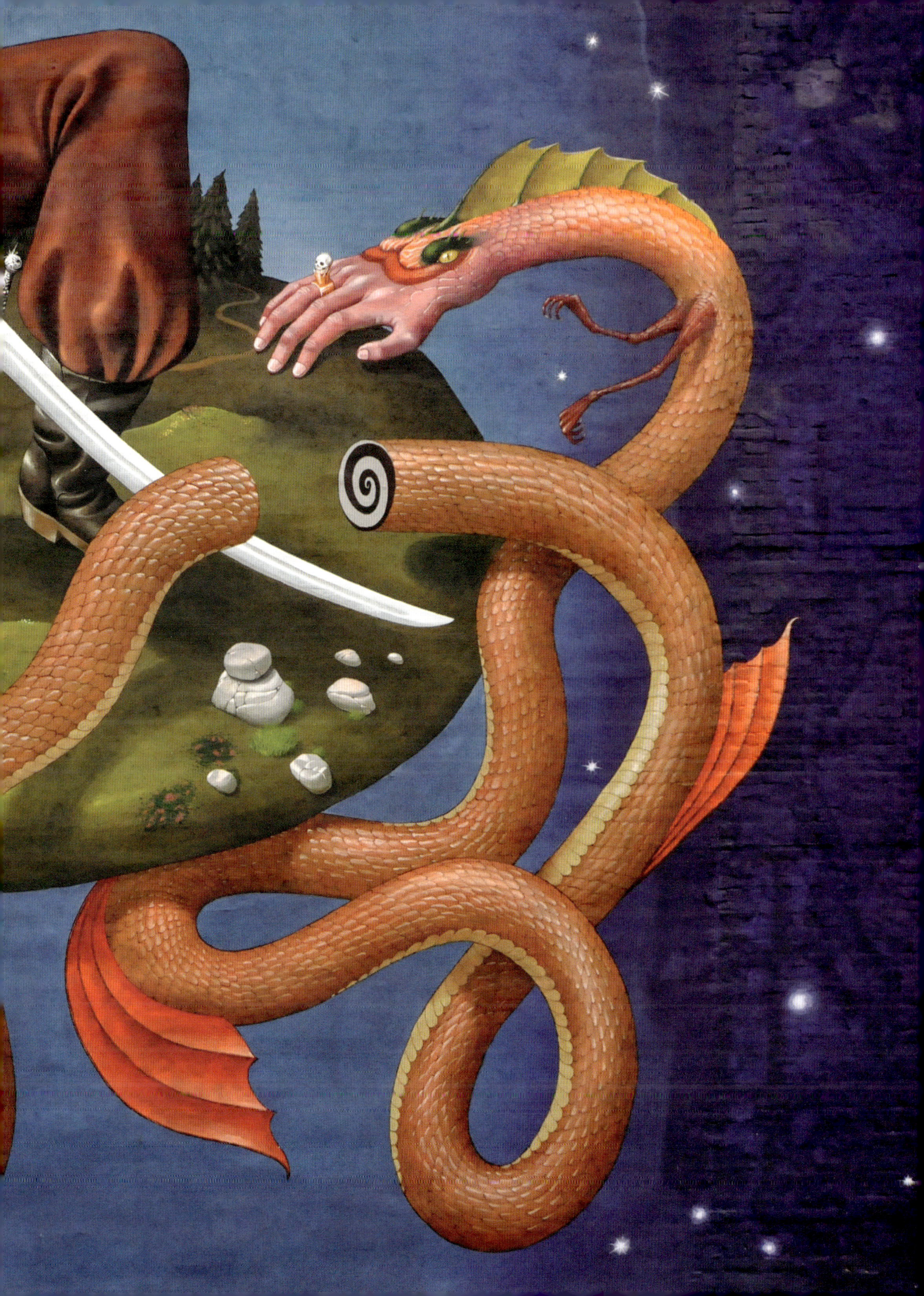

Now, officially, the government and president have changed but all society, and the structure of the country, have stayed almost the same – corrupt politicians have only changed their clothes and taken on patriotic colors, and corrupted the way of life of most people. People got the illusion of freedom but in fact have stayed under the control of corrupt politicians and businessmen who actually ruled the country before the revolution and continue now, covering themselves with 'patriotism' and using war as a tool for manipulation," AEC continues sadly, showing his political vision and deep love for his native country.

Besides his work in Ibiza, probably the most difficult in his career, he remembers another really risky situation: "Once, I painted a mural in Wynwood, Miami, in 2011, and there was a shooting just around the corner. Another time, the same thing happened in São Paulo, Brazil, while we were taking pictures of a completed mural. But more often, painting on the street is very joyful – local people are very thankful and friendly, even bringing tea and food. It happened in India, for example, and in Cape Town, South Africa, in a pretty dangerous, criminal neighborhood. It was very nice and unexpected."

He has his own perspective for street art: "I have a strange feeling about the dispute over art as street art. It is the same as asking the absurd question: is art art? It exists and has the right to exist. Drawings and paintings on walls have existed for millions of years, since ancient men took a piece of coal in their hands. Another question is the popularity of the 'street art' movement now. In the last few years, it has become extremely popular. It came out from wild graffiti that had been forbidden – the underground hip hop movement in the United States – but now the street art movement evokes 'hype'. Mostly, it doesn't have an ideology, because it is too connected with business. Companies involved in commercial projects and developers use street art a lot, so it is used just as bright images on buildings, which have to be politically correct, avoiding any awkward topics . . . "

AEC reconsiders his artistic development in this universe, on a certainly difficult journey: "At the beginning of my journey, no one understood my interest in painting on trains and abandoned walls, especially my parents and friends. I shared my passion with a community of artists. After seven or nine years' hard work without any recognition from society, someone noticed me for my projects in Eastern Europe and began to invite me to Spain, Portugal, France, and then the United States", he states, looking back at his past. Looking to the future, on the other hand, he meditates on what he could still do. "I love to travel and to paint in unique places, to discover new and interesting local cultures. I would love to paint more in Latin America, in Asia and Japan.

Memory of The Land, 2015 - The contrast between past and present, between aboriginal and colonial Australia, is the theme of this mural created in Perth. The protagonist is a man whose head is constituted by a Banksia flower, a native Australian plant.

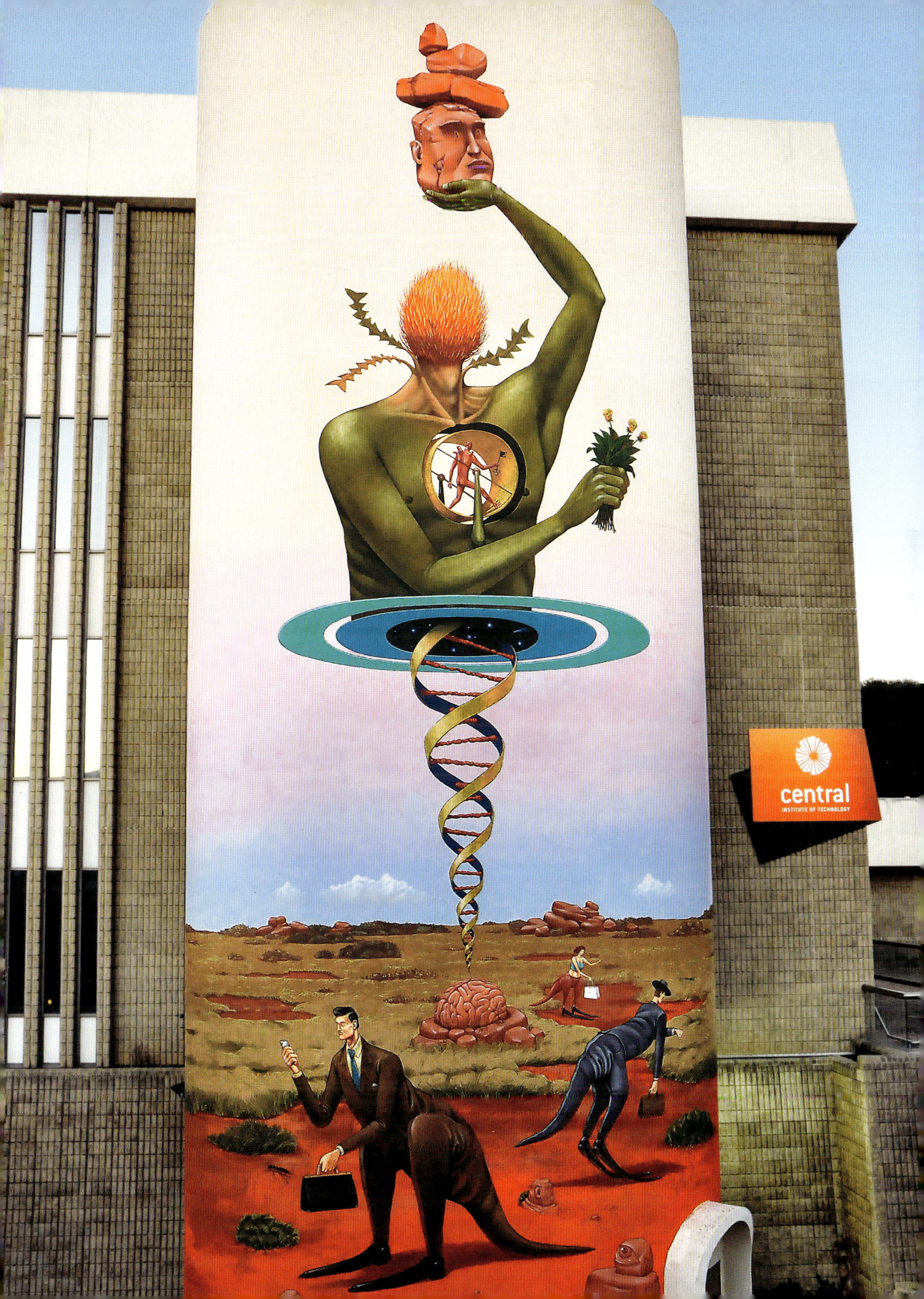
central
INSTITUTE OF TECHNOLOGY

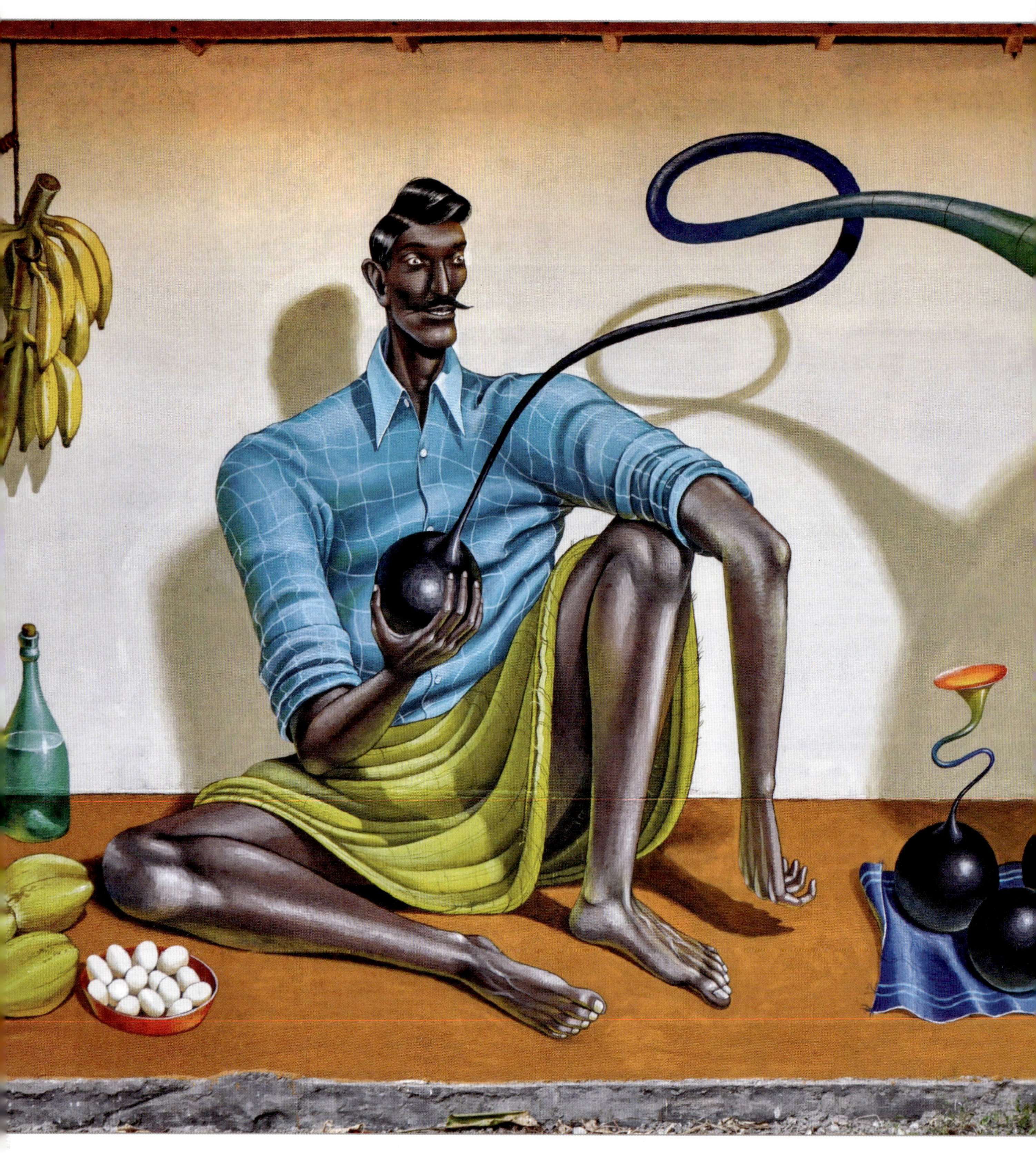

***Seller of Black Holes*, 2015** - The protagonist of the mural sells eggs, bananas, fish . . . and black holes capable of devouring tourists who come too close: a metaphor for the huge fascination of India for the West.

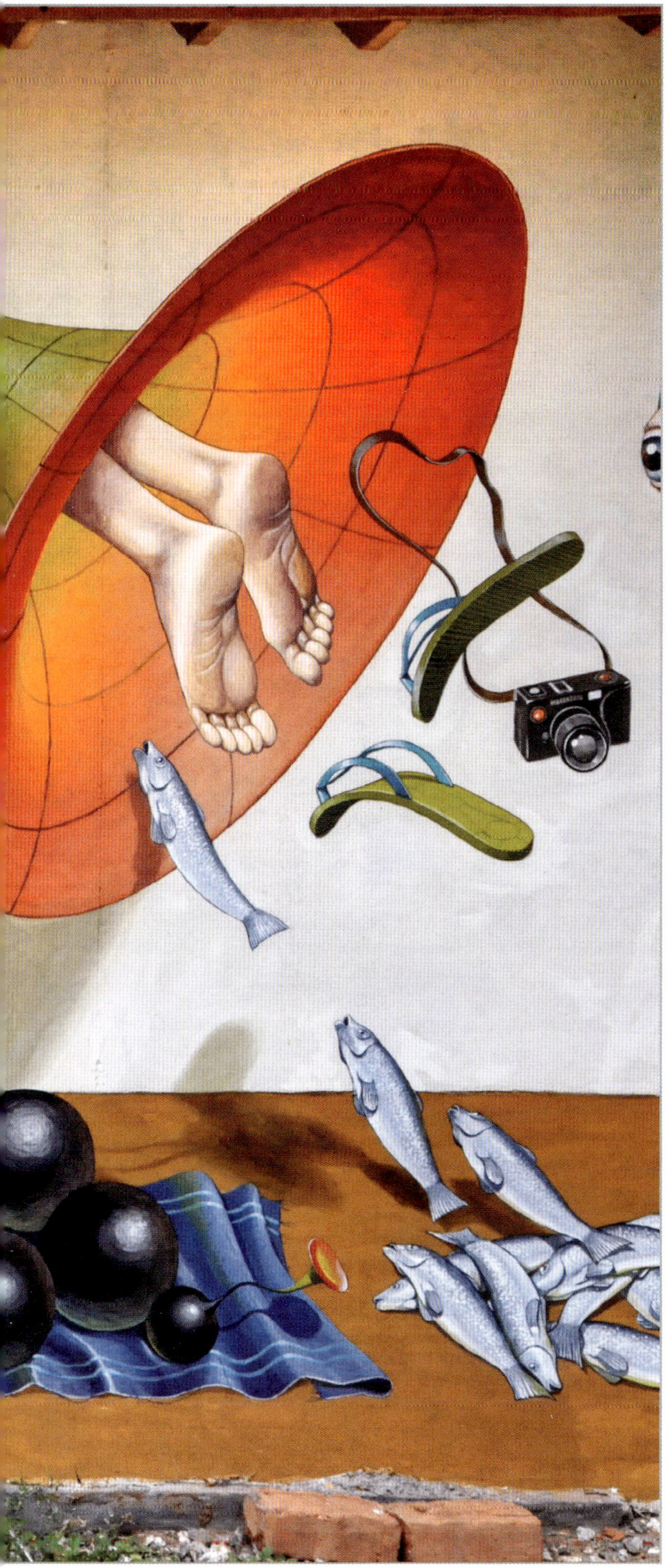

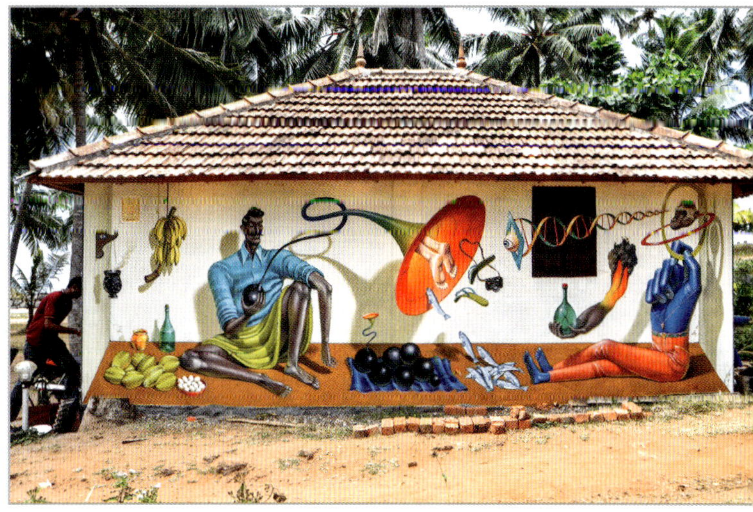

I really love South Africa and the Azores for their nature, places I have visited and worked in. And I really love to work close to the sea." Ukraine is still intensely in his blood: "I really love my city Kiev and Ukraine. It is the place where I grew up, developed as a person and an artist, where my family is, where I met my wife. But life in Ukraine is pretty difficult, because of revolution, and war in the East of the state. People are stressed by the bad economy all the time, by bad news, by the low level of life. And it is very difficult to be an artist here now, because people are more focused on material things, how to survive, and nobody really cares about art," AEC admits reluctantly. However, he maintains his innate positivity: "I prefer to live in the present, not to forget yesterday and not to be afraid of tomorrow's changes. Usually not to plan too much," he says, with great hope in his eyes. What does he hope for to achieve a better world? "More love and tolerance between people."

Seller of Black Holes, 2015

The great blue hand, on the right of the mural – which was created in Varkala, a town on the south-western coast of India – symbolizes the spirit of the local divinity.

M-CITY
Wizard of the Metropolitan Stencil

His works are characterized by a strong metropolitan spirit. They often show shipyards and ships, which he has loved since he was a child, but also factories, rooftops, chimneys, bridges, tunnels, trams, and airplanes. We also find in his work figures resembling cartoon characters, although they are drawn in his unmistakable style. Well integrated into the architecture and surrounding settings, his work mesmerizes and induces the spectator to look more closely. "From far off, they are captivating and pleasant, but as soon as you come close enough to see the details you notice more serious references, to pollution and other social and political themes," explains the artist, Mariusz Waras, in his study in Gdańsk, Poland. He signs his work M-City, and his metropolitan project has spread through hundreds of murals throughout the world. From Warsaw, Berlin, Paris, London, Bolzano, Prague, and Budapest, and as far off as São Paulo, Rio de Janeiro, and Jakarta, M-City shows us how, from many points of view, cities can be considered diverse and appear also as industrial and multi-structural projects.

Born in 1978 in Gdynia, Poland, he graduated from the Department of Graphic Art at the Academy of Fine Arts in Gdańsk, where he obtained his PhD in 2013. From 2008 to 2016, moreover, he has worked in the same Academy as teaching assistant for painting courses. Since 2015 he runs the Street Art Studio at the Academy of Art in Szczecin. He also curates a gallery in Gdynia and an art space in Gdańsk, nearby his studio. However, the mural interventions he realized in the form of actual commentary on the dynamic political situation - like the famous Power of Fantasy at the BOZAR in Brussels - can be admired in galleries and open spaces in Poland and abroad.

"Shipyards work like small-scale cities and are made up of many different elements. There you can discover names, shops for workers, places . . . I've been fascinated by them since I was a child," he says. As a child he lived near the Elektrociepłownia Yard and from his window he saw its many smoking chimneys. His father worked in the yard, and thus he was able to visit him and admire the ships being built.

"I think it was with my father that I traced my first drawings. We spent a lot of time together drawing, and so my parents decided to send me first to a photography school and then to a graphics and design school. I approached this path gradually," he

> You can take a photograph, publish it on Facebook, and say you're in the United States. Online is reality. The place you're in doesn't count anymore. What you want to express counts.

M-City at work, among colors and shapes in evolution.

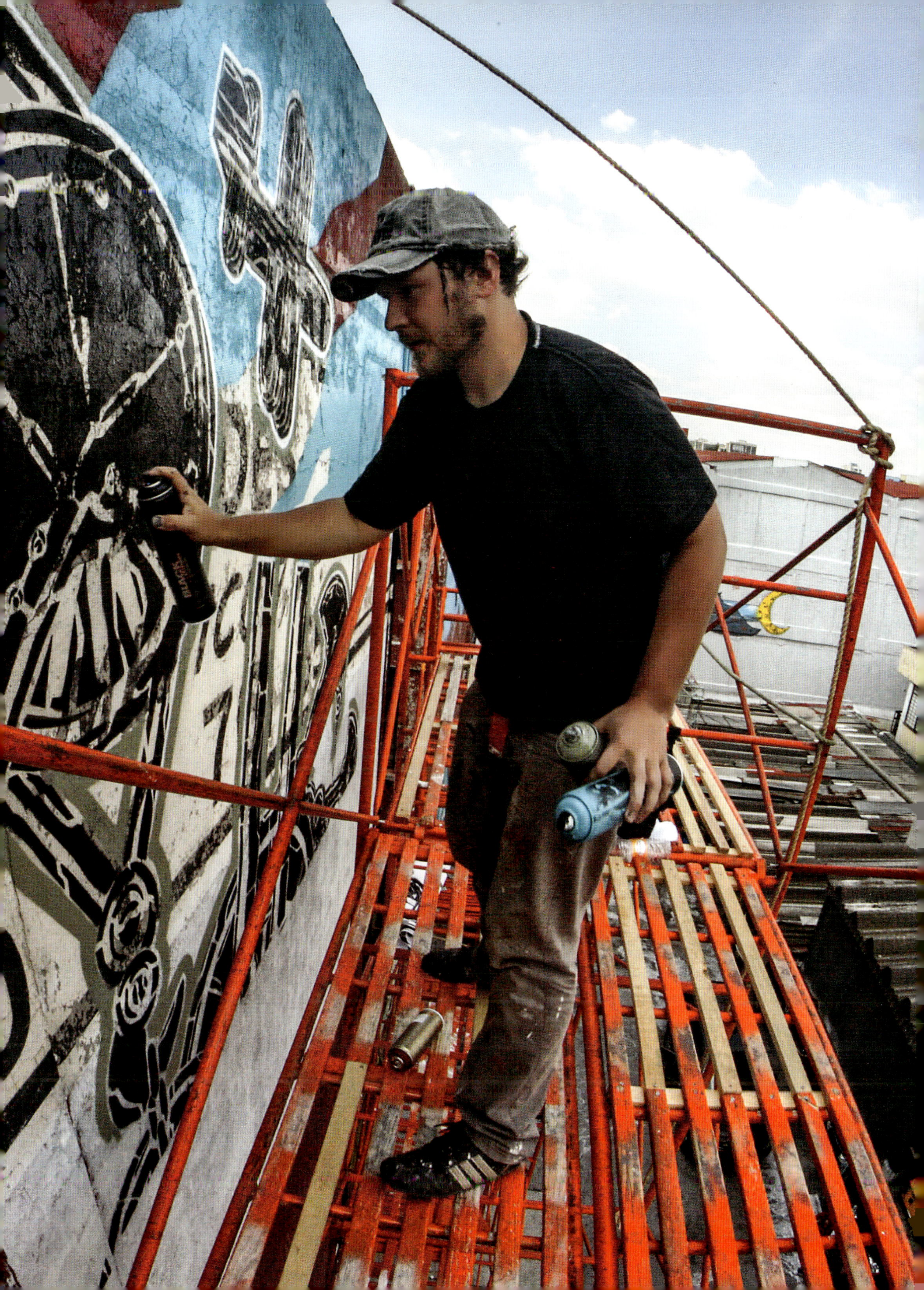

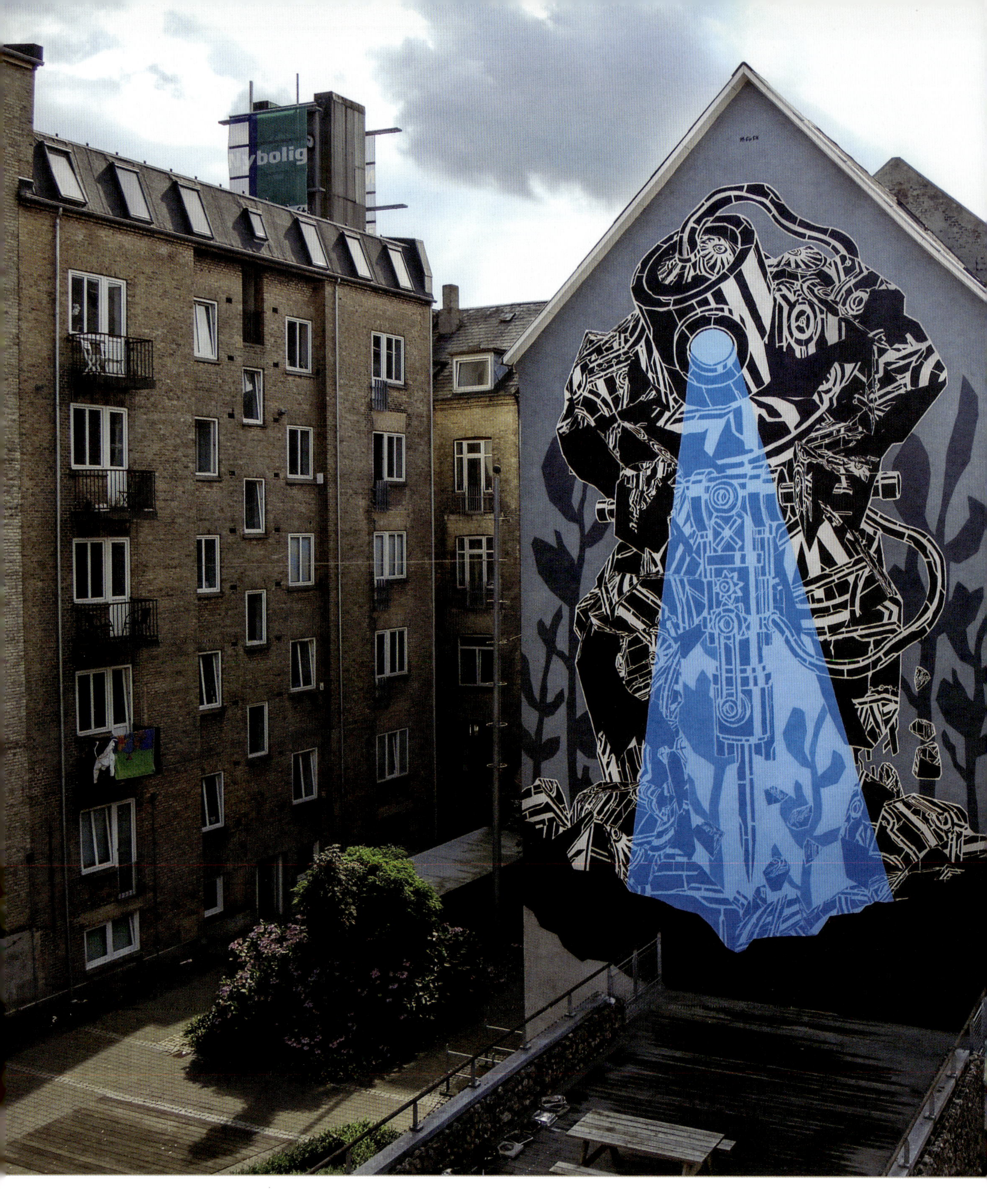

Aalborg, 2015 - The subject of this work created for the WE AArt Festival seems to shed a new light on Aalborg – a Danish city that is living an extraordinary urban revitalization.

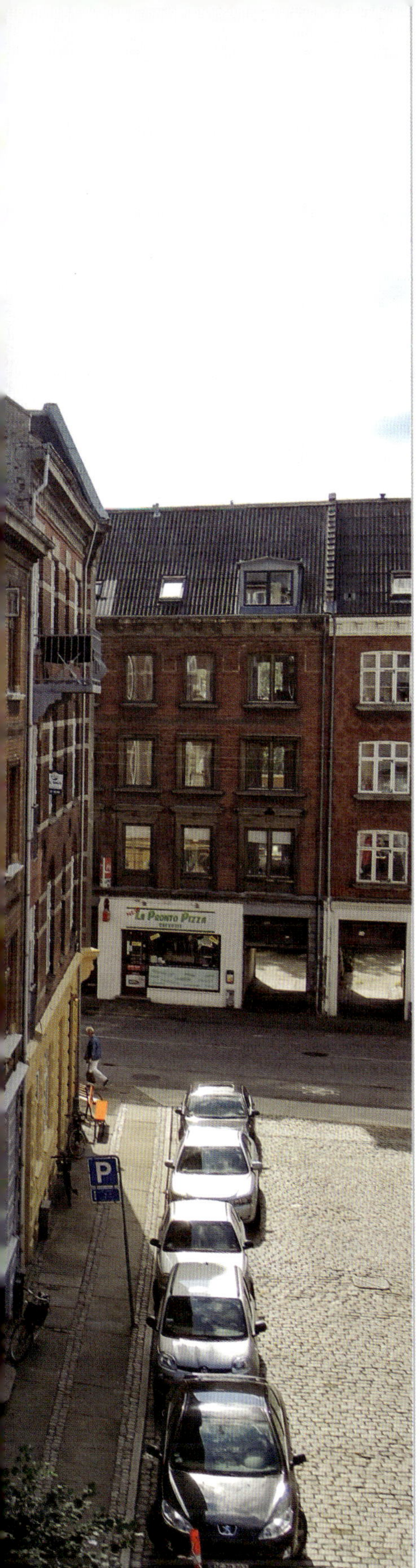

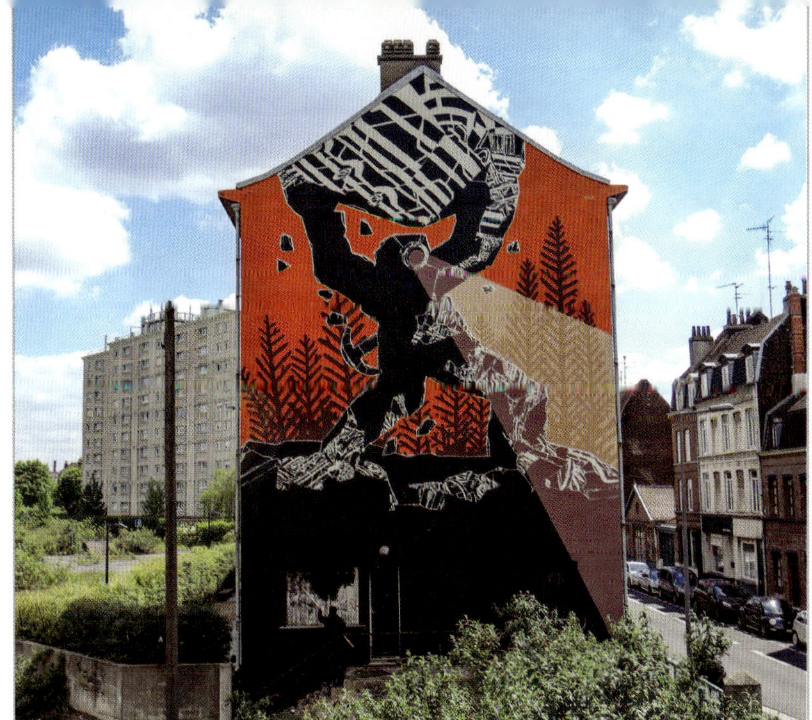

reflects, considering his artistic journey. "I'm primarily an artist of the stencil. I was very young when I became interested in murals. Among the few memories I have of the communist period and the years just afterward are those of the independent artists who expressed their dissent from government and politics on city walls. They wrote short sentences, with big letters, using no particular graphics."

Today M-City draws inspiration from different sources. "I don't have a specific artist in mind. I teach art and therefore, in some way, I love all artists. But perhaps my production is inspired more by the graphic design typical of the period between the World Wars, by linotype printing techniques and by certain comic strips. As far as my ideas are concerned, they are fundamentally anarchic and funky." This foundation was present in his first important work: "I was very young. It was a work of about twenty-seven inches across, with many people, many faces – and in the middle there was an anarchist symbol," he recalls.

M-City has developed a unique technique, embodying an almost mathematical order. "You cannot change dimensions with a stencil. You cut it and apply the paint, it is an exact technique. It occurred to me, however, to put different stencils together, like Lego bricks. In this way the dimensions of the wall didn't matter because I could use as many as ten or fifteen, like the pieces of a puzzle," he explains, and he adds that he came up with the idea due to the work he did before becoming an artist.

Lille, 2015
A postmodern Cyclops, with a headlight eye, encapsulates the artistic path of M-City: dark, spare masses, heightened by the intense red of the background.

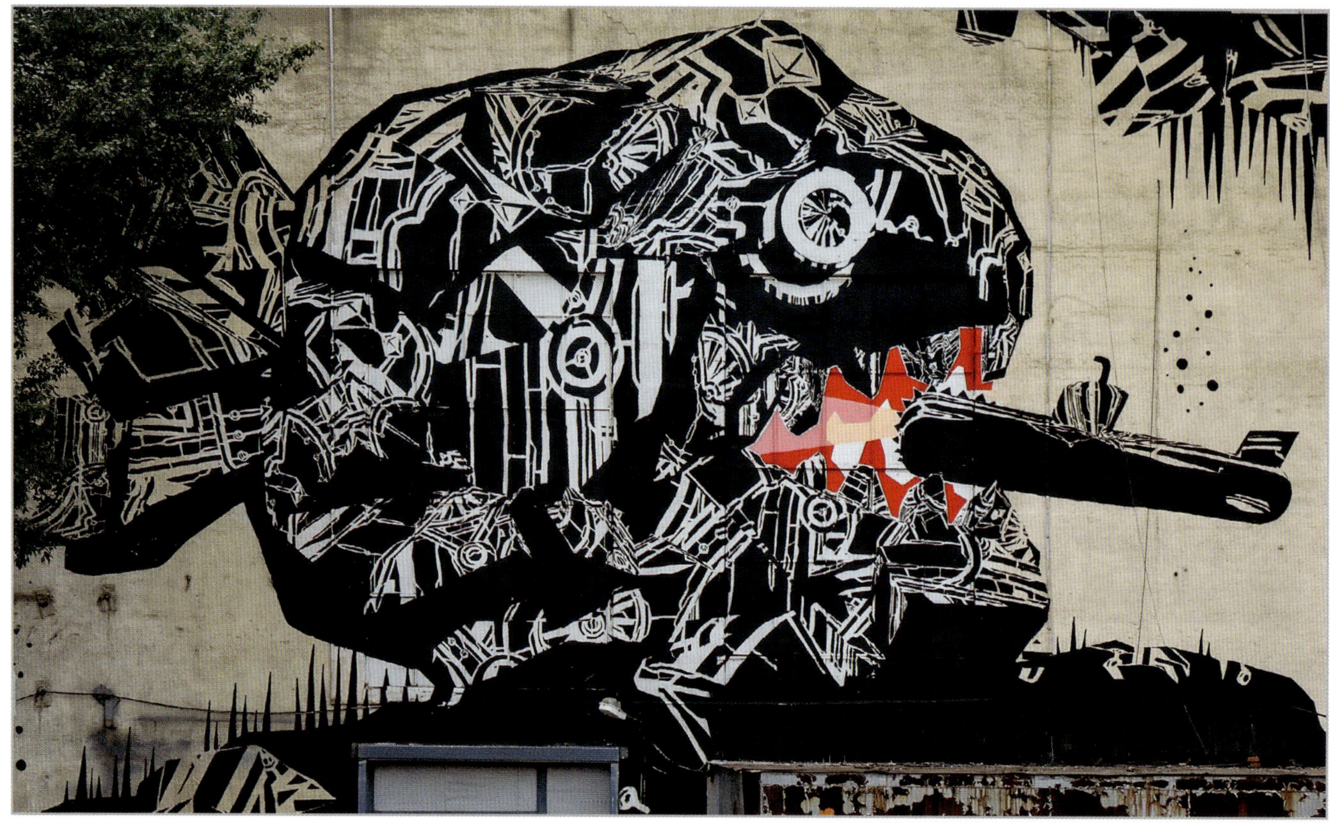

Moscow, 2015 - To Moscow the Outline Festival has bequeathed a disturbing mechanical fish called 822, which is capable of devouring submarines: at night, the lighting makes it still more disquieting.

Poznań, 2014 - On the walls of the Polish city of Poznań, an apocalyptic battle is staged, as in a science fantasy film, between the police and a monstrous giant insect.

"Before devoting myself completely to painting, I worked as a graphic designer for Commodore 64 videogames, and to create them it was necessary to combine symbols, letters, sounds, so many different elements. Certainly that experience stimulated my creativity. In particular, I loved the ones in which you could conquer a city or take the part of a hero . . ."

M-City does not think that all his works contain a message. He states quite frankly that sometimes they are only decorative. "But other times they have deep significance. It also depends on context: whether I'm taking part in a festival, or I'm the guest at a gallery, or in a private capacity, far from everything. If there is a building that I have chosen in front of me, then perhaps I express something polit-ical. Inspiration can come from everything. Recently I created a work for the Native Americans in North Dakota. What is interesting today is that it doesn't matter where you are: you can take a photograph, publish it on Facebook, and say you're in the United States. Online is reality. The place you're in doesn't count anymore. What you want to express counts."

He likes to travel, even if he feels very close to his cities in Poland, where he grew up and has many friends. "I think that Europe in general is more boring than other places – more exotic places, like India, Colombia, Brazil, and Indonesia. I've never been to Japan. I'd like to visit it because it fascinates me. And perhaps if I have inspiration I paint. It always happens like this: the artistic moment takes

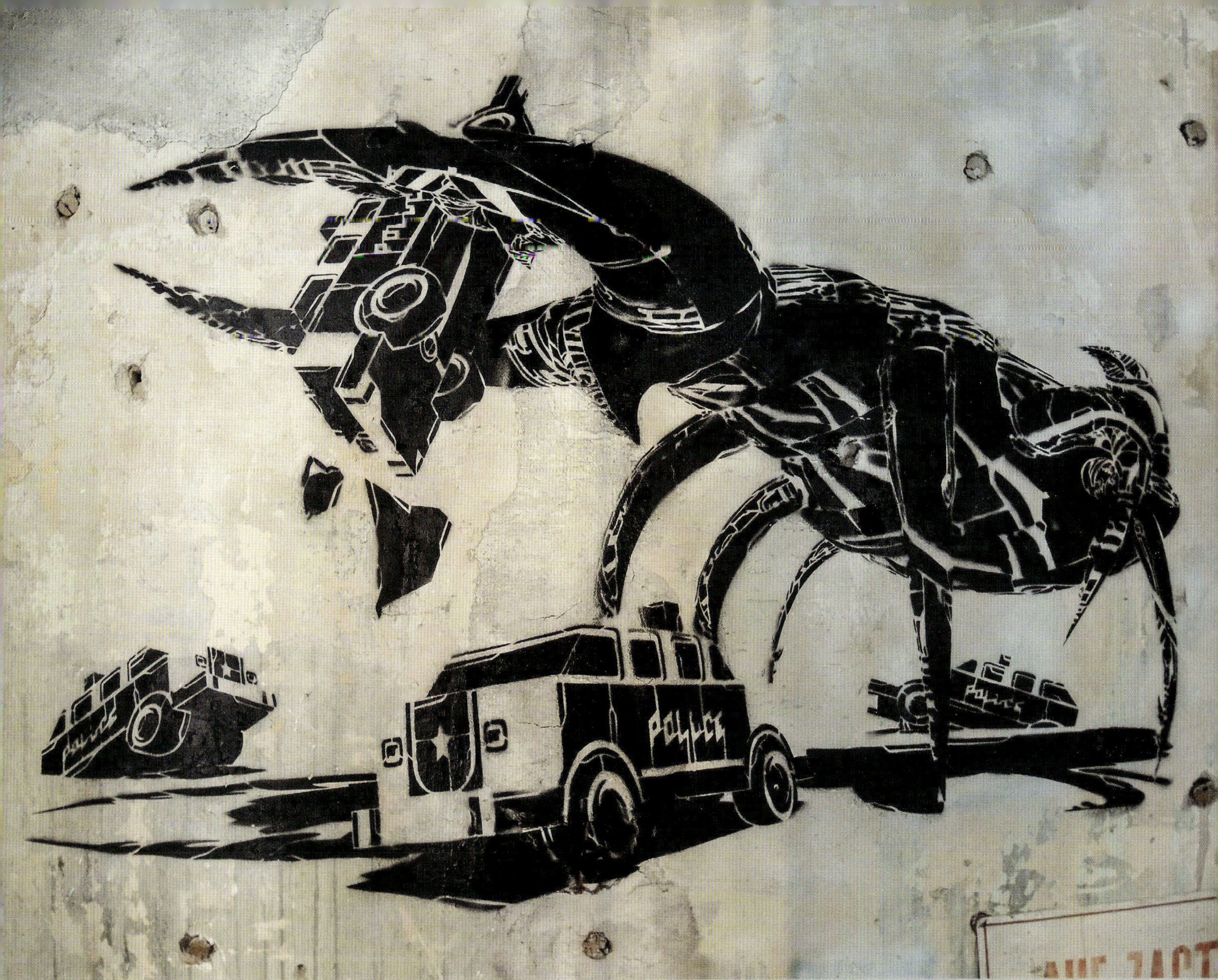

me by surprise. And it doesn't matter if you're painting legally or illegally – you feel the need to paint, you just do it." However, he adds that he has never had great problems choosing sites: "Usually I look for distant places where I can be alone. When I'm traveling I get someone local to help, someone who knows the scene well and can show me suitable places," he says.

"My favorite color is certainly black, which I often combine with white. Sometimes I apply shades of red or another color, but it is always a decorative effect, and so it doesn't matter too much which color it is," he explains. Despite everything, M-City does not have a very positive vision of contemporary street art: "I have the impression that it's sinking, instead of improving. At least this is the vision that I have from Poland, which perhaps is different from the rest of the world. But it seems to me that street art is transforming into a great factory, with so many festivals and artists. There are murals everywhere. In the beginning, everything was inspired only by the desire to make art. Now it is as if artists parachute into a place, stay long enough to complete their work, and then leave. There are too many low-quality murals."

Looking to the future, he hopes above all for a world without war. "The election of Donald Trump was shocking, but in Poland we also have a similar politics. It is a strange situation which sometimes reminds me of the one before Hitler's rise to power," he says.

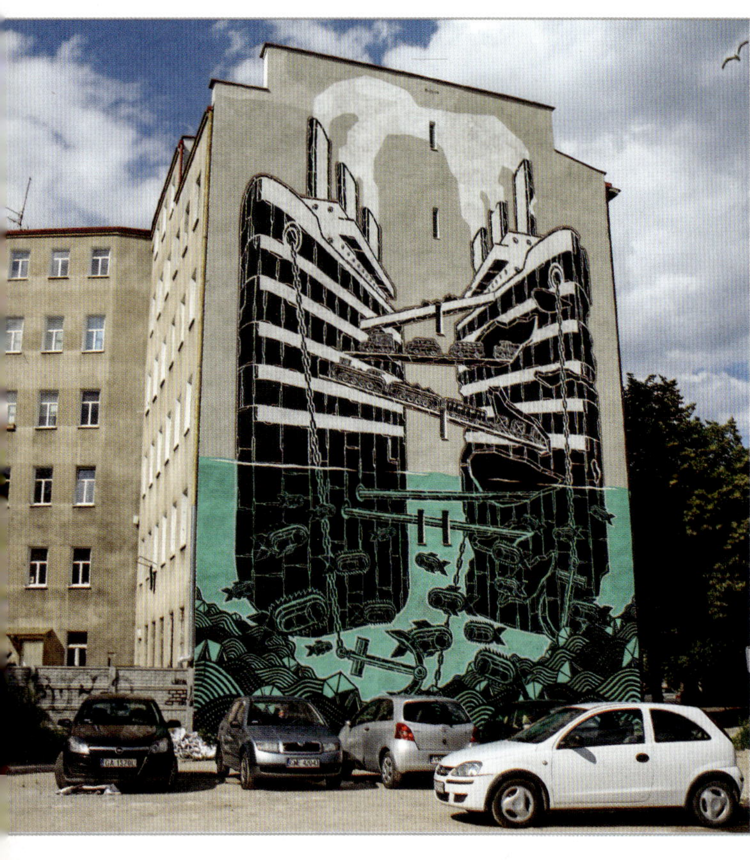

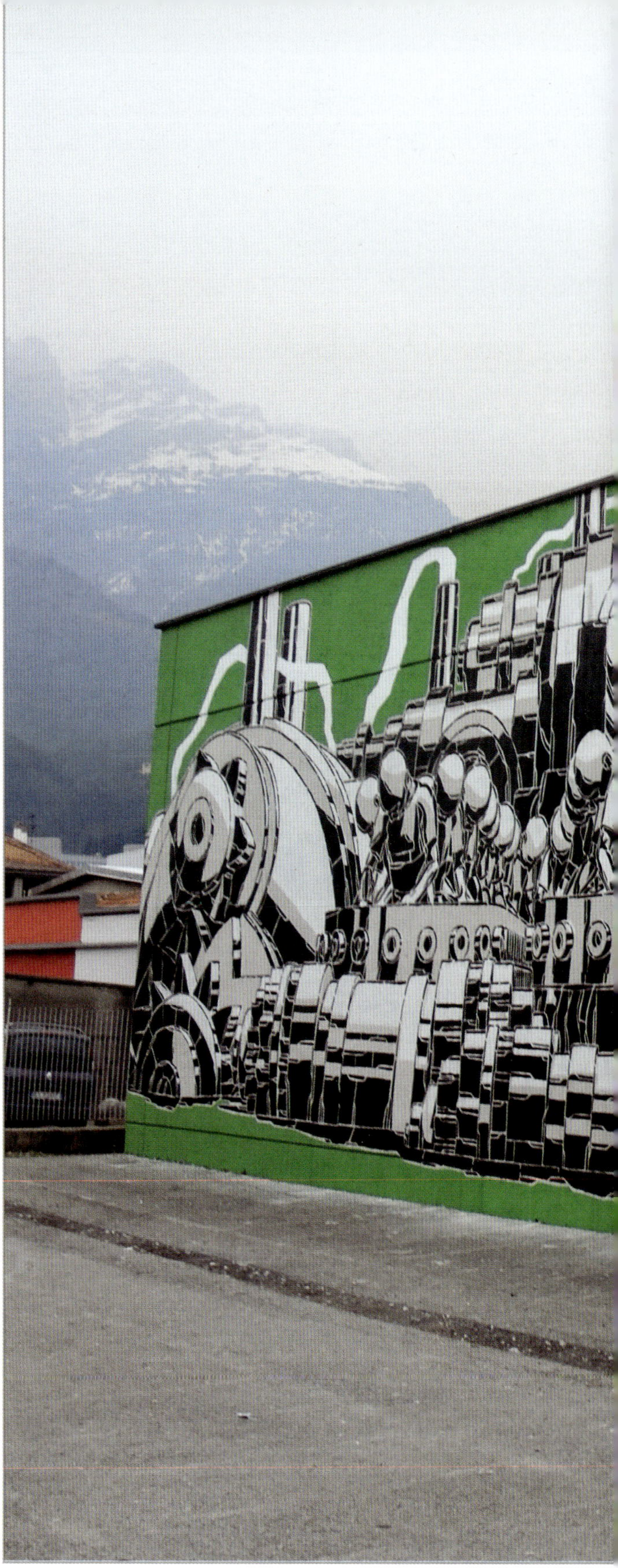

But he has faith in art. "It is precisely the artists who can contribute to changing the world, especially street artists, who have the chance to express themselves freely and create works accessible to everybody." His work as a teacher also fills him with hope. "In India I bought a tuk-tuk and went around with my students. I love to teach. I direct a class in the Academy of Fine Arts in Szczecin and a street art studio focused on public art. I'm stimulated by the energy of young people and I'm an inspiration for them. They make me feel young." He doesn't have a favorite work of those he has produced. "My favorite is always the latest. I think I've made more than 800 works. It's difficult to choose. But as soon as I finish something, I remember every detail. The latest is a Native American. Behind him is the wreckage of a police car. He is the winner."

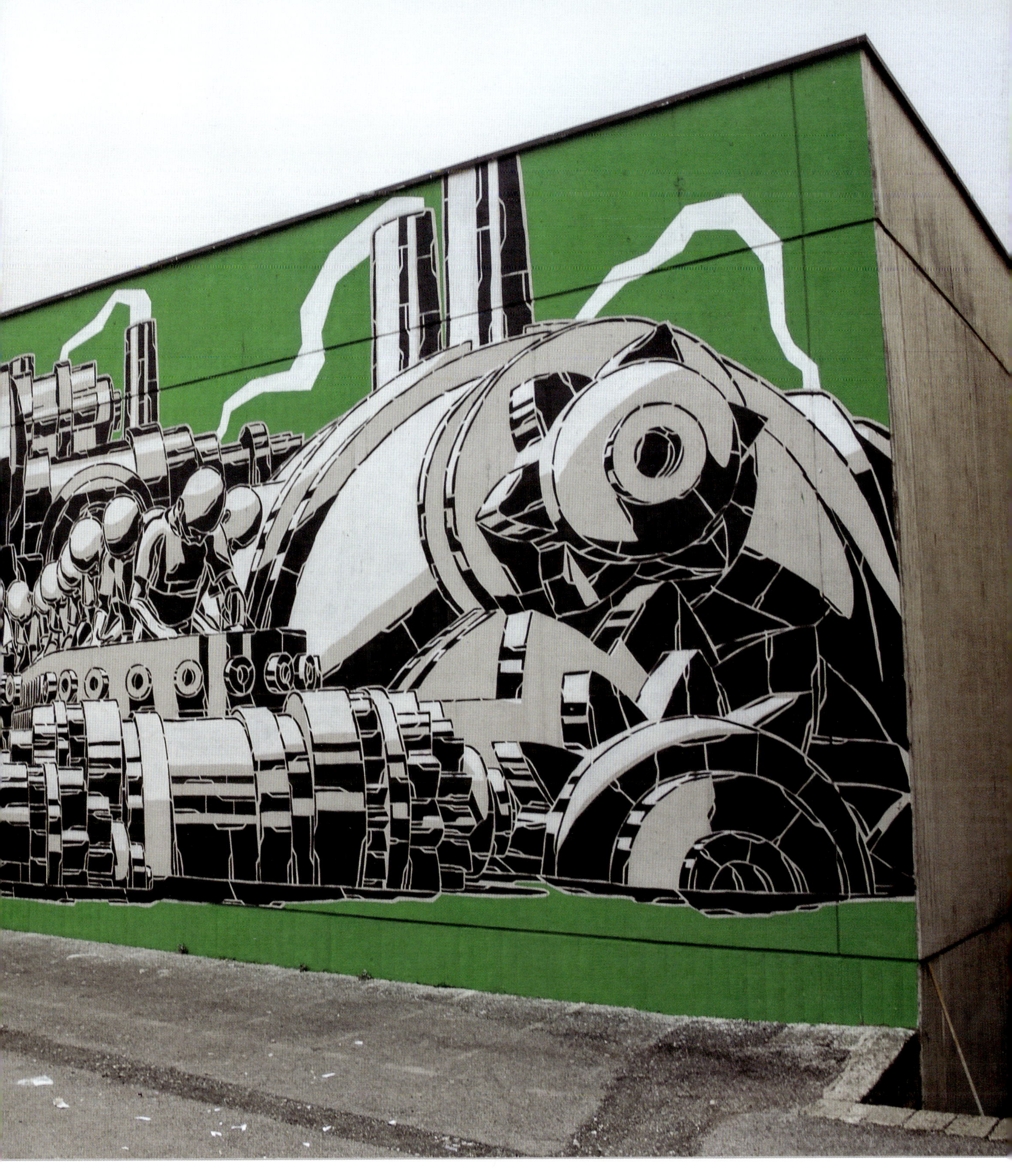

Gdynia, 2015 - Two ocean liners as imposing as skyscrapers are moored in Gdynia, a Polish seaport a short distance from Gdansk, where M-City was born and his imagination was formed.

Lecco, 2015 - In Lecco, an Italian city with a past of heavy industry, M-City creates a sort of giant factory-steam engine, in which humans are dominated by mechanical elements.

NUNCA

The "Charon" Between Indigenous and Modern Culture

His artist name means "never" in Portuguese and indicates the fact that NUNCA doesn't feel limited by either cultural or psychological constrictions. When Francisco Silva thinks of his credo, answering us from São Paulo, in Brazil, where he lives and works, he says: "Spinning around a fireball on the middle of the infinite 'nowhere.'"

He then thinks back to his roots. "I started drawing when I was still a child, around six years old, just like any kid. But when I was eleven I started to go out on the streets with my friends in the neighborhood where I used to live and I was fascinated by the tags and the fact that I could draw anywhere and people would see it. So almost instantly I started to go out and write my name or paint at the weekends with my older friends," he remembers. He was born in 1983: at the time, the streets of Itaquera were marked by the different gangs spraying *pichações* – slogans and graffiti – but NUNCA soon started developing his own style, albeit unconsciously. "It was something I was looking for but I had no idea what it was. I learned from the older kids how to do it, the rules of painting on the street and not getting caught by the police, lessons I've carried with me for a long time and every time I paint on the street. With time I wanted to create bigger and bigger pieces in the most visible spots with my friends and we were all learning this new discipline that united us more and more, using tools like spray, latex paint and rollers and doing letter and symbols that only we could understand. It was our dirty outlaw and secret teenager club that with time brought me to do what I do nowadays," he says.

His art, which is almost always figurative, soon stood out for his close relationship with indigenous Brazilian culture compared to the contemporary and urban culture. In this way, NUNCA moved from the streets to the most prestigious museums and galleries, such as the Tate Modern in London.

He has worked with some of the best Brazilian artists, such as Otávio and Gustavo Pandolfo, known as Os Gemeos, and with Otàvio's wife, Nina.

> We have more power nowadays to make changes in the world than we have ever had before and it is making us become this new and unknown kind of people.

NUNCA, nickname of the Brazilian Francisco Rodrigues da Silva, at work in the Vila Mariana district, in São Paulo.

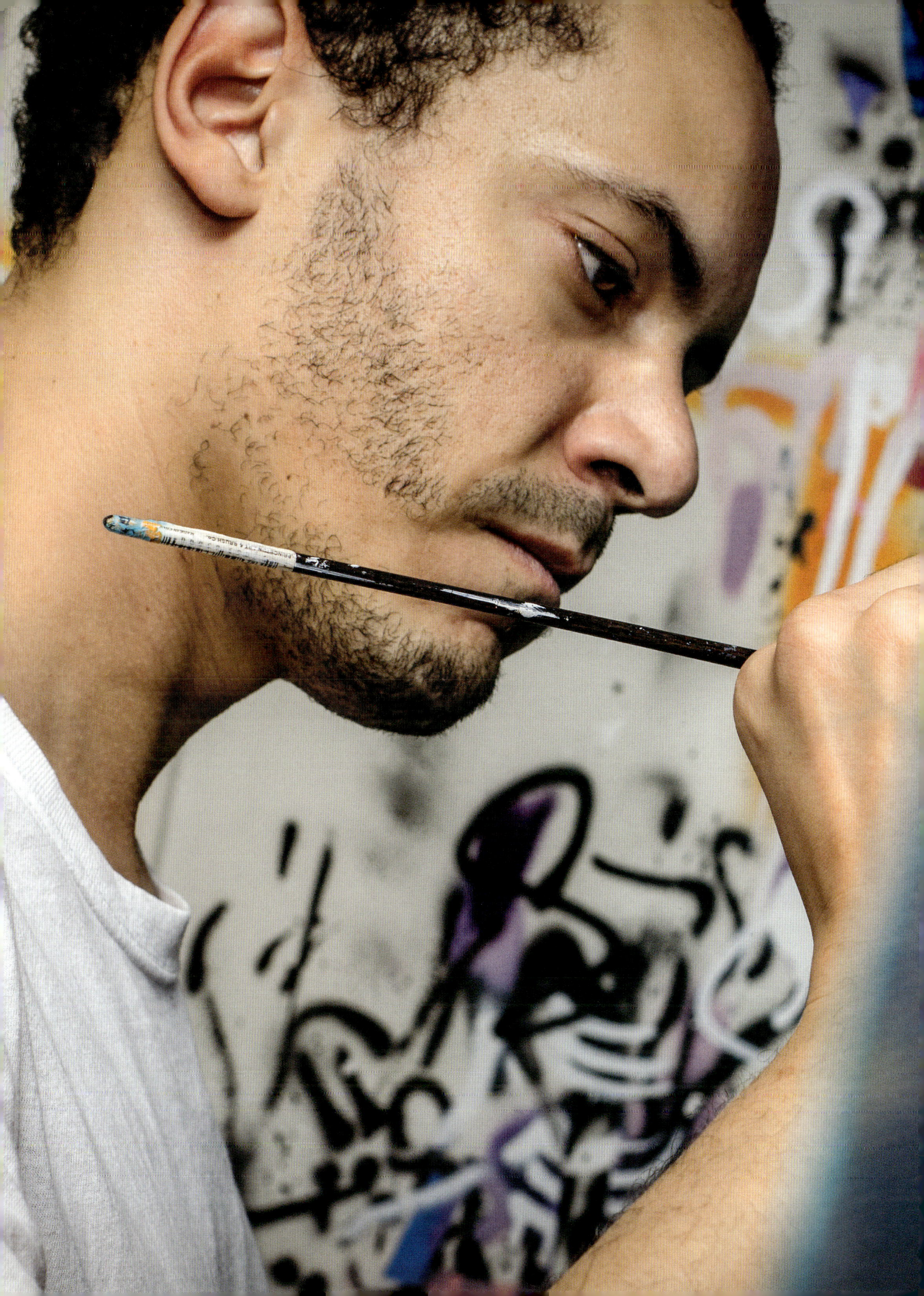

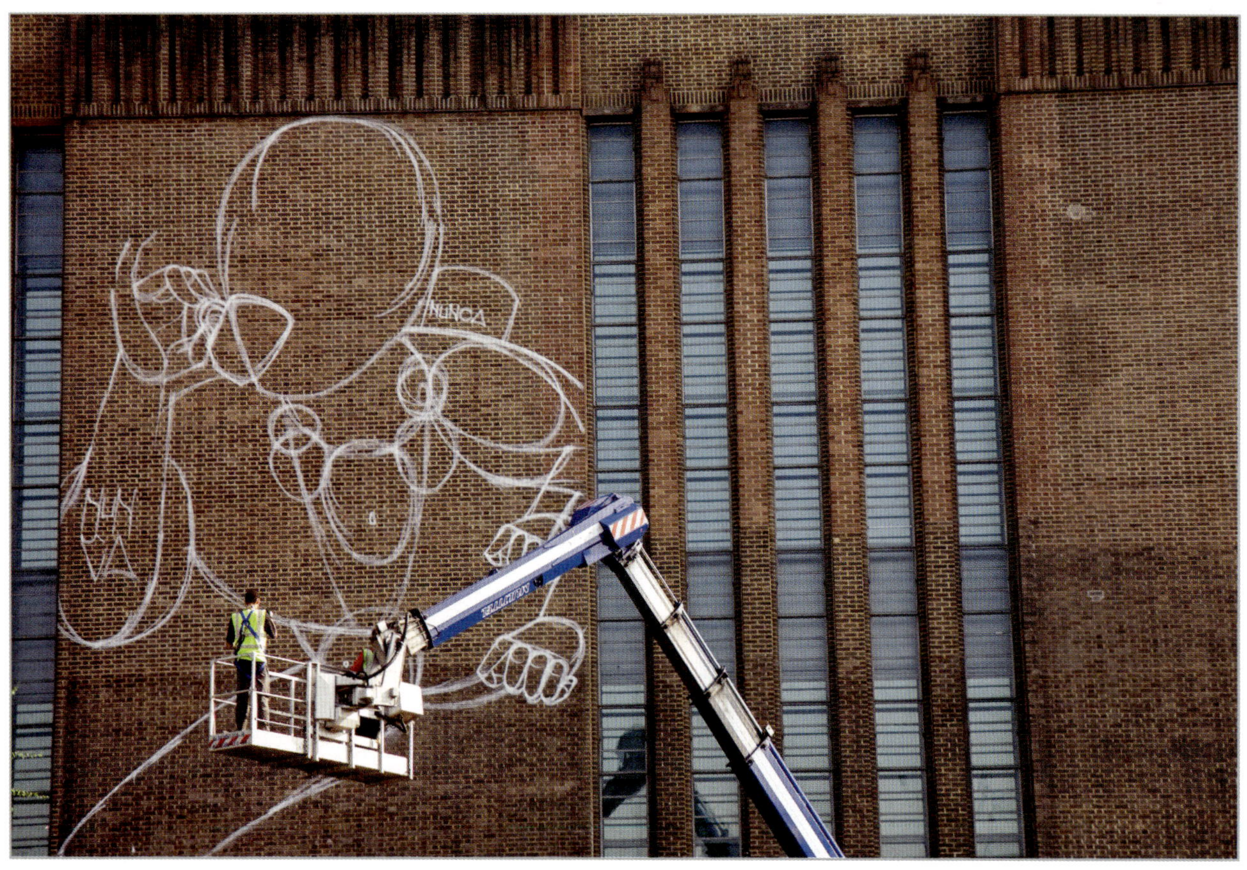

London, 2008 - NUNCA has just begun the great mural painted on the facade of the Tate Modern in London for the *Street Art* exhibition held in summer, 2008.

London, 2008 - The finished mural represents a "metropolitan Amerindian", who drinks coffee and paints on walls with his roll.

His work mainly aims at the juxtaposition, blending and contamination of cultures, the interaction between the modern life style and the tribal one, between the values of contemporary society and those that have characterized the existence of indigenous cultures for centuries: what is most interesting is his understanding of the world and its evolution. And this is why he uses such a wide range of colors, his favorite of which is red.

"I use the engraving technique – in particular for metal engraving – from the 16th century when the first colonizers that came to what they called the 'New World,' Brazil and South and Central America, made an anthropological portrait of the indigenous peoples, the slaves, the fruits, the landscape and the cultural aspects at the time. I borrowed, adapted and developed it in order to use it with spray paint and acrylic paint on my murals and canvasses to create scenes, portraits, fruits based on my own experience of the cultural aspects of the globalized and contemporary world I live in and its cultural exchange, the cultural invasion and cultural creation we take part in all the time, every day."

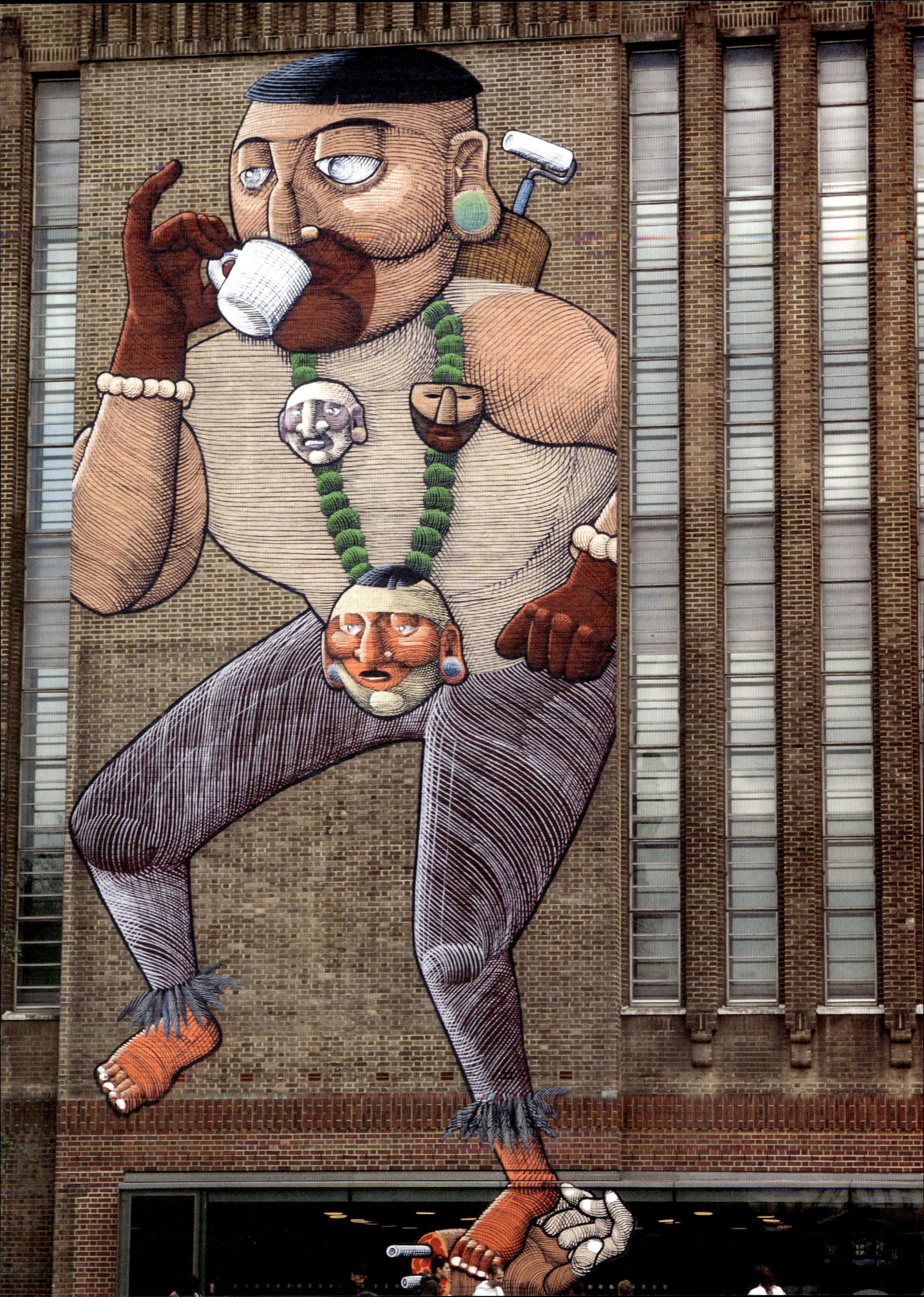

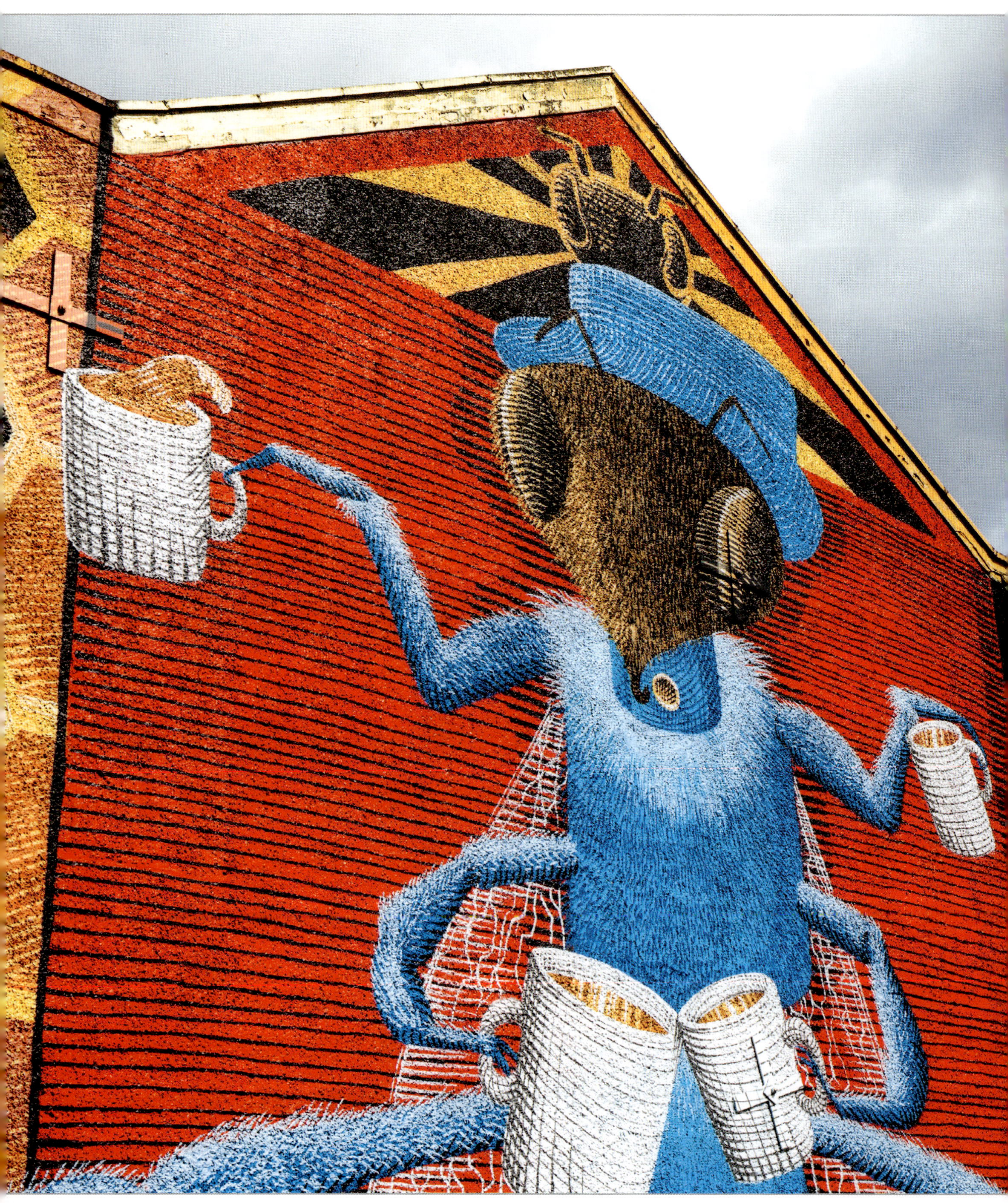

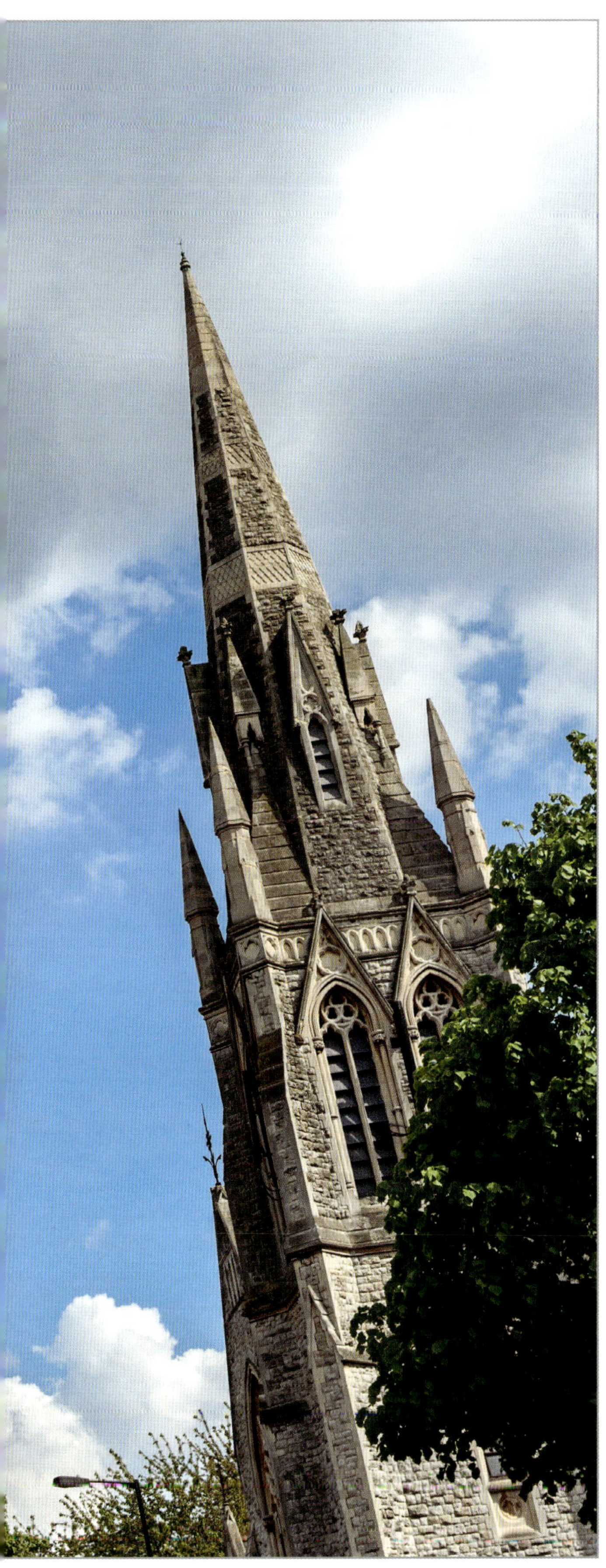

London, 2013
The red background heightens the figure of the enormous blue insect: a visionary fragment of Amazonia at the Dulwich Street Art Festival in London.

If he were to summarize it all in a single image, it would be: "Something like an indigenous blonde using Naique shoes (fake Nike shoes) and a cellphone to talk with his French girlfriend in China." The basic message is "that we have more power nowadays to make changes in the world than we have ever had before and it is making us become this new and unknown kind of people."

The question of what art is, for NUNCA, is a political one. "I don't care at all for street art, really. But what's real art? Is it just what you can see in museums? Is an artist merely someone who makes money through art?" he asks himself. "I have done work for shows in museums and galleries and all I understood is that there is a different mindset between working on a street and working in an institutional space and what you are required to create in each place is completely different. The same difference that there is between those people who only know of artists whose work is exhibited in museums and galleries and those who follow the work of artists that mainly work in public areas. In the end it's all political: it means being democratic, free and respectful of artistic creation. Anyone who denies that certain works can be described as 'art' do so only because they want art to be a culture of the elite. Why are there more and more conceptual and contemporary artists working in the public arena, painting murals, using the same tools as street artists and graffiti artists and yet a big part of the institutional artistic circle of directors, gallery owners, curators and artists themselves do not consider graffiti or street art to be art?

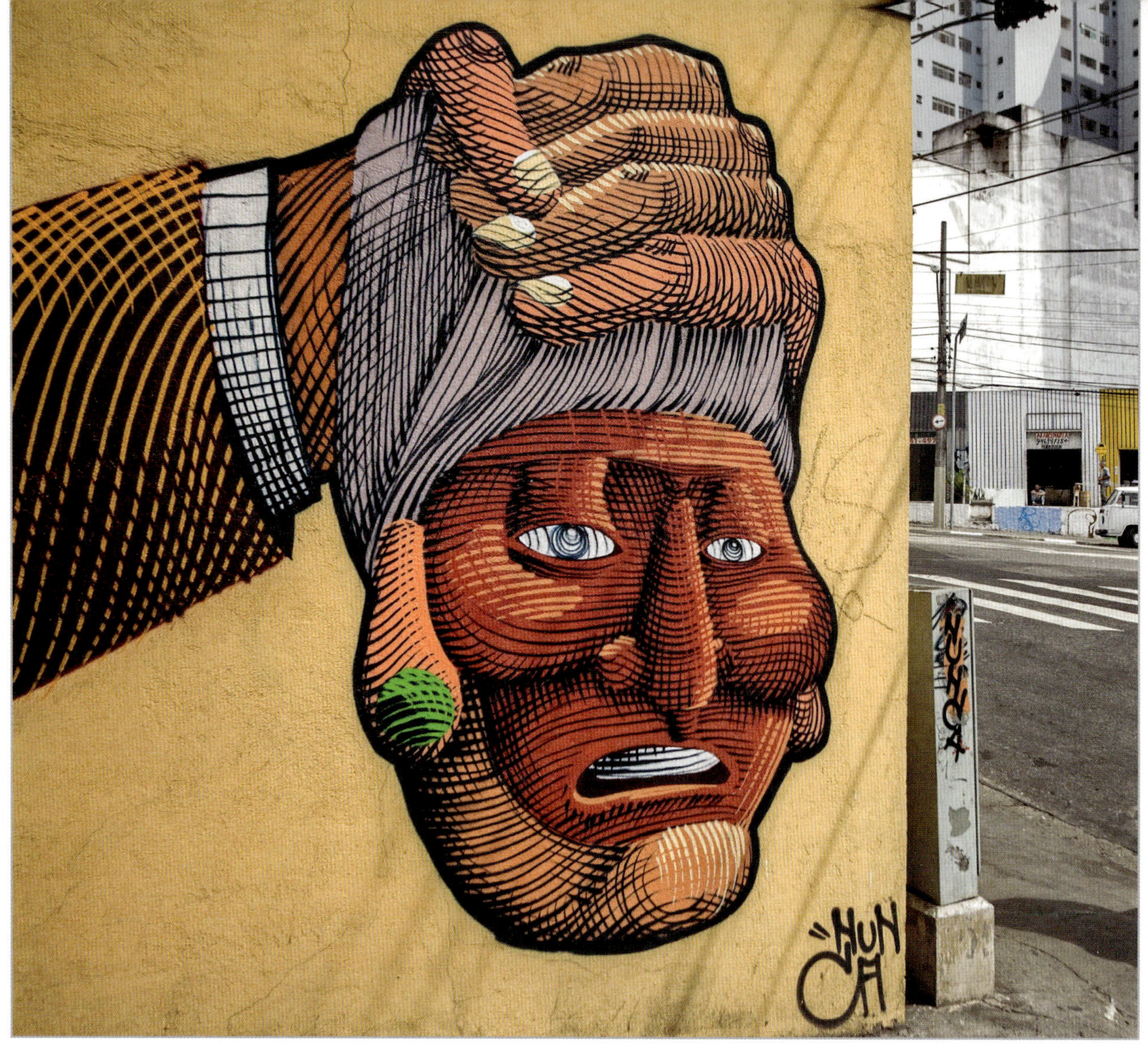

São Paulo, 2008 - This mural seems to accuse contemporary Brazilian society of decapitating ancient autochthonous cultures.

Frankfurt, 2013 - Despite the blonde subject with blue eyes, in this mural NUNCA proves to be attracted by the aesthetic of the indigenous people of South America.

Even when the most important artists of this discipline are exhibited in some of the greatest museums throughout the world?" and adds, "It's too cynical to say a train painted with graffiti is not art but to argue that a mural painted by a contemporary artist with no roots in street art or graffiti is. I don't consider myself a street artist, I was painting on the streets way before this became an issue and the only attempt made by artistic institutions to understand what we have over the years was to pigeonhole it as 'art.' So no, I don't consider myself a street artist."

And yet he remembers those years with affection: "I am very proud of most of the murals I created when I was painting trains illegally. I like painting, I love creating and showing people my work," he confesses openly.

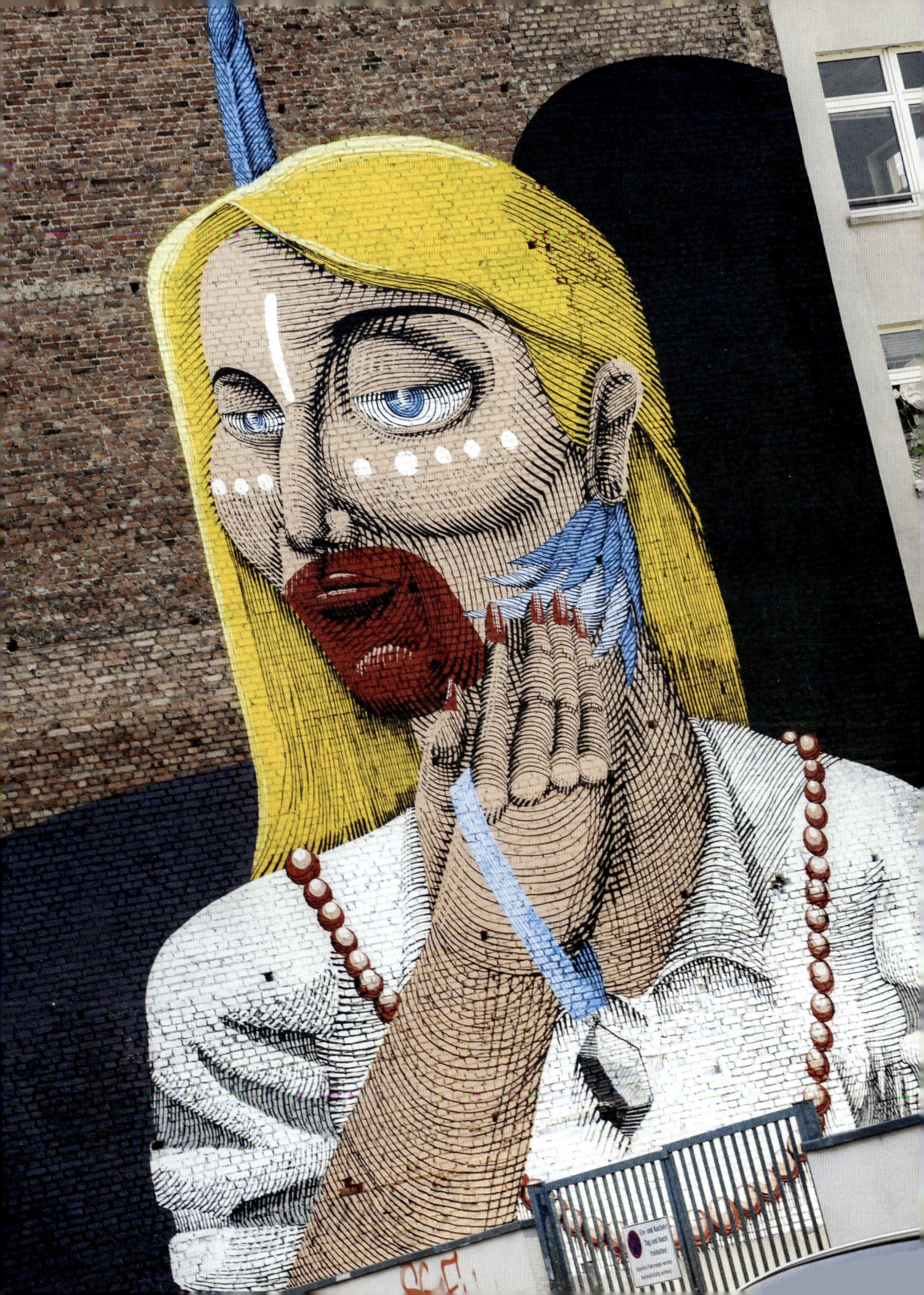

"I remember everything. And perhaps one day I will reproduce my memories in a large piecc and people will then get to know about it, but for now it is a hidden part of me," he confides, perhaps thinking of a certain event that for now he cannot reveal. But NUNCA still has a lot of unrealized dreams, for example "painting a train in Singapore."

There are three cities in particular where he loves to work: São Paulo, Los Angeles and Paris. "These are the places where, until now, I have had the most intense experiences of my life and where today some of my best friends live." Special honor is, of course, reserved for his hometown: "São Paulo is where the whole world meets and it has a cosmic ethnicity. And that's all I need to continue creating."

His vision for the future is rather negative, a bit like – he explains – in Pearl Jam's video, *Do the Evolution.* What he would like for a better world is "No more electricity." Adding, almost prophetically, "Be safe."

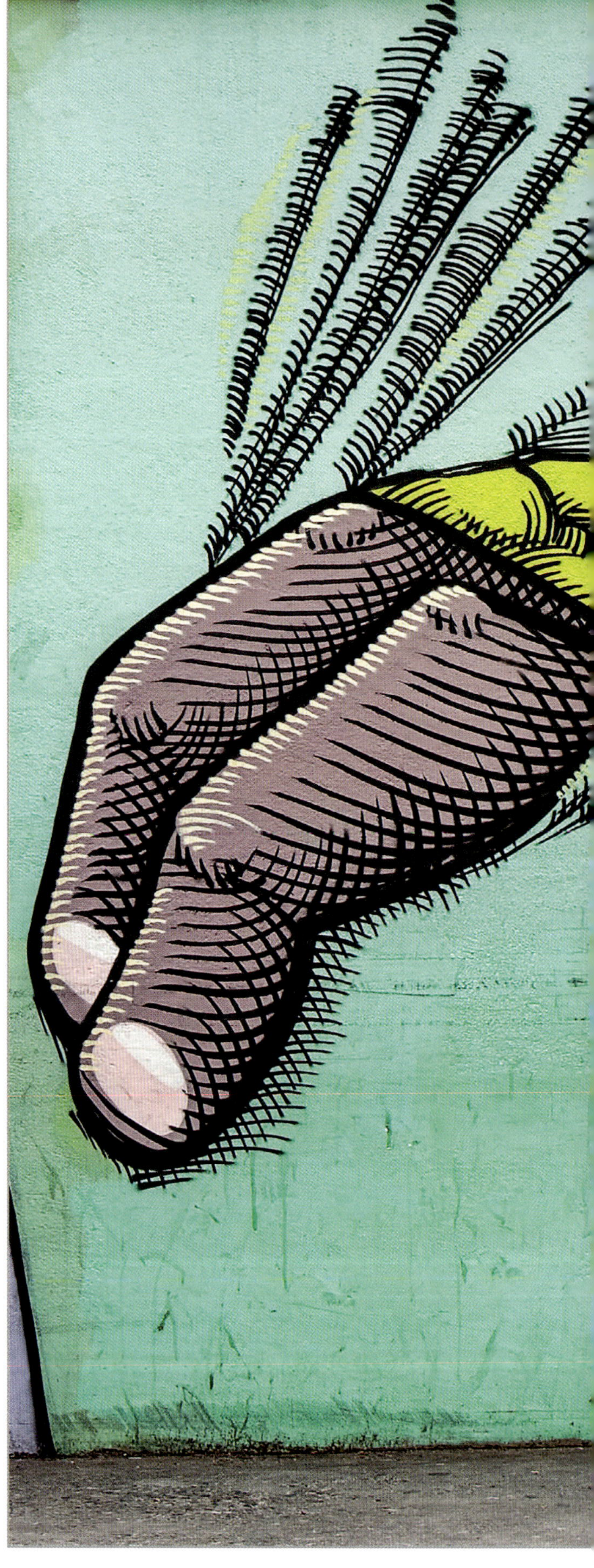

São Paulo, 2008
NUNCA's figures show the essence of the Pre-Colombian civilization thanks to strong lines and bright colors, just like this composite face.

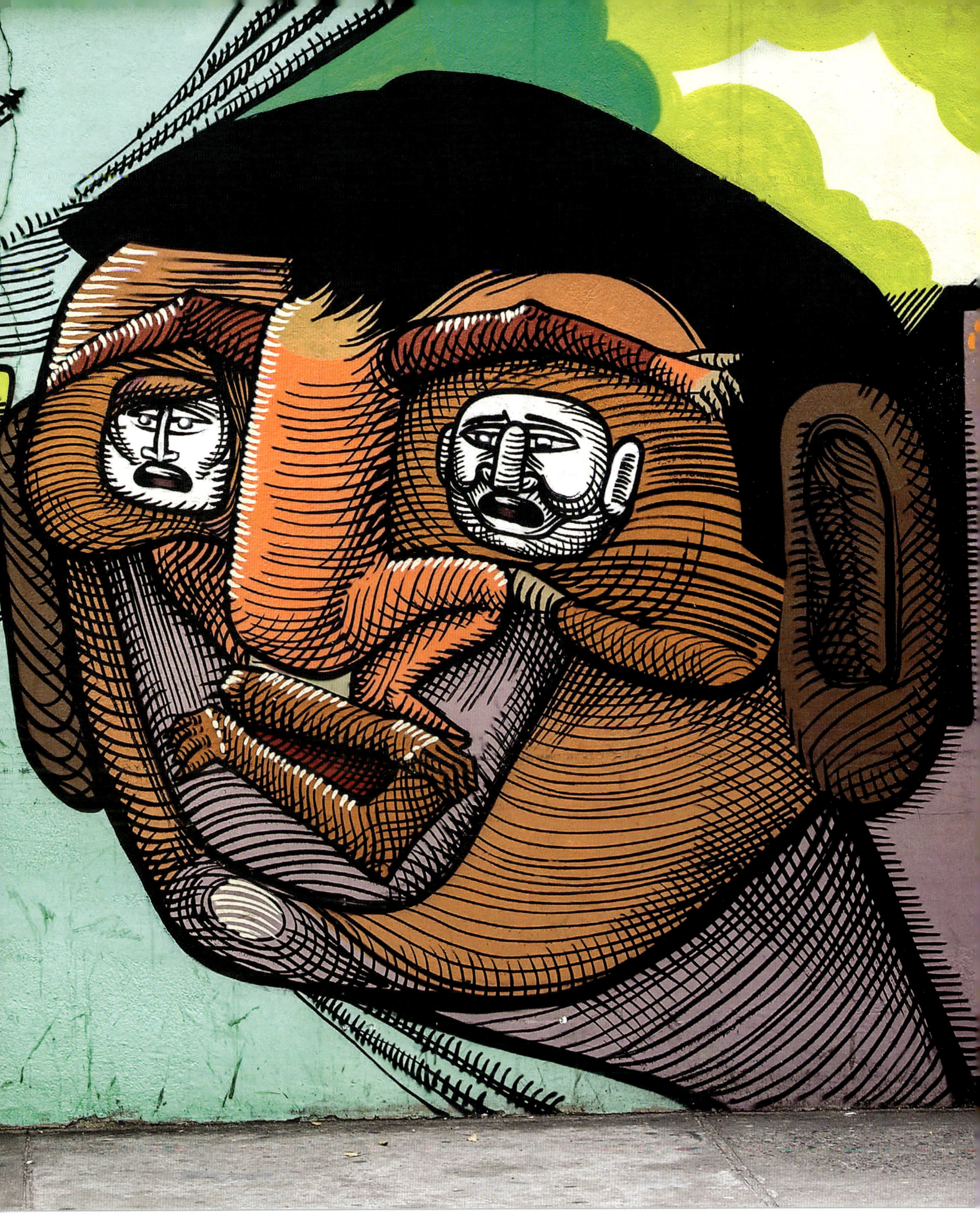

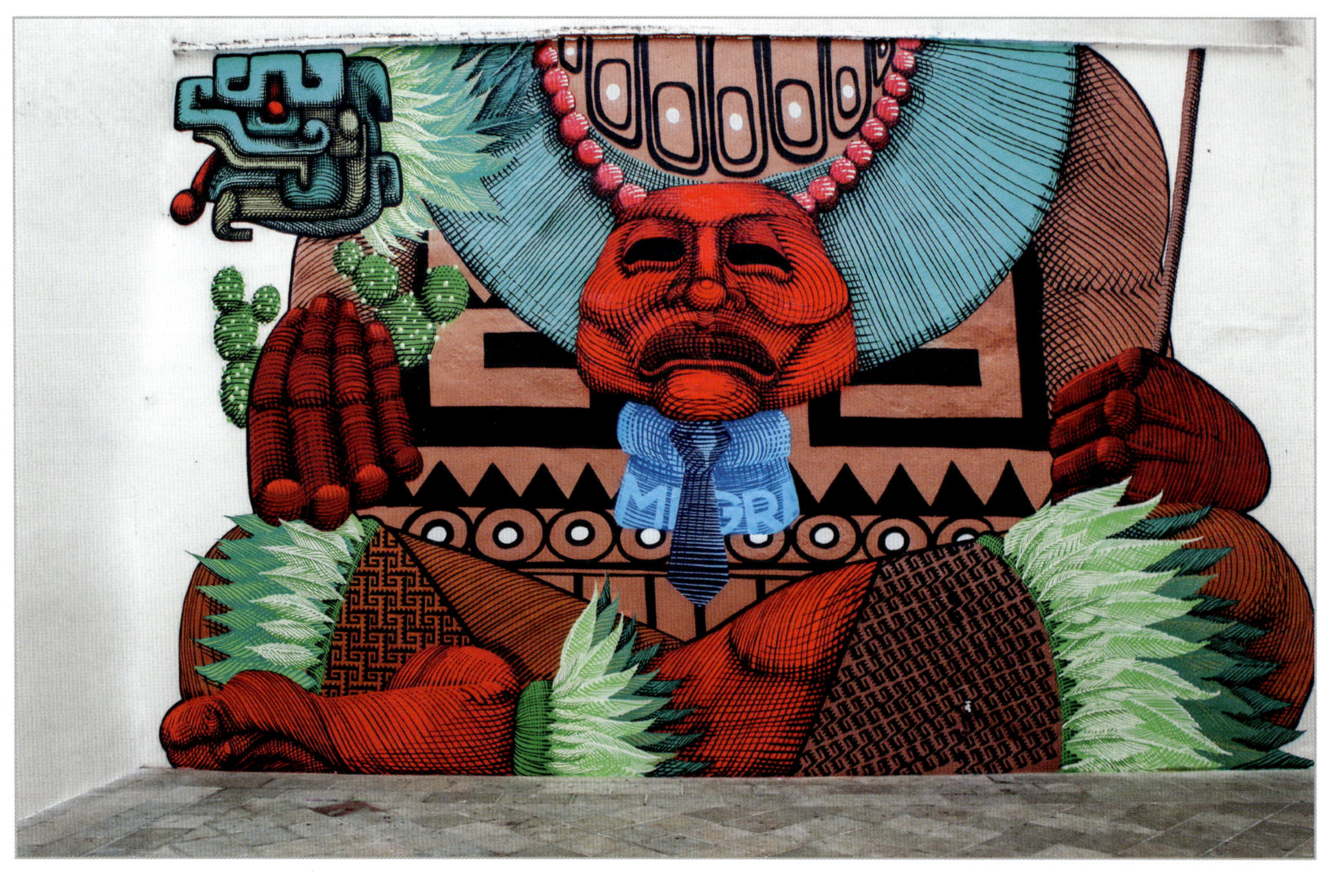

Oaxaca, 2013 - For the Museum of Contemporary Art in Oaxaca de Juárez, a Mexican city of Mixtec and Zapotec origins, NUNCA paints a enigmatic and totemic figure whose face is replaced by a large mask hanging from the neck.

Kiev, 2015 - This mural depicting a Ukrainian Cossack seems to paint itself. In reality, this work in Podil, in the center of Kiev, cost NUNCA much effort.

"I have done work for shows in museums and galleries
and all I understood is that there is a different mindset
between working on a street and working in an institutional space
and what you are required to create in each place
is completely different."

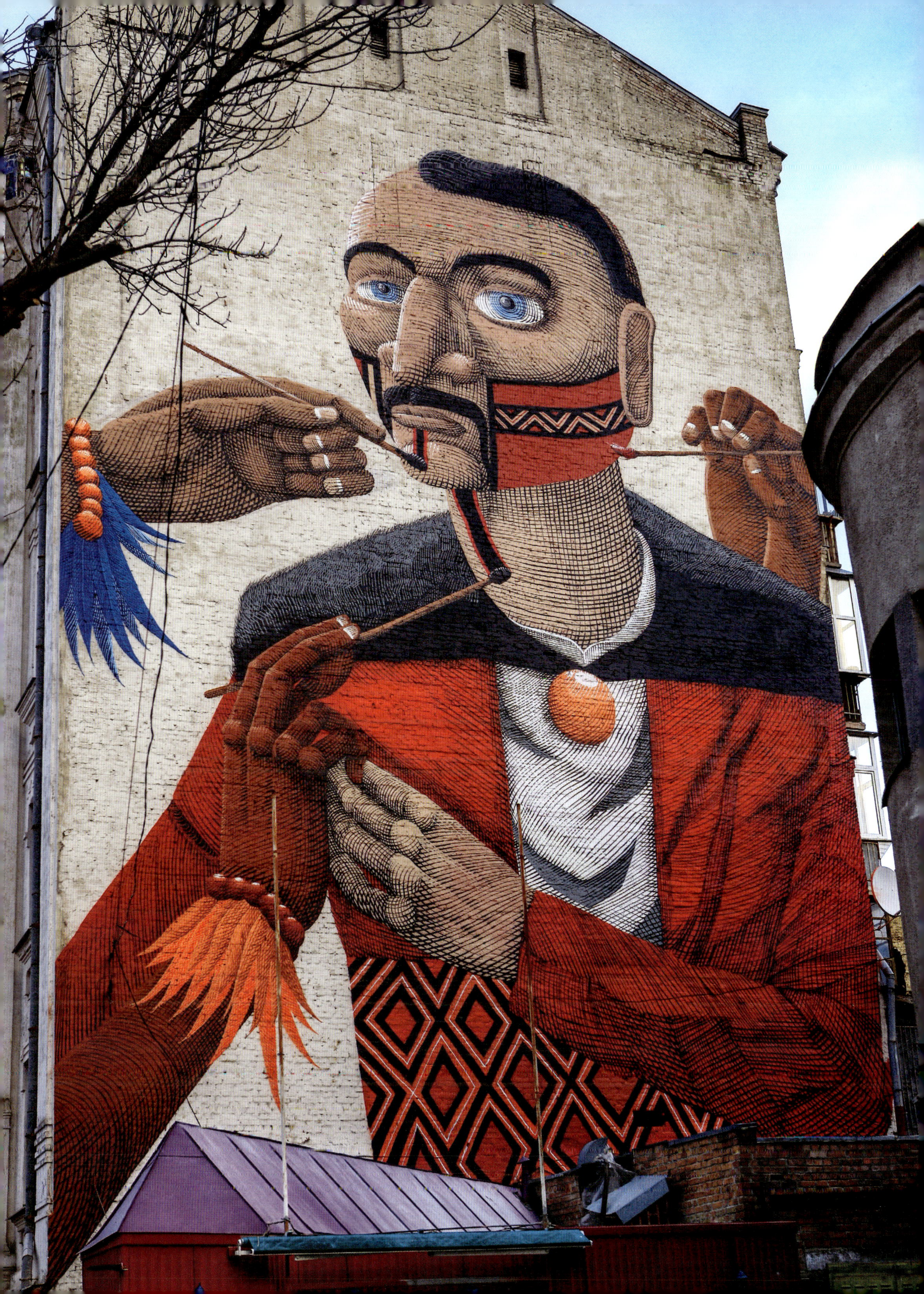

ROA
Expert in Animals and Anatomy

"I tend not to define myself too much: *panta rhei.* To me, the process is more intense than the outcome, what emerges from everything," ROA begins, trying to express his credo. The essence of his art is animals: birds, mice, elephants, rabbits, but also rare species (such as the famous Numbat created in Fremantle for the FORM Gallery in Perth, Australia). Some of them are portrayed in anatomical detail: skulls, bones, internal organs. He "captures" them in his characteristic black and white style, in a rather dark vein, often large, gigantic, so that they are still more striking. ROA values his anonymity because he is sure that it can guarantee him more freedom in artistic creation. He only reveals his origins: "For many Belgians, Belgium feels small, because it is small, although it's pretty centrally located. European capitals like Paris, London, Amsterdam, Berlin [. . .] are all very easy to travel or drive to. In the last few years I haven't spent that much time there anymore, but it's the place where I grew up, and many of my friends are there. It changes through traveling continuously.

I like to return to places and meet the same people, with whom I establish a connection. I'm often in New York and London. But I can't define a 'favorite' city or place. Every place has its uniqueness, and I paint local animal species specific to the location. Thus, travelling keeps me inspired."

His passion for drawing goes back a long way: "As a kid, I never considered doing anything else than drawing or being a *bricoleur*, from an early age I was doing these things, because that was what I liked to do. There was not a defining moment that I recall becoming an artist. It was only when people started to refer to me as an artist that I realized that I might have succeeded in making a life out of my passion!" he confesses. His style developed just as spontaneously. "A friend and I had been fascinated by graffiti for a long time, we were thirteen or fourteen years old and so one day we did something with letters on a bridge in our hometown (Ghent). Now he is an important musician and I continue to paint on walls. But that was my first work ever!" he recalls nostalgically.

> Every culture connects with animal species in different ways, above all today when we live in an era full of challenges.

Dresda, 2016 - ROA at work in Dresden during *Magic City - The Art of the Street*, a festival dedicated to the most diverse forms of street art.

Whale, 2012 - During the Komafest in Vardø, in the North of Norway, ROA painted a whale skeleton on a building corroded by saltwater: a choice that reinforces the idea of dereliction.

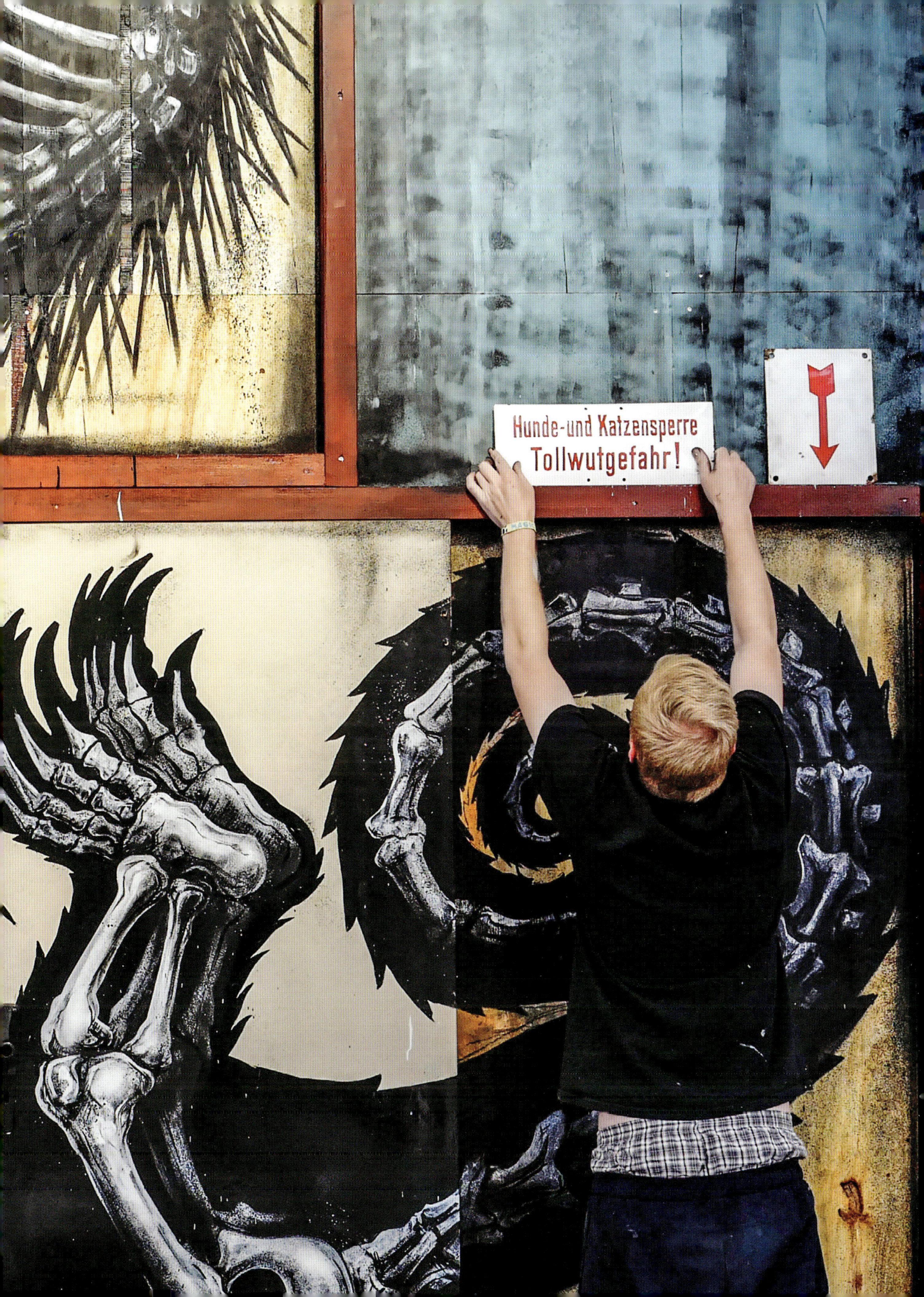

Hunde- und Katzensperre
Tollwutgefahr!

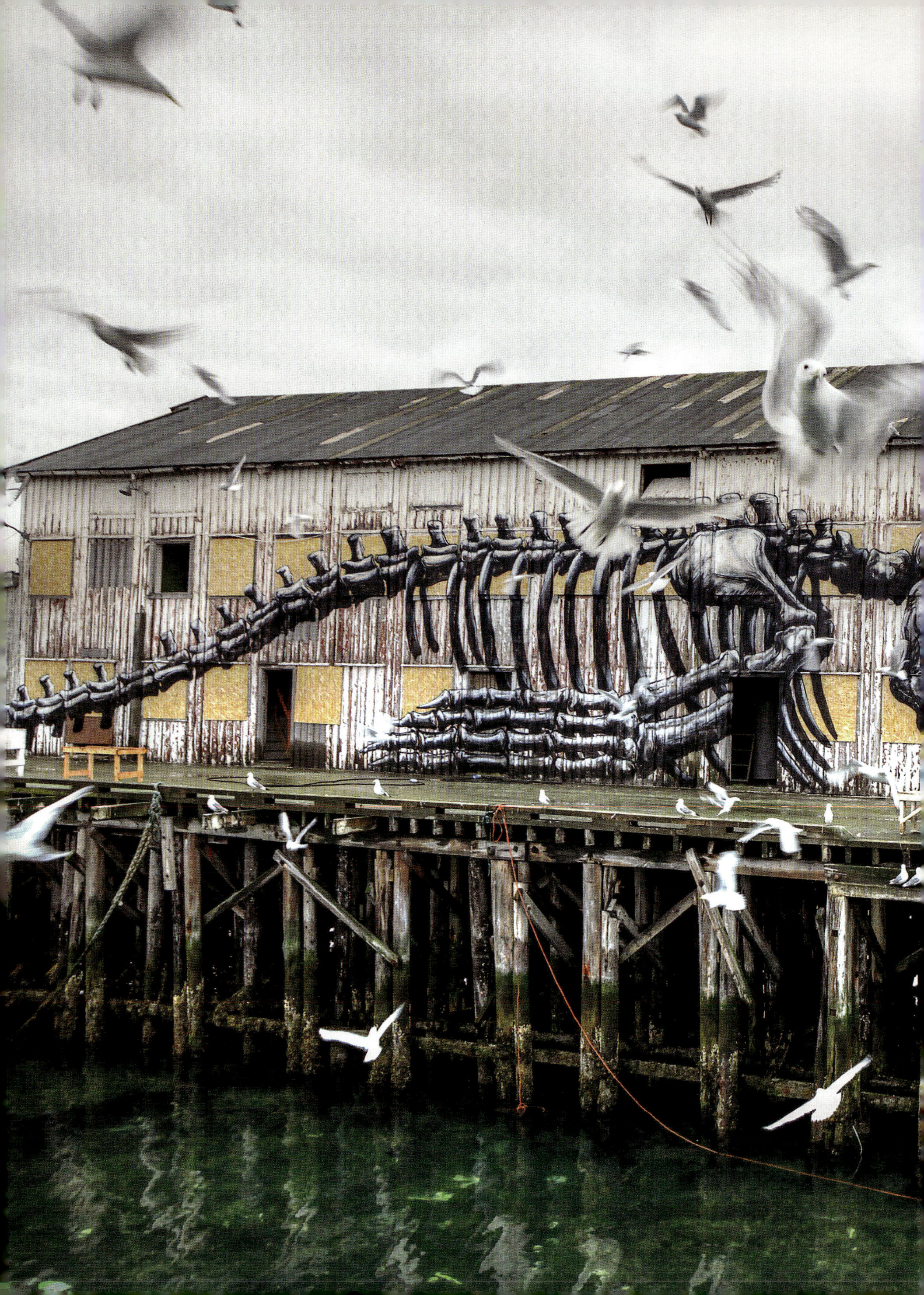

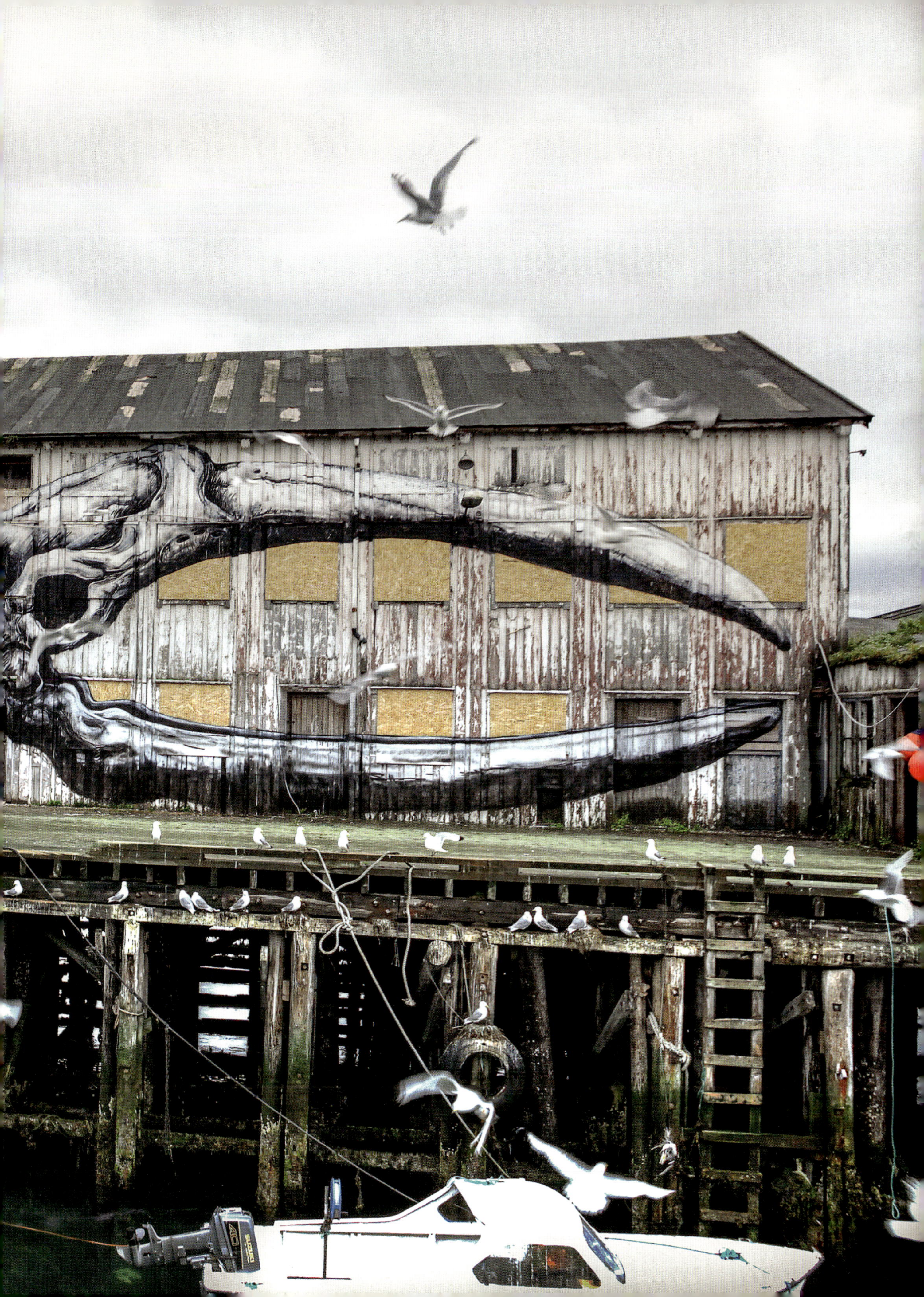

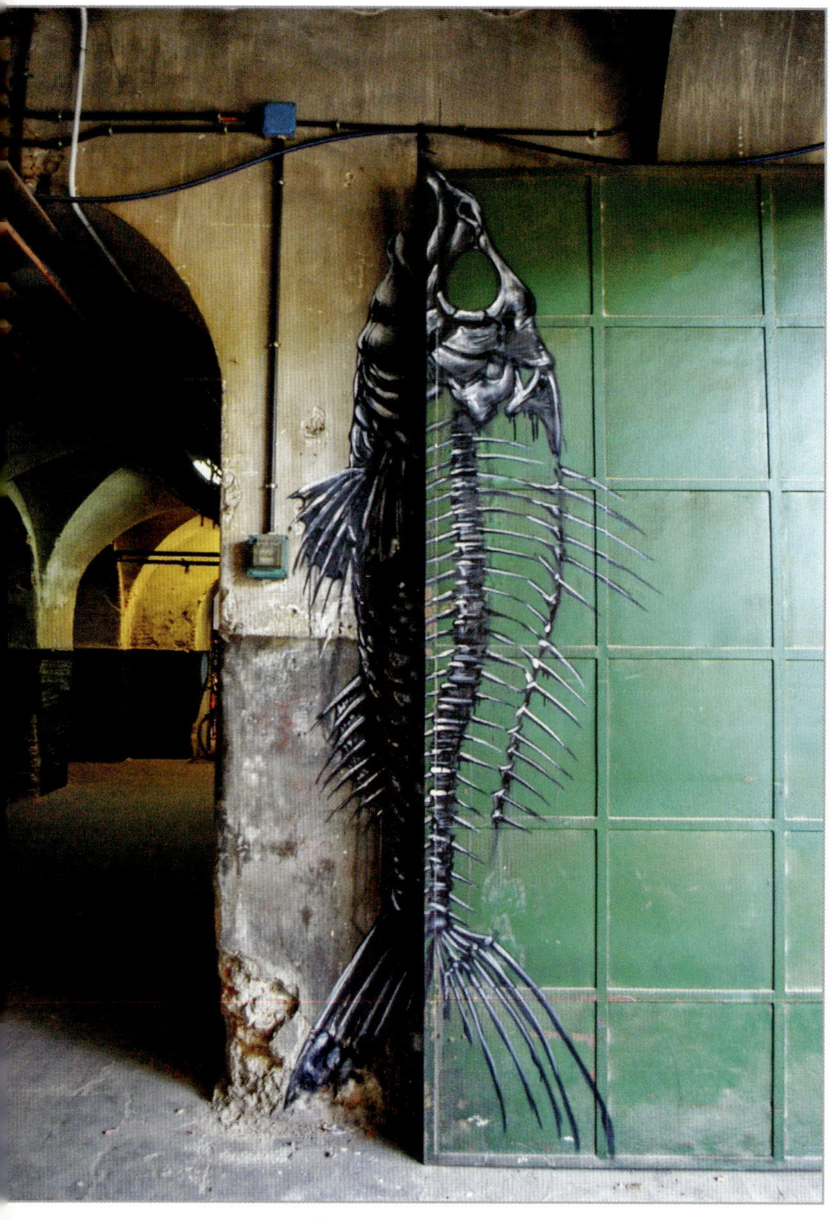

ROA then explains that the technique depends on the kind of work. "My technique depends on what I am doing. Outdoor and indoor practices are different. Both are based on painting, although my technique is derived from my sketches. The black and white pallet, the hatchings . . . much is derived from drawing into painting. However, I consider painting as a different action, a much more physical act," he explains, "but I'd rather others described my art. I try not to reflect too much on what I'm doing in order to keep it pure. Certainly, in the last few years I have mainly painted animals . . ." he says, and admits that they have always fascinated him. "It's interesting to see how they adapt to modern society and how they change in relation to their environment. By observing them in different situations we discover humanity itself, our surroundings, and our values. This journey makes me do research on the species that live in the places I visit, and sometimes I create a little encyclopedia of the local fauna." For ROA, the interaction between human beings and animals is fundamental: "Every culture connects with animal species in different ways, above all today when we live in an era full of challenges," he adds. But this is not the only interpretation possible of his works: "In my opinion, the message is the medium, because I'm convinced that each one of us perceives things in a personal way and that this is what counts.

Fish, 2010

Sometimes ROA depicts transformative murals. As a door or gate is opened, a partial or total skeleton view of the painted creature is revealed: as in the case of this fish in the social center La Tabacalera in Madrid, not far from the museum Reina Sofia, which houses *Guernica* by Picasso. A game that is both ironic and macabre, like the *memento mori* in the Baroque tradition.

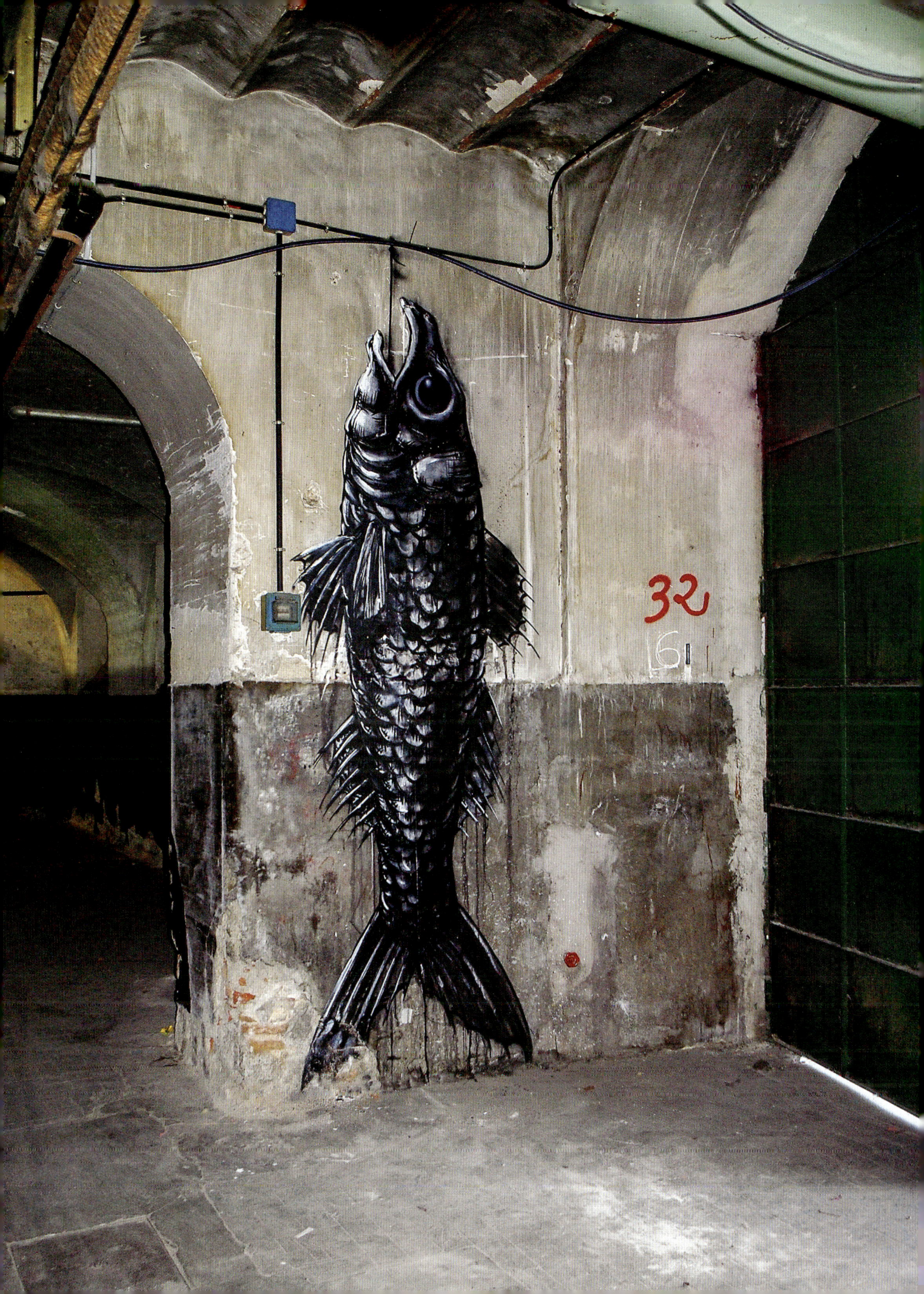

32

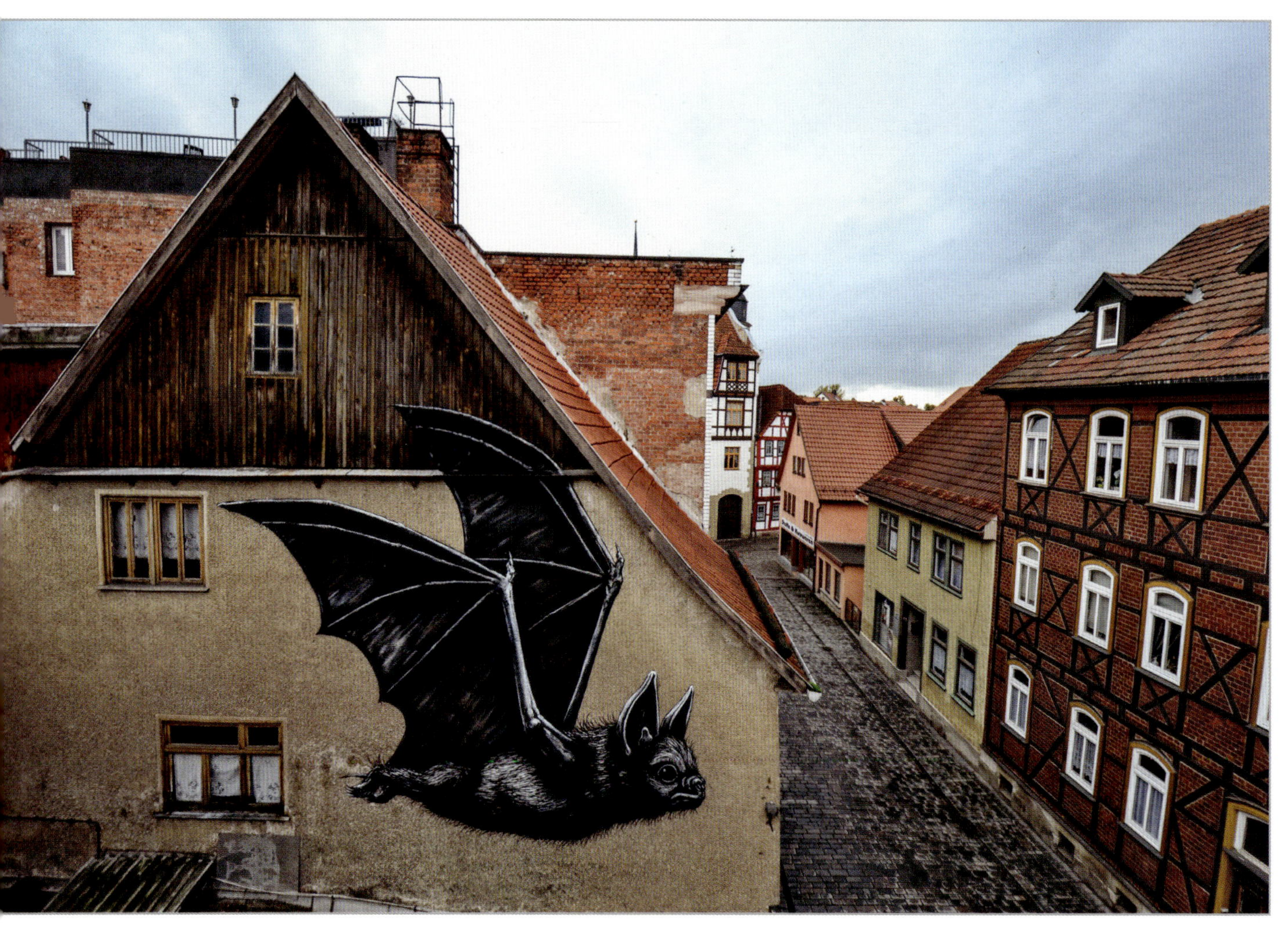

Bat, 2014 - Inspired by a bat seen immediately on arrival in Schmalkalden, ROA creates this mural in the German city, along Stumpfelsgasse, on the occasion of the WallCome Festival 2014.

I don't want to impose explanations on people, but leave them free to develop their own thought," he states. For ROA, every artist has probably been influenced by the history of art and by contemporary reality. "As far as I'm concerned, I feel subject to different influences, which are at play in me directly and indirectly, and range from graffiti to works of the great masters of the past and contemporary artists. I can only mention some, like Chardin for his still lifes, Zurbarán for his contrasts of light and dark, Dürer for his powers of observation, Bernini for his Baroque sculptures . . . and, more recently, Gordon Matta-Clark for his involvement with his surroundings and his love for abandoned places. I love to see artists working outside the studio, in an urban context, like, for example, Matthew Barney, who in *River of Fundament* mixes mythological and metropolitan aspects of New York, Los Angeles, and Detroit," he relates, reflecting on that infectious and compelling desire to paint great walls and immense open spaces.

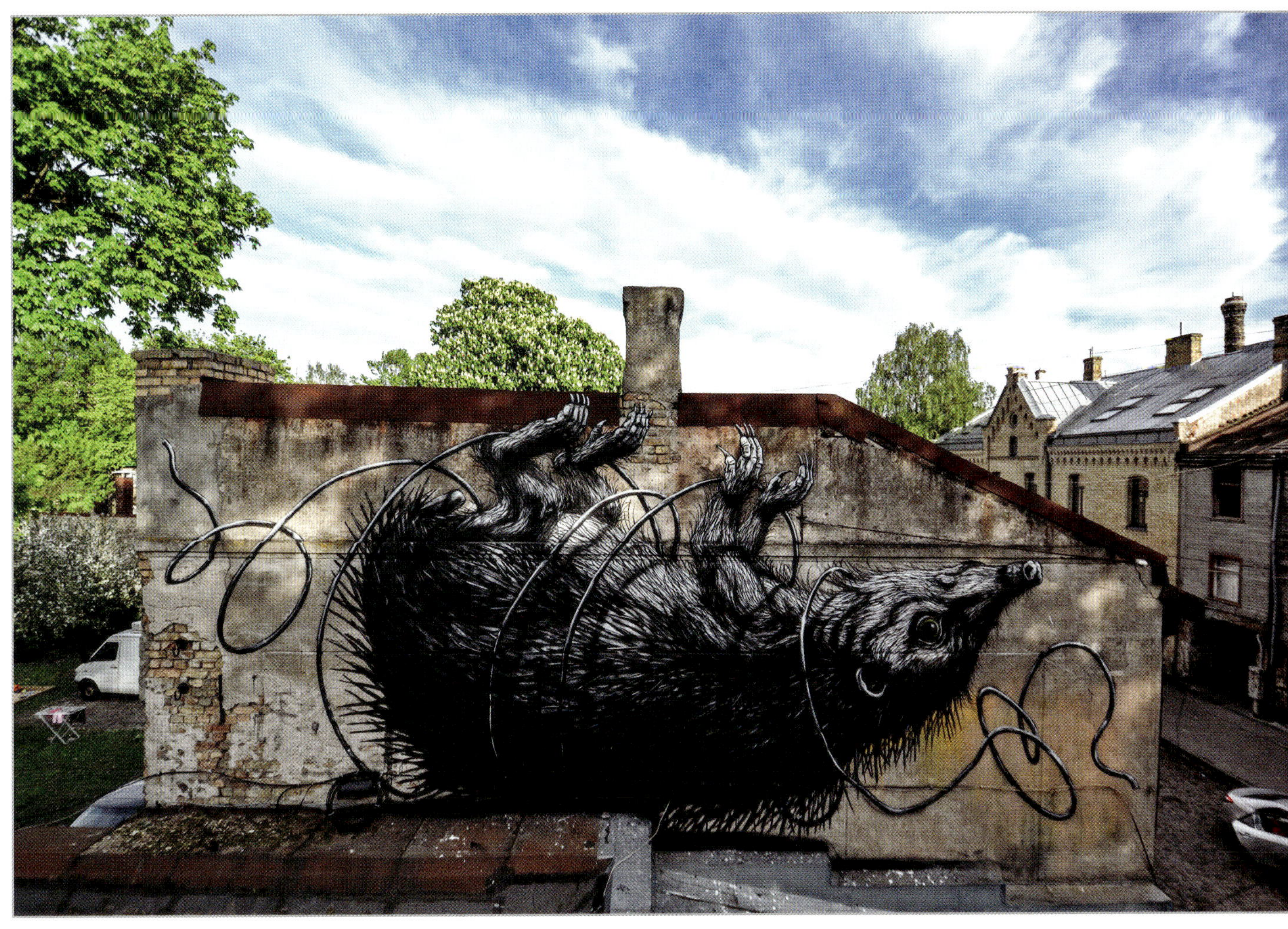

Hedgehog, **2014** - At the entrance to the Ziedoņdārzs park in Riga one can admire one of the ROA's crudest murals:
a hedgehog in a trap, a metaphor for wild animals besieged by man.

"Every person decides for themselves what art is. Classifying it into rigid categories like street art is like branding art itself. At this moment, there are various approaches. What unites us all is that it happens in public space, which is, moreover, independent of the institutions," explains ROA, trying to find a definition for a creative phenomenon that is revolutionizing the world and the very way of viewing artistic production. And then he meditates on how his journey is down to fate. "As I said, I had no idea I'd become a street artist. When I was young I went to an art school, I had books for the sketches and I did graffiti with spray cans; and then I was asked to draw stories and backgrounds, but straightaway I realized that I needed to produce my works, I didn't want to change my passion into work serving others. And in my free time I went to isolated places and painted where I happened to be. In short, I made abandoned factories my studio. I didn't have a studio in my home, but I had all these ideas and I wanted to experiment: I needed

"This journey makes me do research on the species
that live in the places I visit, and sometimes I create
a little encyclopedia of the local fauna."

'private' and remote spaces, so as to explore the different techniques in a kind of oasis," he relates. Isolation and the surrounding desolation have fascinated him since he was a child. "And so one day some explorers of 'urban wastelands' noticed my works, photographed them and put them on Internet. And so I became viral."

"I haven't got a favorite color. We need all the colors," explains ROA. However, fundamentally, he favors almost all the shades of black and white; he reserves the bright colors for drawing internal organs. For him, every wall is different, ready to be filled with meaning. "Honestly, most murals I painted have their story. Working in the public space creates unexpected encounters and site-specific complexities. When I manage the walls myself, it's much more interpersonal: I learned to know some amazing people by just ringing their doorbells to ask if I could paint their wall. Most precious were maybe the residencies in Gambia and in Western Australia were you actually spent time with people and talked about life, nature, and art. Most of the time the best backstage stories happen when for a few days I become part of a certain corner of a big city, or a small African village. Spending time in a certain place in Bangkok, Chicago, Johannesburg . . . or somewhere in no man's land in the dark north of Norway, offers a good barometer on what's going on there. You get immersed in the social life of that specific area," explains ROA, who now knows many countries well and adapts to them with the same ability to "mutate" as his animals. "The most difficult mural? It depends on how you look at it . . . Painting in Sweden while the cans are frozen? Or painting during the night to avoid the humidity of the day in a prostitute suburb in Atlanta? Or painting in Curundu in Panama City . . . or next to the police office in Mexico City? Sometimes I did wonder how I got there, and I experienced some craziness, but I don't want to emphasize those stories too much, as it mythologizes the practice of mural painting, while there is more to tell about it," he reflects. "There are ideas that are not accomplished yet; they need the right context and conditions that will hopefully come my way," he continues. And, visionary that he is, he adds: "I can't predict the future and I try to stay in the present. Of course, I want to continue with my paintings and installations on buildings for exhibitions . . . and to watch where my future will take me."

African Animals, 2012 - Are the animals sleeping or have they been killed? This is the question raised by ROA in Johannesburg, in a South Africa that sees its fauna threatened by poaching.

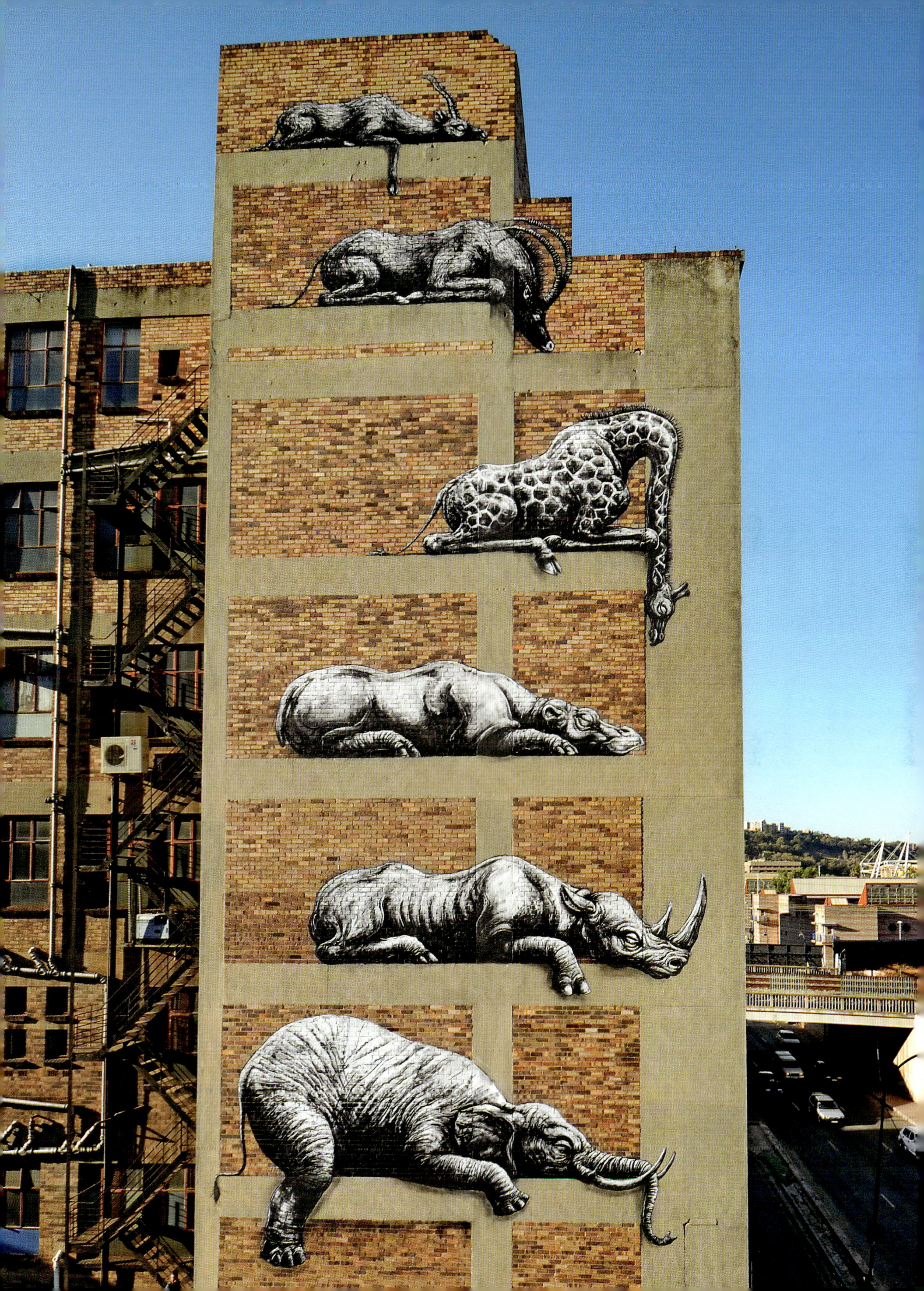

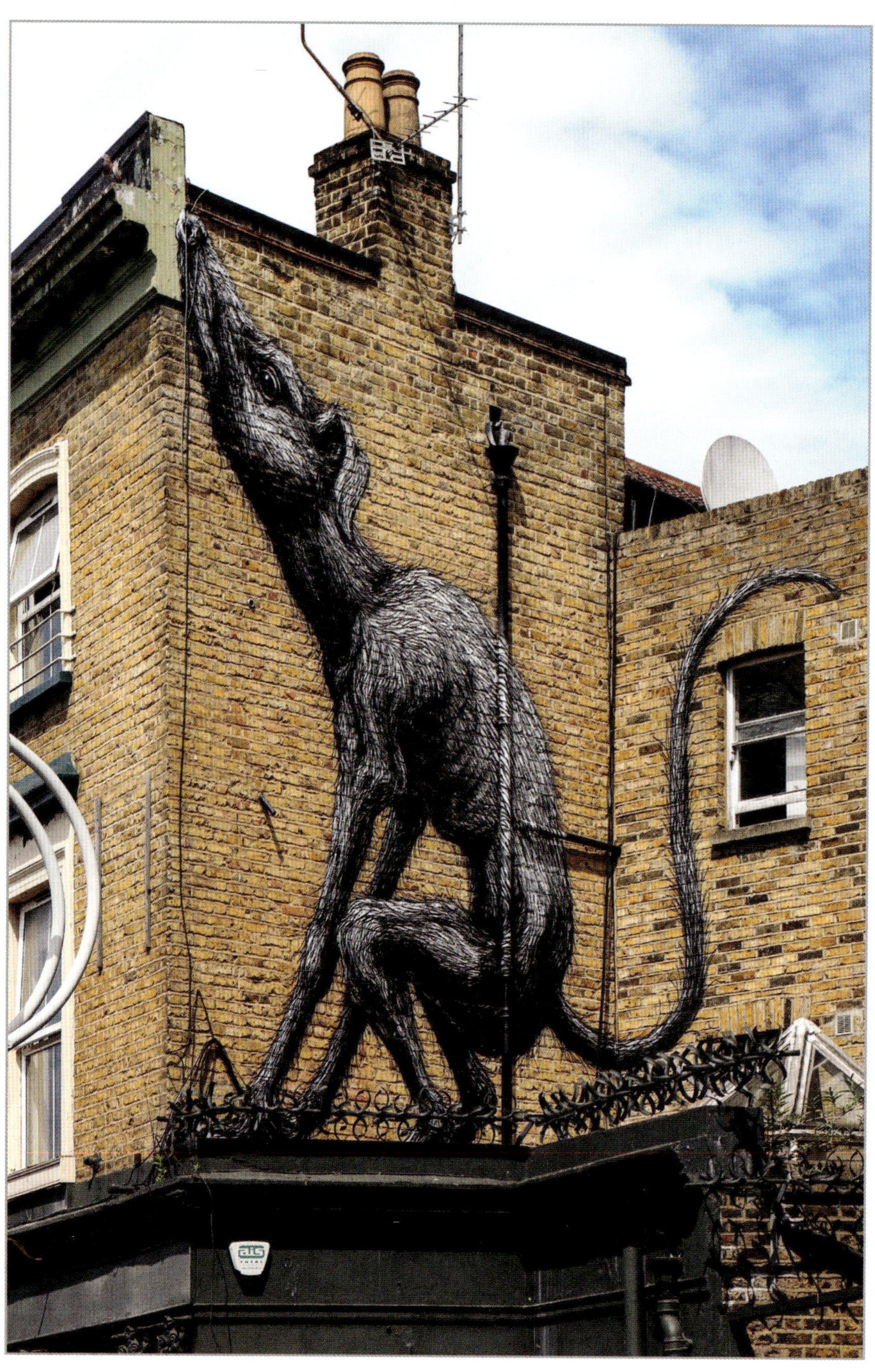

***Shitting Dog**, 2013*
The mural, which was created in Bellenden Road in London, was controversial. But the same subject can be found in a 1665 painting by Adam Pynacker, preserved in a nearby museum.

***Jumping Wolf (Hunted Wolf)**, 2014*
In via Galvani in Rome, the artist has reinterpreted the iconography of the Capitoline Wolf by painting a frightened wolf baring its fangs, intent on defending itself.

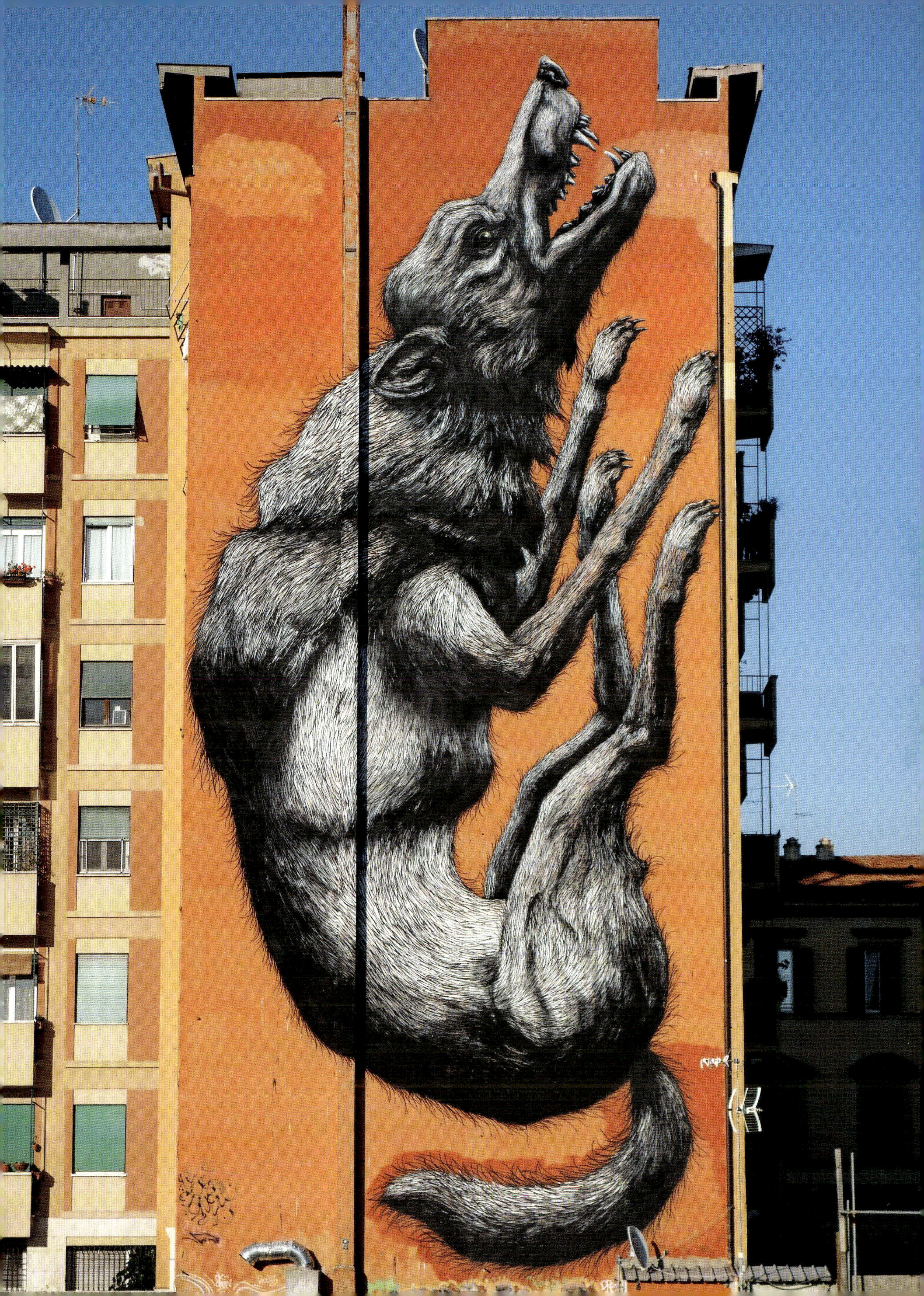

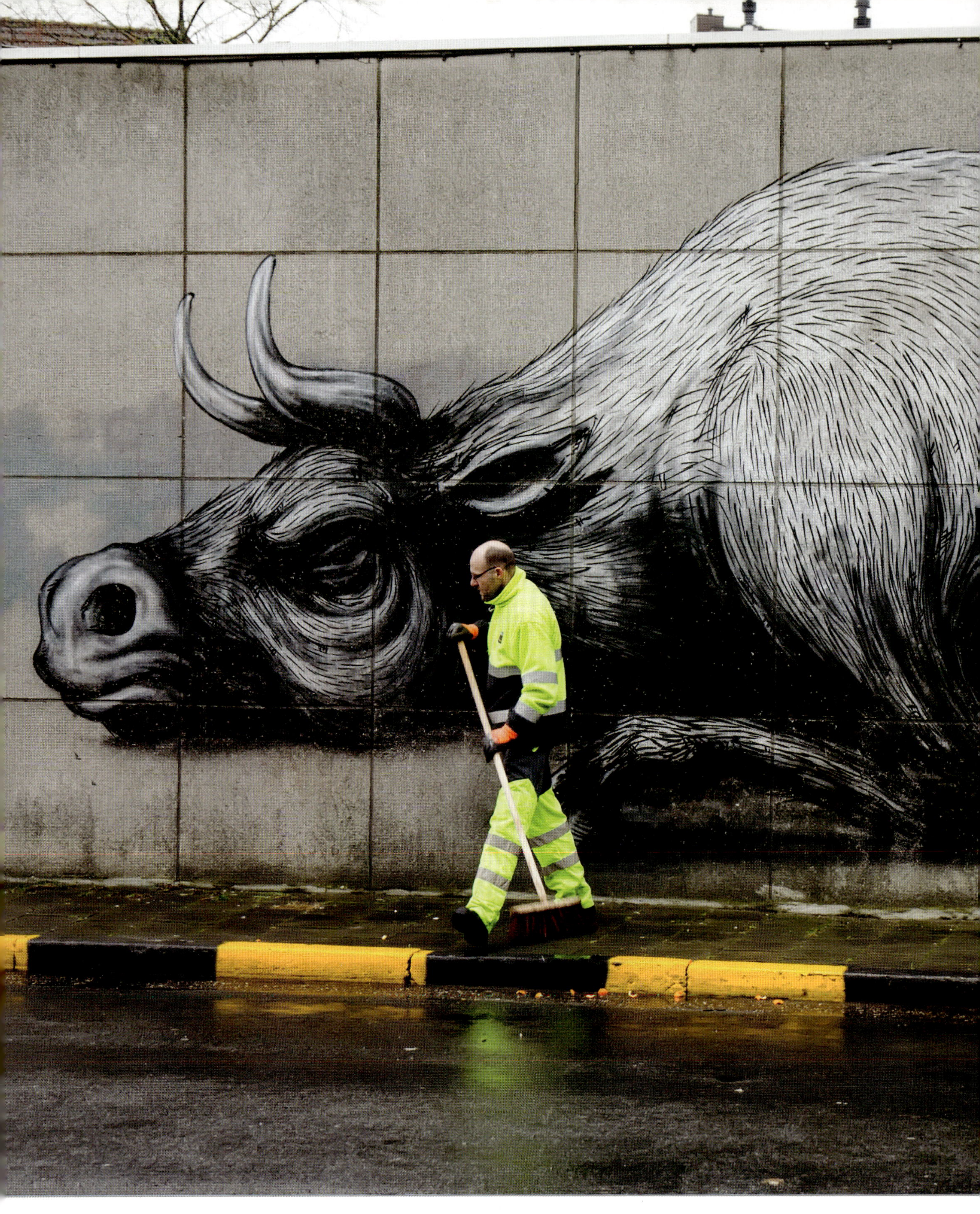

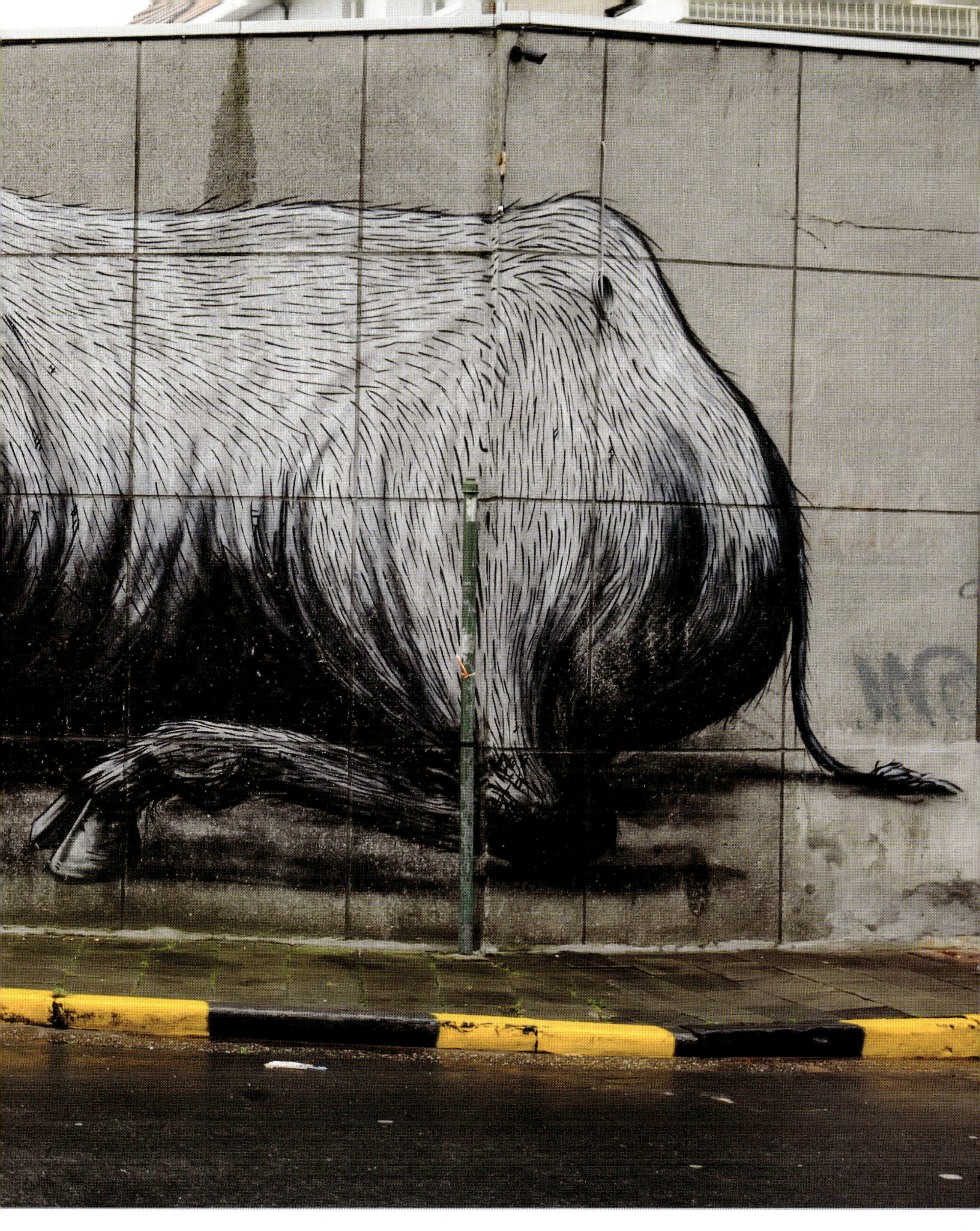

***Bull (Buffalo)*, 2014** - Along Kapelaanstraat in Ghent one can admire one of the works that ROA has scattered through the streets of his city; today they are the subject of thematic tourist itineraries.

SLINKACHU

Miniature Lover

"My dream is to spark the viewer's imagination," Slinkachu admits from London, where he has lived for some time. The uniqueness of this original artist, who in 2016 confessed to being thirty-three years old, is that of building small everyday scenes with miniature figures. He has been doing this since 2006, when he began what he called *The Little People Project*. First, he sets up the scene in the street; then he photographs it; and he the leaves it there to illustrate the loneliness and melancholy of living in a big city. And he does so with a bit of British humor, he is keen to point out. How did all of this begin? Slinkachu, Stu for his friends, also knows how to charm with words and draw viewers into his magical universe: "Some of my earliest and fondest memories are of making miniature dioramas from cereal boxes with my mother. I grew up in a fairly rural area in Devon, in the United Kingdom, and left when I was nineteen to study graphic design, advertising and illustration at university. My first job was as an art director and it was while I was working that I started making miniature street installations as a creative release from my more restrictive day job. It was a hobby that slowly became more and more important in my life. In 2008, I left my job to pursue my art full time. It was difficult at first, but also liberating. My challenge now is not to be too self-critical!" he confesses.

His first street installation was in the autumn of 2006. "I was so excited about the idea of the project and the buzz of creating and leaving a work in the street. I would doodle ideas during the day and then create new works at home in the evenings. My daily commute would often incorporate a detour to leave a miniature somewhere in London and my free time at the weekends was taken up with exploring the city for new locations," he remembers fondly. He explains his technique with the same enthusiasm: "The process is the same for each installation I create. I spend a long time coming up with ideas and keep sketchbooks full of drawings and notes. Once I have an idea that I like, I can make the figures for it, at a 1:87 scale. I cut them up, repose them, add new elements with modeling clay and then paint them.

> My work has different stages that encompass a few different mediums so it can be hard for me to nail down an exact definition of what I do. Its sculpture, photography and street art all at once.

A portrait of Slinkachu at the Andipa Gallery in Kensington (London), where in 2011 he presented *Concrete Ocean*: reproductions on a 1:87 scale of the common people of Britain.

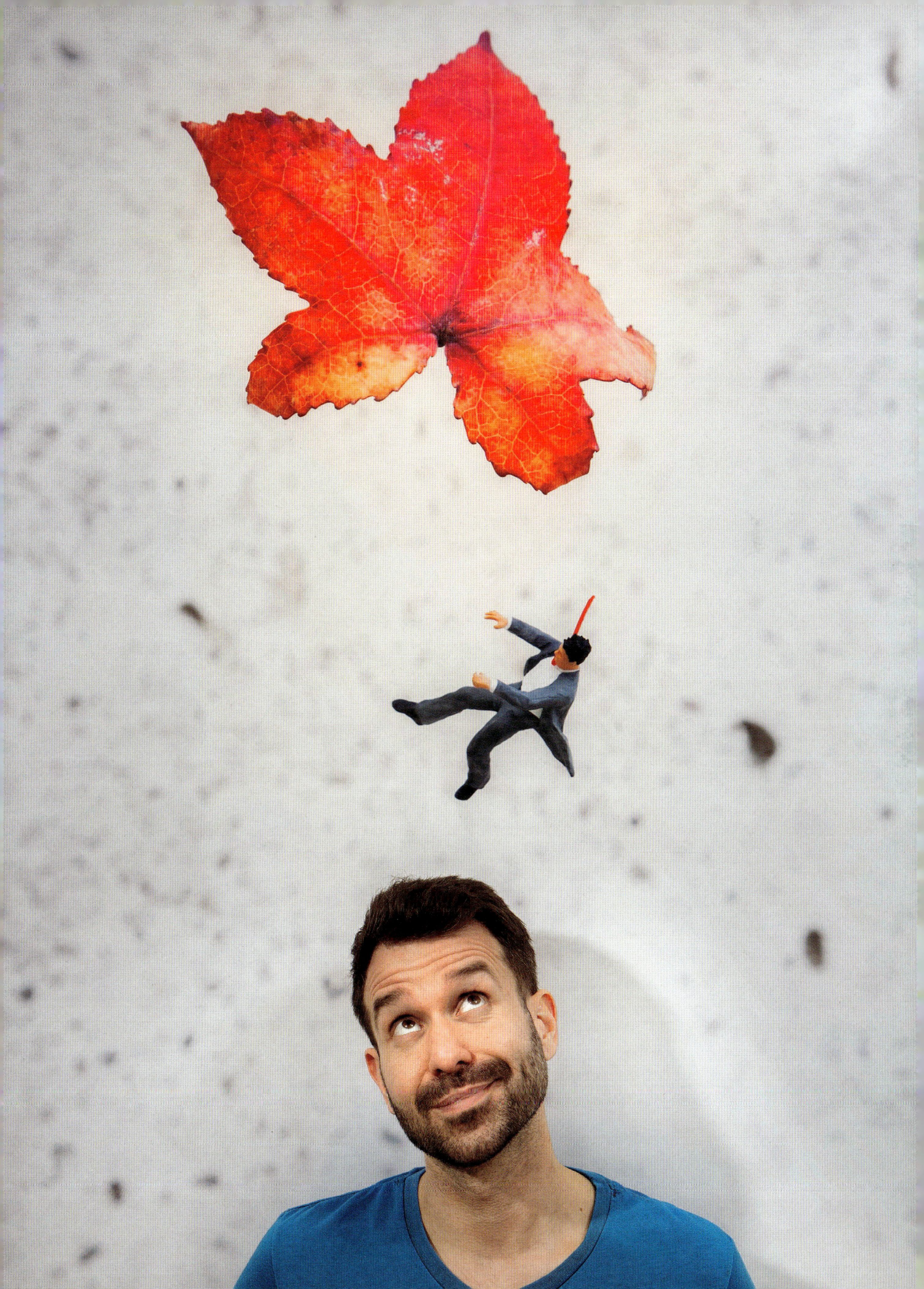

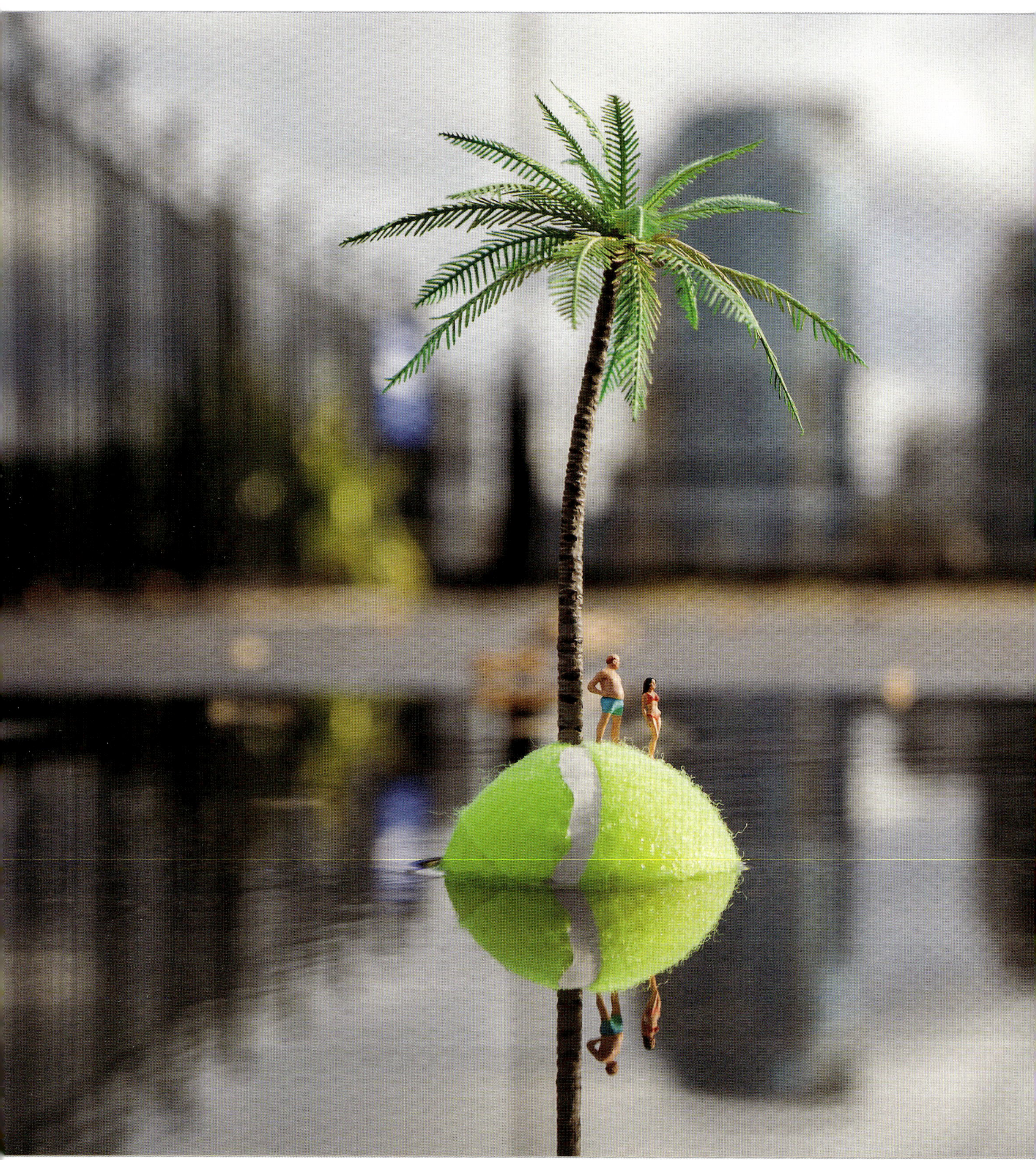

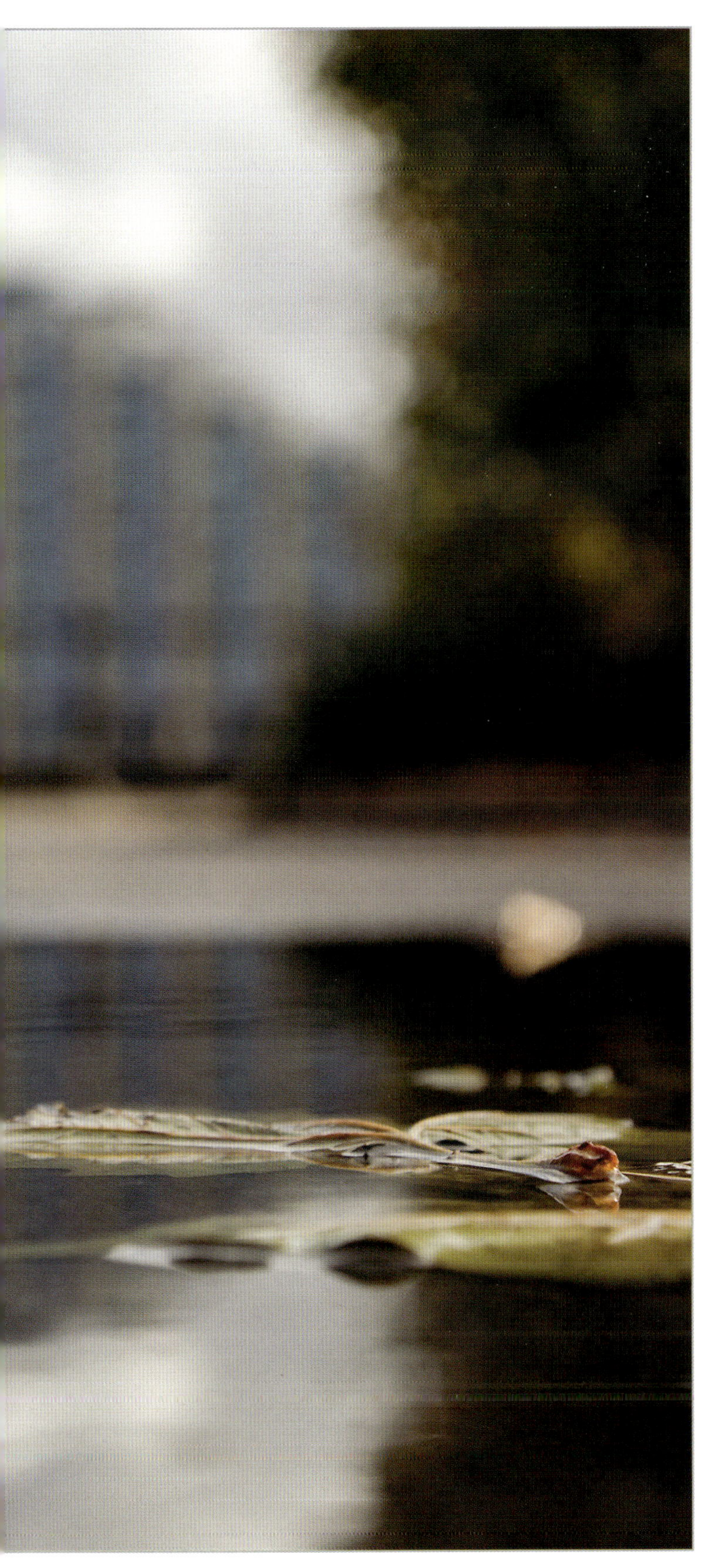

The Last Resort, **2011**
Slinkachu creates a scene of a married couple sunbathing in the middle of . . . a London puddle. The palm tree creates a little shade on the boiling tennis ball.

Often the scene will need props of some sort, so I sometimes find objects that I collect from the street, such as dead insects or bits of litter, or sometimes miniature items from websites, such as eBay. Often I make things from scratch using bits of modeling kits or household objects. For instance, I recently made a 'cave' from a crisp packet. Once the figures are made, I take them out on to the street to place and shoot. I usually have a rough location in mind, for instance I will know I need a letterbox, but I then spend a long time walking around the city to find the specific letterbox that feels right for an image. The scenes take roughly five to ten minutes to set up, depending on the complexity, and then thirty minutes to an hour to shoot, using multiple angles and depth of field. The figures are then left on the street."

His art is far more complex to make than it seems: "My work has different stages that encompass a few different mediums so it can be hard for me to nail down an exact definition of what I do. Its sculpture, photography and street art all at once – or perhaps only sculpture, if I am making a physical artwork specifically for a museum or gallery. Photography 'in and of itself' isn't really a passion of mine.

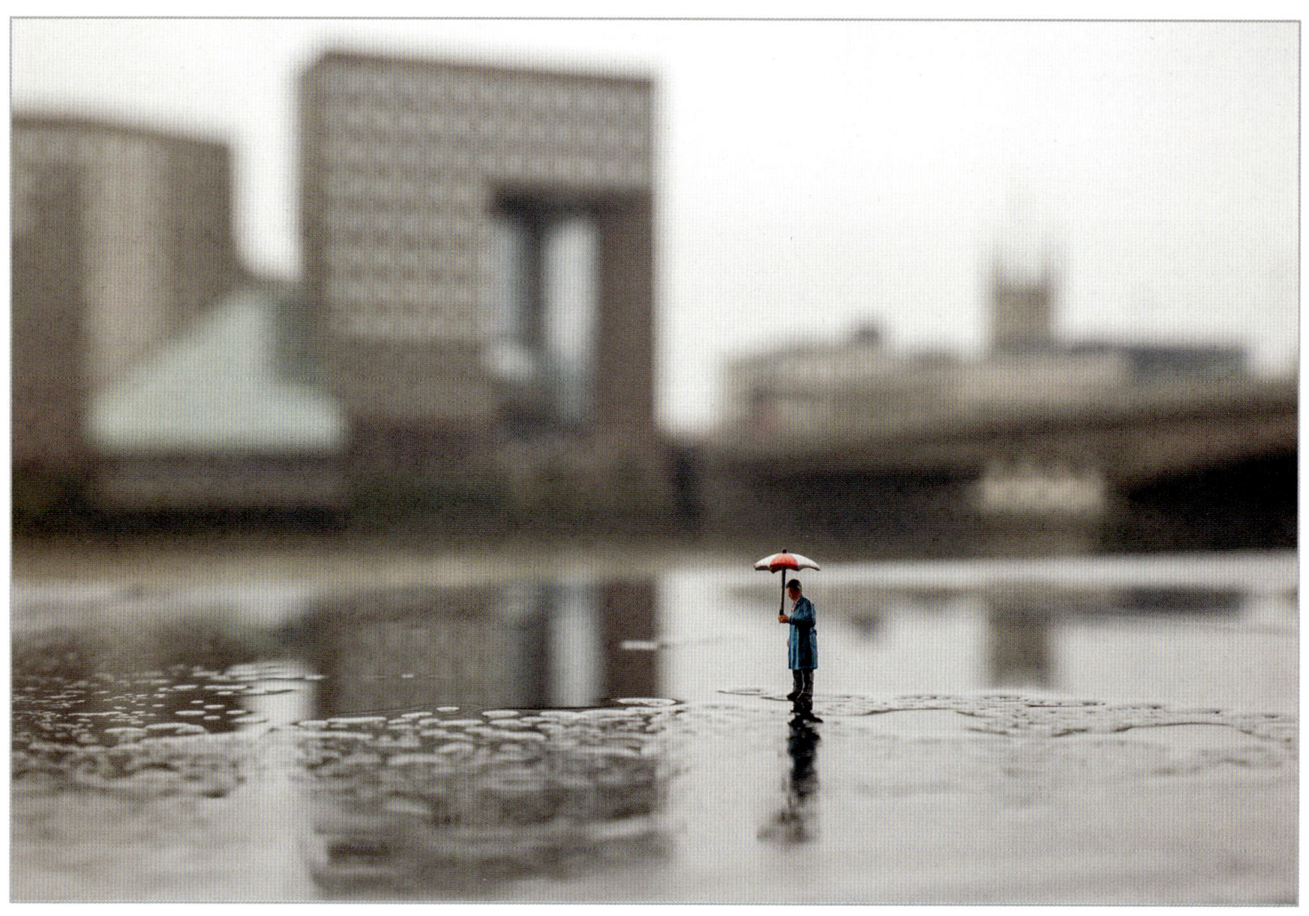

Downpour, **2010** - Every person lives in their urban island: this little man with an umbrella faces the London rain alone.

Taxi!, **2009** - It is always difficult to find a taxi in London, still more if the unfortunate prospective passenger is only a few inches tall.

I think of photography as more of a means-to-an-end – a way to record my installations, instead of an art itself. I am trying to tell a story through the images and installations, or create an emotional response of some sort. The fact that my work involves different mediums is part of the fun for me. There are lots of different processes to learn and explore."

And the message that Slinkachu wants to convey is no less articulate: "I like being able to tell stories with my work and my objective is to get an emotional reaction. I am often fascinated by the different ways that my photography, in particular, is interpreted by different people. I'm interesting in exploring the ways in which living in a city affects us and the problems of urban life. We tend to ig-nore what is going on around us, we are often wrapped up in our own little worlds, so I hope that in some small way my work (or at least the idea of my work) can encourage people to become more aware of the world, and people, around them," he explains. "I've certainly been inspired by other artists who work on the street, such as Swoon and JR, but my main inspiration comes from more traditional artists. I love the work of Edward Hopper: how he works with light in his painting and creates an unsettling atmosphere in an otherwise mundane scene. I am also a huge fan of the American comic artist and author Chris Ware. His ability to tell a story and create emotion, sometimes through the most minimal changes to a comic panel, are amazing."

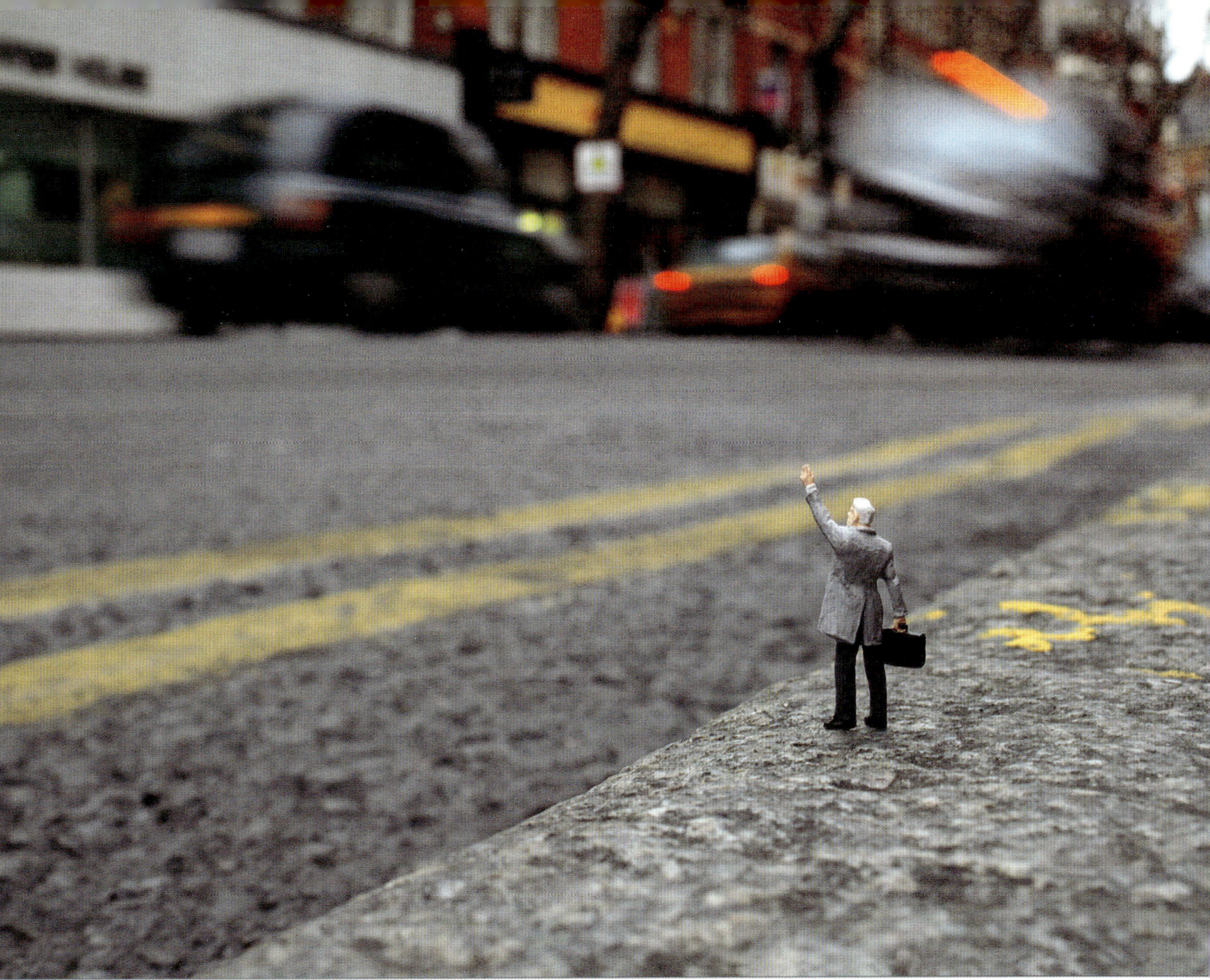

Slinkachu has a clear vision even when it comes to criticism: "I think almost all art movements and artists over the years have faced the 'criticism' of 'That's not real art.' I think 'street art' encompasses such a range of disciplines now that it is hard to sum it up in one term. Often, all that ties this work together is that it began life on the street. Imagine how stupid it would sound to group together all 'traditional' art – sculpture, painting, video and more – as 'Gallery Art' and then judge it all, as a whole entity. It is impossible to do, of course . . ."

Among all of his works, he fondly recalls those in which the installation phase was particularly memorable and those in which chance played in his favor, allowing him to make a better picture than he expected. "I like *All Alone* – a giant CCTV camera emerging from the snow to intimidate a young couple – as it was a challenge to shoot in the freezing cold of Moscow. Lying in the snow for an hour, I was so absorbed with shooting that I didn't realize I had lost all feeling in my body! I was really pleased with *The Last Resort*, too – the sun came out at just the right moment to bring a tropical island scene to life on an otherwise dull and rainy winter's day."

These are the kind of adventures Slinkachu stumbles upon when working the street. "Not much of my work is dangerous in the same way that a graffiti artist might put themselves in danger by scaling a great height, but I do face other difficulties.

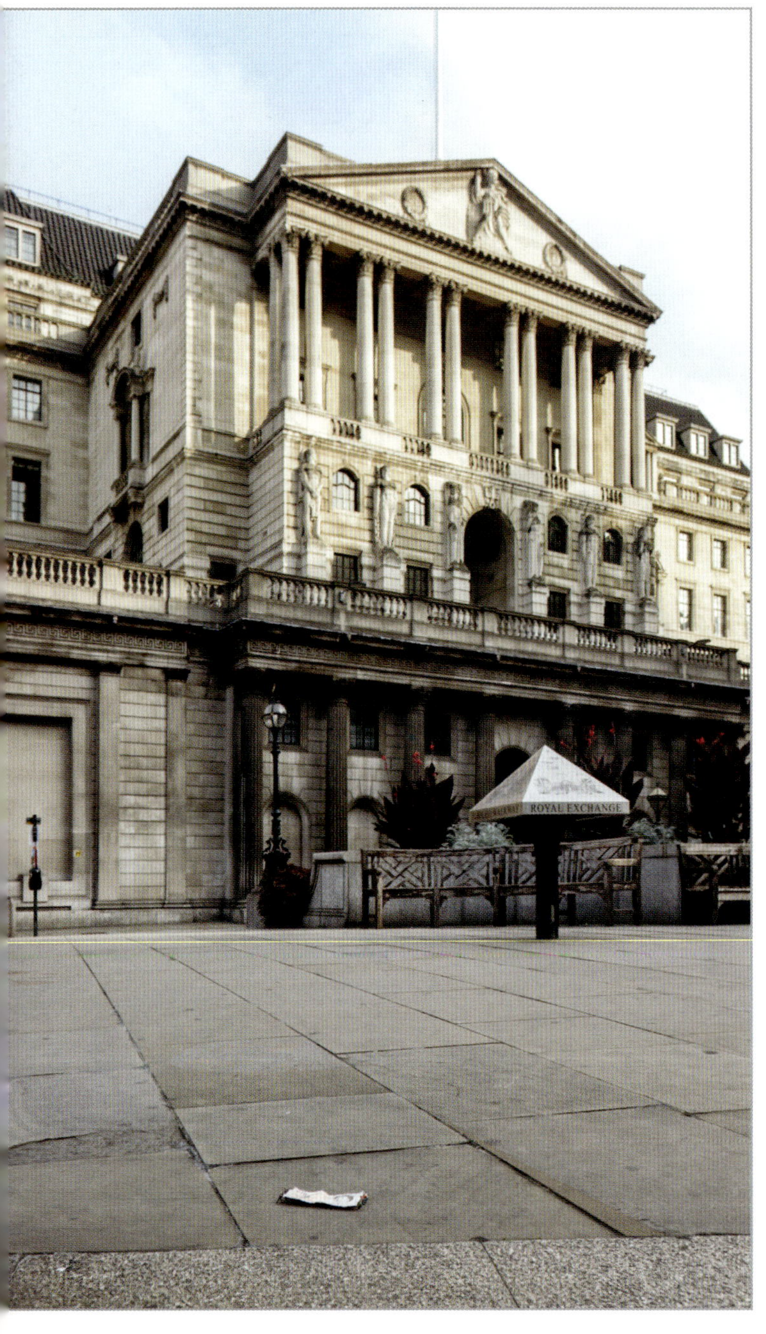

***Tug of War*, 2014** - Four white-collar workers and four young men face off in a duel which is between generations, social, and above all economic, in front of the Bank of England in London. This is the eternal conflict between "the haves" and "the have-nots": the banknote longed for by everyone seems about to tear apart.

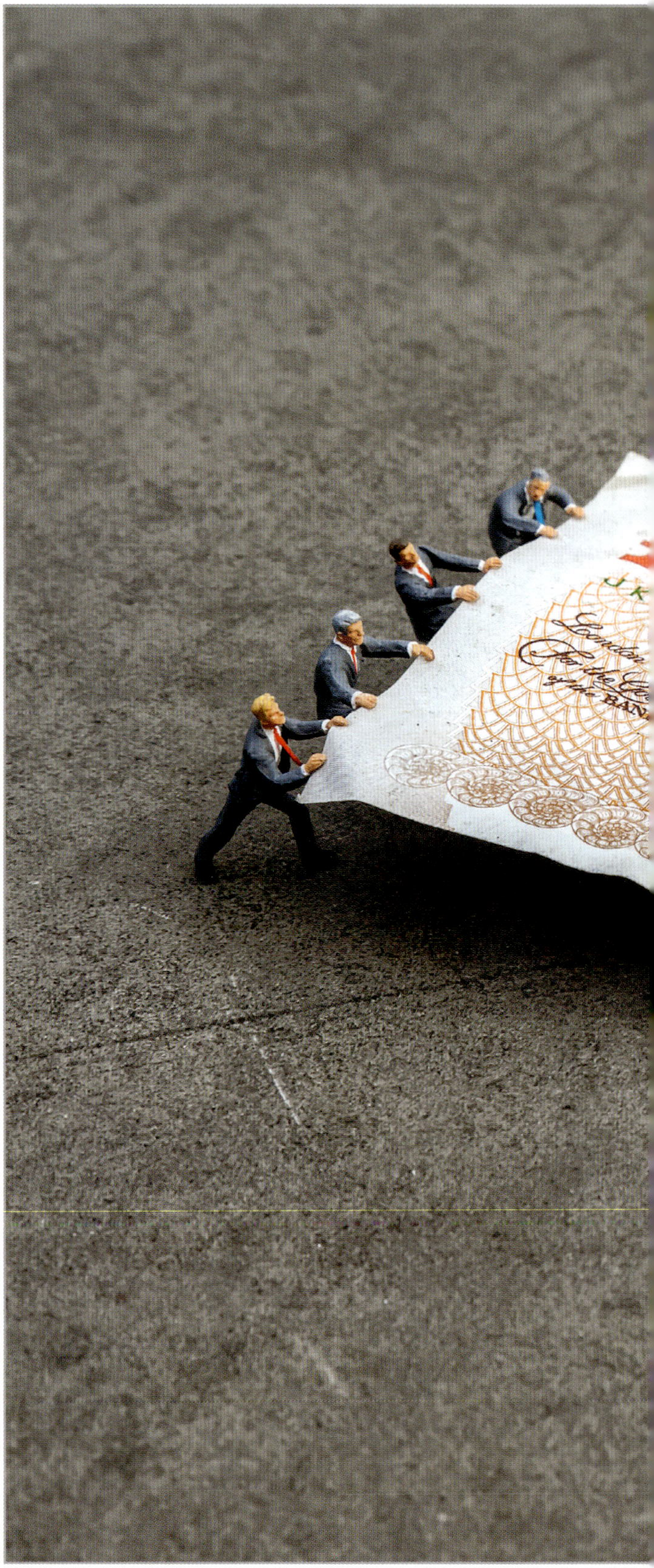

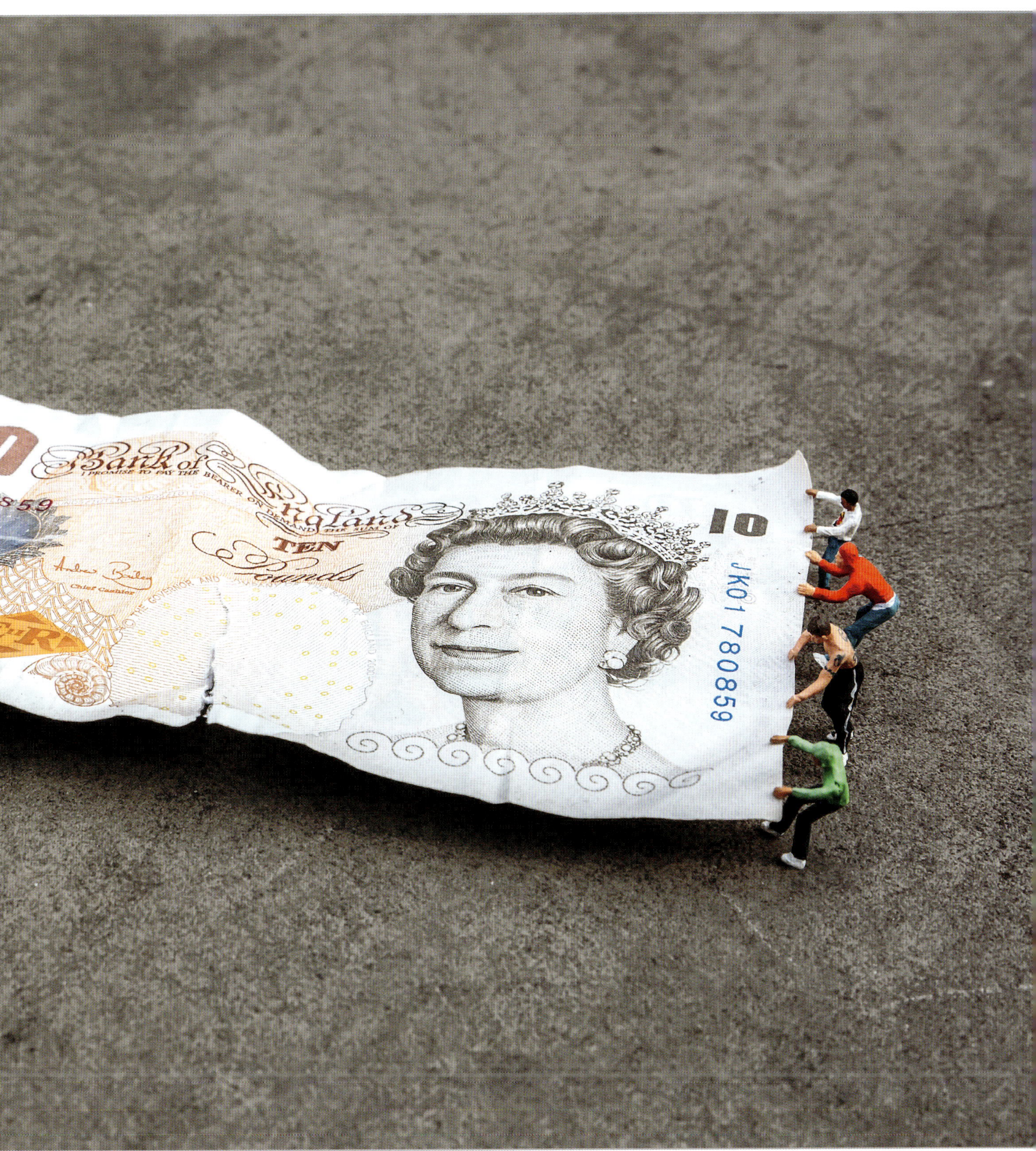

Bank of England
I PROMISE TO PAY THE BEARER ON DEMAND THE SUM OF
TEN
Pounds
859
TO THE GOVERNOR AND
JK01 780859
10

I often have to lie down in the street to set up and photograph my work and once I narrowly missed stabbing myself with a hypodermic needle. Dog crap is a problem. And chewing gum. I've twice been approached by firemen, who thought that I had collapsed in the street. Someone tried to steal my camera bag once, too," he recalls, ironically. "Usually, the most difficult works that I do are the most complicated ones. For instance, I once created a miniature washing line that stretched across a street in Italy, where each item of clothing had to be glued on individually, with passersby ducking under the line as they came and went. The weather can make things difficult, too; I've been in the middle of setting up and shooting an installation and it has started raining, ruining the scene," he adds. He has lots of ideas for the future: "I'd love to create more elaborate scenes, miniatures on a larger scale. I'd love to work in Pyongyang, but I doubt that will ever happen! My favorite city is London; this is where my heart is. I also adore Hong Kong and would love to go back and do more work there. The tension between the scale of the city and the proximity of the city dwellers is really interesting to me," he explains. And to think that he was born far from the city: "I was born in a picturesque retirement town by the sea and went to school in the countryside. That sense of being surrounded by nature is something that, strangely, has crept in to my urban work over the past few years," he reflects. "What I can say is that I see my future in a crystal ball in miniature . . . And for a better world, I hope there is more open-mindedness."

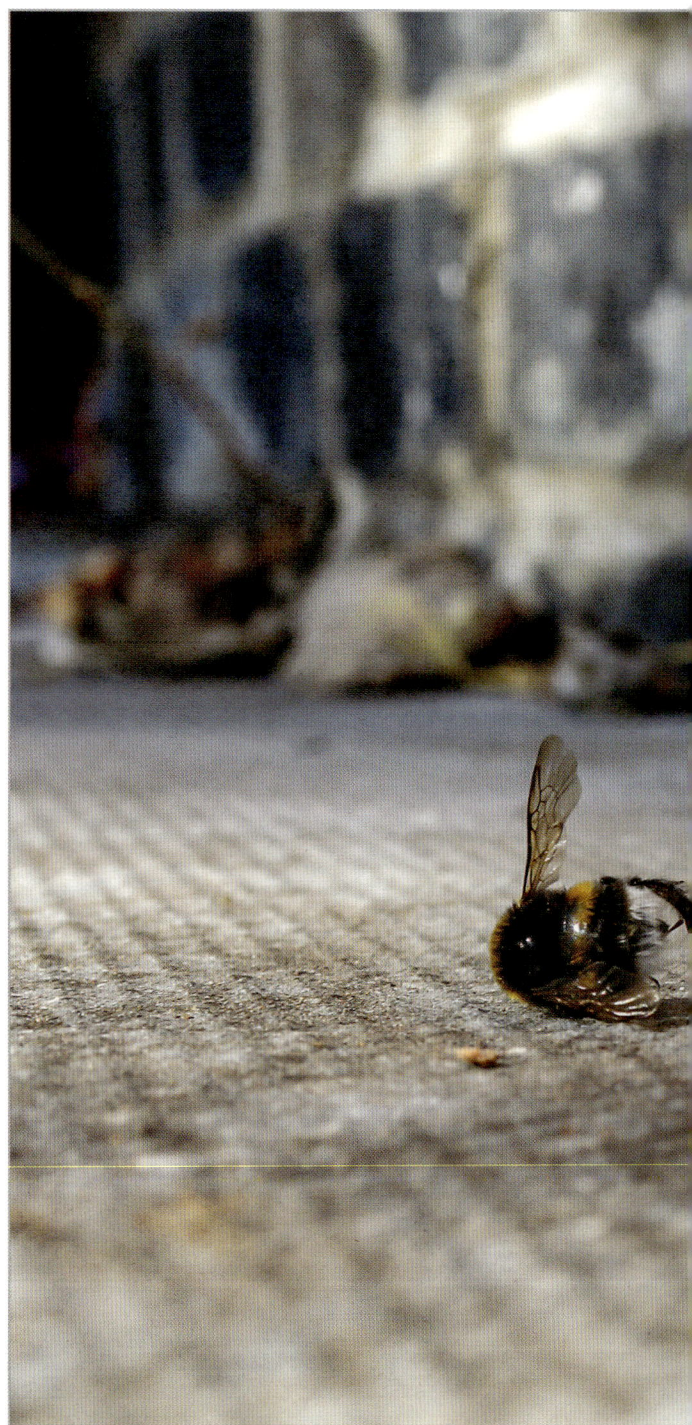

They're Not Pets, Susan, 2008

Dad takes up his gun to defend his frightened little daughter and teach her a lesson in life, in a ferocious and unequal hunt of a bee (the work is part of the project *Little People in the City,* which Slinkachu developed for years in the streets of London).

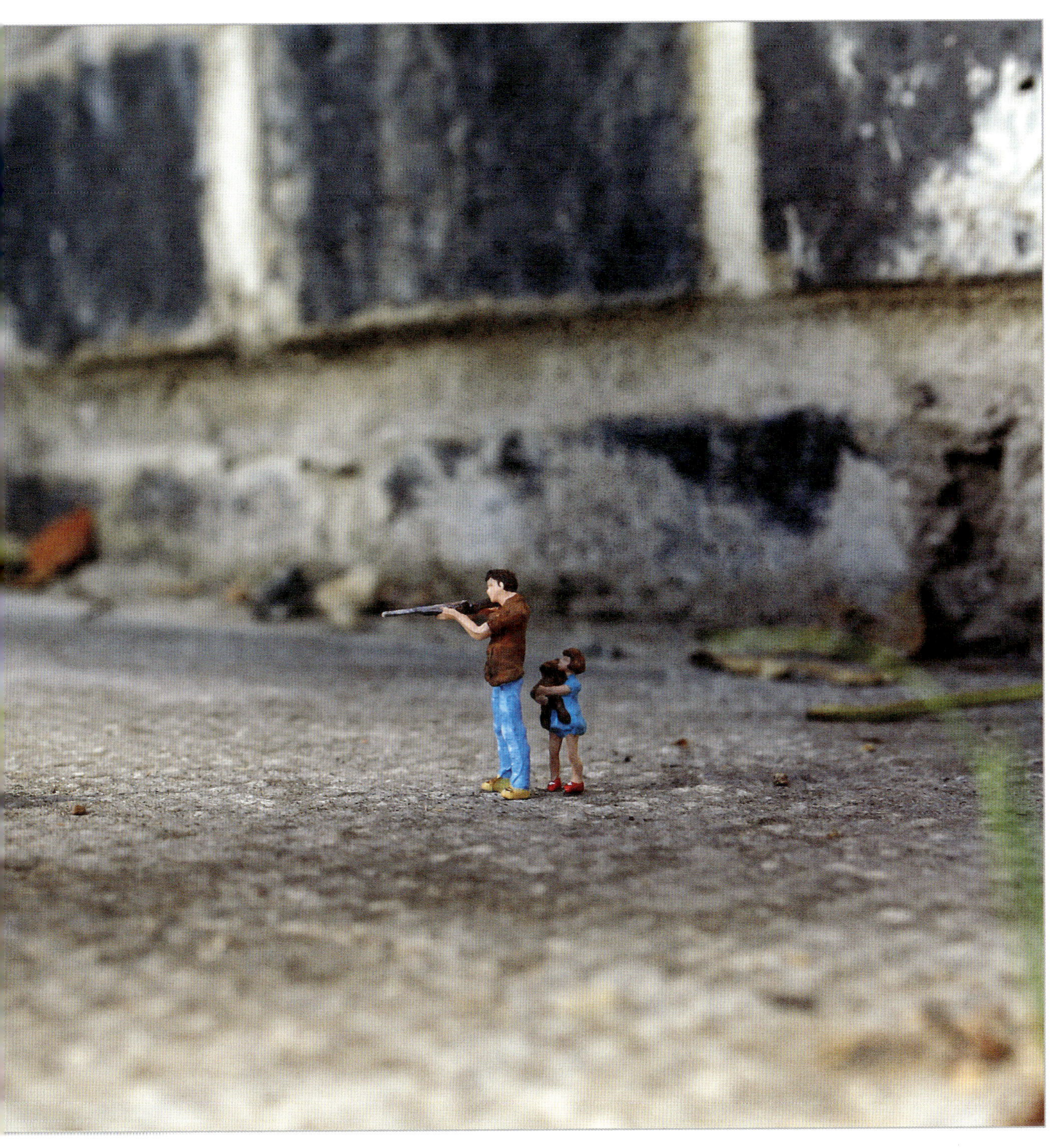

***Fantastic Voyage*, 2011** - In the urban jungle, adventure is around the corner: the green string of a tennis shoe becomes
a sea monster to fight on board a beer cap, in the London district of Acton.

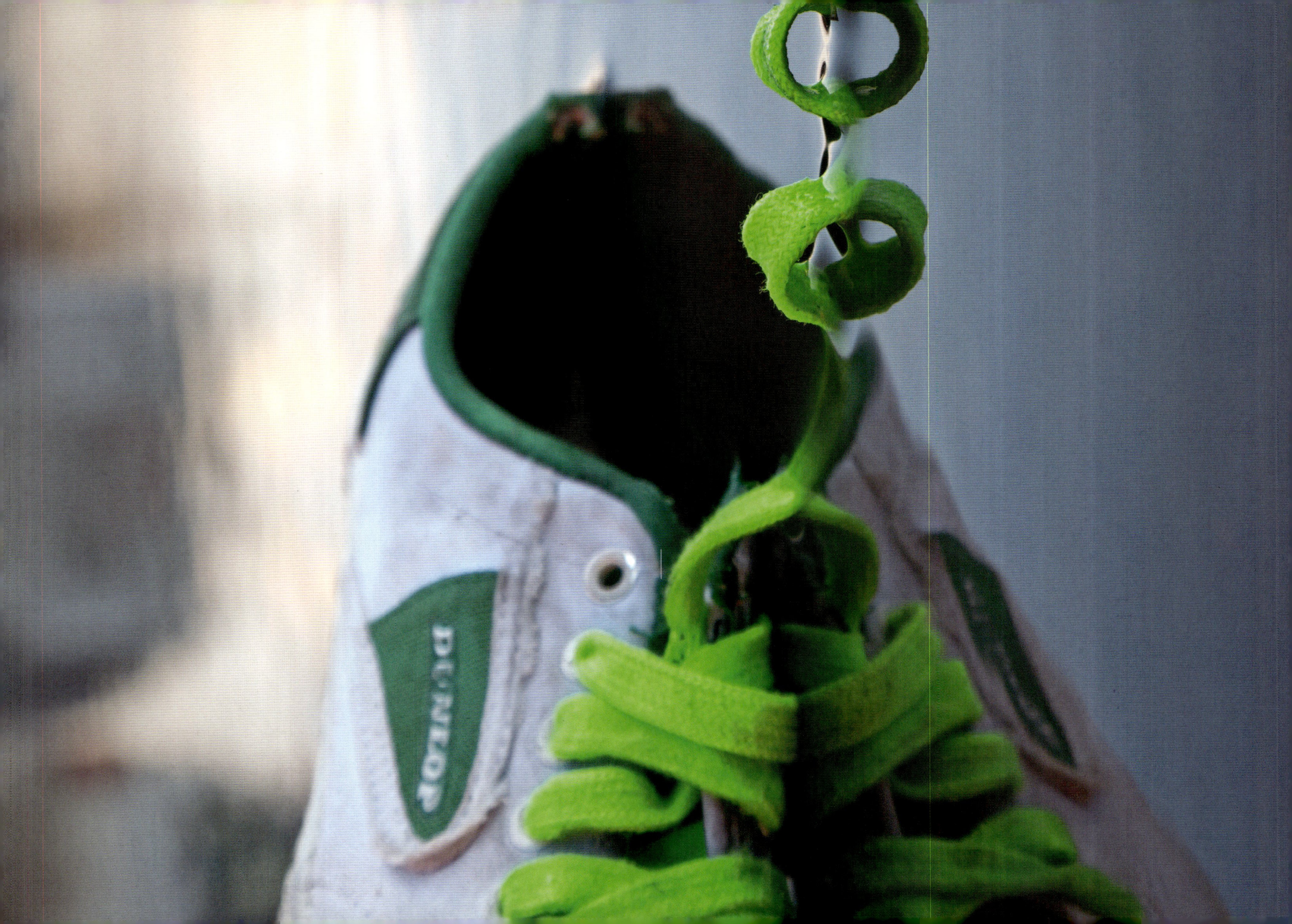

DUNLOP

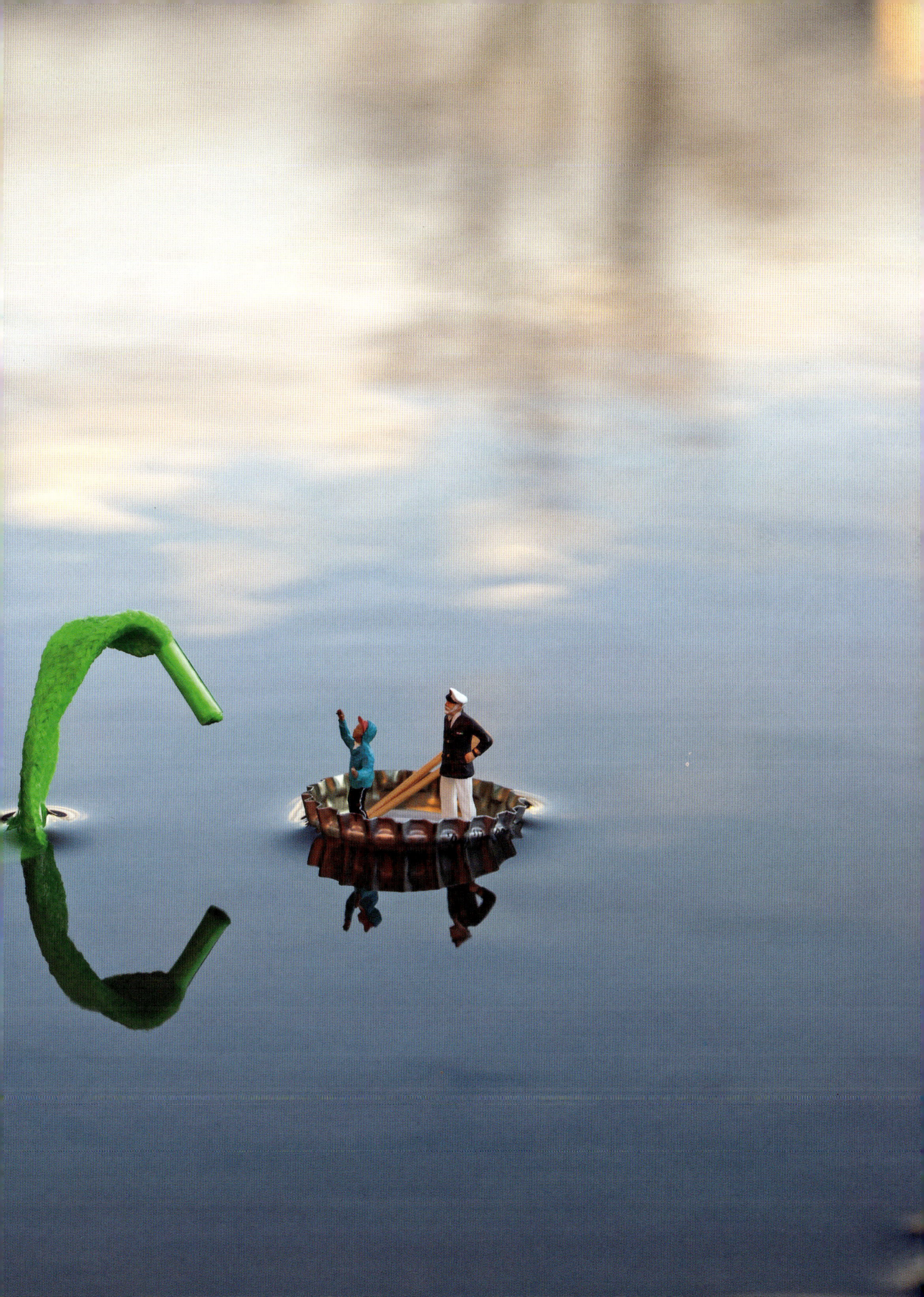

SPECTER

Street Art Ghost

He calls himself "Specter" because he is like a ghost: he says that, when he works, he has the ability to make himself invisible to others. "The secret is to pretend that you are there to do something that's perfectly legal: in this way, often, you're not even seen. Another secret is knowing how to transform yourself, as though you were working undercover. If I shave or not, if I comb my hair one way or another, I know I can look like a totally different person every time," says Gabriel Reese, also known as Gabriel Specter, from his studio in Brooklyn, where he lives among canvases, brushes, a computer and everything else he needs to make his art. He has banged up a leg, due to a recent accident on his bicycle, with which he enjoys doing acrobatics in the streets. "Even with my leg like this, the other night with an artist friend we climbed up onto the roof of a building that is being turned into a luxury complex. We knew we'd have a view for which people will soon pay millions of dollars to see, and we created a work on the façade of the construction yard: I think it'll stay there for a few months. It is really big, so I got help from a friend. It was early in the morning and no one stopped us."

> I've never felt the need to sign my works; I know I have to when they are commissioned, but otherwise, I know myself that I made it and that's enough for me.

Half Canadian and half American, for years he has worked using different techniques: he creates murals, paintings, prints, installations, and photographs. He fights gentrification and homogenization. He is attentive to the world of the homeless and marginalized and, with the same passion, he enjoys creating works that please the eye of the beholder, like abstract ones, in a fabulous kaleidoscope of colors. He became famous in the mid-1990s by chance. "As a child, I didn't draw at all, unlike many of my artist friends. The first sign of talent was perhaps when, on my grandparents' anniversary, I assembled a plate of vegetables in a really creative way," he jokes. "Two years later, I was about sixteen or seventeen – I never remember exact dates – I made my first graffiti with a friend. In the beginning, I wasn't very good, but I learned quickly, as if I had always had it inside me. And within a year, I had become famous, in spite of myself. I can't even explain how it happened, but suddenly I was an inspiration to others and I was gaining recognition. So, I found myself, at eighteen, already with a reputation that I hadn't at all worked to gain," he recalls.

The Canadian-American artist Gabriel Reese, nicknamed Specter, in his studio in New York. You can come across his works in Paris, London, and St. Petersburg.

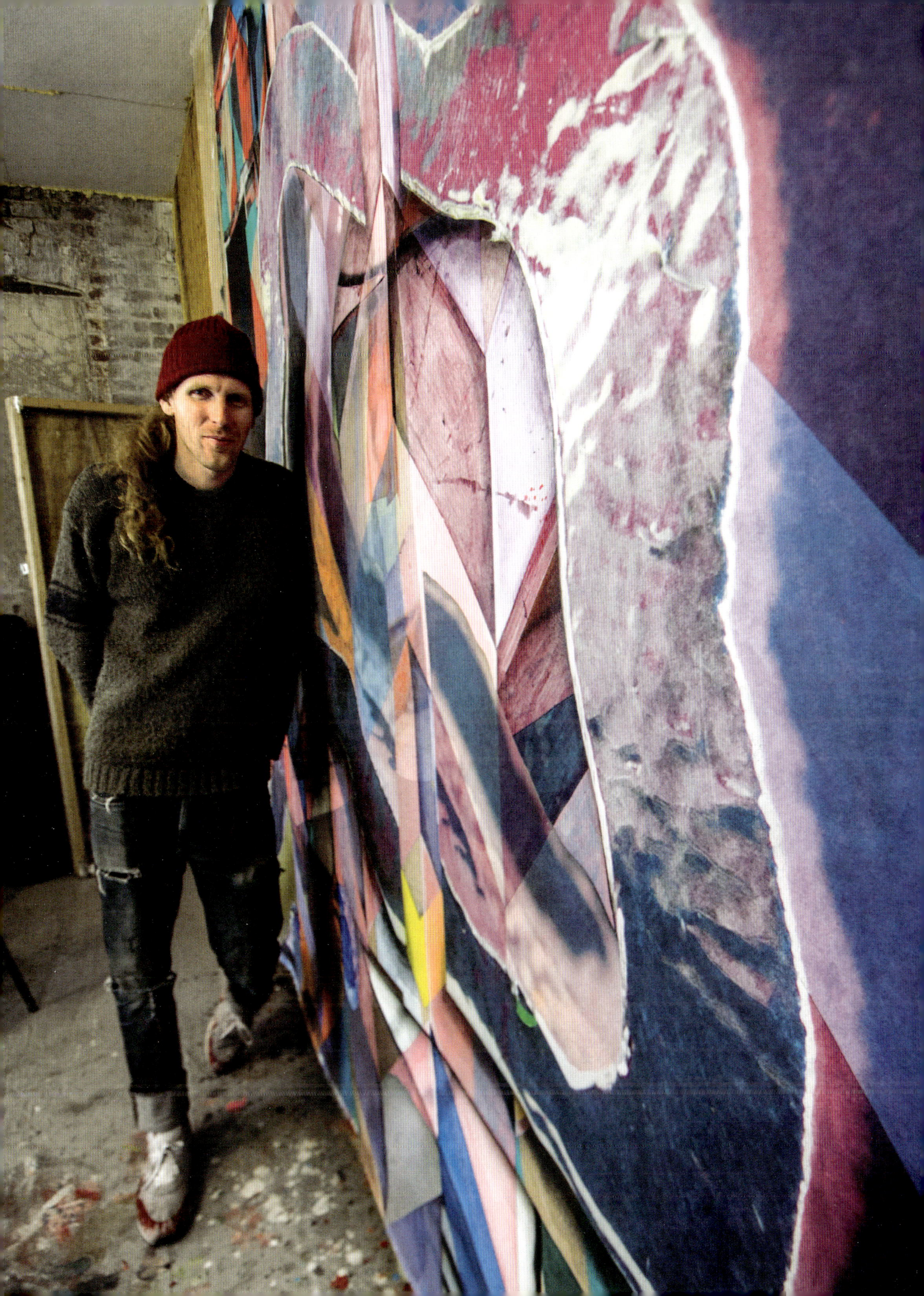

"It all started with our egos: we were a group of teenagers competing with each other; we were pioneers of a movement. We inspired each other, and we all wanted to prove we were better than the next guy. It was a very different attitude than my own today, which is now aimed at sharing my art with others, at making a difference, at evoking emotions. My perspective has definitely changed. It's true that, perhaps, there is that part of the ego that wants the recognition, but this may differ from artist to artist. Without the recognition, in the end, it is very difficult to continue to work because, unfortunately, we need it in order to survive economically. Despite this, I've never felt the need to sign my works; I know I have to when they are commissioned, but otherwise, I know myself that I made it and that's enough for me," and, thinking back to his early days, he adds: "Besides, I also had great passion - at the time, I was being punished for what I was doing, it certainly wasn't remunerated." And then he recalls how he won an art scholarship from the Canadian government, which allowed him to spend some time in New York. "I'm Canadian but also American. I've never noticed a difference between the two countries because I have good friends both here and there. At first, they gave me an apartment in Chelsea, in a very trendy area, then I entered the city 'scene' and now I live in Brooklyn. I love New York and I share my studio with another artist, who is a painter and musician," he adds. While he is talking, you can hear someone moving at the back of the studio: there seem to be various workshops there, all of which are pretty underground. "I started painting on walls, but then I began to develop other works, and with these experiences I started to do what I wanted. I never put myself under pressure. I don't force myself to make art all the time; maybe I'll stop for a while and then start again. For me, what's important, first of all, is to be free. When I can earn enough to support myself, I do not feel the need for more," he clarifies.

"My first graffiti that caught people's attention was illegal and was in the courtyard of a school in Montreal, in the NDG neighborhood, where I grew up. At first, I had this wild sense of rebellion that led me, first of all, to want to vandalize. I did not know much about art then. Now, for example, when I come across a street sign that prohibits people from entering, I enter all the same and record it on video. I violate the law when it unreasonably limits individual freedom," he says.

A female figure that is elusive and mysterious, like many of the subjects depicted by Specter,
who directs his artistic sensibility toward unexpected apparitions.

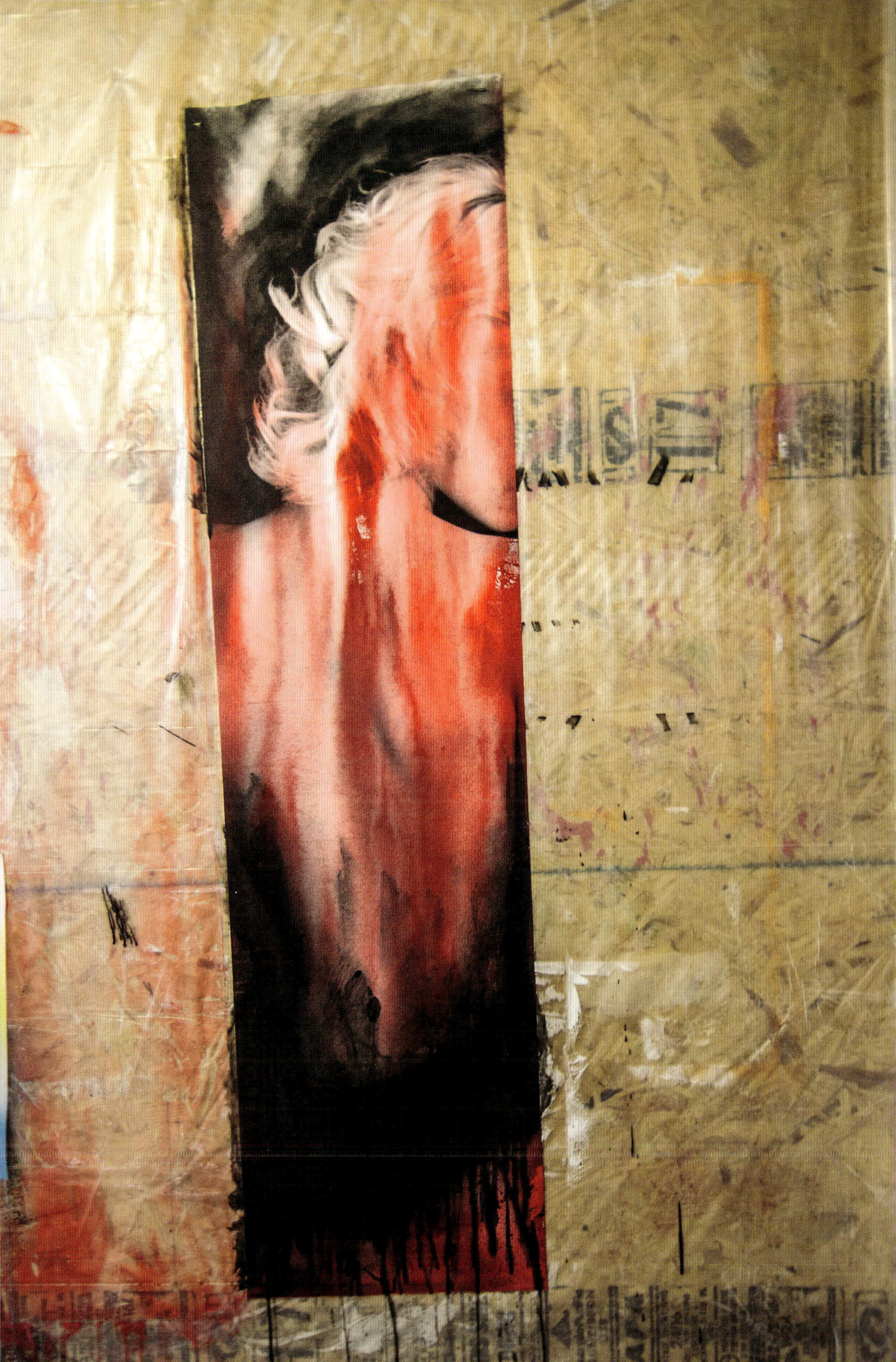

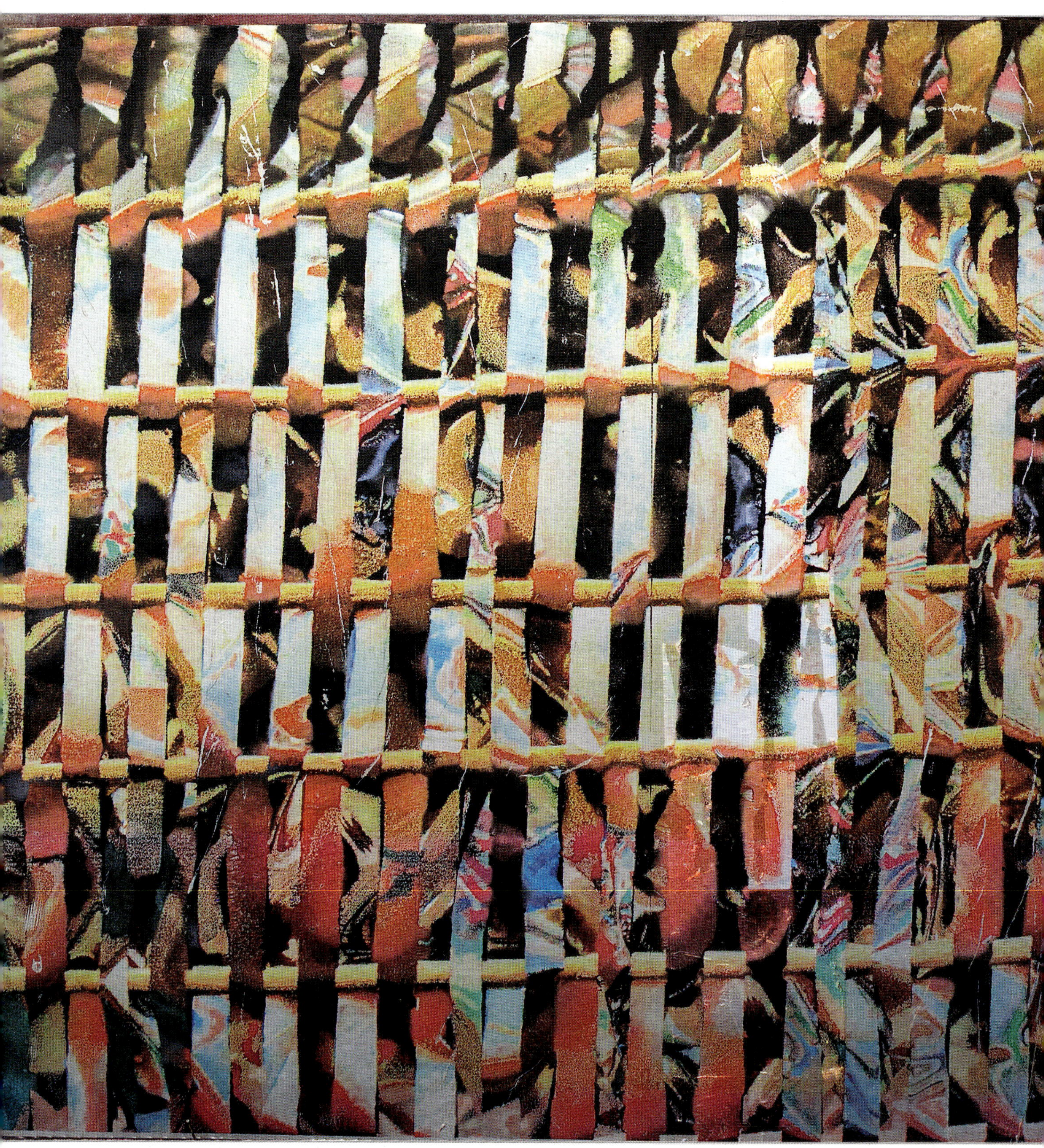

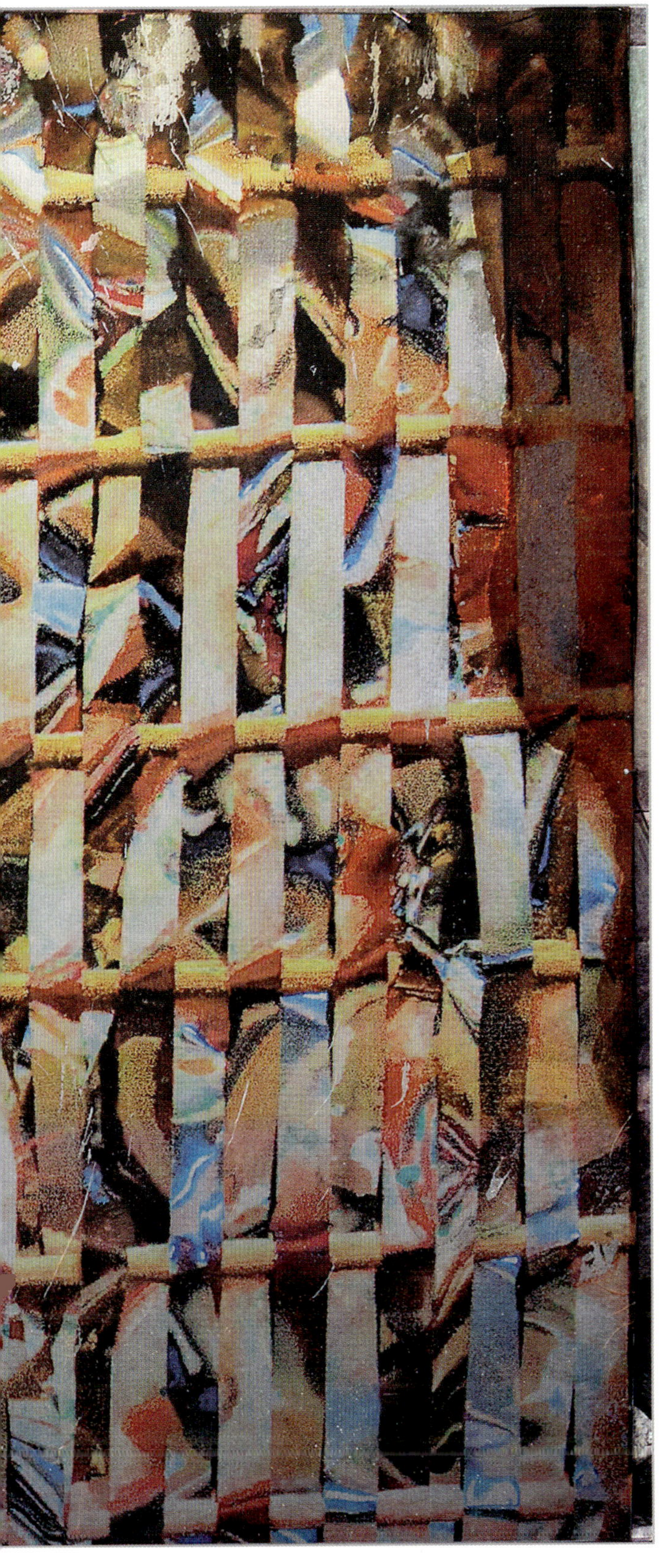

In 2013, Prada presented, as part of the project, *In the Heart of the Multitude*, the works of several different graffiti artists: in addition to Gabriel Specter, there was El Mac and Mesa, and illustrators Jeanne Detallante and Pierre Mornet. "I like fashion, it is a form of art, and I consider Miuccia Prada a great artist," he explains, showing me a few T-shirts and garments with writing or symbols drawn by him.

He confesses that he considers himself very lucky because he is never short of inspiration: "I have at least a hundred ideas swirling in my head every day and I end up realizing a fair share of them. Creativity has never been a problem. One of the artists I respect the most is Blu, for his attitude rather than his style. In 2010 the MOCA Museum in Los Angeles decided to remove his wall mural because it was considered too provocative and anti-capitalist; in 2016 he destroyed all of his works in Bologna and he now lives in a community of squatters. It was definitely a move against the system: he protested because he did not want his works to be put on display in an exhibit, in a museum or in a book. I am also inspired by my artist friends, who work with me or who are close to me, like Dan Bergeron, with whom I have collaborated on several works in Toronto."

Thinking about his work, he says: "Right now, I really like this work behind us; I made it here in my studio, it is a superimposed work of different shapes, colors, lines in which I used at least twenty or thirty different techniques. It should be observed from a distance; it doesn't have a meaning but it plays before your eyes. I find that even the colors are interesting. I mix them and create them I myself, it's my thing: all I need is red, blue, yellow, black and white, and I can invent lots of different ones," he explains, speaking of his technique, which is very diverse and complex, and continuously evolving and under experimentation.

Specter claims the right to use urban spaces taken up by advertising: in these, he proposes forms like these and invites his audience to reconstruct them, thus encouraging critical thinking.

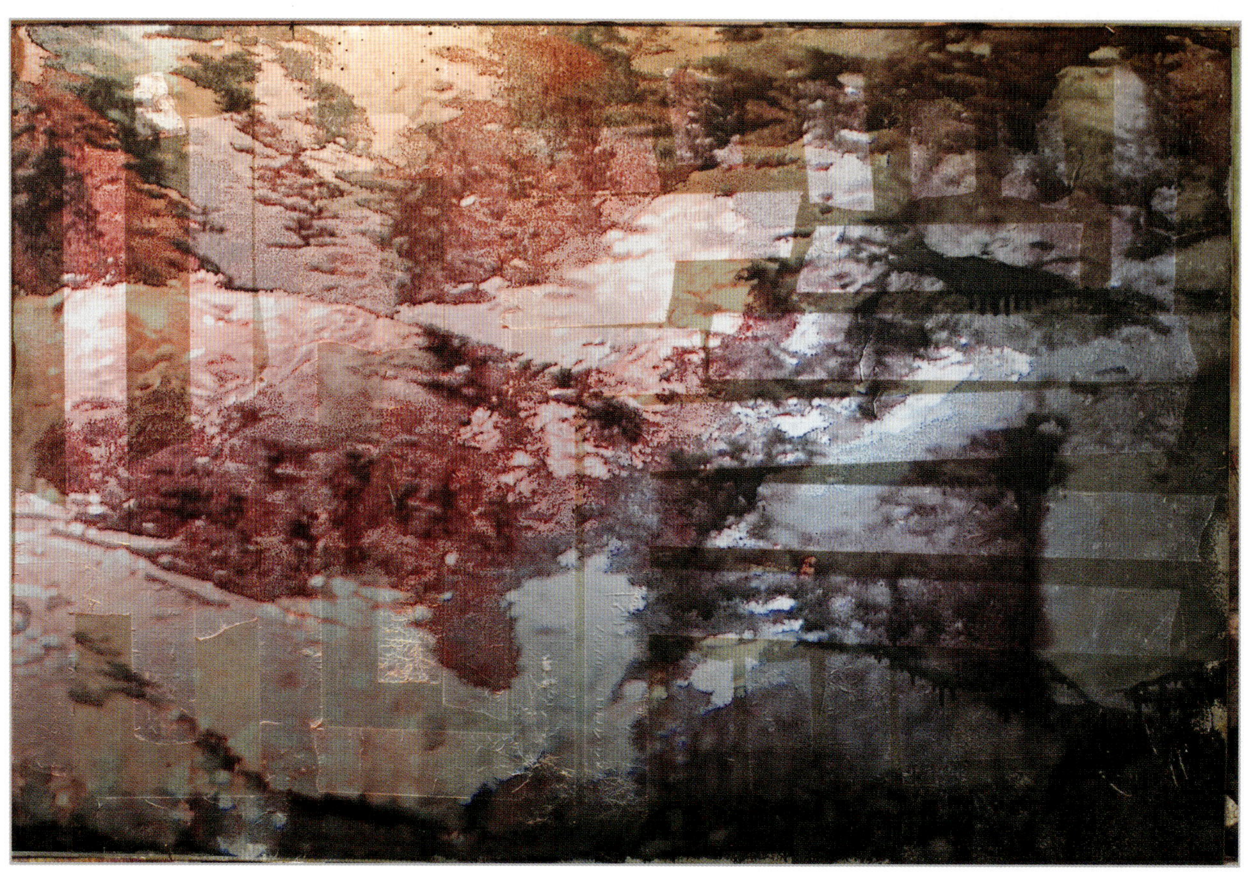

New York, 2016 - Abstract images similar to this were proposed by Specter in Chinatown and on the entrance to the Astor Place subway station in New York in 2016, in the series *Public Access Newsstands*.

***Public Access Billboard*, 2015** - A large billboard in the Sentier Paris Metro station "taken up" by an installation by the American artist.

"I have at least a hundred ideas swirling in my head every day and I end up realizing a fair share of them. Creativity has never been a problem."

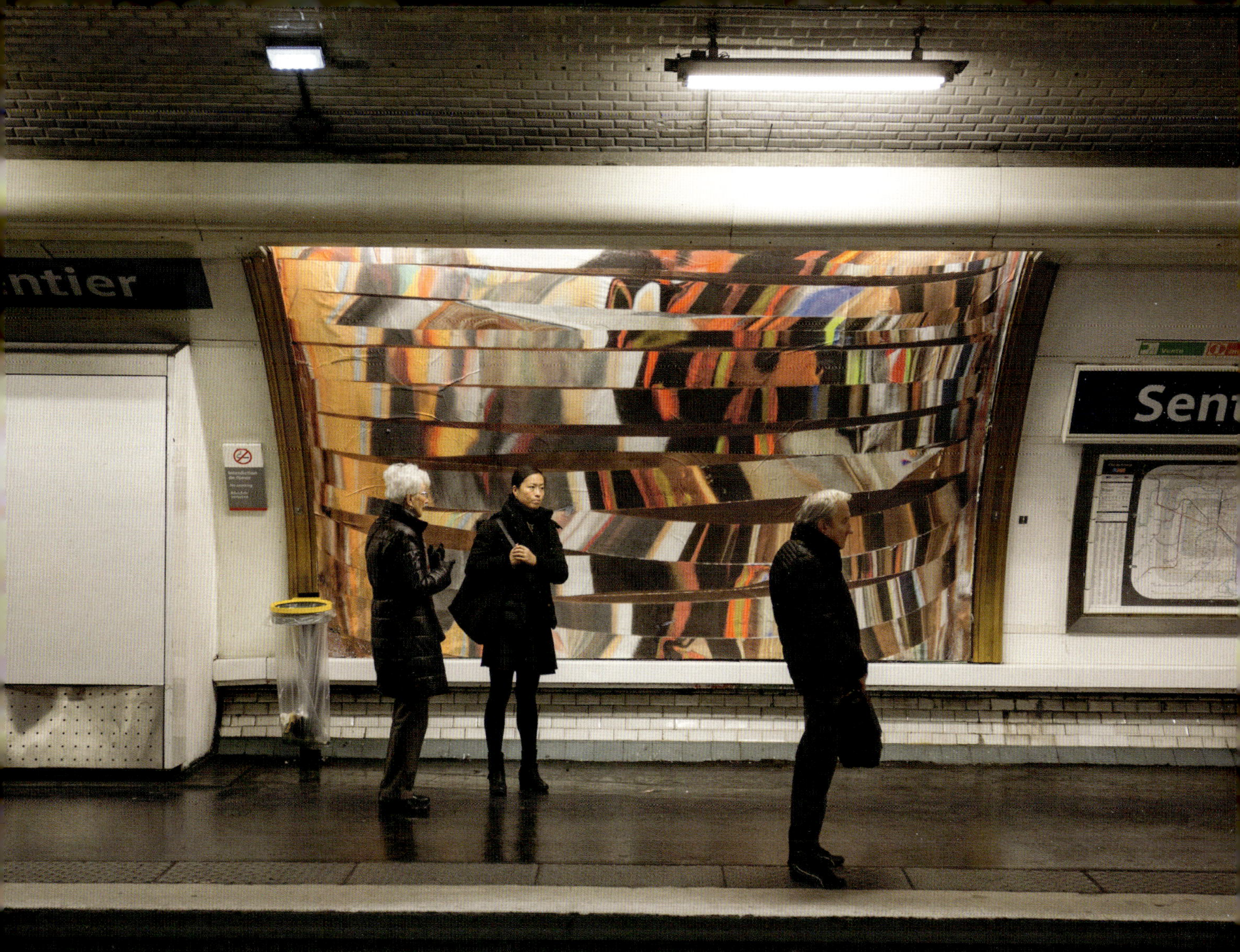

Working illegally, he has often had problems with the authorities, including a rooftop chase with the police, an arrest, and a badly spraining ankle while running away: "I am rebellious, but in the end, I am a good person. I like people and I would never make problems for someone else. Sometimes, in street art, you have to be aggressive to get what you want, but I never exaggerate. I am quite calm. It is more a matter of 'pressing the right buttons' and causing a reaction. But, I also like evoking a good feeling in others. That's why I alternate my more rebellious works with the more abstract or visual ones. Recently, I have been getting more into videos with which I use fun music. I use my camera for everything, from murals to this kind of work. For a while, I boycotted advertising on buses and subway cars, as well as advertising on walls. Recently, I have also been developing a particular technique for collages." Specter doesn't think much about the future; he prefers to live in the moment: "I try to live now, doing what I love: art, drink a beer with friends, hang out with a girl, feel good about myself, and feel balanced. But I have a dream: in the future, I see myself doing something important for a community; it doesn't matter where or if I don't speak the language. Better, though, if in a place where you eat well, like Italy, for example. Like when I was in Portugal, I made a painting on a house and the family invited me to eat and they were so proud of what I had created. Even though I grew up in a very poor family, my parents were fantastic people and I was very lucky to have a special life that allows me to do what I love. I feel the need, therefore, to give something to others to share the art which I was given the ability to create."

SWOON

Portrait Master

Her name sounds like the title of a lovely song: Caledonia Dance Curry. "In general, I prefer to be known as Callie, but I adopted the stage name Swoon when I was creating works illegally. A friend of mine suggested it: he had dreamed I was called this. 'Swoon' is something you see and overwhelms you so you almost feel faint," she says, smiling. Swoon is in an isolated locality in Wisconsin, where she's working in an artist residency, where she is experimenting with prints of her works. "It's an enormous space, and I work in collaboration with the university, where a team specializing in printing helps me to fulfill my ideas," she explains.

Caledonia Dance Curry was born in 1977 in New London, Connecticut, and grew up in Daytona Beach, Florida. She works with different materials, which include: prints, which she applies with wheat paste, a gel or liquid adhesive, prepared with wheat flour and water, already used in ancient times for book binding; *découpage*; collage; *papier-mâché*, the attachment of posters and other things to walls. Swoon became well known through her portraits and drawings of human figures cut out in paper. She studied art at the Pratt Institute in Brooklyn. "I grew up in Florida and I moved to New York when I was nineteen years old. I was not a city girl and I was fascinated by the energy presence in the Big Apple, by all those people who live together and produce culture. For me, the city in itself was a work of art," she recalls. She was immediately struck by the graffiti she saw on the walls. "The graffiti were an incredible discovery. I saw people writing, drawing, and applying materials to walls, sometimes following a precise design, other times at random . . . I, too, felt that I wanted to do something, I wanted to be part of all that," she continues. Art immediately became her life. "In my upbringing, in the academic tradition, art was something that only the rich could enjoy, but I wanted to create something that was public, that became an integral part of the city and of my life," she explains.

Swoon began to be successful around 1999, when she produced large installations and exhibited in various museums, including the Museum of Modern Art and the Brooklyn Museum. "Brooklyn is peopled by numerous artists and has certainly had a influence on me.

> I wanted to create something that was public, that became an integral part of the city and of my life.

Swoon engaged in the preparation phase of one of her works.

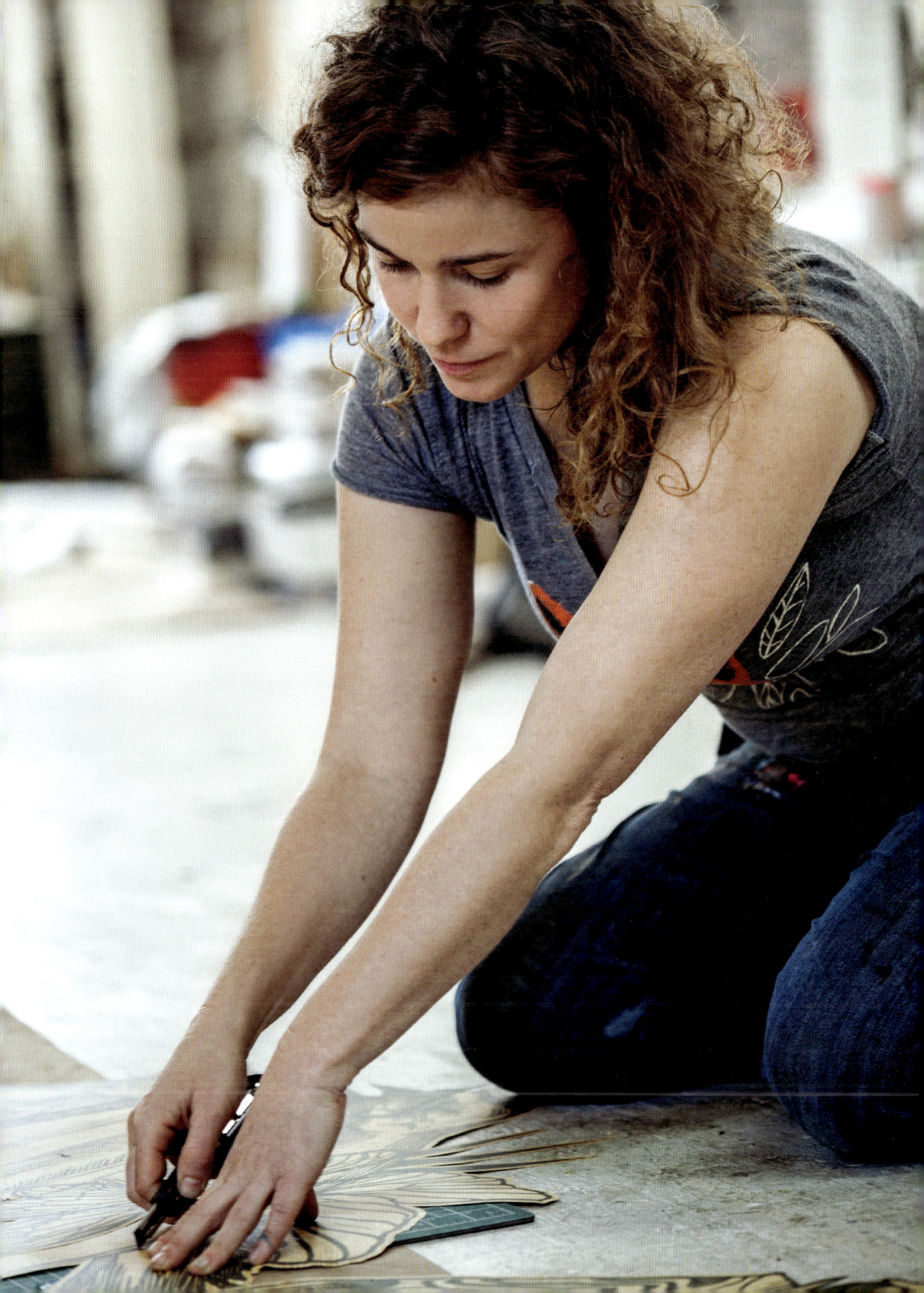

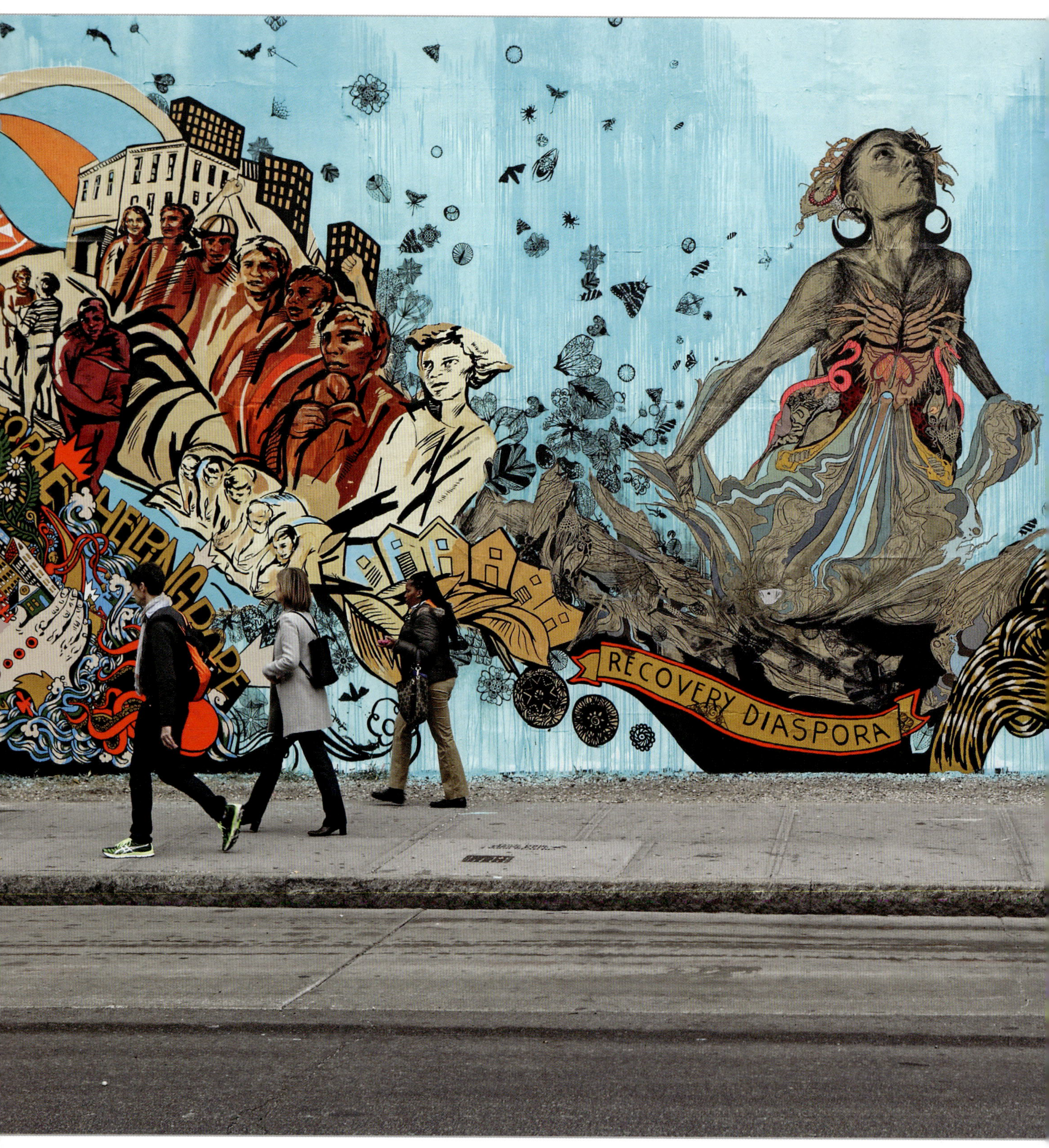

RECOVERY DIASPORA

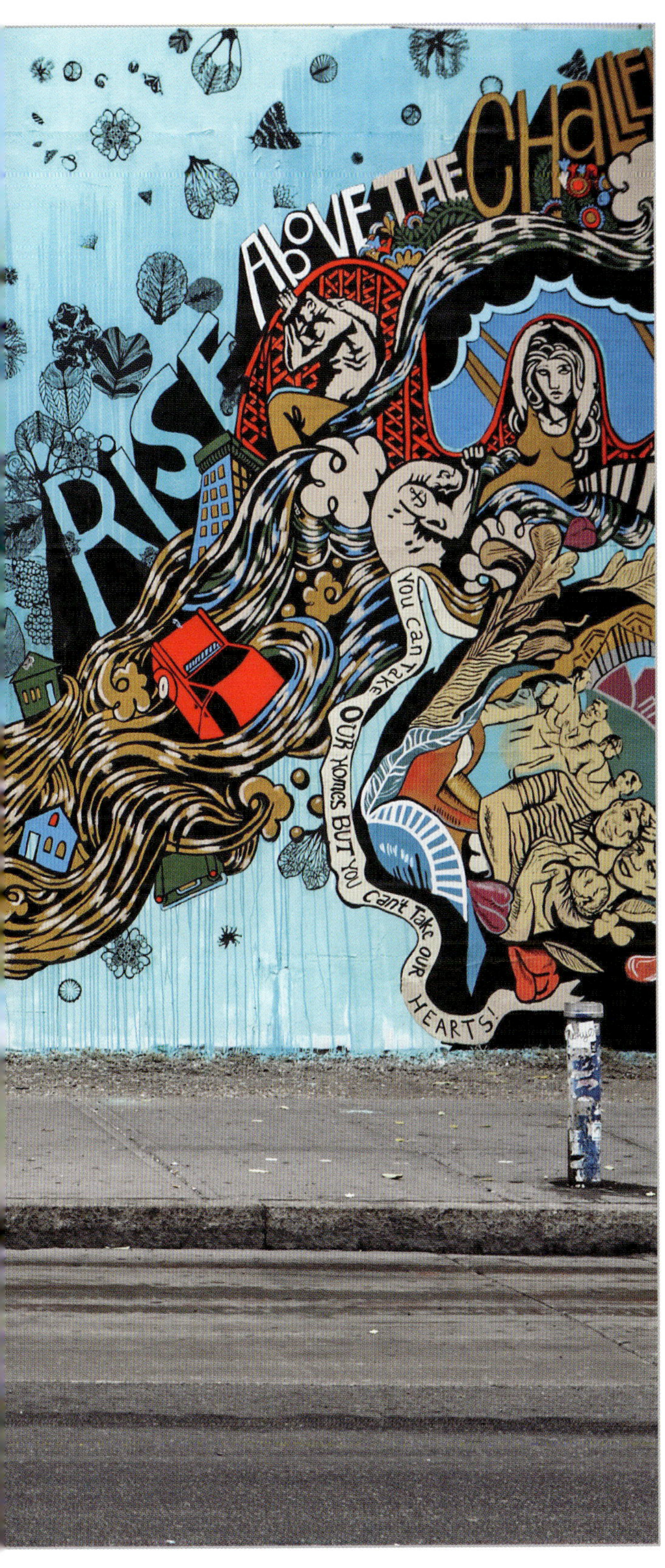

New York, 2013
This multicolor creation applied by Swoon to the Bowery Mural Wall in Houston Street pays homage to the victims of Hurricane Sandy, exactly a year after the disaster.

In the beginning I lived in Fort Greene, and then I moved to Bushwick and Gowanus, and for a short time I also lived in Queens, in Bridgewood. These districts, real urban wildernesses, contributed a lot to my development, like so many street artists that I met, even if I've always tried to follow my own path," she relates.

For a short period, she belonged to a few groups of artists, such as Grub, and founded the cooperative Toyshop . . . "We did projects all over Manhattan and Brooklyn, many on the Lower East Side, but not only." But her first graffiti was in Chinatown: "It was a linoleum print on transparent paper which allowed one to see the wall underneath. I applied it on the other layers already present. I had an artistic education and I'm used to thinking about every detail of what I want to grow or produce. I needed about six months to achieve that result."

Her works have been found in isolated areas, amid abandoned buildings, bridges, alleys, fire exits, road signs, water containers . . . They often portray the faces of family and friends, but she emphasizes that she does not limit herself to this: "I like to look at faces, I can do it for a long time without ever getting tired of it. It is the subject that inspires me most; I try to discover their secrets and particularities and to reproduce them to communicate them to others. It's true that I portray my friends and family, but also people I work with or I happen to meet: sometimes they are people with significant experiences, sometimes not." There is one person, of the people she has portrayed, whom she cannot forget: "A man, in Pennsylvania.

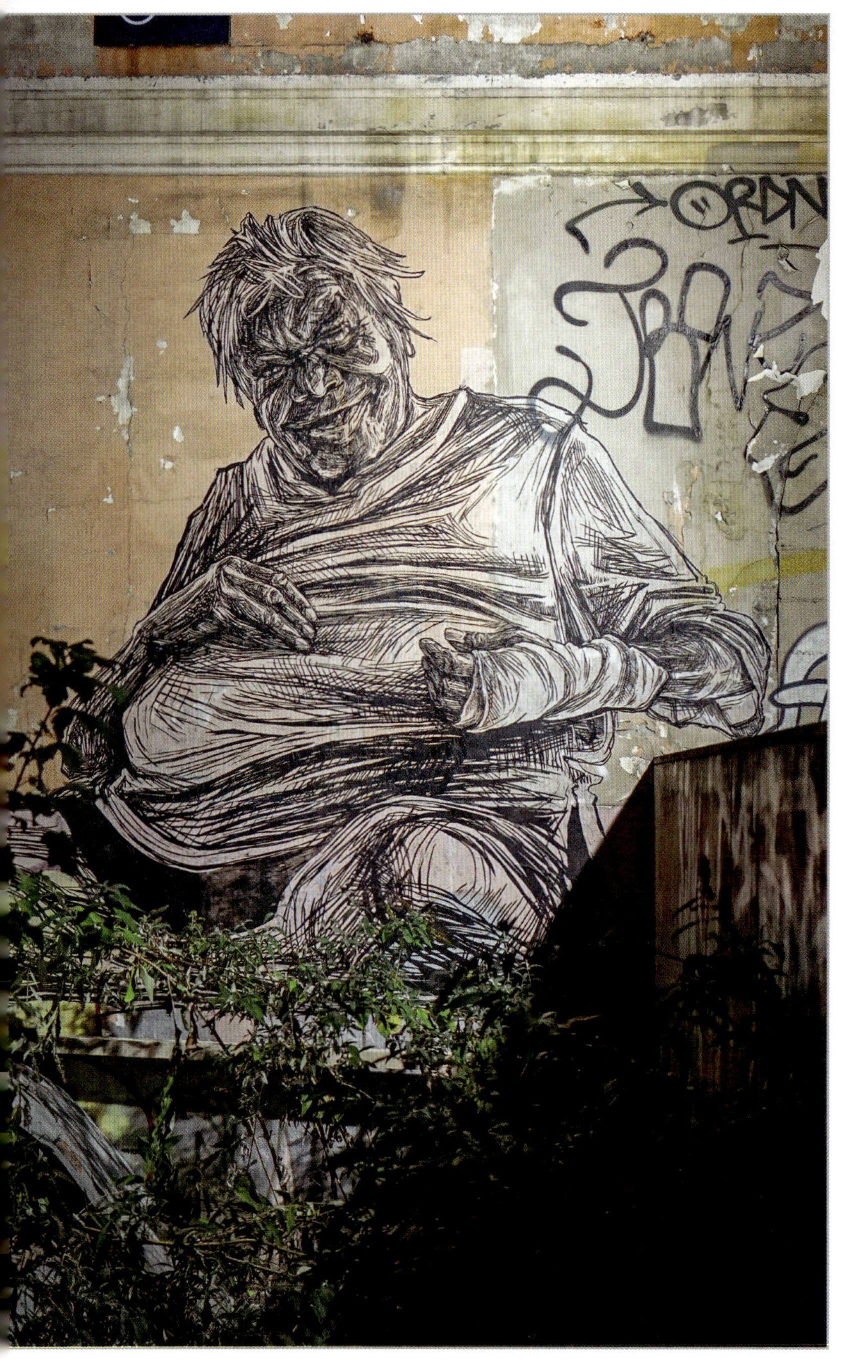

I met him in prison, where he would spend the rest of his life. In America we have an extremely high number of prisoners and I wanted to explore that world. This man was sixteen when he committed a crime. He has never undergone psychological therapy. I was interested in communicating with him, finding out the reasons for his gesture and his perception of the world. Then I put his portrait everywhere."

From a technical point of view, her working method is time-consuming: "I spend a lot of time drawing or painting or cutting out each of the figures and then I apply them to the walls. Since I use adhesive materials that make them easy to remove, I have never had problems with the law, not even when I was working underground. I work a lot with linoleum block printing."

Among her most significant works, there are *Anthropocene Extinction*, *Swimming Cities of Serenissima*, presented at the 2009 Venice Biennale, *Konbit Shelter*, created in 2010 in Haiti, and *Transformazium*, in Pennsylvania. We must also mention the Heliotrope Foundation, a non-profit organization created by Swoon in 2015 to support projects in Haiti, New Orleans, North Braddock, Pennsylvania, and elsewhere. "I believe I've made progress in my activity.

Paris, 2014
For the Nuit Blanche, in the ex-railroad station, Masséna, Swoon creates greatly differing female figures: this is taken from a previous installation, *Anthropocene Extinction*, by the same artist.

Melbourne, 2011
Complexity, fragility, and beauty are perfectly represented by the delicate intaglios of paper surrounding the curious figures of the three children, in an Australian city alley.

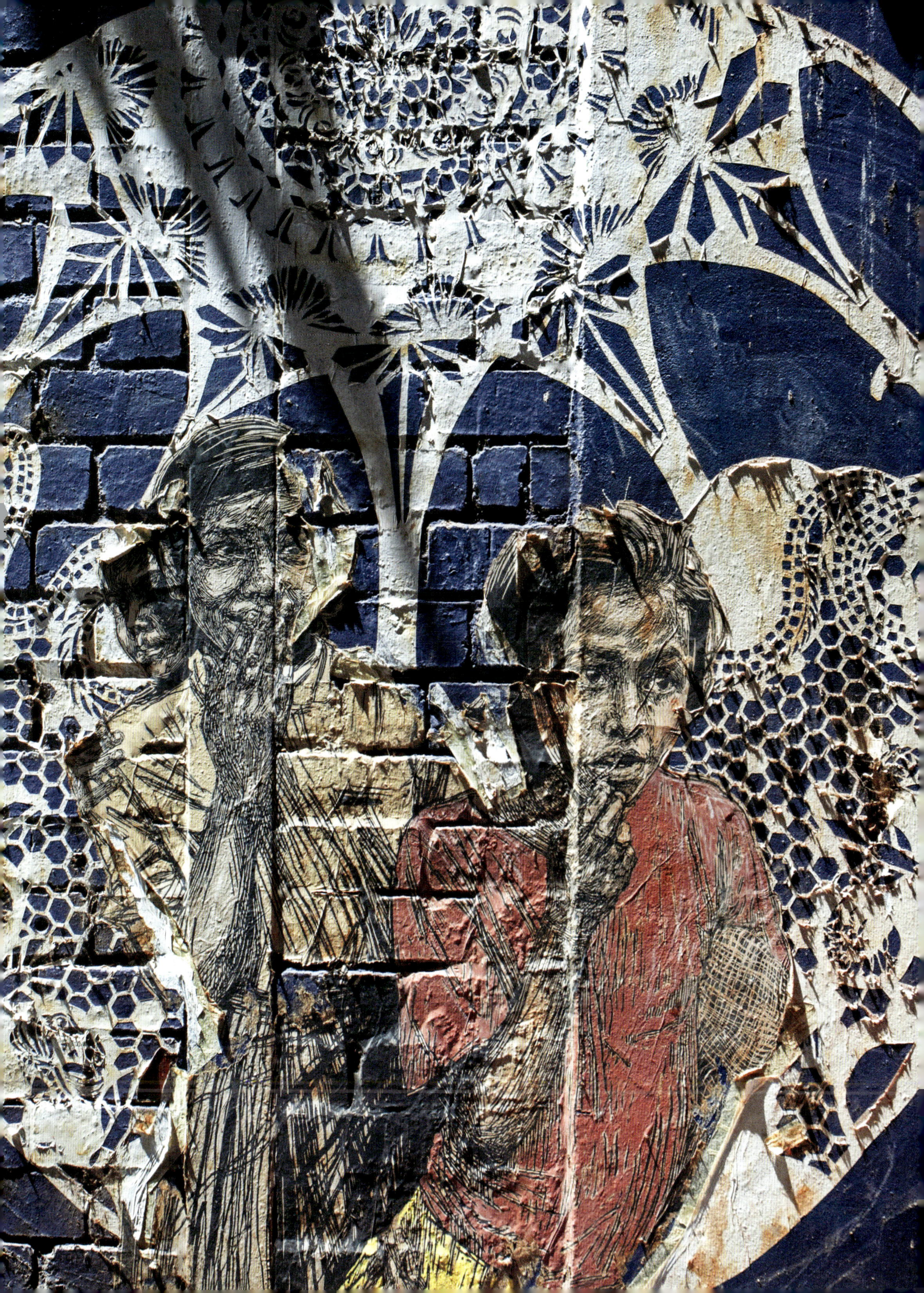

All my projects aim to use creativity to investigate a crisis, which may be an environmental disaster or a situation to resolve," she thinks. "At the moment, I'm involved, with other artists, in creating a residential complex in a Haiti village, I'm working on a project of musical architecture in New Orleans. Also for this reason, I adore Yogyakarta, a place in Jakarta, Indonesia, where graffiti is legal and many artists meet. In particular, there are groups of radical Indonesian artists who seek to do something important for their culture, for freedom. The only time I didn't feel safe was in Cuba, where the Communist government tries to control all forms of expression and asked me many questions. Besides freedom, the most important values for me are compassion and equality, in all fields. But with the choice of Donald Trump as President the United States seems to have chosen the opposite direction. I'm also committed to protecting nature and the environment and to improving the impact that humankind has had and continues to have on the planet. I go scuba diving and recently I've learned to surf, so in the future perhaps I'll supplement my production with elements inspired by the oceans," she says, and with a trace of emotion in her voice she speaks about her vocation: "I've always wanted to become an artist. I've been drawing since I was ten and I feel really complete when I know I'm part of everything and I'm making a difference. What excites me about graffiti is that today it is the most important phenomenon in contemporary art."

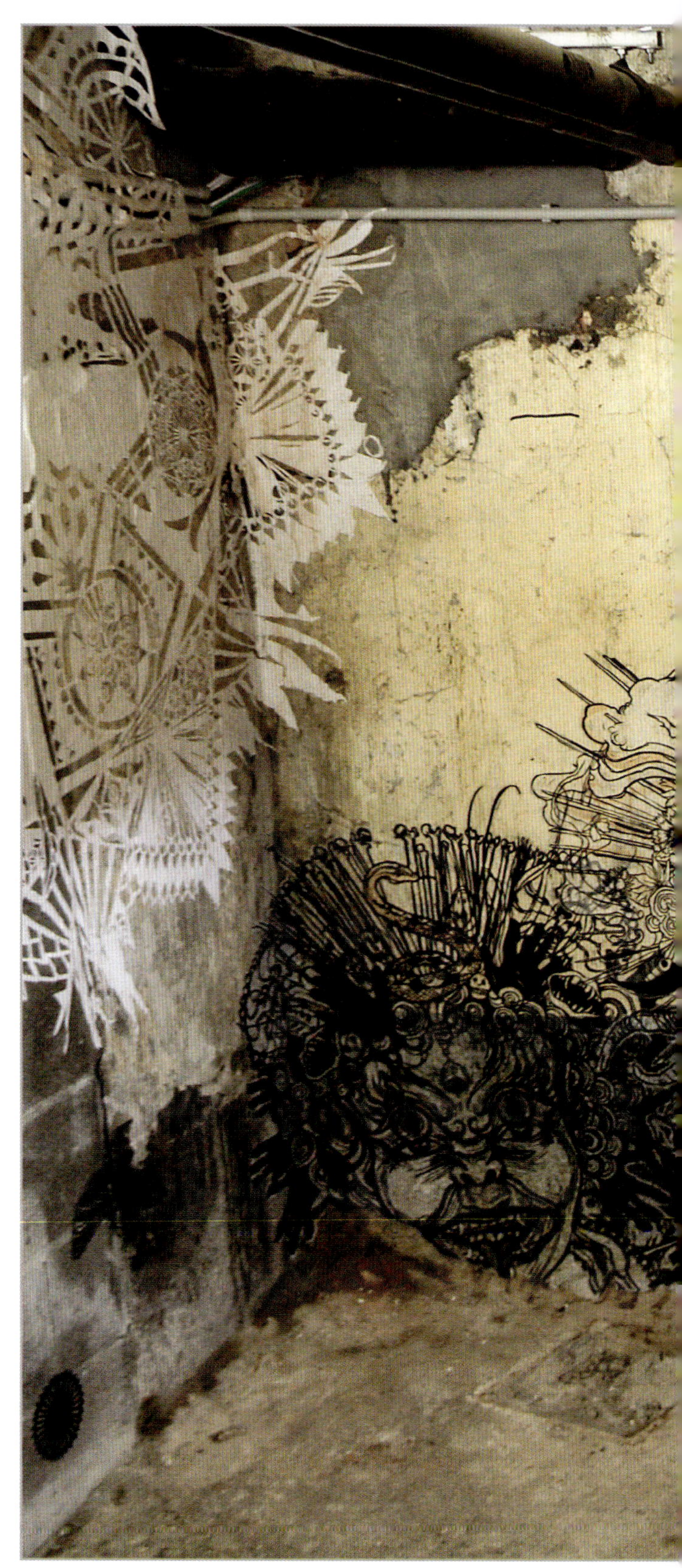

Bruxelles, 2016
A great paste-up from the exhibition *City Lights*, created in the red-brick basement of the Millennium Iconoclast Museum of Art (Mima) in Molenbeek, Brussels.

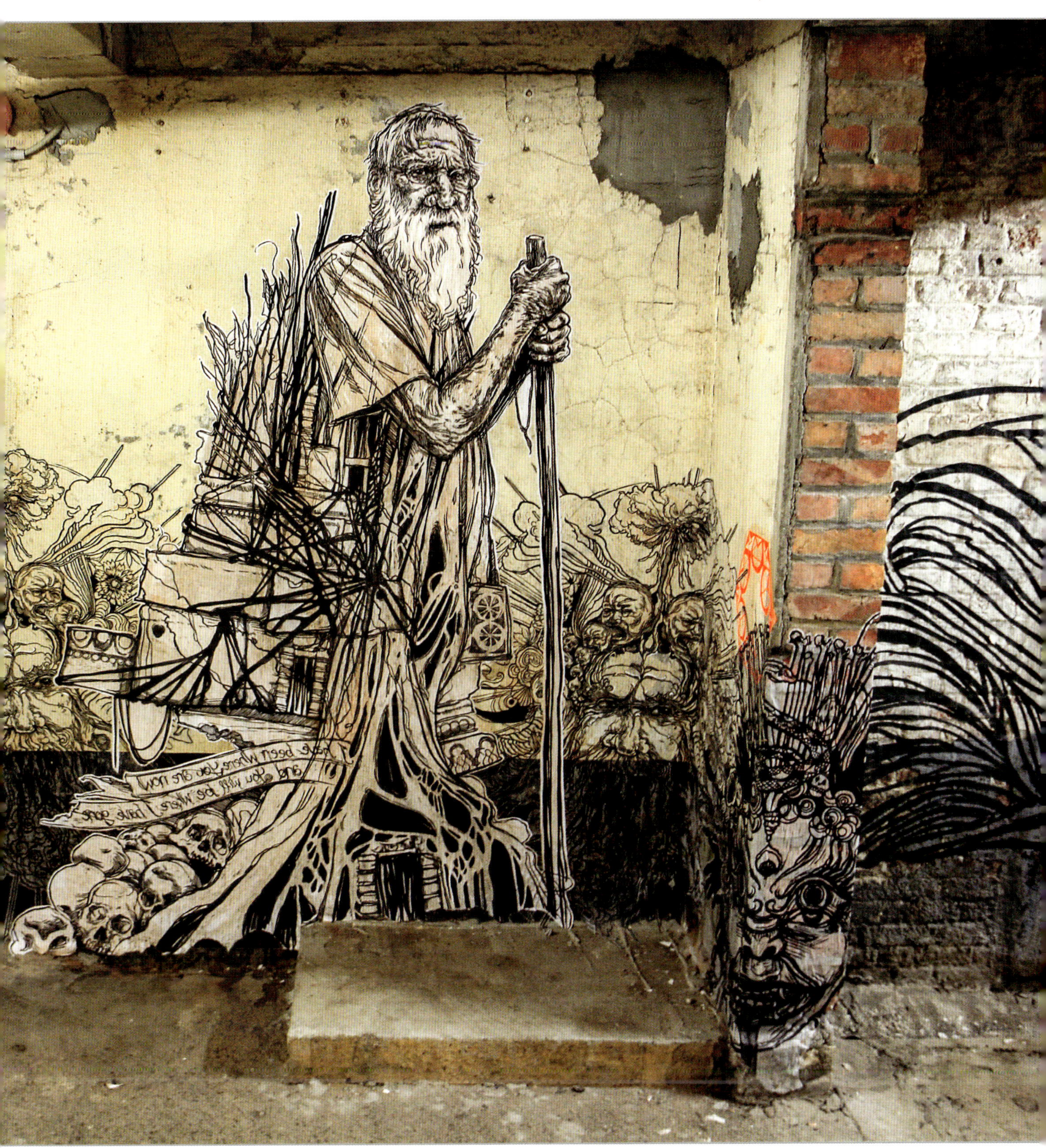

ALEX VAU
Creator and Destroyer

Even if his real identity has been revealed online, he prefers not to be quoted by name and to hide behind a pseudonym. He is passionate, instinctive, cheerful, just like his art. And he conquers his audience with the same strength. He speaks with contagious enthusiasm about his beloved homeland, Greece, and discusses everything, showing great irony, curiosity, and a sense of humor. Alex Vau differs from many other street artists in his rather dark spirit. He confesses he does not like to talk too much: he prefers to be concise, rather than to lose himself in endless complex discussions on his creative vein and artistic production. In his opinion, one can understand everything by looking at his work: he enchants through a universe of smiling, apparently merry figures, or through a maze of warm feelings and emotions, as if we were involved in a game of empathy that is impossible to resist.

His credo, he states simply without too much thought: "Sea, sex, and sun." When asked to explain, he smiles and recalls a song that represents that atmosphere for him. "*Sea, Sex and Sun* by Serge Gainsbourg often rings in my ears. I admire so much this guilt-free approach to life."

Alex studied at the Academy of Fine Arts in Athens, and then at the Academy of Fine Arts, Architecture, and Design in Prague. He had two passions when he was young: "As a child I mainly played football. My love for graffiti began in my teens. It is this element of dirt and freedom that lures many teenagers. And then it was important when I realized that graffiti was illegal. I was a 'bad boy,' in the sense that I was attracted by the things that were forbidden, and for me being 'bad and creative' at the same time was an irresistible temptation . . . In the 1990s, graffiti was spreading like a wild-fire, and so I met various artists like me. We even worked in groups of twenty. It was like an initiation to a new type of culture, like entering a special universe," he recalls. He adds: "So with graffiti it was love at first sight. But then I needed to work hard to develop my own style."

He recalls his first time: "My first tags were done in 1992 and my first quick piece a couple of years later. It felt like losing my virginity."

> So with graffiti it was love at first sight. But then I needed to work hard to develop my own style.

Vau, at work in Karditsa in Greece, seems to converse with the creatures taking shape on the wall.

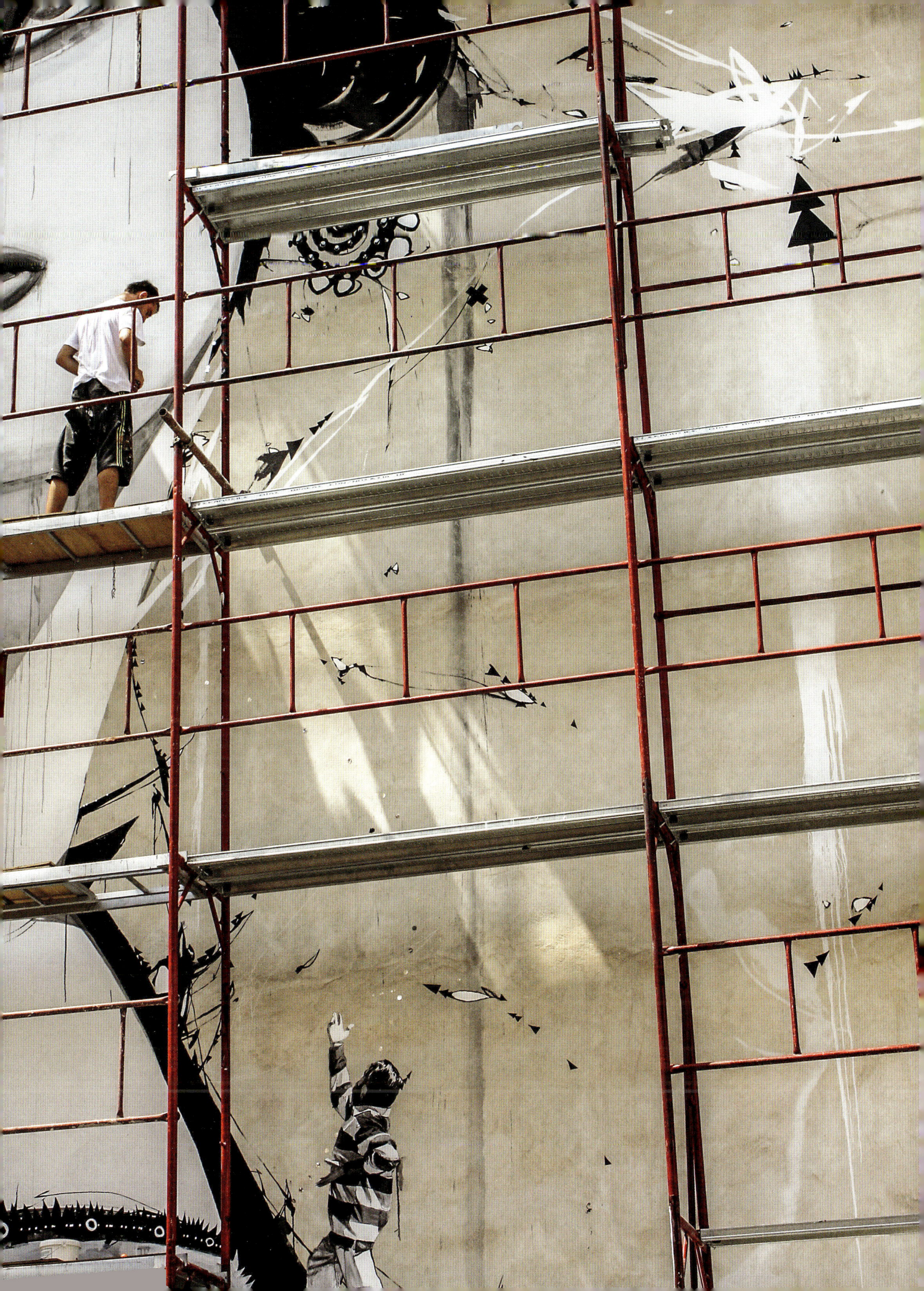

He pauses, and then begins again, remembering those times as a great and exciting adventure: "Everything was focused on how to experiment with letters in different ways, so as to ensure that uniqueness which can lead to being recognized. The message was finding its own style."

"My technique is mostly based on creation through destruction. My methods are no longer those of a teenager. I operate on many strata in my work, from the first to the last layer, and it takes days to destroy and create through them. It is a game of strata. It feels like a tug of war between the layers," he says in describing his method. Creating new layers by destroying the old ones.

When he has to describe his art, he comes up with the expression "carrot and stick," which he states abruptly. "It is as if my work were a combination of recognition and punishment. The former is represented by the achievements, the latter by the frustrations of the work process."

Alex admits that for him, in the final analysis, communication is the most important factor in his work. "It is fundamental for me to reach the greatest audience possible and for all my works to move people. I never have a particular message to communicate – excepting creativity itself," he says, contemplating the idea, "and I am completely open to this."

"Believe it or not, I had no difficulties, all happened rather smoothly. In the beginning, when we did graffiti, my friends and I didn't call ourselves artists. We didn't intend to describe ourselves in this way. I don't even have extraordinary backstage stories to tell," he says, concluding. But then he thinks again and something comes to mind. "To be honest, I've been caught several times and ended up at the police station. I've been arrested, but they've never held me overnight . . . And for a teenager it was something cool, something to joke about with my friends, to pretend I was a hero! In several cases," he confesses, "I had to climb some walls, and got cut up or injured . . . But nothing serious, these things usually happen to every graffiti or street artist out there. I consider the scars as souvenirs, I'm happy to have them!"

Alex Tries, 2008 - A tiny man climbs up a woman with an endless neck, as fascinating as a dark tale: Vau's painting on a wall in Karditsa is a dialog of love, homage to beauty.

Looking at Marc Chagall, 2007 - In Athens, in the "rebellious" quarter of Exarchia, Vau pays homage to Chagall by painting a couple floating on a gray wall, supported by poetry and by their very embrace.

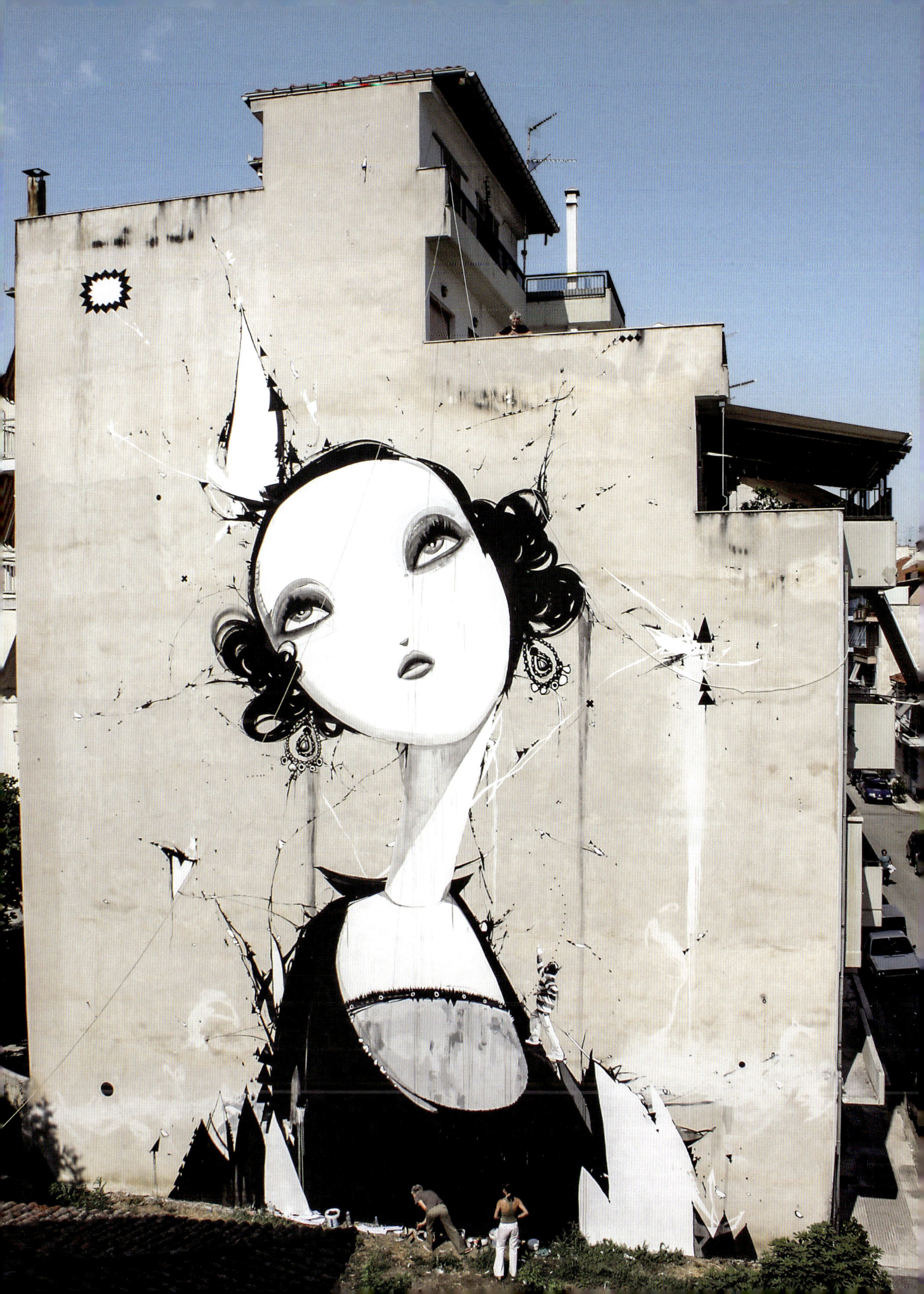

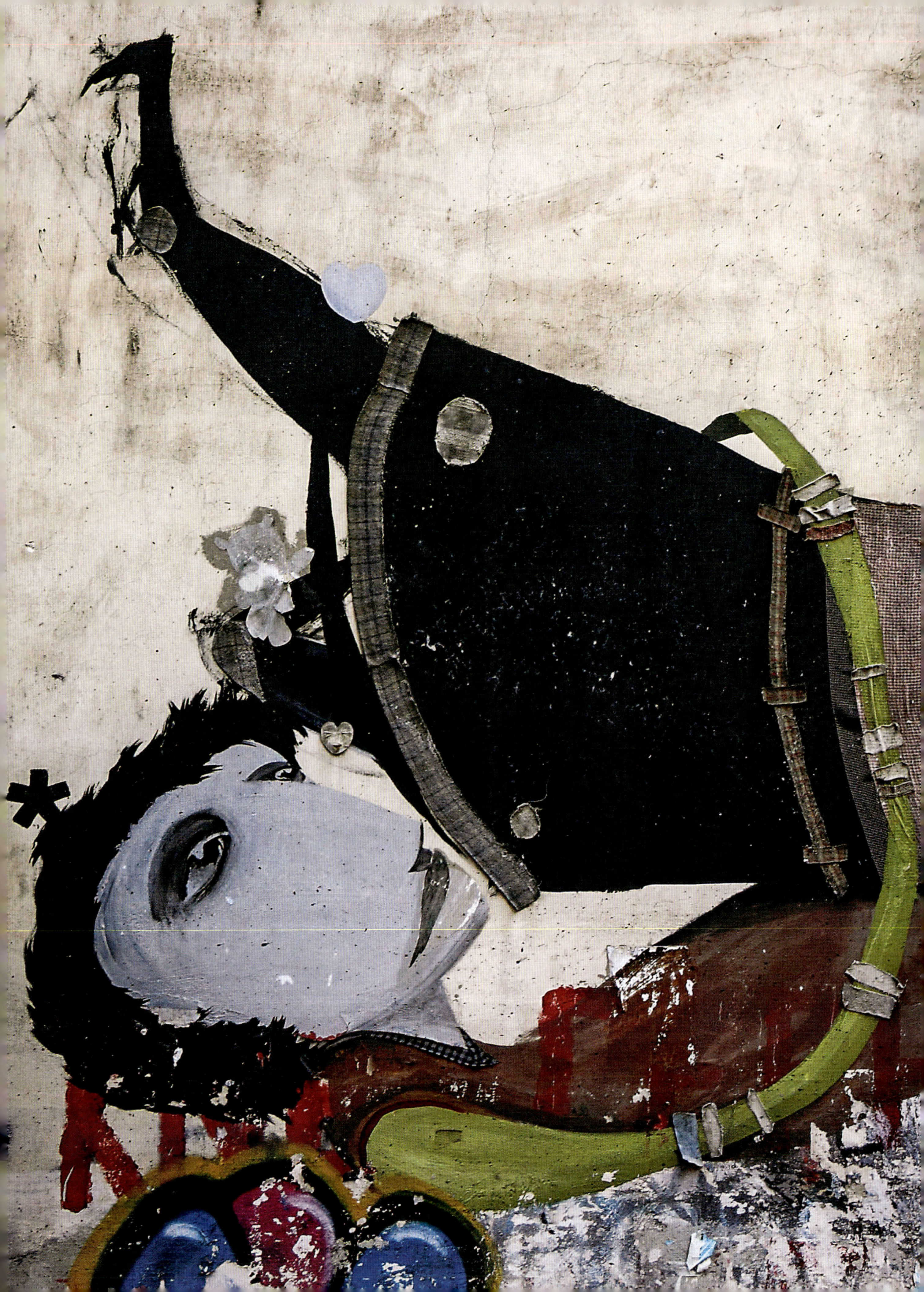

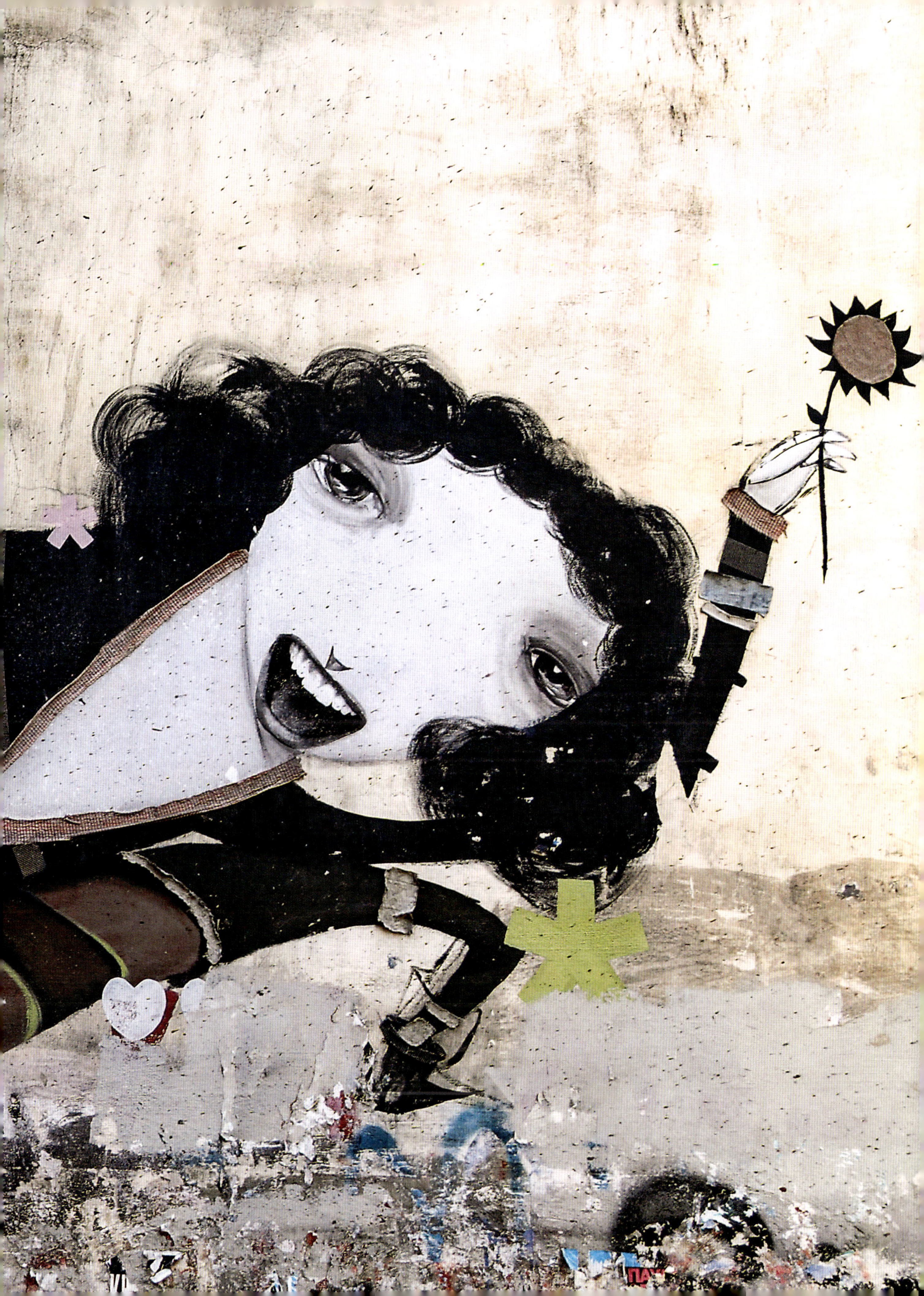

He has had many sources of inspiration, some eccentric or unusual. "As a teenager, I admired M.C. Escher, an artist who took my breath away with his wonderful work. I don't feel like naming others, because it seems like wronging someone: too many have inspired me, however, Escher was my first love. Then, as in life, there have been others . . . If I really had to mention someone, I might add Diego Maradona for his way of playing soccer – theatrical, full of character . . . I'm convinced he's an artist in his field!" he adds, laughing.

Alex Vau likes working with color, but he hasn't got a favorite one. "My palate of colors is enormous. It depends on the day, on the weather, on the temperature, on how I slept the night before . . ." When asked to give some examples, he replies: "My favorite colors . . . Purple when I sleep well! Cold white when I'm moody. While if I'm happy I use cobalt blue which gives to the painting great depths by itself."

From the artistic point of view, Alex Vau says that he does not have an unfulfilled project: "I think I've produced a lot and sometimes I hate all my work. It depends upon the moment . . . sometimes I like it. I know that there really is a question about whether street art is a worth-preserving art . . . These guys are actually right. More often than not street art and graffiti are painful disaster pieces, 'visual pollution' - to say the least. Usually I like less than a 10% of the works I see in the streets. However, at times this 10% can be stunning!"

For Alex, what's fundamental is not the place he works in, but what he succeeds in creating. "I am more concerned with what I make, rather than where I make it. A combination of London, where I'm drawn to the British temperament, of Greece, where I love the sea and the mountains and my friends and where I grew up, and Buenos Aires, a really interesting place: This mixture would be an earthly paradise" he concludes.

Alex also likes the idea of transhumanism. "This cultural movement envisions humans with technological implants, and I'm convinced that this is a great opportunity for further evolution. Having a computer inside my head? Fascinating."

***Superman (Apocalypsis)*, 2011** - In the Athenian quarter of Psyrri, with many bars and nightclubs, Vau leaves a complex mural with a strange effect, which hides a deep apprehension behind a show of jollity.

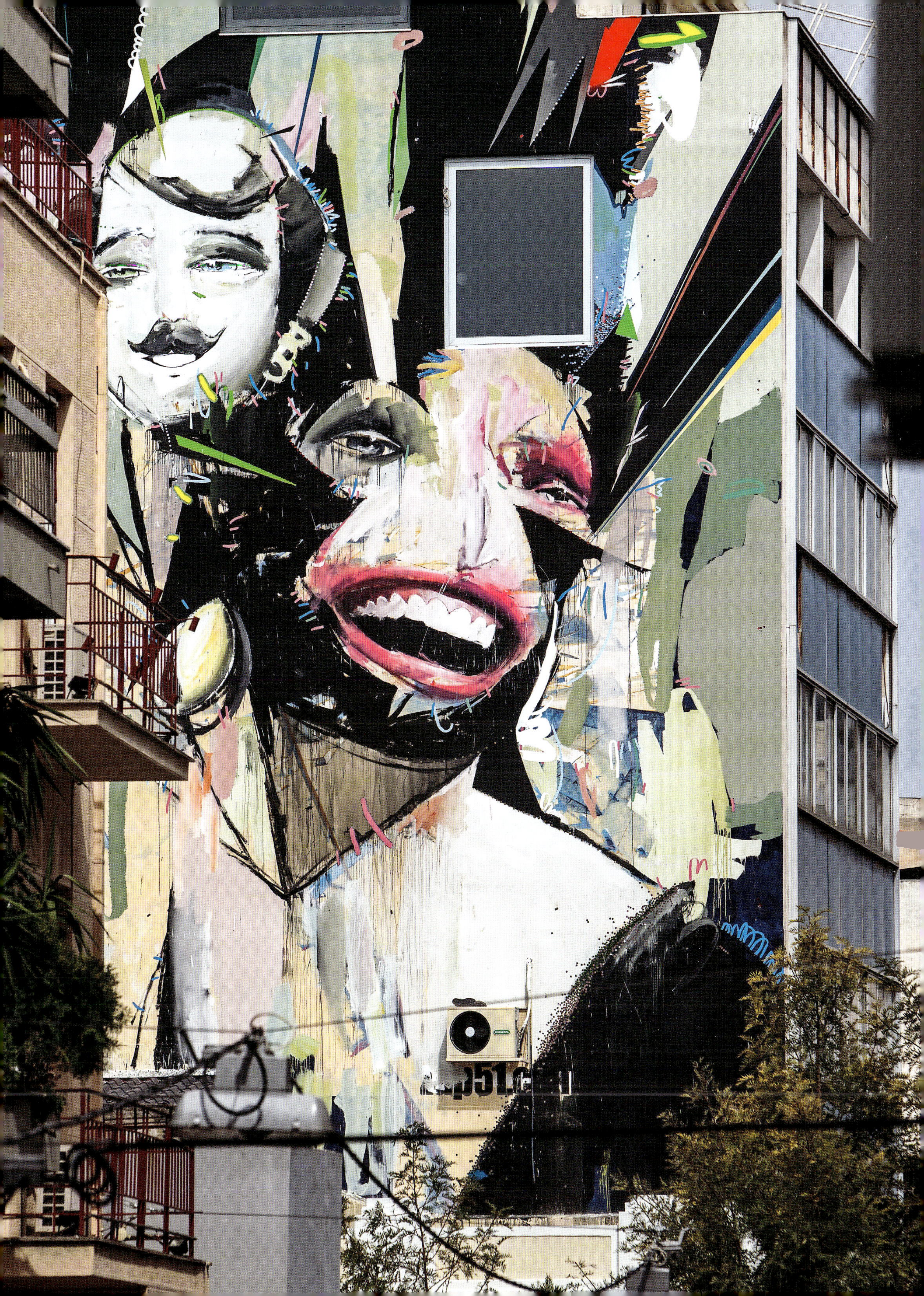

VHILS

Humanizer of Urban Spaces

"I believe in working with the forces of chaos present in the city and making them part of an art that is as transient as the material reality that surround us. I try to harness something of these forces of destruction to create an organic, evolving art that in turn can help humanize our urban spaces," says Vhils, who moves between his native Lisbon and London, another place that has played an important role in his career.

The Portuguese artist Alexandre Farto, born in 1987, attained considerable success as a 'writer' in 2000 under the name Vhils, but he continues to draw. "I used to draw a lot when I was a child, to the point that one day my mother was called to my school where she was told I spent too much time drawing and wasn't paying attention in class. At the age of ten, I started noticing more and more graffiti on the walls in my hometown and was immediately attracted to it. I soon started drawing and sketching inspired by what I saw. One thing led to another and eventually I became involved with the local graffiti scene. This became my gateway to the visual arts. Although it was something I liked doing, there was never a conscious plan for me to become a full-time artist, things just went naturally in that direc-

> The main themes present in my work are mostly connected with trying to reflect on the complex reality of the urban spaces we live in and the globalized model of development we are following.

tion," he explains. Like many other graffiti 'writers' I started tagging with markers on walls on my way to school. The first pieces I painted were very crude things that I tried out in an abandoned factory after saving up to buy some spray paints. What I remember clearly is the thrill that painting graffiti gave me. It was nothing like I had experienced before. It involved risk and creativity. I was hooked from day one. Sometime later, when I became better at painting and started 'bombing' trains this feeling increased to a point where it took over my life, and for a few years I simply lived for the thrill." He goes on to describe his artistic vision, "My technique plays with the notion of aesthetic vandalism by resorting to destructive means in order to create. It is based on the practice of removing some of the formative layers that give shape to our material reality in order to expose and bring to light some of the essence that, symbolically, lies buried beneath. In other words, I use a stencil-based technique as a symbolic window that helps reveal what lies hidden beneath the surface of things."

He continues, "My art can be seen as an ongoing work of exposure by means of subtraction and removal. It helps make visible what is invisible."

Portrait of Vhils, an artist fascinated by the human face, with its lights and shadows.

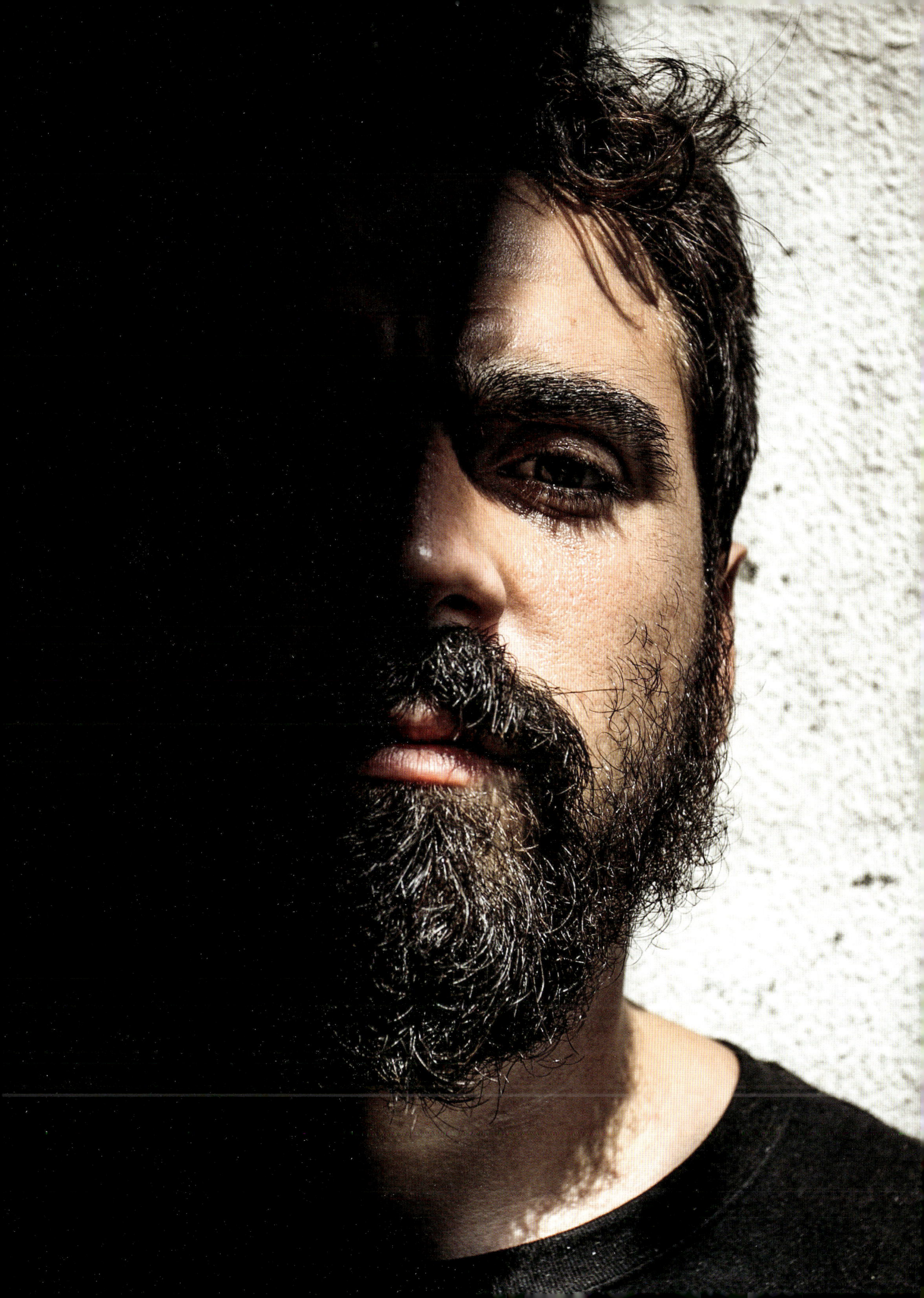

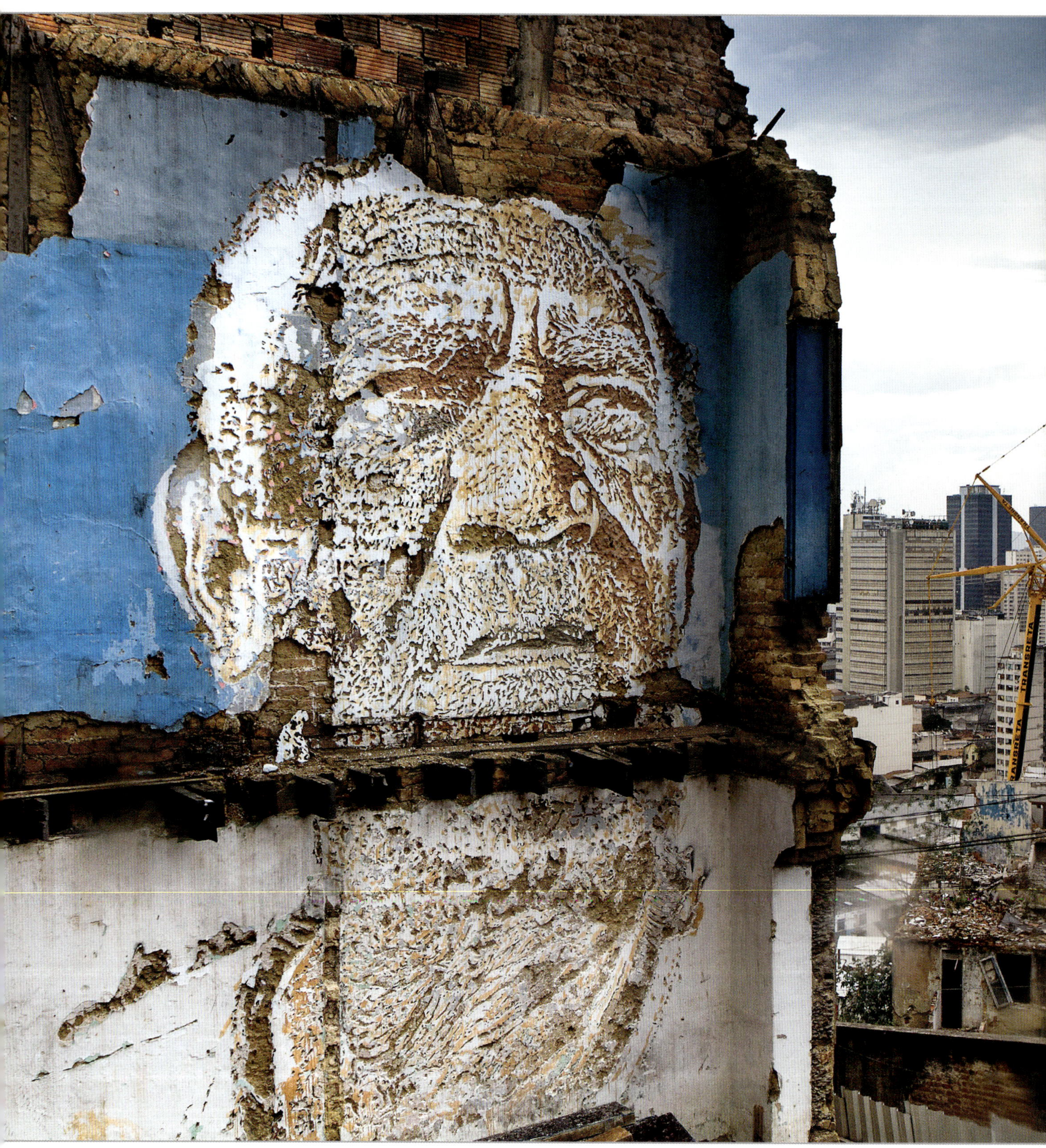

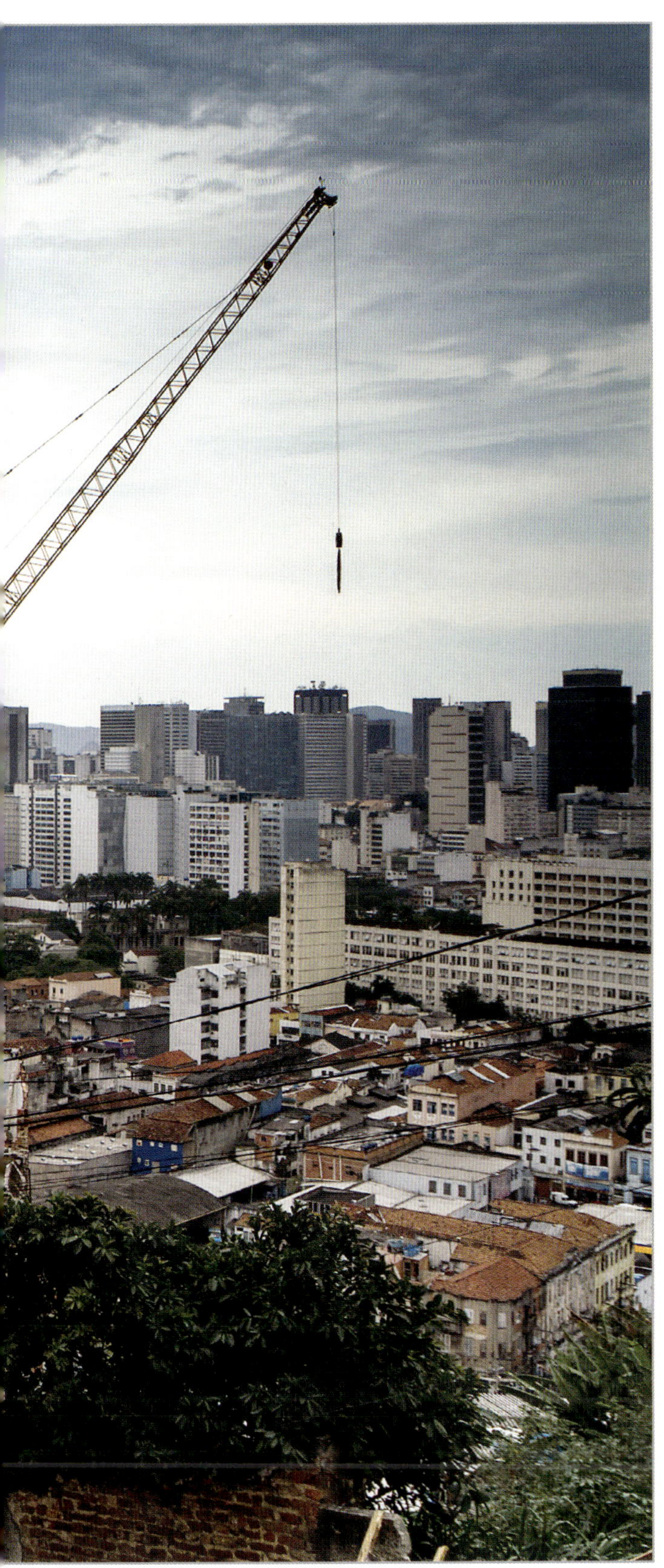

His message, therefore, is deeply rooted in reality. "The main themes present in my work are mostly connected with trying to reflect on the complex reality of the urban spaces we live in and the globalized model of development we are following; how we are losing touch with our human nature by following a path that seems to be leading us to destruction for the sake of profit and exploitation. Development and growth are good, but not only should they be based on our needs and not on our desires, they should also be inclusive and sustainable in the long run. In many of the pieces though, I just tend to highlight some detail that pertains to a human dimension I want to emphasize. I also look into the notions of identity and how people and the places they live in are locked in a cycle of reciprocal shaping through which they develop a shared character. Additionally, I explore the themes of randomness and the ephemeral nature of things, both of which are deeply connected with what I do and how I do it. I'm interested in incorporating these elements into my work and making them a part of the pieces themselves, working along with nature and the way time changes materials and surfaces," he says, expressing a thoughtful, complex and elaborate vision of his art.

Asked if he has a favorite color, he answers, "Not really. Most of the colors present in my work are usually already part of the materials. I like to work mainly with black and white in order to create sharp contrasts and keep things simple."

Vhils grew up in Seixal, an industrial suburb of Lisbon and was strongly influenced by the urban transformations of the region, such as the 1974 revolution in his country; he has often testified to the destruction and the pain of the war in his works.

Rio de Janeiro, 2012
A dubious, critical gaze up from the favela Morro da Providência, the oldest in Rio, while below it the city is being transformed for the 2016 Olympics.

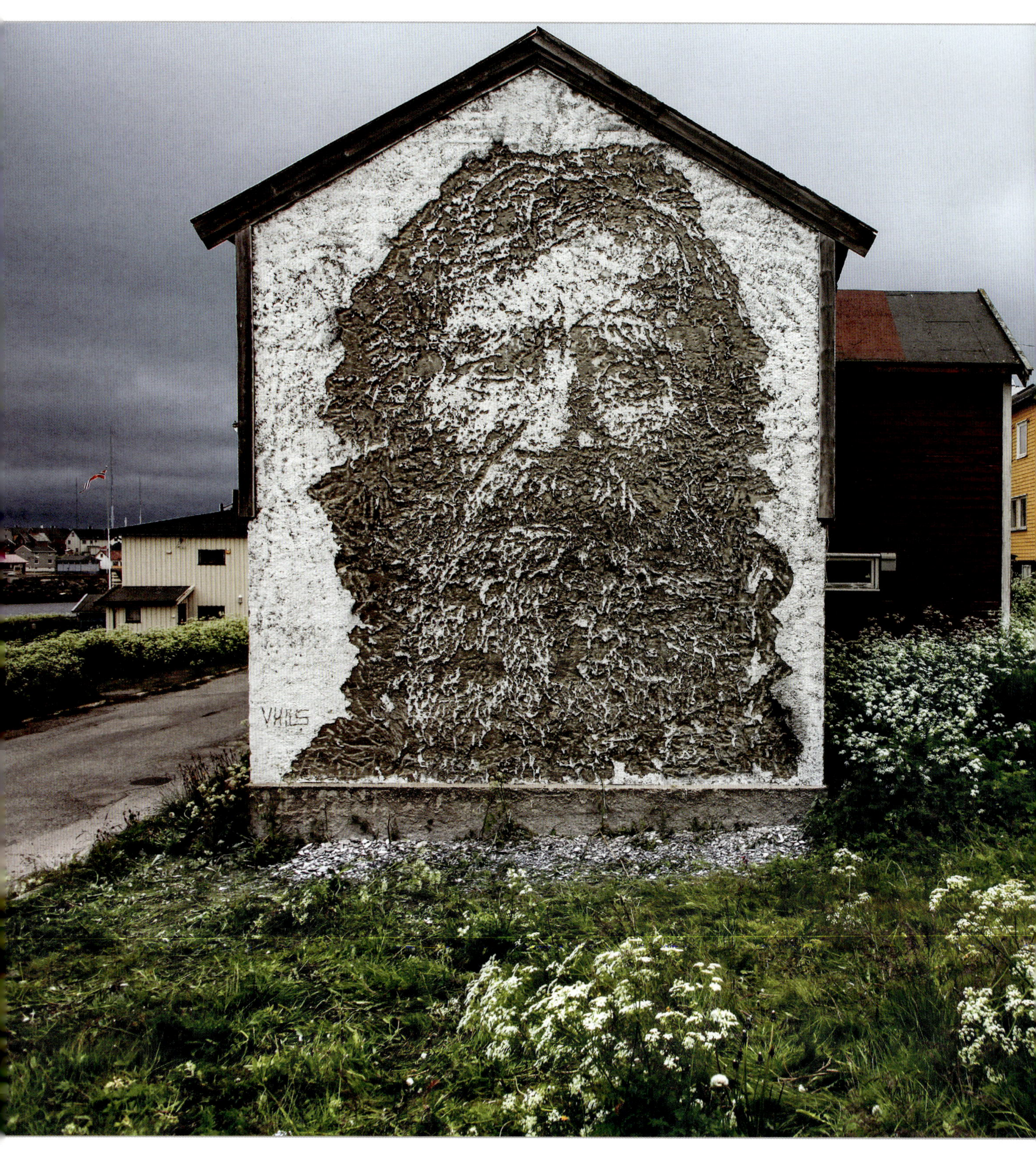

Vardø, 2012 - From a light-colored wall emerges an enormous bearded face, rich in detail. It is created for the Komafest in Vardø, Norway: the texture of the background contributes to heightening its expressiveness.

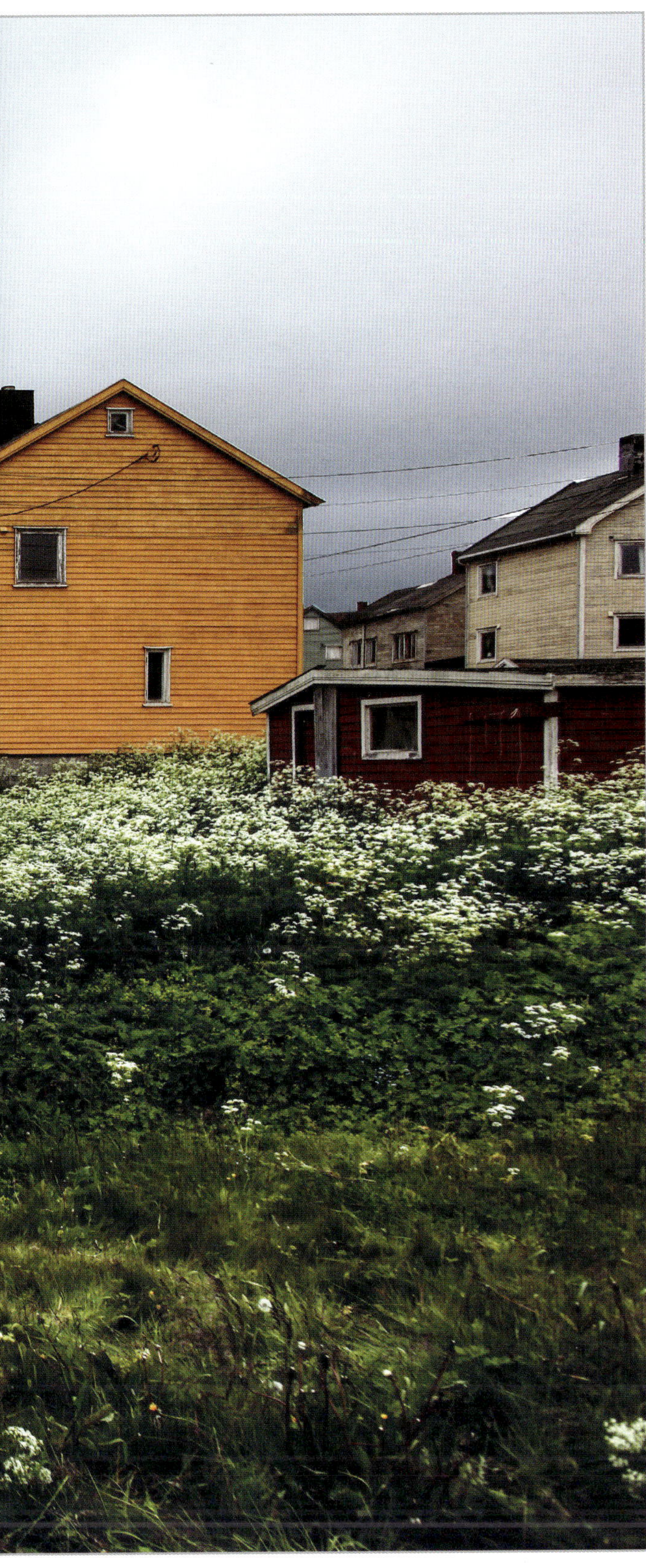

He studied at the Byam Shaw School of Art in London and the first recognition of his work came in 2008, at the Cans Festival in London, when one of his works, a face dug out of a wall, stood alongside a work by Banksy. He has taken part in any number of important projects, although one of his best-known works is an original image of the first female Australian senator carved on the exterior wall of the Norfolk Hotel, during the Fremantle Street Arts Festival in 2013.

"I have always found it difficult to claim particular influences," he says thoughtfully, "as I honestly believe we are constantly being influenced and changed by literally everything and everyone that surrounds us. When I first started out, I used to follow closely the work of other graffiti writers, especially those who were active around Lisbon at the time. It was graffiti that sparked my interest in the visual arts, and there are quite a few artists whose work I do admire, although I feel that my work has been more influenced by the small, mundane details of life than by other people's work. Having said that, Banksy's attitude and approach on how to use the public space effectively to communicate your ideas and interact with a large audience were pivotal in shaping my own ideas and approach.

I admire his work and what he's accomplished, although I don't claim any direct influence in terms of visual language or style. Gordon Matta-Clark is also a major reference for his ability to work with architectural structures in connection with a reflection on urban decay and its effects on people and communities living in the urban environment.

I also admire the work of many other artists, including Katharina Grosse, Anish Kapoor, AkaCorleone, ±MaisMenos±, Os Gemeos, Barry McGee, Faile, Interesni Kazki, Cyrcle, JR, Blu, Word 2 Mother, Martha Cooper, Conor Harrington, How & Nosm, Finok, and Pixel Pancho, to name but a few."

With regard to those who criticize street art, he retorts, "I strongly believe that art is art, regardless of the context in which it's being created or presented."

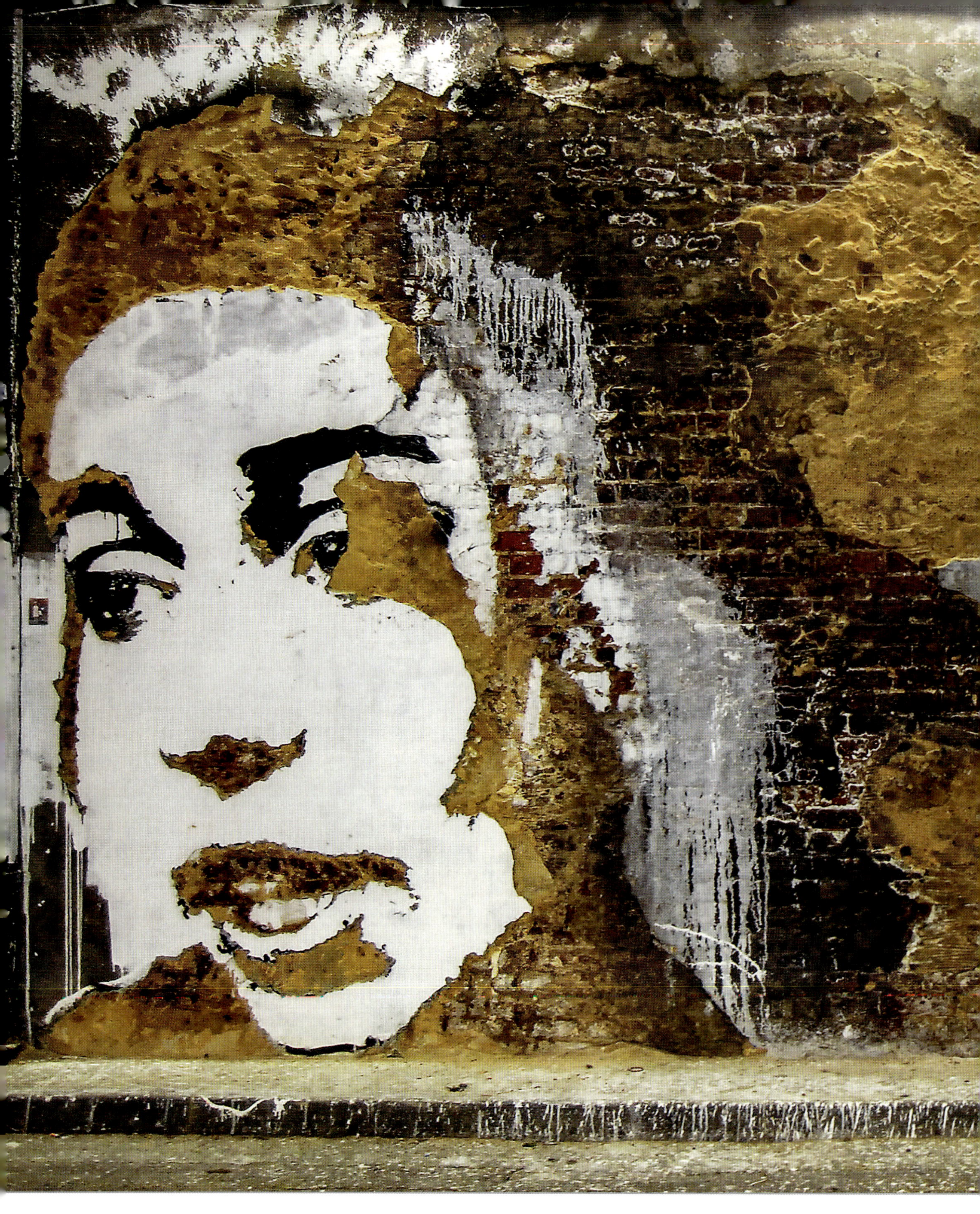

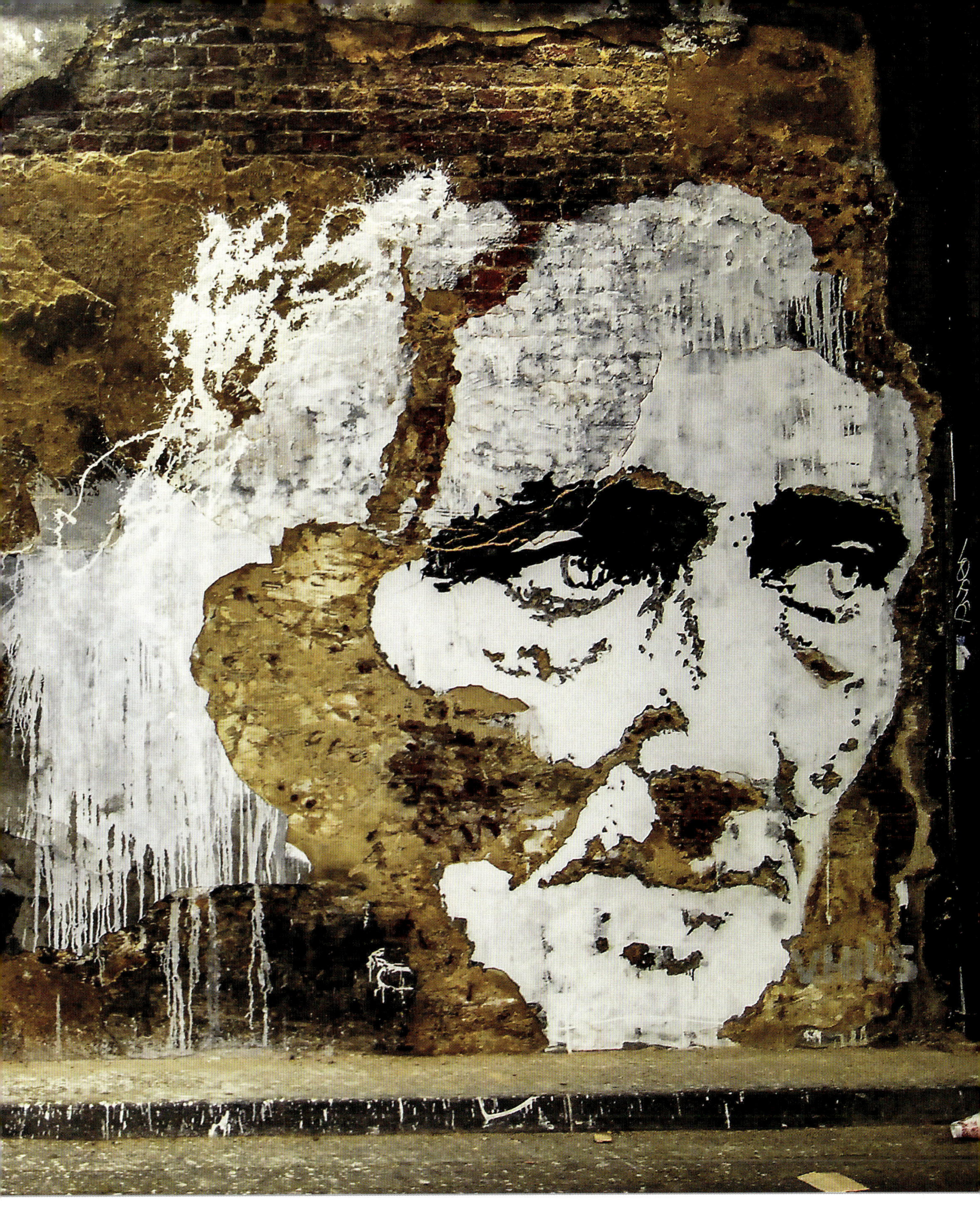

London, 2008 – Youth and old age look in opposite directions on the wall of the Cans Festival in the Leake Street tunnel, Waterloo Station, London.

In any case, he has never encountered complications or mishaps. "I can't say that I have experienced any difficulties as an artist creating in the streets, except the obvious problems with the authorities. The difficulties I did face came about when I was moving into the institutional art world with a background in graffiti and street art, and in this context I faced the usual prejudices when I was starting out; however, then I was lucky enough to meet the gallerist Vera Cortês, who gave me her full support and believed in my work from the very beginning. Many people still classify my work as street art, whereas I find it easier to think of it simply as art, regardless of the context."

Then he adds, "Despite owing a lot to graffiti in conceptual and even material terms, my artwork is not graffiti. I find it very hard to choose a favorite piece, as I value all of them equally, even those that came out wrong. In many ways, all the community-related projects I've done in Portugal, Brazil, China and other countries have been very rewarding mostly because you're working with people who are dealing with real-life issues and it feels good to help them in a very modest way. But all projects and pieces have their special significance." He continues his reasoning, "Again, my artwork is not graffiti. I have found some difficulties in creating some of the wall pieces, but you have to adapt to the particularities of every sur-face. I once had to carve a piece on super thick concrete used to build missile-proof and bullet-proof walls, and that was tough. Placing a site-specific piece aboard the International Space Station in 2015 (a portrait of Danish astronaut Andreas Mogensen of the European Space Agency) was also demanding due to the logistics involved. On the other hand, putting up large solo exhibitions, such as the 2014 show at the EDP Foundation in Lisbon and the 2016 show with HOCA Foundation in Hong Kong, have been some of the most demanding and consuming experiences of my life."

"I think my art is best expressed in the context in which it's produced, regardless of the location. Although I do like to establish connections and correlations between places, people and subject matter, most of my work is conceived as being site-specific. As for a favorite city, I would have to say Lisbon and Hong Kong, as each of them gives me something the other cannot. Hong Kong has given me a type of peace I was struggling to find in Lisbon, enabling me to focus more on my artwork and less on the bureaucracy of running a studio. It's a blend between hi-tech efficiency and the chaos inherent to city life, representing everything that is positive and negative in contemporary urban societies. It is a city of sharp material contrasts and home to many cultures.

Rio de Janeiro, 2012 - Vhils favors irregular walls "with a past": his intervention seems to bring out faces already present under the plaster.

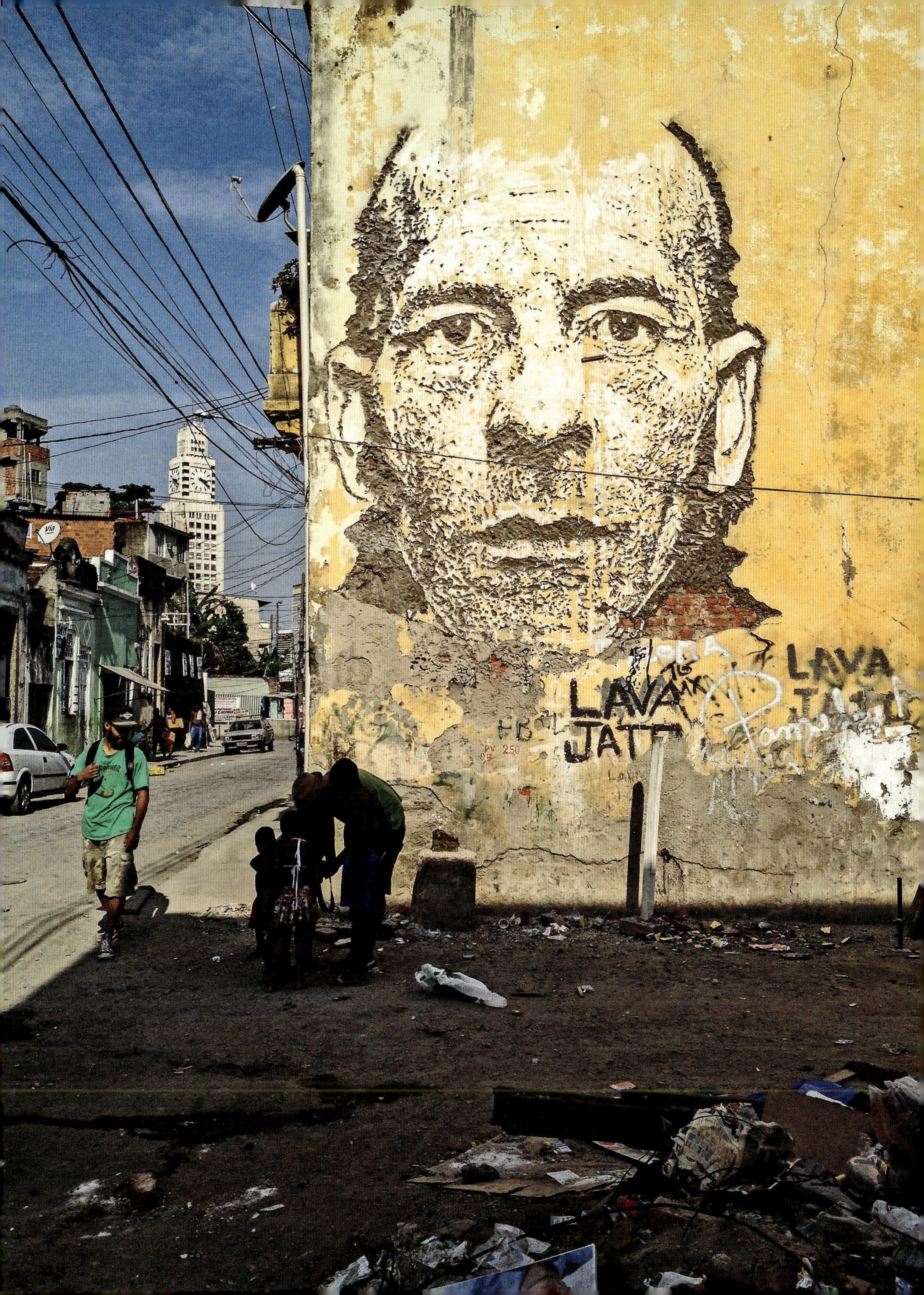

LAVA
JATT
LAVA
JATT

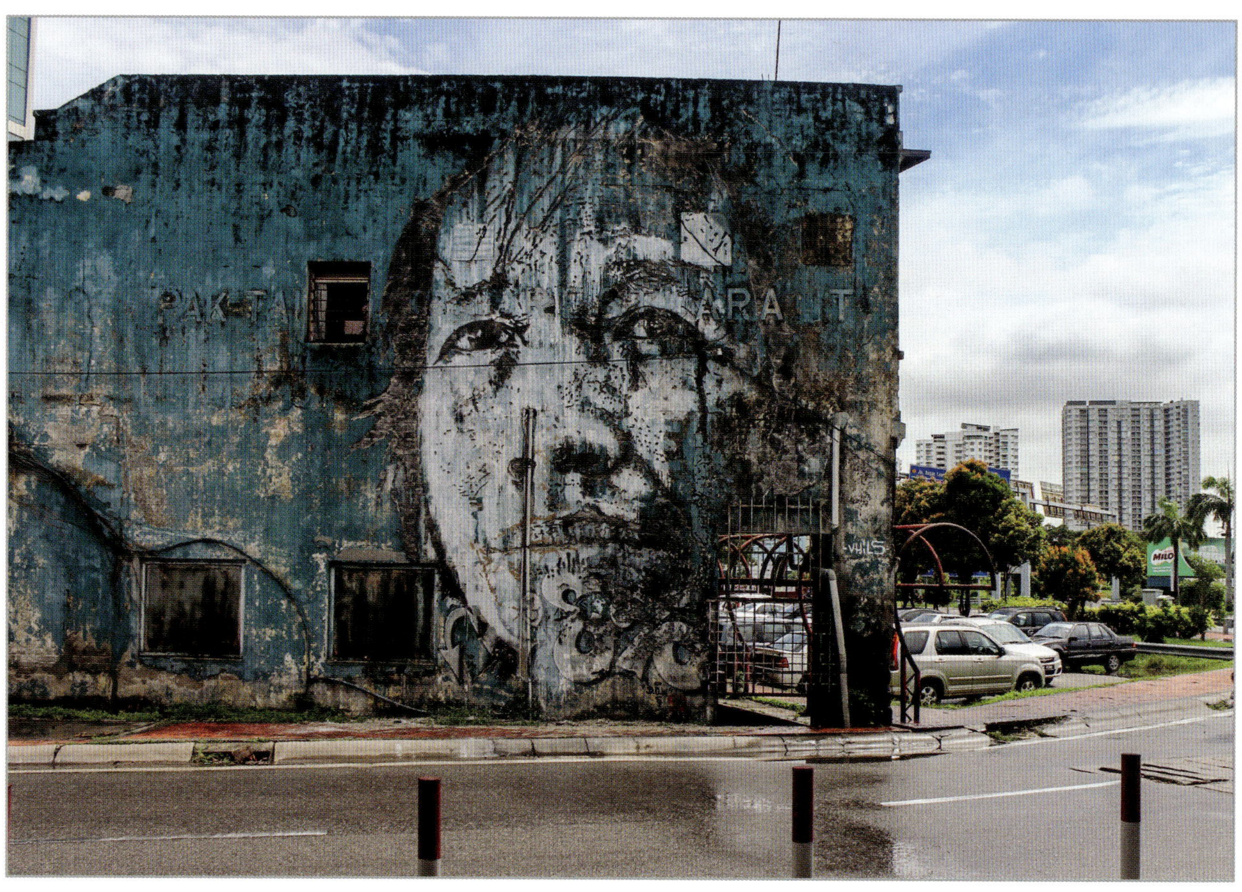

Butterworth, 2015 - The portrait of a resident of Butterworth, Malaysia, emerges from the blue of a wall. The work, both delicate and intense, was created during the Urban Xchange Festival.

Grottaglie, 2010 - This penetrating gaze seems to blend in with the stone in the historic center of Grottaglie, in Italy.

You can stand in one place and see the contrast between the high-rise developments and the surrounding mountains, a striking statement on our relationship with nature and technology. It is the past, the present, and the future all rolled into one. Lisbon, on the other hand, has a unique poetic ambience emanating from its very particular faded glamour. It is an old city, steeped in culture and the past. Once the capital of a thriving global empire, it spent half of the 20th century stifled under a conservative dictatorship, falling into disrepair. It only really began regenerating itself in the last two decades, and is now seen as one of Europe's most stylish and appealing cities. Lisbon is a city of small nooks and hidden details – it differs greatly from one area to the next, depending on when it was built, so it's really like several different towns rolled into one. Its decaying, peeling walls, their layers thick with history, inspired me to develop my visual language." He admits that the place he was born continues to exercise a strong affective and professional attraction for him. "I feel a huge connection with Lisbon, where I was born, and with Seixal, a small suburban town close to Lisbon where I grew up. Growing up in this particular suburban reality definitely shaped my world view. I believe that the environment we grow up in and live in plays a pivotal role in shaping our personality. My work has been exploring at length this relationship of interdependence between people and the surrounding environment, based on the con-

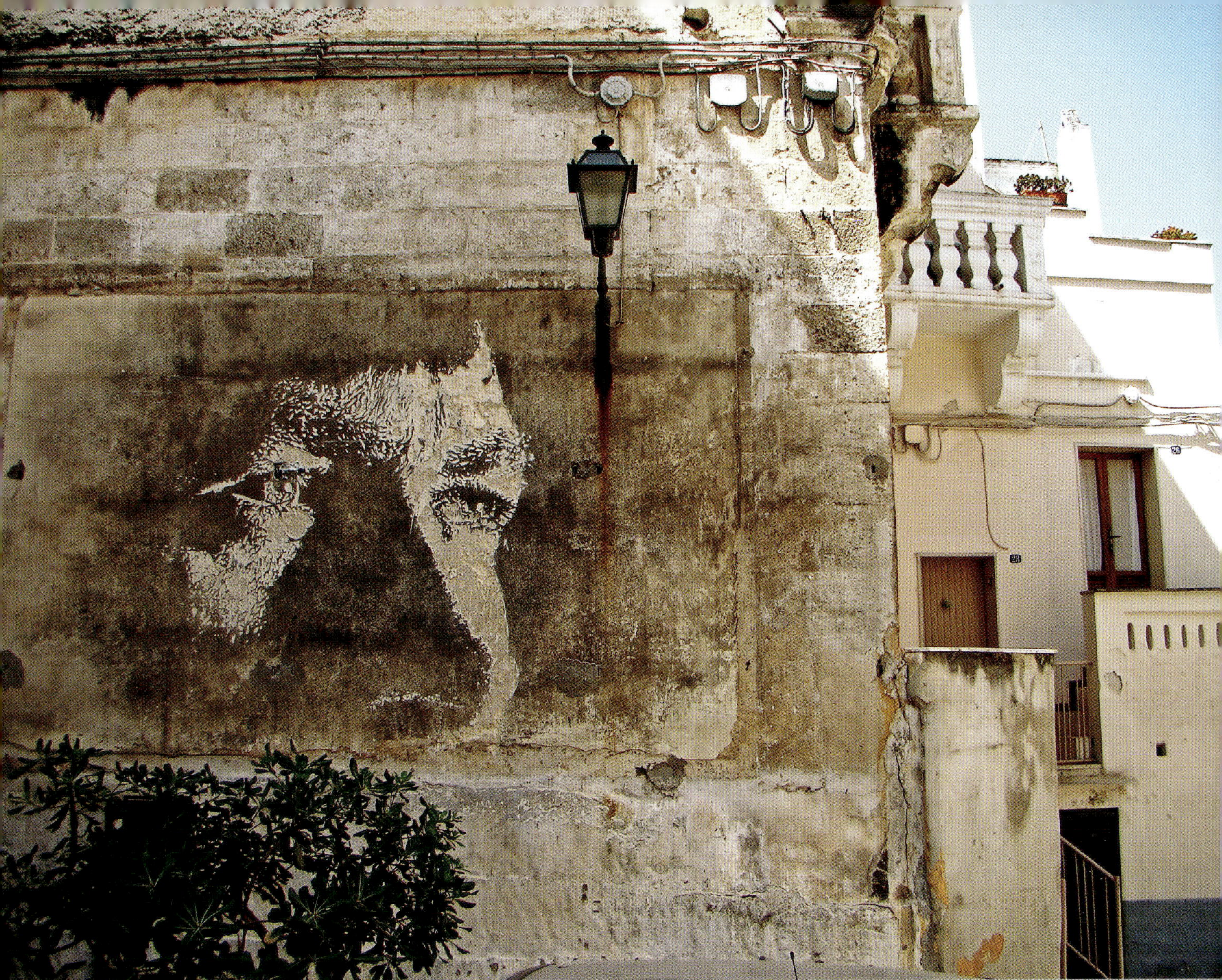

cept of reciprocal shaping. Seixal and the entire South Bank were peripheral areas, a contrasting landscape of heavy industry and farmlands which, over the years, was transformed by an intense process of urban development as the city's suburbs expanded. This rapid transformation left a deep impression on me. I was also affected by the fast-changing reality I saw on its walls, how the impressive political murals and paintings that had taken over the landscape after the Carnation revolution faded away and were replaced by the advent of capitalist advertising and later on by graffiti. This process taught me a lot about visual communication in the streets and how history leaves its traces on public walls. I was also heavily influenced by graffiti itself, which was important in shaping my perception of the world, of the urban landscape and the way in which cities operate and how we can operate in them," he states. Still, there is a place where he would like to do a piece: Antarctica.

Lisbon, 2012 - Vhils' work gains a new aesthetic dimension in contact with the lively tones of Pixel Pancho, who together with him creates this work for the *Underdogs* project in Lisbon.

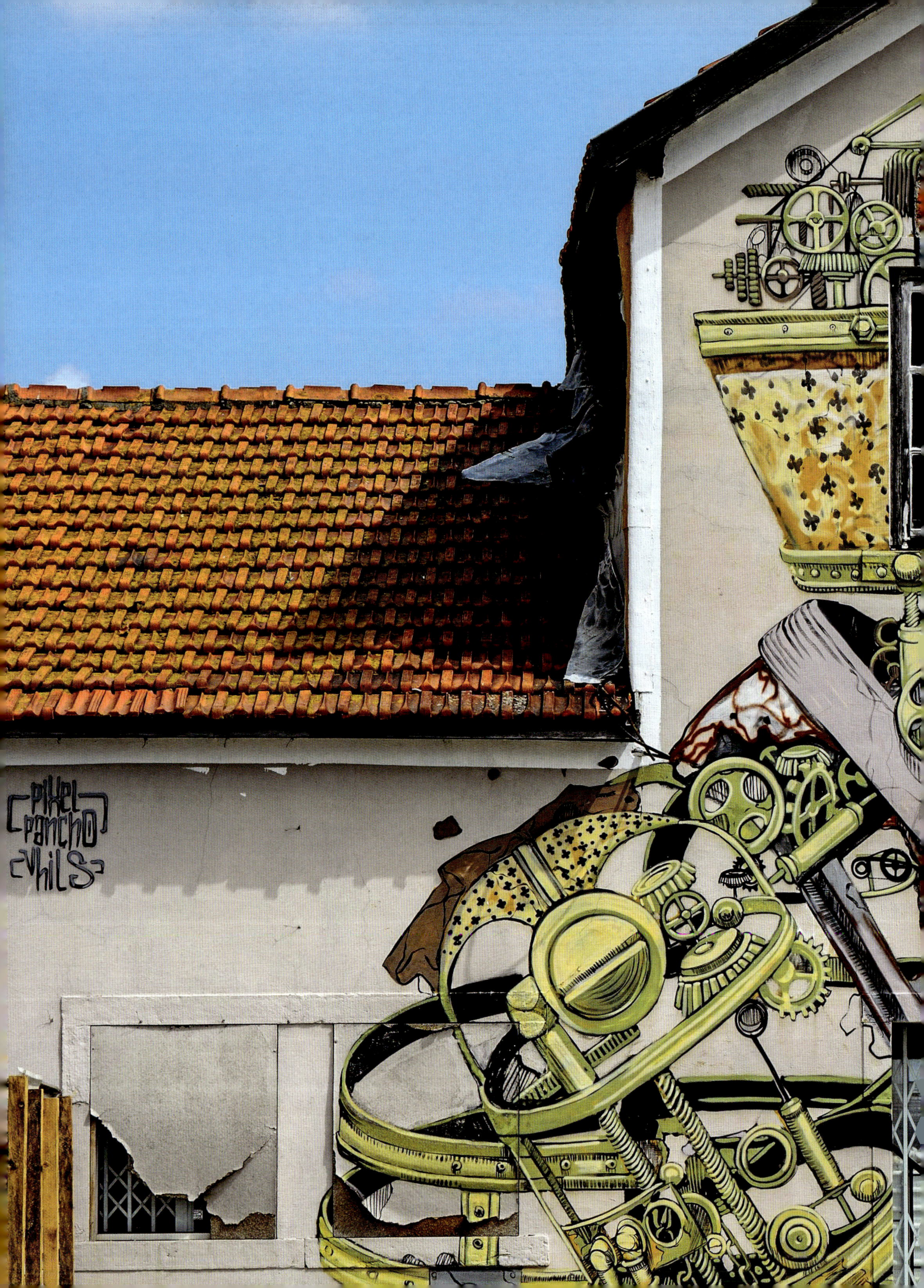

pixel
pancho
vhils

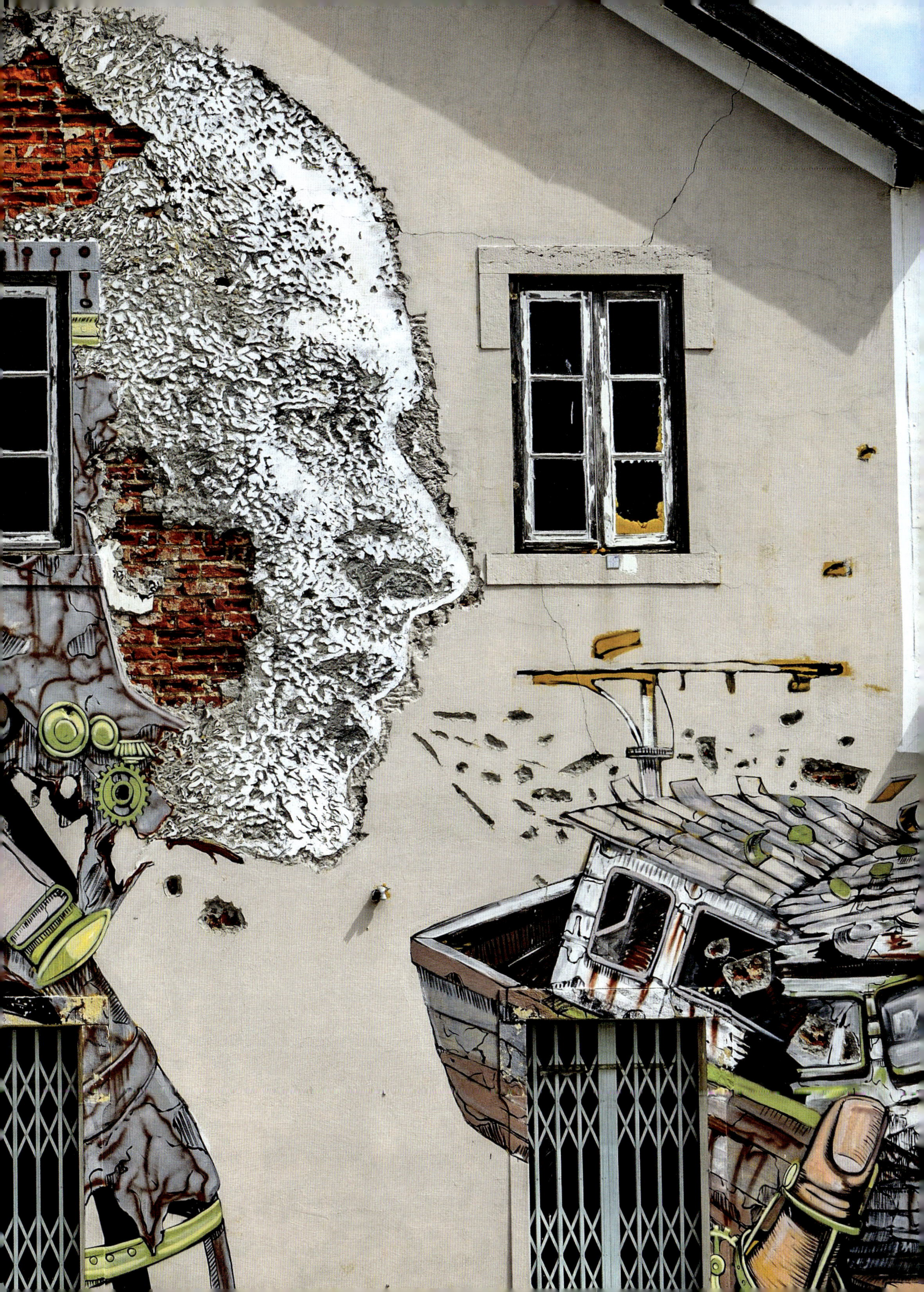

Authors

ALESSANDRA MATTANZA, writer, screenwriter, and fine art photographer, has lived in New York and Los Angeles for a number of years. At the moment, she works as a foreign correspondent, contributor, and editor for several publishing houses and magazines; she collaborates on interviews and mini-documentaries for TV Studio Universal. She is also the author of novels, screenplays, illustrated travel books, and tourist guides. In 2014, she came first in the category "Personality Profile – International Journalism" of the Annual Southern California Journalism Awards in Los Angeles, and in 2016 she was third. She obtained third place in the category "nonfiction books" at the 56th SoCal Journalism Awards in Los Angeles. White Star has published, in the same series, her "My New York: Celebrities Talk About the City" and "My Paris: Celebrities Talk about the Ville Lumière."

CHRIS VERSTEEG, lives and works in Rotterdam, the Netherlands, as a graphic designer and illustrator at Project C. He is the editorial director and Editor-in-chief of the magazine SAM (Street and More) and co-founder of the collective of artists Lastplak. After attending the Grafisch Lyceum and the Willem de Kooning Academie in Rotterdam, he specialized in the field of graphic design, illustration, and painting.

Photo Credits

Alan Gallery/Alamy Stock Photo/IPA:
    page 181
Philip Game/Alamy Stock Photo/IPA:
    page 229
Jean Gaumy/Magnum Photos/
    Contrasto: pages 60-61
Janusz Gniadek/Alamy Stock Photo/
    IPA: page 29
FRANCOIS GUILLOT/AFP/Getty
    Images: page 119
Mark Hamilton/Alamy Stock Photo/
    IPA: page 105
Isa Harsin/Sipa/IPA: pages 32-33, 135
Anthony Hatley/Alamy Stock Photo/
    IPA: page 180
Hemis/Alamy Stock Photo/IPA:
    pages 252-253
David S. Holloway/Getty Images:
    pages 130-131
PHILIPPE HUGUEN/AFP/Getty Images:
    pages 54-55
In Pictures Ltd./Corbis/Getty Images:
    page 103
Marcos Issa/Bloomberg/Getty Images:
    pages 184, 186-187
Kim Kaminski/Alamy Stock Photo/IPA:
    pages 202-203
Michael Kemp/Alamy Stock Photo/IPA:
    page 104
LE BLEAVEC Antoine/Age Fotostock:
    page 228
simon leigh/Alamy Stock Photo/IPA:
    pages 38-39
Matthew Lloyd/Getty Images:
    page 102
JOHN MACDOUGALL/AFP/Getty
    Images: page 191

AC Manley/Alamy Stock Photo/IPA:
    pages 182-183
Steven May/Alamy Stock Photo/IPA:
    pages 40-41
Kyodo News/Getty Images: pages 12-13
Eolo Perfido: page 6
Picture Hooked/Kieran Orwin/Alasmy
    Stock Photo/IPA: pages 246-247
robertharding/Alamy Stock Photo/IPA:
    page 43
Stacy Walsh Rosenstock/Alamy Stock
    Photo/IPA: pages 14-15
David L. Ryan/The Boston Globe/Getty
    Images: pag, 107
Joem Sackemann/Alamy Stock Photo/
    IPA: page 27
Ted Soqui/Corbis/Getty Images:
    pages 44, 45, 139
Kristy Sparow/WireImage/Getty
    Images: page 63
Homer Sykes/Alamy Stock Photo/IPA:
    page 99
Ramin Talaie/Bloomberg/Getty
    Images: page 89
Natalie Tepper/ArcaidImages/Getty
    Images: page 101
Simon Turner/Alamy Stock Photo/IPA:
    page 200
CARINE VAISSIERE/Alamy Stock
    Photo/IPA: pages 236-237
Victor VIRGILE/Gamma-Rapho/Getty
    Images: page 57
WENN.com/IPA: page 37
Matt Writtle/Contrasto: page 205
ZUMA Press, Inc./Alamy Stock Photo/
    IPA: page 7

Courtesy of the:
Aryz: pages 28, 30-31, 34, 34-35
Dan Bergeron/Fauxreel: pages 141, 142,
    143, 144-145, 146, 147, 148-149, 150-151
Aleksei Bordusov - Aec Interesni
    Kazki: pages 153, 154, 155, 156, 157, 159,
    160, 161, 162, 163, 164-165, 167, 168-169,
    169
C215: pages 73, 74, 74-75, 76-77, 77, 78, 79,
    80, 81, 82-83, 84-85, 86-87
David Choe: pages 90-91, 92, 93, 94,
    94-95, 96, 97
El Mac: pages 108-109, 110-111, 112-113,
    114, 115, 116, 117
Evol e Adagp: pages 120-121, 122, 123,
    124, 124-125, 126, 127
Jennifer Jaimes: pages 65, 66-67, 68-69,
    70, 71
M-City: pages 171, 172-173, 173, 174, 175,
    176, 176-177
Chia Messina: page 225
Nunca: pages 179, 188, 189
Roa: pages 192-193, 194, 195, 196, 197,
    199
Slinkachu: pages 210, 210-211, 212-213,
    214-215
Gabriel Specter: pages 217, 219, 220-
    221, 222, 223
Alex Vau: pages 233, 235, 239
Vhils: pages 241, 244-245, 249, 250

Cover: Banksy, London.
© Barry Lewis/Alamy Stock Photo/IPA

Backcover: Banksy, New York.
© Zuma Press, Inc./Alamy Stock
Photo/IPA

Original Edition by

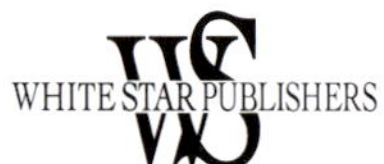

WHITE STAR PUBLISHERS

WS White Star Publishers® is a registered trademark
property of White Star s.r.l.

©2017 White Star s.r.l.
Piazzale Luigi Cadorna, 6 – 20123 Milan, Italy
www.whitestar.it

This edition published by Shelter Harbor Press by arrangement with White Star s.r.l.

SHELTER HARBOR PRESS
NEW YORK

SHELTER HARBOR PRESS
603 W. 115th Street, Suite 163
New York, NY 10025
www.shelterharborpress.com

Cataloging-in-Publication Date has been applied for and may be obtained from the Library of Congress.

ISBN: 978-1-62795-163-0

Translation and Editing: Iceigeo, Milan (translation: Jonathan West, Emma Jane Williams, Brenda Dionisi,
Katherine M. Clifton; editing: Joshua Burkholder, Paola Paudice)

For sales please contact info@shelterharborpress.com

Printed and bound in Turkey

10 9 8 7 6 5 4 3 2 1